# Flex 3 Component Solutions
## Build Amazing Interfaces with Flex Components

Jack Herrington

*an Apress® company*

# Flex 3 Component Solutions: Build Amazing Interfaces with Flex Components

ISBN-13 (pbk): 978-1-4302-1598-1

ISBN-13 (electronic): 978-1-4302-1599-8

Printed and bound in the United States of America 9 8 7 6 5 4 3 2 1

Distributed to the book trade worldwide by Springer-Verlag New York, Inc., 233 Spring Street, 6th Floor, New York, NY 10013. Phone 1-800-SPRINGER, fax 201-348-4505, e-mail orders-ny@springer-sbm.com, or visit www.springeronline.com.

For information on translations, please contact Apress directly at 2855 Telegraph Avenue, Suite 600, Berkeley, CA 94705. Phone 510-549-5930, fax 510-549-5939, e-mail info@apress.com, or visit www.apress.com.

Apress and friends of ED books may be purchased in bulk for academic, corporate, or promotional use. eBook versions and licenses are also available for most titles. For more information, reference our Special Bulk Sales–eBook Licensing web page at http://www.apress.com/info/bulksales.

The source code for this book is freely available to readers at www.friendsofed.com in the Downloads section.

## Credits

| | |
|---|---|
| **Lead Editor**<br>Clay Andres | **Associate Production Director**<br>Kari Brooks-Copony |
| **Technical Reviewer**<br>Winsha Chen | **Production Editor**<br>Kelly Winquist |
| **Editorial Board**<br>Clay Andres, Steve Anglin,<br>Mark Beckner, Ewan Buckingham,<br>Tony Campbell, Gary Cornell,<br>Jonathan Gennick, Michelle Lowman,<br>Matthew Moodie, Jeffrey Pepper,<br>Frank Pohlmann, Ben Renow-Clarke,<br>Dominic Shakeshaft, Matt Wade, Tom Welsh | **Compositor**<br>Dina Quan<br><br>**Proofreader**<br>Lisa Hamilton<br><br>**Indexer**<br>Broccoli Information Management |
| **Project Manager**<br>Sofia Marchant | **Interior and Cover Designer**<br>Kurt Krames |
| **Copy Editor**<br>Ami Knox | **Manufacturing Director**<br>Tom Debolski |

*This book is dedicated to my father, who gave me another lesson in how to face your fears with dignity as I was writing this book.*

*"Just machines to make big decisions,*
*Programmed by fellas with compassion and vision.*
*We'll be clean when their work is done,*
*We'll be eternally free and eternally young."*

*—Donald Fagen, "I.G.Y."*

# CONTENTS AT A GLANCE

# CONTENTS

# ABOUT THE AUTHOR

**Jack Herrington** is an engineer, author, and presenter who lives and works in the Bay Area. He lives with his wife, daughter, and two adopted dogs. When he is not writing software, books, or articles, you can find him on his bike, running, or in the pool training for triathlons. You can keep up with Jack's work and his writing at http://jackherrington.com.

# ABOUT THE TECHNICAL REVIEWER

**Winsha Chen** is an engineer at Adobe. She started at Macromedia as an engineer on Dreamweaver 3 and worked on it through the MX 2004 release. Since then, she has been working on building authoring tools for Flex.

# ACKNOWLEDGMENTS

The author would like to acknowledge the outstanding work of Winsha Chen in reviewing the applications presented in this book. He would also like to acknowledge Clay Andres' invaluable work in helping develop the content for the book.

# LAYOUT CONVENTIONS

To keep this book as clear and easy to follow as possible, the following text conventions are used throughout:

Important words or concepts are normally highlighted on the first appearance in **bold type**.

Code is presented in fixed-width font.

New or changed code is normally presented in **bold fixed-width font**.

Menu commands are written in the form Menu ➤ Submenu ➤ Submenu.

Where I want to draw your attention to something, I've highlighted it like this:

> *Ahem, don't say I didn't warn you.*

Sometimes code won't fit on a single line in a book. Where this happens, I use an arrow like this: ➡.

```
This is a very, very long section of code that should be written all ➡
on the same line without a break.
```

# 1  A QUICK INTRODUCTION TO FLEX

  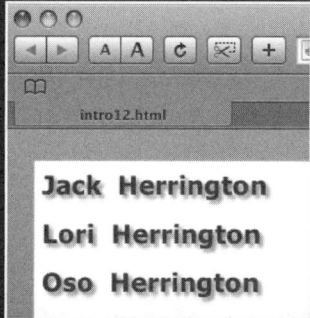

Updated 6/21/08

# Getting started with Flex

So why would you want to build Flash applications? Let me give you a few reasons. First, the Ajax model, while fine for small applications, turns into a maintenance nightmare when you try to maintain browser compatibility in large applications. The Java VM doesn't have the browser share that Flash does, so applets, while interesting, will bring you installation and versioning headaches.

Flash, on the other hand, is everywhere. Who hasn't gone to YouTube to watch a viral video or two, and the only way to watch the video is to have an up-to-date, easy-to-install, Flash Player. And what's more, Flash comes with an amazing set of tools for building rich applications, including excellent support for multimedia. The Flash VM also works the same regardless of browser or operating system. So it's a lot easier to build applications that work everywhere.

Then there is the Flash developer community, including the people and companies who build reusable components that you can use in your application. That's the focus of this book. Because you might find yourself looking at a Flash application and saying, "How did they do that? It must have taken years." It may, but probably not, because the Flash community has a rich set of tools and libraries outside of the default framework that you can make use of in your own application.

The place for developers to get started in the world of Flash is to use Flex 3. Now you could use the SDK (http://flex.org) and a text editor to develop and compile applications, but there is a much better option. Flex Builder 3 (http://adobe.com/flex) is available for a trial basis from Adobe. It's an IDE specific to Flex 3 that is built on the Eclipse IDE core. That means code hinting, code coloring, project management, real-time compilation, and excellent debugging tools are all at your fingertips. The trial period should give you enough time to realize whether Flex (and Flex Builder) are worth the investment. After you try some of the examples in this book, I'm sure you will be convinced.

If you are already familiar with Flex and Flex Builder, you can easily skip ahead to the next chapter. If you aren't familiar with these tools or think you need a refresher, then stick around, and I'll walk you through the basics so that all of the code in the rest of the book will make sense.

After downloading and installing Flex Builder, the next step is to create your first project. You can call it whatever you like; I called mine "intro." Flex Builder will automatically create an intro.mxml file for you to correspond to the "intro" project name.

Replace the auto-generated code with the following:

```
<?xml version="1.0" encoding="utf-8"?>
<mx:Application xmlns:mx=http://www.adobe.com/2006/mxml
  layout="vertical">
  <mx:Label text="Hello World" fontSize="30" />
</mx:Application>
```

Then click the Run button in the toolbar, and you should see something like Figure 1-1.

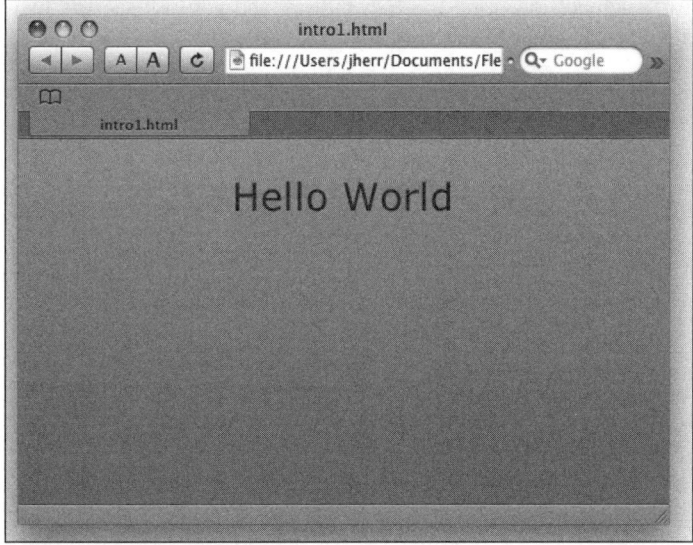

**Figure 1-1.** A very simple Flex application

This is the Flex equivalent of the Hello World application, and it has a few important elements to convey. The first is MXML. MXML is the user interface definition language of Flex. You can think of it as roughly equivalent to HTML. It's an easy shorthand way of specifying what Flex controls (and any custom controls you download or write yourself) should be placed where and how they should be styled.

In this case, the <mx:Application> tag is at the root of the file. The base tag of a Flex application is always the <mx:Application> tag (for AIR applications, it's <mx:WindowedApplication>). From there, we specify that a single Label control be created. And that default values for text and fontSize be replaced by a text value of Hello World and a fontSize value of 20 pixels.

The layout of the Label control is handled by the Application object, which acts as a container. In this case, we specify that the layout should be vertical. This means that each control that is added to the Application container will be laid out vertically down the application's stage.

## Adding some interactivity

The next thing to try is to add a little interactivity to the demonstration. Replace the code in the previous example with the following:

```
<?xml version="1.0" encoding="utf-8"?>
<mx:Application xmlns:mx=http://www.adobe.com/2006/mxml
  layout="vertical">
  <mx:Label text="Hello" id="txtLabel" fontSize="30" />
  <mx:Button label="Change" click="txtLabel.text='Goodbye'" />
</mx:Application>
```

Now launch the application using the Run button, and you will see the two controls, a Label and a Button, as you can see in Figure 1-2.

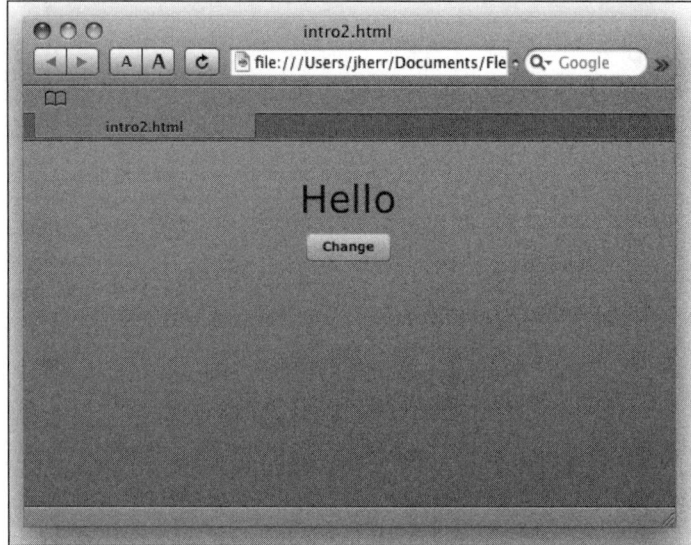

**Figure 1-2.** A label with an interactive Change button

You can then click the Change button, and the label will change as shown in Figure 1-3.

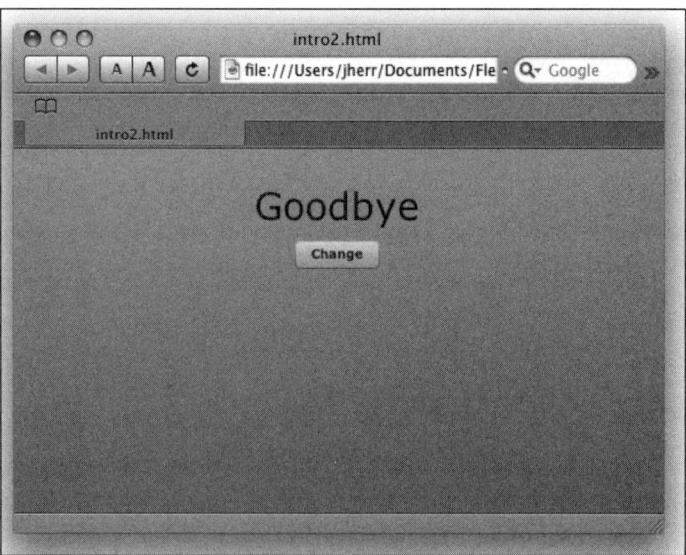

**Figure 1-3.** Click the Change button, and the label changes from Hello to Goodbye.

Let's look back at the code to see how this is accomplished. First, we have added an id attribute to the Label control. This ID is used as the name of the variable that will reference the Label object. For this reason, the id attribute has to be unique within the Flex file.

In the Button tag, we then add some ActionScript 3 to the click handler, which will be invoked when the user clicks the button. ActionScript 3 is the scripting language for Flex. It's very powerful, and we will get more into it in a bit.

In this case, the ActionScript code sets the text parameter of the Label object to Goodbye by referencing the Label through the txtLabel variable that was defined in the id of the Label tag.

So there are some critical elements you learned here: First, the id parameter, which is associated with every Flex object, is used by the MXML compiler to set the variable name for use with ActionScript. Second, controls (e.g., Buttons, Lists, DataGrids, etc.) fire off events in response to certain actions by the user. We can then associate ActionScript code with those events to respond to them.

Next, we are going to refine the code a little bit. Have a look at this:

```xml
<?xml version="1.0" encoding="utf-8"?>
<mx:Application xmlns:mx="http://www.adobe.com/2006/mxml"
  layout="vertical">
<mx:Script>
<![CDATA[
public function onChangeClick( event:Event ) : void {
  txtLabel.text='Goodbye';
}
]]>
</mx:Script>
<mx:Label text="Hello" id="txtLabel" fontSize="30" />
<mx:Button label="Change" click="onChangeClick(event)" />
</mx:Application>
```

Here I have replaced the inline code in the click handler with a call to a local onChangeClick method that is defined in an <mx:Script> tag. The <mx:Script> tag is how you add larger sections of ActionScript code to the interface. As you will see later, you can create independent ActionScript files to define classes, but this technique of using an <mx:Script> tag can be handy for defining small portions of code as shown in this example.

To further refine this example, I want to show how conditional logic is represented in ActionScript 3. Have a look at the following code:

```xml
<?xml version="1.0" encoding="utf-8"?>
<mx:Application xmlns:mx="http://www.adobe.com/2006/mxml"
  layout="vertical"
  creationComplete="onChangeText(event)">
<mx:Script>
<![CDATA[
```

```
    public function onChangeText( event:Event ) : void {
      if ( txtLabel.text == '' || txtLabel.text == 'Goodbye' )
        txtLabel.text='Hello';
      else
        txtLabel.text='Goodbye';
    }
  ]]>
  </mx:Script>
  <mx:Label id="txtLabel" fontSize="30" />
  <mx:Button label="Change" click="onChangeText(event)" />
</mx:Application>
```

Everything remains the same with the exception of the onChangeText handler, which now toggles the label between Hello and Goodbye using a conditional. As you can see, the basic structure of ActionScript, as well as its keywords and control structures, is very similar to that for JavaScript, C, C#, and Java. If you are fluent in one or more of these languages, ActionScript should feel very familiar to you.

# Managing and displaying data

In this next example, I'll show a DataGrid control that displays an array of ActionScript objects. The code for this example is shown here:

```
<?xml version="1.0" encoding="utf-8"?>
<mx:Application xmlns:mx="http://www.adobe.com/2006/mxml"
  layout="vertical">
<mx:Script>
<![CDATA[
import mx.collections.ArrayCollection;

[Bindable]
private var addresses:ArrayCollection = new ArrayCollection( [
  { first: 'Jack', last: 'Herrington', email: 'jack@donotreply.com' },
  { first: 'Lori', last: 'Herrington', email: 'lori@donotreply.com' },
  { first: 'Oso', last: 'Herrington', email: 'oso@donotreply.com' }
] );
]]>
</mx:Script>
<mx:DataGrid dataProvider="{addresses}" />
</mx:Application>
```

In this example, we set up a member variable called addresses, which is initialized with an array of ActionScript objects. Each of these objects contains three parameters: first, last, and email. This curly bracket ({}) syntax for defining Objects is straight out of JavaScript, which is at the root of ActionScript.

The address member is then defined to be Bindable. This means that controls can bind to it and watch it for changes. The DataGrid control takes the addresses member variable as the dataProvider for display. This assignment is accomplished using the binding syntax in MXML. If we were to put addresses into the dataProvider field without the curly braces, the dataProvider member of the DataGrid control would be initialized with a string object with the value addresses. By using the curly brace syntax, we are telling the MXML compiler to send a reference to the object with the name addresses.

When we launch this from Flex Builder, we see something like Figure 1-4.

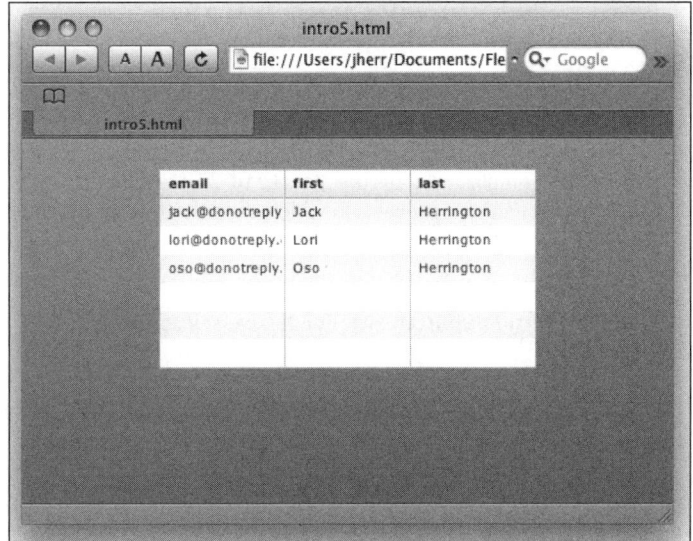

**Figure 1-4.** The data grid with the default settings

The DataGrid has helpfully examined the array referenced in the dataProvider, deduced what columns should be presented, and then created columns for each and displayed it. Nice, huh?

## Refining control presentation

To refine our application a little more, we can make the changes shown here:

```
<?xml version="1.0" encoding="utf-8"?>
<mx:Application xmlns:mx="http://www.adobe.com/2006/mxml"
  layout="vertical">
<mx:Script>
<![CDATA[
import mx.collections.ArrayCollection;

[Bindable]
private var addresses:ArrayCollection = new ArrayCollection( [
  { first: 'Jack', last: 'Herrington', email: 'jack@donotreply.com' },
  { first: 'Lori', last: 'Herrington', email: 'lori@donotreply.com' },
```

```
    { first: 'Oso', last: 'Herrington', email: 'oso@donotreply.com' }
  ] );
]]>
</mx:Script>
<mx:DataGrid dataProvider="{addresses}" width="100%">
<mx:columns>
  <mx:DataGridColumn dataField="first" headerText="First Name" />
  <mx:DataGridColumn dataField="last" headerText="Last Name" />
  <mx:DataGridColumn dataField="email" headerText="Email Name" />
</mx:columns>
</mx:DataGrid>
</mx:Application>
```

In this new code, the addresses remain exactly the same, but now we have added three DataGridColumns to the initialization of the DataGrid. These column objects will tell the DataGrid which object fields to present, in which order, with what header text, and so on. You can define the width of the column, whether it should be sortable, how it should be rendered, and so on.

When we bring the new version up from Flex Builder, we see something like Figure 1-5.

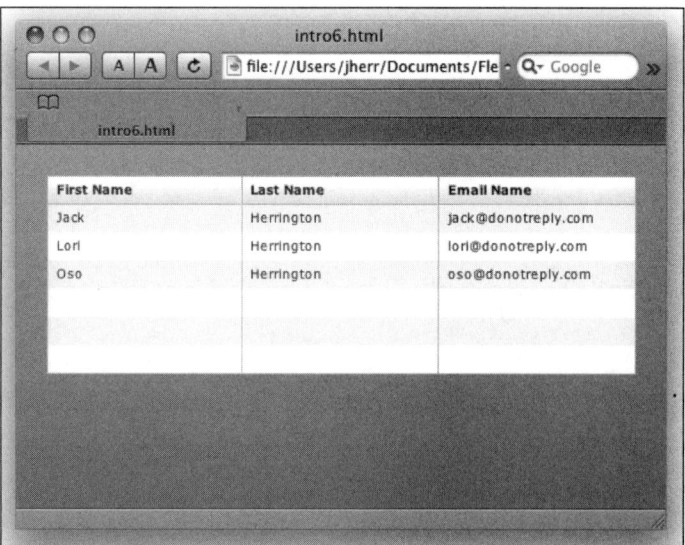

**Figure 1-5.** The data grid with customized columns

Now that's much nicer.

## Building ActionScript classes

To refine the data side of the equation, let's start by defining an Address class. The original address list had an array of anonymous objects of type Object with some fields assigned. As applications grow in size, the use of these anonymous objects of type Object is frowned upon because you don't know the type of the Object, and you can't predict what fields will be there.

Here's the new Address class, which has real fields and a constructor:

```
package com.jherrington
{
  public class Address
  {
    private var _first:String = '';
    public function set first( str:String ) : void { _first = str; }
    public function get first( ) : String { return _first; }

    private var _last:String = '';
    public function set last( str:String ) : void { _last = str; }
    public function get last( ) : String { return _last; }

    private var _email:String = '';
    public function set email( str:String ) : void { _email = str; }
    public function get email( ) : String { return _email; }

    public function Address( inFirst:String, inLast:String,
  inEmail:String )
    {
      first = inFirst;
      last = inLast;
      email = inEmail;
    }
  }
}
```

There are a few things to take note of when you look at this code. The first is the package definition right at the top. I put this Address class in the com.jherrington package, which means that the Address.as file needs to be in the jherrington folder within the com folder located at the root of the project directory. This package namespacing makes it easy to maintain larger projects that might have similar class names between different packages.

The next thing to note is the use of the class keyword. ActionScript 3 has **first class** objects. That means that each object has a **type**, and that type is defined by a **class**. This should be very familiar to you if your background is in C++, C#, or Java.

Within the class, we define three member variables: _first, _last, and _email. All are of type String and initialized to be empty strings. Associated with each is a get and set function. These get and set functions are called when the first, last, or email member variables are requested or set. The code in these functions can be as complex as the code in any method. The value of having get and set functions is that you can maintain the handy dot syntax of getting and setting values on an object, without sacrificing the ability to have code triggered in response to the get or set event.

The final element is the constructor, which takes three parameters and sets the values of first, last, and email to the values that are sent in with the constructor call.

The new version of the MXML, which uses this Address class, is shown in the code here:

```
<?xml version="1.0" encoding="utf-8"?>
<mx:Application xmlns:mx="http://www.adobe.com/2006/mxml"
  layout="vertical">
<mx:Script>
<![CDATA[
import mx.collections.ArrayCollection;
import com.jherrington.Address;

[Bindable]
private var addresses:ArrayCollection = new ArrayCollection( [
  new Address( 'Jack', 'Herrington', 'jack@donotreply.com' ),
  new Address( 'Lori', 'Herrington', 'lori@donotreply.com' ),
  new Address( 'Oso', 'Herrington', 'oso@donotreply.com' )
] );
]]>
</mx:Script>
<mx:DataGrid dataProvider="{addresses}" width="100%">
<mx:columns>
  <mx:DataGridColumn dataField="first" headerText="First Name" />
  <mx:DataGridColumn dataField="last" headerText="Last Name" />
  <mx:DataGridColumn dataField="email" headerText="Email Name" />
</mx:columns>
</mx:DataGrid>
</mx:Application>
```

The DataGrid definition at the bottom remains exactly the same. But now I've changed the addresses array to be a list of Address objects instead of anonymous objects. To do that, I've had to add the import statement that references the Address class within the com.jherrington package.

## Using containers for layout

Now that we have had a pretty good look at some controls, how ActionScript works, how events are handled, and so on, it's time to dig a little more into how user interfaces are laid out.

To do that, I'll start out with an MXML application that shows several different container objects. Following is the example file application:

```
<?xml version="1.0" encoding="utf-8"?>
<mx:Application xmlns:mx="http://www.adobe.com/2006/mxml"
  layout="vertical">
 <mx:Panel title="Horizontal" width="100%"
  paddingBottom="5" paddingLeft="5" paddingRight="5" paddingTop="5">
  <mx:HBox>
    <mx:Button label="A" />
    <mx:Button label="B" />
    <mx:Button label="C" />
  </mx:HBox>
</mx:Panel>
  <mx:Panel title="Horizontal" width="100%"
   paddingBottom="5" paddingLeft="5" paddingRight="5" paddingTop="5">
  <mx:VBox>
    <mx:Button label="A" />
    <mx:Button label="B" />
    <mx:Button label="C" />
  </mx:VBox>
</mx:Panel>
<mx:Panel title="Divider" width="100%"
   paddingBottom="5" paddingLeft="5" paddingRight="5" paddingTop="5">
  <mx:HDividedBox width="100%">
    <mx:Button label="Left" />
    <mx:Button label="Right" />
  </mx:HDividedBox>
</mx:Panel>
</mx:Application>
```

The application has three Panel objects, each of which contains a different container type and some controls. The Panel object is a nifty window-ey type container that has a title and looks fairly elegant.

Now the first panel has an HBox in it. The HBox container lays out all of its children in one long horizontal line. If that line becomes too long for the width of the HBox, the container puts in a scrollbar (though you can turn that off).

The second panel contains a VBox which, as you might have guessed, does the same as the HBox but does it vertically.

The third panel contains two controls that are within an HDividedBox. The HDividedBox container puts a little grabby widget between the two left and right elements that allows the user to resize the container.

You can see all of these containers in action in Figure 1-6.

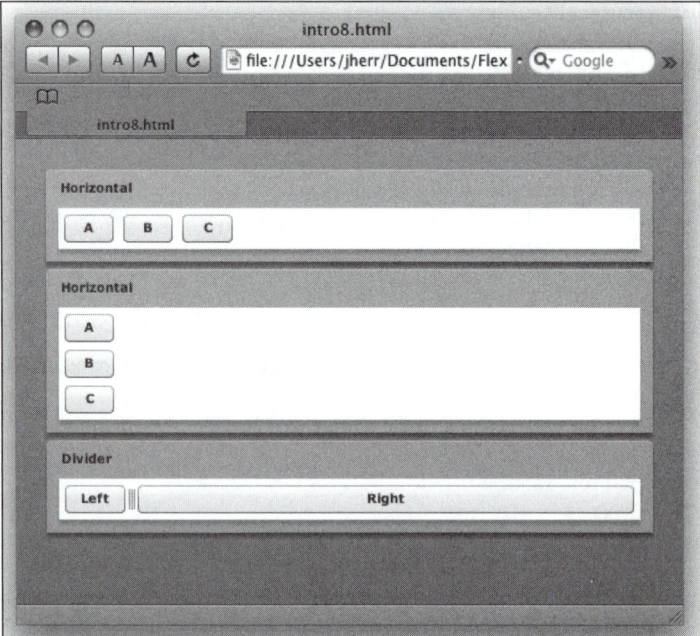

**Figure 1-6.** Three different container schemes with some panels

I think one of the great things about Flex is the fact that even when the interface is kind of arbitrary, or at least not very well designed, as it is in this example, the final product still looks nice and clean. It's just my own opinion, but I don't find the same elegance in other layout-based user interface toolkits.

## Laying out controls absolutely

Another layout method is absolute positioning. This method is fairly straightforward, as you can see here:

```
<?xml version="1.0" encoding="utf-8"?>
<mx:Application xmlns:mx=http://www.adobe.com/2006/mxml
  layout="absolute">
<mx:Label x="10" y="10" text="First"/>
<mx:Label x="10" y="36" text="Last"/>
<mx:Label x="10" y="62" text="Email"/>
<mx:TextInput x="57" y="8"/>
<mx:TextInput x="57" y="34"/>
<mx:TextInput x="57" y="60"/>
<mx:Button x="57" y="90" label="Add"/>
</mx:Application>
```

The Application tag's layout attribute is set to absolute, and each of the controls has an x and y value associated with it that positions it. You can use ActionScript to move the controls around. There are states and effects mechanisms that you can use to animate their movement and so on, if you want to get really fancy.

This example, when it's launched from Flex Builder, looks like Figure 1-7.

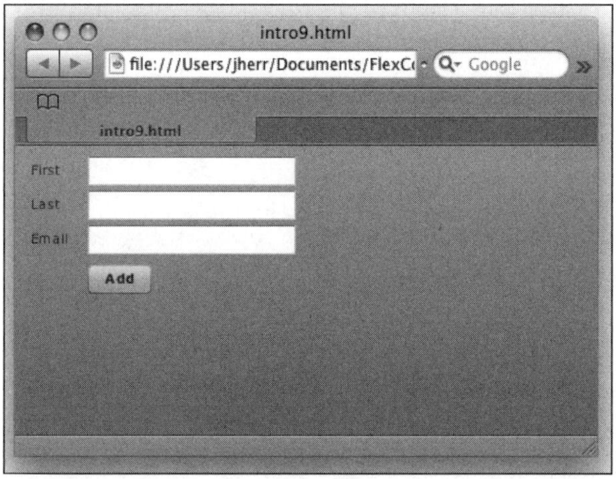

**Figure 1-7.** An absolutely positioned layout

This example looks as nice as it does because Flex Builder 3 has a **Design mode** that you can use to interactively move controls around the stage with the mouse or the keyboard. And that Design mode does some intelligent **snapping** to line up controls into neat columns and space them evenly vertically.

That being said, I don't think that this particular example is the best use of Flex. If you change the font size, for example, the controls will just overlap each other instead of giving each other the room to spread out.

The best way to lay out a form is to use the Form object, which is a container designed for just that purpose. An example of the Form container is shown here:

```xml
<?xml version="1.0" encoding="utf-8"?>
<mx:Application xmlns:mx=http://www.adobe.com/2006/mxml
  layout="vertical">
  <mx:Form>
    <mx:FormItem label="First">
      <mx:TextInput />
    </mx:FormItem>
    <mx:FormItem label="Last">
      <mx:TextInput />
    </mx:FormItem>
    <mx:FormItem label="Email">
      <mx:TextInput />
    </mx:FormItem>
```

**13**

```
      <mx:FormItem>
        <mx:Button label="Add" />
      </mx:FormItem>
    </mx:Form>
  </mx:Application>
```

Sure, it's a lot of tags, but it's really pretty simple. A Form object expects all of the children to be of type FormItem. Each FormItem can have a label associated with it. And then the FormItem contains one or more controls associated with that form item.

The result of this particular MXML code is shown in Figure 1-8.

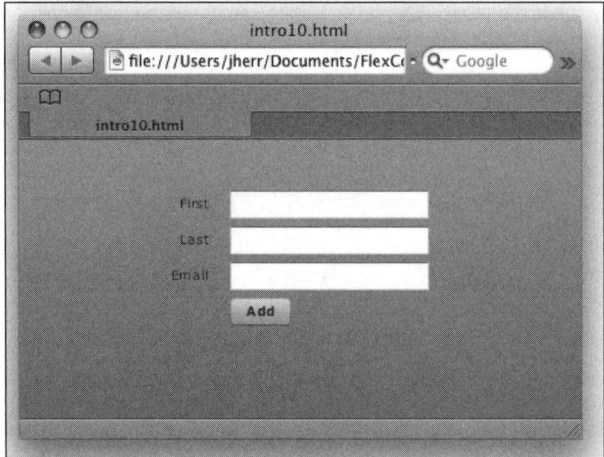

**Figure 1-8.** A form-based layout

Flex has a number of different container classes, and of course you are free to develop your own as well. This small sampling I've provided shows most of the containers that I use in the example code throughout the book.

# Custom rendering

The final element of Flex that I'll cover in this chapter is the ability to define custom renderers and custom components. This is one of the most powerful aspects of Flex and one that distinguishes it from other GUI frameworks.

To demonstrate providing a custom renderer, I'll show the original addresses example, but this time with the addition of a new column that contains a Button.

```
<?xml version="1.0" encoding="utf-8"?>
<mx:Application xmlns:mx="http://www.adobe.com/2006/mxml"
  layout="vertical">
<mx:Script>
<![CDATA[
import mx.collections.ArrayCollection;
import com.jherrington.Address;

[Bindable]
private var addresses:ArrayCollection = new ArrayCollection( [
  new Address( 'Jack', 'Herrington', 'jack@donotreply.com' ),
  new Address( 'Lori', 'Herrington', 'lori@donotreply.com' ),
  new Address( 'Oso', 'Herrington', 'oso@donotreply.com' )
] );
]]>
</mx:Script>
<mx:DataGrid dataProvider="{addresses}" width="100%">
<mx:columns>
  <mx:DataGridColumn dataField="first" headerText="First Name" />
  <mx:DataGridColumn dataField="last" headerText="Last Name" />
  <mx:DataGridColumn dataField="email" headerText="Email Name" />
  <mx:DataGridColumn dataField="first">
    <mx:itemRenderer>
      <mx:Component>
        <mx:Button label="Edit {data.first}'s record" />
      </mx:Component>
    </mx:itemRenderer>
  </mx:DataGridColumn>
</mx:columns>
</mx:DataGrid>
</mx:Application>
```

The important code here is in the final DataGridColumn definition. I've created a subtag of type <mx:itemRenderer> to define the controls that will be used to populate this column instead of the usual text rendering. That <mx:itemRenderer> in turn contains an "inline" <mx:Component> tag that has in itself the <mx:Button> that will be used to populate each cell of this column in the data grid.

When this is launched from Flex Builder, you see something like Figure 1-9.

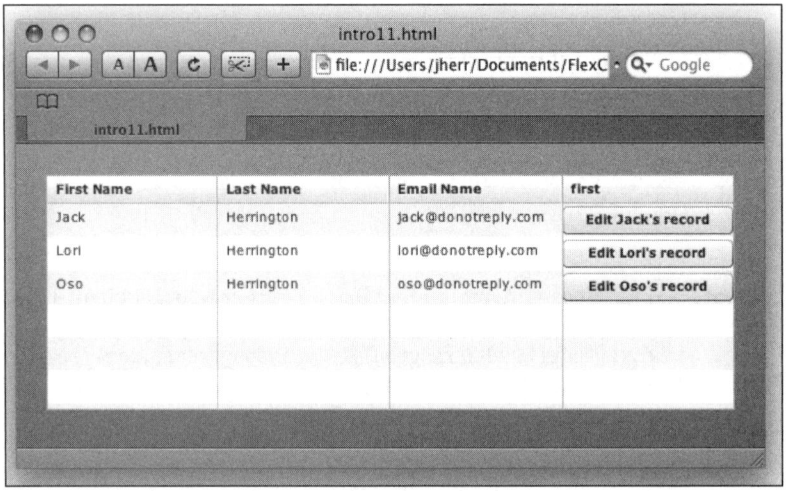

**Figure 1-9.** A DataGrid that renders a button into a column

Now have a look at the last column there. Yes there is a button, and that's cool, but what's more interesting is the label of the button has that first name of the record from that row. How is that done? Well, that's in the magic of Flex's data model.

As the DataGrid builds the controls that go into each cell, it sets the data member of the component specified by the itemRenderer to be the object for that row. The component can in turn reference the original row object through its data member. Almost every control you are going to use, or subclass from, in Flex has a data member. You can also attach code to the dataChange event that will be triggered when an update is made to the data member.

## Building renderer modules

My final example for this chapter will be to show how this same type of custom component work can be done with a component that is described in another file. The user interface parent code for this is shown here:

```
<?xml version="1.0" encoding="utf-8"?>
<mx:Application xmlns:mx=http://www.adobe.com/2006/mxml
  layout="vertical">
<mx:Script>
<![CDATA[
import mx.collections.ArrayCollection;
import com.jherrington.Address;
```

```
[Bindable]
private var addresses:ArrayCollection = new ArrayCollection( [
  new Address( 'Jack', 'Herrington', 'jack@donotreply.com' ),
  new Address( 'Lori', 'Herrington', 'lori@donotreply.com' ),
  new Address( 'Oso', 'Herrington', 'oso@donotreply.com' )
] );
]]>
</mx:Script>
<mx:List dataProvider="{addresses}" width="100%"
  itemRenderer="com.jherrington.PersonRenderer">
</mx:List>
</mx:Application>
```

This is the same address list example as before, but in this case the DataGrid has been replaced by a List control that references a custom itemRenderer by class name instead of defining one in this file.

The code for the PersonRenderer is contained within the com/jherrington folder and is defined by the following code:

```
<?xml version="1.0" encoding="utf-8"?>
<mx:HBox xmlns:mx="http://www.adobe.com/2006/mxml" width="100%">
<mx:rollOverEffect>
  <mx:Glow duration="800" />
</mx:rollOverEffect>
<mx:filters>
  <mx:DropShadowFilter color="#999999" />
</mx:filters>
  <mx:Label text="{data.first}" fontSize="20" fontWeight="bold" />
  <mx:Label text="{data.last}" fontSize="20" fontWeight="bold" />
</mx:HBox>
```

Here I have done a few things of note. First, you will see that the root tag is an <mx:HBox> and not an <mx:Application>. MXML components can have any container type as the root object. In this case, I wanted the cell laid out horizontally, so HBox was the logical choice.

The controls for this component are the two Label controls at the bottom. Their text is defined using the data syntax, which works just as well in these types of components as it does when you define the itemRenderer component in-place.

The fun stuff comes when I define the rollOverEffect and the DropShadowFilter within the filters tag. The rollOverEffect tells Flex to make the component glow for 800 milliseconds when the user moves the mouse over it. The DropShadowFilter applies a fancy drop shadow effect to the children of the component.

Have a look at the result in Figure 1-10.

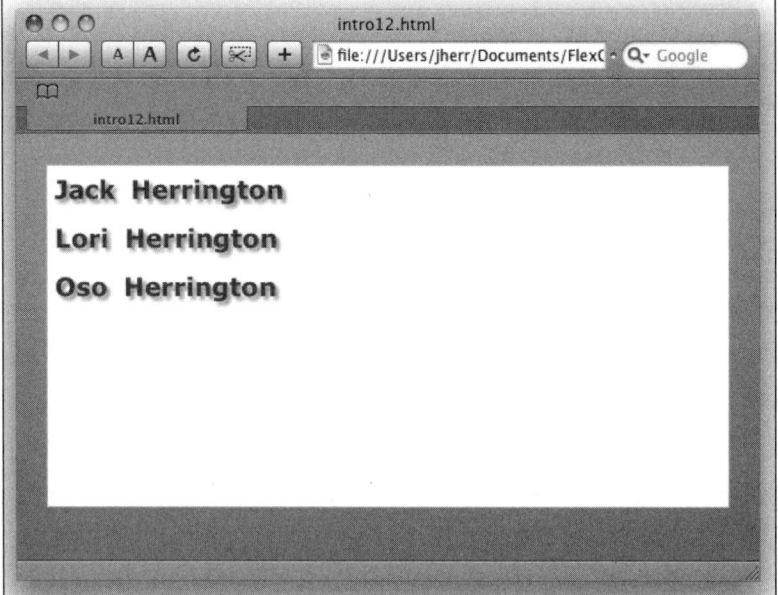

**Figure 1-10.** A list that uses a custom component to render each cell

Notice what happens when you roll your mouse over each cell. The text glows if only just for a brief moment. How cool is that? And how little code to make that happen. This is the kind of thing that people expect from a Flash movie and that Flex makes very easy.

The effects and animations toolkit that is supplied in the Flex framework will knock your customers' socks off. And there is a lot more out there in the community that you can have fun with.

## Where we will go from here

In the chapters that follow, you will learn both more about Flex and what controls are available off the shelf that will allow you to make amazing applications quickly.

# 2 **MAKING STATES ROCK**

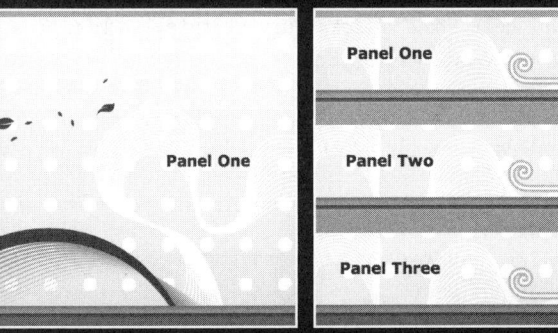
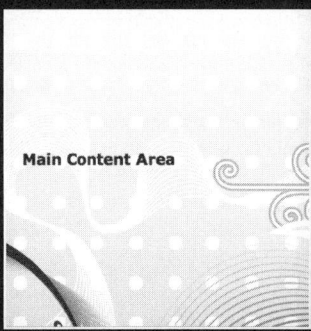

# Recipes for states

States are one of the most important, but least understood, features of the Flex frame-work. One of the reasons stems from their vaguely defined role. A Flex interface can have one or more **states**, defined by you, where each state can change as many or as few attributes as it wants to.

That all sounds great, but what are states useful for? For my Flex application work, I see states as defining the different modes of the interface. For example, let's say you have a HorizontalList showing a series of image thumbnails. When the user clicks one, you want to shrink the space occupied by the list and show a new space that displays an enlargement of the picture. You could call the state where just the HorizontalList is showing collapsed, and the state where both the list and the enlargement are shown detail. Flex will handle the work of flipping between these two states, if you just define them.

In this chapter, I'll demonstrate a bunch of "recipes" for state designs. These are designs that can be used directly in any application, or you can modify them to suit your needs.

# Show/Hide panels

The first example of a state design recipe I'm going to show is the "Show/Hide" recipe. This is where a section of the interface is either hidden or shown depending on the state. I most often use this recipe with side elements that show more detail.

The first version of the code that demonstrates the "Show/Hide" recipe is shown here:

```
<?xml version="1.0" encoding="utf-8"?>
<mx:Application xmlns:mx="http://www.adobe.com/2006/mxml"
  layout="horizontal"
  currentState="hide">
<mx:ApplicationControlBar dock="true">
  <mx:Button label="Hide" click="currentState='hide';" />
  <mx:Button label="Show" click="currentState='show';" />
</mx:ApplicationControlBar>
<mx:Style>
HBox {
  background-image: Embed('background.png');
  border-thickness: 3;
  border-style: solid;
  corner-radius: 3;
  vertical-align: middle;
  horizontal-align: center;
  border-color: #034EA2;
}
Label {
  font-weight: bold;
  font-size: 20;
}
```

```
.shelf {
  font-weight: normal;
  font-size: 15;
}
</mx:Style>
<mx:states>
  <mx:State name="hide">
    <mx:SetProperty target="{panel2}" name="visible" value="false" />
  </mx:State>
  <mx:State name="show">
    <mx:SetProperty target="{panel2}" name="visible" value="true" />
  </mx:State>
</mx:states>
<mx:HBox width="50%" height="100%" id="panel1">
  <mx:Label text="Panel 1" />
</mx:HBox>
<mx:HBox width="50%" height="100%" id="panel2">
  <mx:Label text="Panel 2" />
</mx:HBox>
</mx:Application>
```

Here we have two panels located on the left and right. The right panel, panel 2, starts hidden because the currentState in the application tag is set to hide. When the currentState is set to show, the second panel is shown. This is all defined in the <mx:states> tag.

There is an application control bar at the top of the window that we can use to toggle between the states. The resulting application is shown in Figure 2-1.

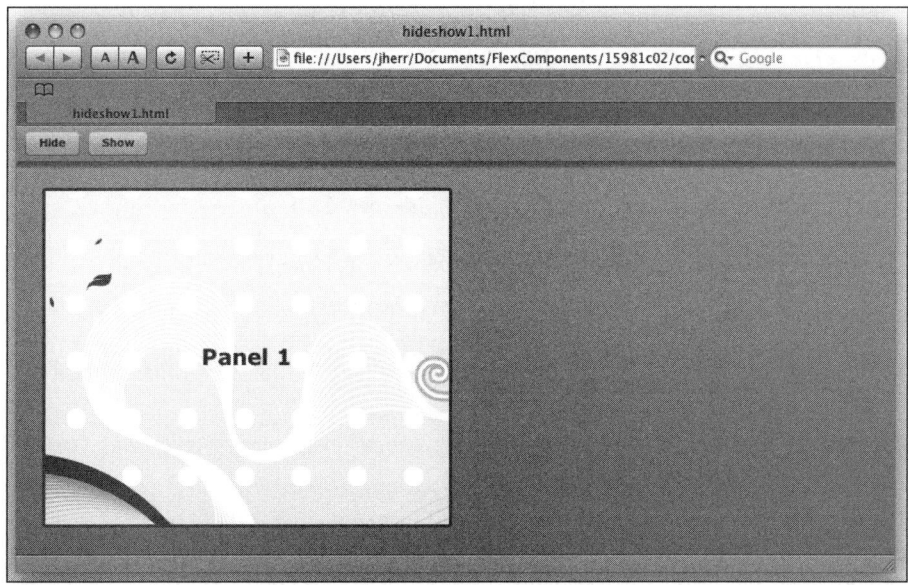

**Figure 2-1.** The application in the hide state

Clicking the Show button sets the state to show, and that brings up the second panel on the right. This is shown in Figure 2-2.

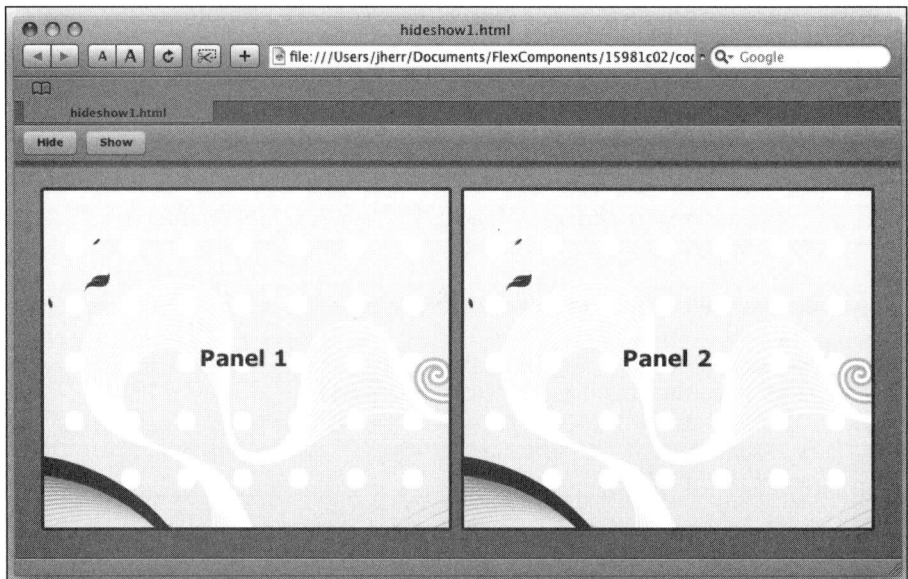

**Figure 2-2.** The application in the show state

The next thing to learn about states is that they are closely coupled to transitions. **Transitions** tell Flex what cool effects should be used to move from one state to another. For example, if we want the second panel to fade in and out, we could do something like this:

```
<?xml version="1.0" encoding="utf-8"?>
<mx:Application xmlns:mx="http://www.adobe.com/2006/mxml"
  layout="horizontal"
  currentState="hide">
...
<mx:HBox width="50%" height="100%" id="panel2">
  <mx:showEffect>
    <mx:Fade alphaFrom="0" alphaTo="1" duration="500" />
  </mx:showEffect>
  <mx:hideEffect>
    <mx:Fade alphaFrom="1" alphaTo="0" duration="500" />
  </mx:hideEffect>
  <mx:Label text="Panel 2" />
</mx:HBox>
</mx:Application>
```

This tells the HBox to run a fade-in-and-out effect when the panel is hidden or shown. The problem with this approach is the fade effect is run when the application starts up. So you end up seeing the second panel disappear just as the application comes up.

Transitions not only make the fade-in effect smoother because it's not applied on startup, but also make it easier to specify all of the effects that should applied to all of the elements that are moving around and how they will be sequenced.

The hide/show code that has transitions defined is shown in the following code:

```
<?xml version="1.0" encoding="utf-8"?>
<mx:Application xmlns:mx="http://www.adobe.com/2006/mxml"
  layout="horizontal"
  currentState="hide">
<mx:ApplicationControlBar dock="true">
  <mx:Button label="Hide" click="currentState='hide';" />
  <mx:Button label="Show" click="currentState='show';" />
</mx:ApplicationControlBar>
<mx:Style>
HBox {
  background-image: Embed('background.png');
  border-thickness: 3;
  border-style: solid;
  corner-radius: 3;
  vertical-align: middle;
  horizontal-align: center;
  border-color: #034EA2;
}
Label {
  font-weight: bold;
  font-size: 20;
}
.shelf {
  font-weight: normal;
  font-size: 15;
}
</mx:Style>
<mx:transitions>
<mx:Transition fromState="hide" toState="show">
  <mx:Sequence>
  <mx:SetPropertyAction target="{panel2}" name="visible" />
  <mx:Fade target="{panel2}" alphaFrom="0" alphaTo="1"
  duration="500" />
  </mx:Sequence>
</mx:Transition>
<mx:Transition fromState="show" toState="hide">
  <mx:Sequence>
  <mx:Fade target="{panel2}" alphaFrom="1" alphaTo="0"
  duration="500" />
  <mx:SetPropertyAction target="{panel2}" name="visible" />
  </mx:Sequence>
</mx:Transition>
</mx:transitions>
```

```
<mx:states>
  <mx:State name="hide">
    <mx:SetProperty target="{panel2}" name="visible" value="false" />
  </mx:State>
  <mx:State name="show">
    <mx:SetProperty target="{panel2}" name="visible" value="true" />
  </mx:State>
</mx:states>
<mx:HBox width="50%" height="100%" id="panel1">
  <mx:Label text="Panel 1" />
</mx:HBox>
<mx:HBox width="50%" height="100%" id="panel2">
  <mx:Label text="Panel 2" />
</mx:HBox>
</mx:Application>
```

The transitions tag, located between the style tag and the states tag, tells the Flex framework what effects to apply when going from one state to another. In this case, it tells the framework that when going from the hide state to the show state, it should first make the panel visible, and then fade in the alpha from 0 to 1. The transition from show to hide does just the reverse.

# Implementing a two-panel interface

The next recipe is very commonly used in applications that have a list of objects where detail is presented when a user selects one of the objects. The first panel is used to show the main object list, and the second panel is used to show the detail.

The following code shows a simple two-panel interface:

```
<?xml version="1.0" encoding="utf-8"?>
<mx:Application xmlns:mx="http://www.adobe.com/2006/mxml"
  layout="vertical"
  currentState="one">
<mx:Style>
Panel {
  background-image: Embed('background.png');
  vertical-align: middle;
  horizontal-align: center;
}
Label {
  font-weight: bold;
  font-size: 20;
}
</mx:Style>
<mx:ApplicationControlBar dock="true">
  <mx:Button label="One" click="currentState='one';" />
  <mx:Button label="Two" click="currentState='two';" />
```

```
      </mx:ApplicationControlBar>
      <mx:states>
        <mx:State name="one">
          <mx:SetProperty target="{p1}" name="height" value="100%" />
          <mx:SetProperty target="{p2}" name="height" value="0%" />
          <mx:SetProperty target="{p2}" name="includeInLayout"
      value="false" />
          <mx:SetProperty target="{p2}" name="visible" value="false" />
        </mx:State>
        <mx:State name="two">
          <mx:SetProperty target="{p1}" name="height" value="50%" />
          <mx:SetProperty target="{p2}" name="height" value="50%" />
          <mx:SetProperty target="{p2}" name="includeInLayout"
      value="true" />
          <mx:SetProperty target="{p2}" name="visible" value="true" />
        </mx:State>
      </mx:states>
      <mx:Panel id="p1" title="Panel One" width="100%">
        <mx:Label text="Panel One" />
      </mx:Panel>
      <mx:Panel id="p2" title="Panel Two" width="100%">
        <mx:Label text="Panel Two" />
      </mx:Panel>
    </mx:Application>
```

When we bring this up in Flex Builder 3, we see something like Figure 2-3.

**Figure 2-3.** The two-panel example in one state

Clicking the Two button sets the interface to the two state, which brings up the second panel where the detail information would be located. This is shown in Figure 2-4.

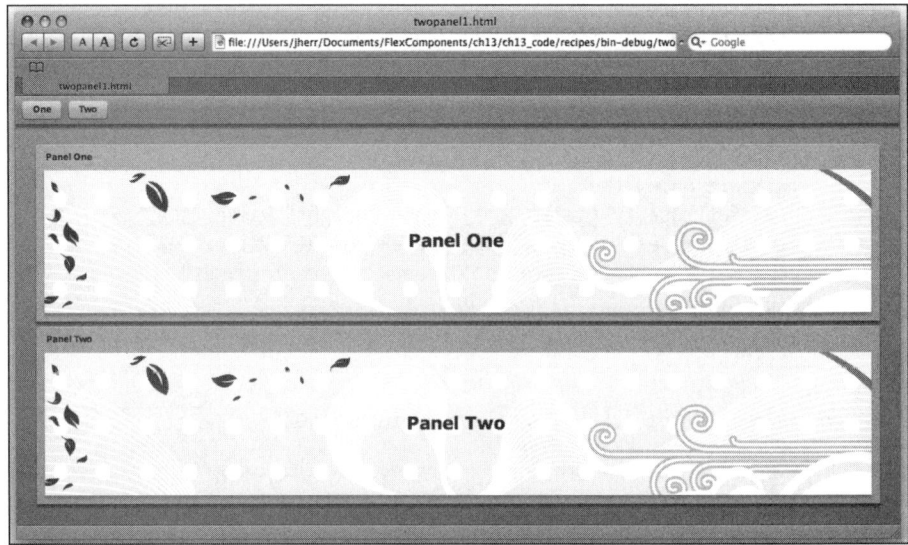

**Figure 2-4.** The two-panel example in two state

To smooth the transitions between the two states, we can use the transitions tag shown here:

```
<mx:transitions>
  <mx:Transition fromState="one" toState="two">
   <mx:Sequence>
    <mx:SetPropertyAction target="{p2}" name="includeInLayout" />
    <mx:SetPropertyAction target="{p2}" name="visible" />
    <mx:Resize targets="{[p1,p2]}" />
    </mx:Sequence>
   </mx:Transition>
   <mx:Transition fromState="two" toState="one">
    <mx:Sequence>
    <mx:Resize targets="{[p1,p2]}" />
    <mx:SetPropertyAction target="{p2}" name="visible" />
    <mx:SetPropertyAction target="{p2}" name="includeInLayout" />
    </mx:Sequence>
   </mx:Transition>
  </mx:transitions>
```

This will create an animated resize effect when the first panel shrinks to show the second panel as the application goes from one state to two state. And it shrinks the second panel to just show the first when going from two to one.

If you want, you can change this pattern so that the second panel is above or to the left or right of the first panel by adjusting the states and transitions tags.

# Three panels

Sometimes two panels just aren't enough. You not only have the list and the detail, but also need detail on the detail. So you need a three-panel approach, as shown in the following code:

```
<?xml version="1.0" encoding="utf-8"?>
<mx:Application xmlns:mx="http://www.adobe.com/2006/mxml"
  layout="vertical"
  currentState="one">
<mx:Style>
Panel {
  background-image: Embed('background.png');
  vertical-align: middle;
  horizontal-align: center;
}
Label {
  font-weight: bold;
  font-size: 20;
}
</mx:Style>
<mx:ApplicationControlBar dock="true">
  <mx:Button id="b1" label="One"
  click="currentState='one';b3.visible=false;" />
  <mx:Button label="Two"
  click="currentState='two';b3.visible=true;b1.visible=true;" />
  <mx:Button id="b3" label="Three"
  click="currentState='three';b1.visible=false;" visible="false" />
</mx:ApplicationControlBar>
<mx:states>
<mx:State name="one">
  <mx:SetProperty target="{p1}" name="height" value="100%" />
  <mx:SetProperty target="{p2}" name="height" value="0%" />
  <mx:SetProperty target="{p2}" name="includeInLayout" value="false" />
  <mx:SetProperty target="{p2}" name="visible" value="false" />
  <mx:SetProperty target="{p3}" name="includeInLayout" value="false" />
  <mx:SetProperty target="{p3}" name="visible" value="false" />
</mx:State>
<mx:State name="two">
  <mx:SetProperty target="{p1}" name="height" value="50%" />
  <mx:SetProperty target="{p2}" name="height" value="50%" />
  <mx:SetProperty target="{p2}" name="includeInLayout" value="true" />
  <mx:SetProperty target="{p2}" name="visible" value="true" />
  <mx:SetProperty target="{p3}" name="includeInLayout" value="false" />
  <mx:SetProperty target="{p3}" name="visible" value="false" />
</mx:State>
<mx:State name="three">
  <mx:SetProperty target="{p1}" name="height" value="33%" />
  <mx:SetProperty target="{p2}" name="height" value="33%" />
```

```
    <mx:SetProperty target="{p3}" name="height" value="33%" />
    <mx:SetProperty target="{p2}" name="includeInLayout" value="true" />
    <mx:SetProperty target="{p2}" name="visible" value="true" />
    <mx:SetProperty target="{p3}" name="includeInLayout" value="true" />
    <mx:SetProperty target="{p3}" name="visible" value="true" />
  </mx:State>
  </mx:states>
  <mx:Panel id="p1" title="Panel One" width="100%">
    <mx:Label text="Panel One" />
  </mx:Panel>
  <mx:Panel id="p2" title="Panel Two" width="100%">
    <mx:Label text="Panel Two" />
  </mx:Panel>
  <mx:Panel id="p3" title="Panel Three" width="100%">
    <mx:Label text="Panel Three" />
  </mx:Panel>
</mx:Application>
```

In this case, we use the `includeInLayout` attribute to ensure that the panels are completely removed from the layout of the display when they aren't being used.

When we bring this up from Flex Builder 3, the application first starts in the one state that shows just the panel one contents. This is shown in Figure 2-5.

**Figure 2-5.** The application in one state

From here, we can only select to go to the two state to show more detail. When we click the Two button, we see something like Figure 2-6.

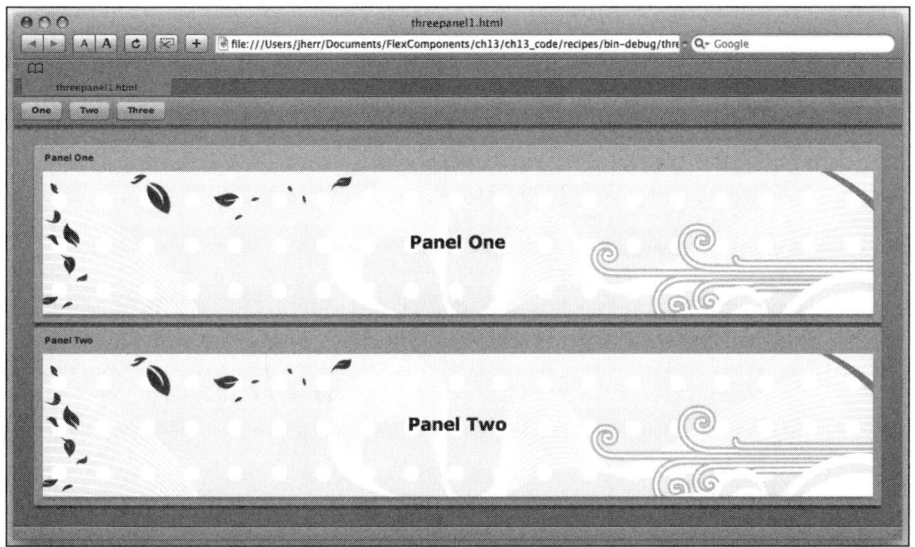

**Figure 2-6.** The application in two state

From here, we can go back to the one state and hide the detail in panel two, or move on to the three state and show the third and final panel. This third panel is shown in Figure 2-7.

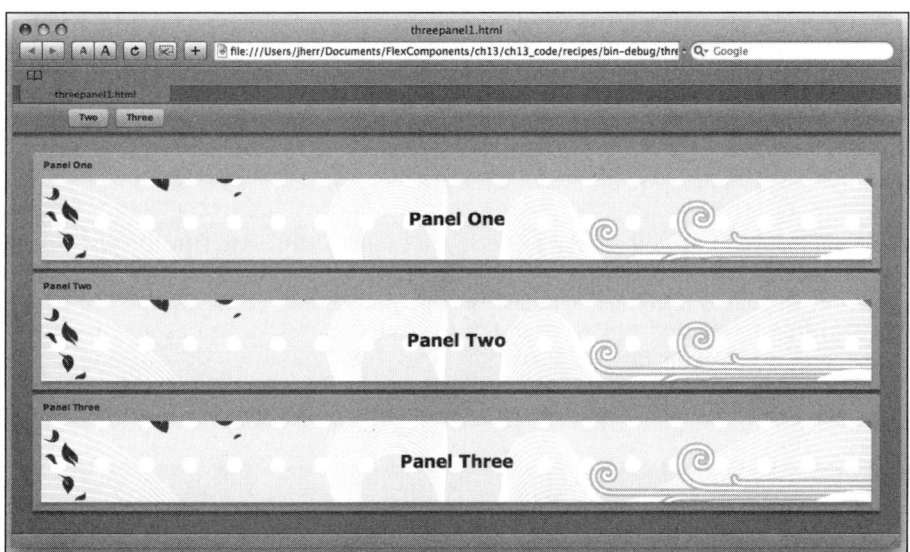

**Figure 2-7.** The application in three state

Just as with the two-panel recipe, a set of transitions makes moving to and from each of the states very sexy.

This transitions code is shown here:

```
<mx:transitions>
 <mx:Transition fromState="one" toState="two">
   <mx:Sequence>
   <mx:SetPropertyAction target="{p2}" name="includeInLayout" />
   <mx:SetPropertyAction target="{p2}" name="visible" />
   <mx:Resize targets="{[p1,p2]}" />
   </mx:Sequence>
 </mx:Transition>
 <mx:Transition fromState="two" toState="three">
   <mx:Sequence>
   <mx:SetPropertyAction target="{p3}" name="includeInLayout" />
   <mx:SetPropertyAction target="{p3}" name="visible" />
   <mx:Resize targets="{[p1,p2,p3]}" />
   </mx:Sequence>
 </mx:Transition>
 <mx:Transition fromState="three" toState="two">
   <mx:Sequence>
   <mx:Resize targets="{[p1,p2,p3]}" />
   <mx:SetPropertyAction target="{p3}" name="visible" />
   <mx:SetPropertyAction target="{p3}" name="includeInLayout" />
   </mx:Sequence>
 </mx:Transition>
 <mx:Transition fromState-"two" toState="one">
   <mx:Sequence>
   <mx:Resize targets="{[p1,p2]}" />
   <mx:SetPropertyAction target="{p2}" name="visible" />
   <mx:SetPropertyAction target="{p2}" name="includeInLayout" />
   </mx:Sequence>
 </mx:Transition>
 </mx:transitions>
```

As an alternative to using the Resize effect, you could use the Fade effect to just fade in the new panel as the other panels are being resized. What effects you want to use is completely up to you, as is the spatial relationship between the three panels. You could have them go from bottom to top, or from left to right, by adjusting the parameters in the states and transitions tags.

# Slide in

Sometimes it's not possible to do all of the state work with MXML tags. One of these cases is the "Slide In" recipe shown in the following code:

```
<?xml version="1.0" encoding="utf-8"?>
<mx:Application xmlns:mx="http://www.adobe.com/2006/mxml"
  layout="absolute"
  currentState="out" horizontalScrollPolicy="off"
```

```
    verticalScrollPolicy="off"
    creationComplete="onResize()" resize="onResize()">
<mx:Style>
HBox {
  background-image: Embed('background.png');
  border-thickness: 3;
  border-style: solid;
  corner-radius: 3;
  vertical-align: middle;
  horizontal-align: center;
  border-color: #034EA2;
}
Label {
  font-weight: bold;
  font-size: 20;
}
</mx:Style>
<mx:Script>
<![CDATA[
private function onResize() : void {
    if ( !initialized ) return;

  inWidth.value = ( ( width - p2.width ) - 30 );
  outWidth.value = width - 20;
  inLeft.value = ( width - p2.width ) - 15;
  outLeft.value = width;

  p1.width = ( currentState == 'out' ) ? ➡
outWidth.value : inWidth.value;
  p2.setStyle( 'left', ( currentState == 'out' ) ? ➡
  outLeft.value : inLeft.value );
}
]]>
</mx:Script>
<mx:ApplicationControlBar dock="true">
  <mx:Button label="In" click="currentState='in';" />
  <mx:Button label="Out" click="currentState='out';" />
</mx:ApplicationControlBar>
<mx:states>
  <mx:State name="in">
    <mx:SetProperty target="{p1}" name="width" id="inWidth"
  value="100" />
    <mx:SetStyle target="{p2}" name="left" id="inLeft" value="100" />
  </mx:State>
  <mx:State name="out">
    <mx:SetProperty target="{p1}" name="width" id="outWidth"
  value="100" />
    <mx:SetStyle target="{p2}" name="left" id="outLeft" value="100" />
  </mx:State>
```

```
    </mx:states>
    <mx:HBox id="p1" top="10" left="10" height="95%">
      <mx:Label text="Main Content Area" />
    </mx:HBox>
    <mx:HBox id="p2" top="10" left="10" width="250" height="95%">
      <mx:Label text="Side Content Area" />
    </mx:HBox>
    </mx:Application>
```

The "Slide In" recipe is a variation on the "Two Panel" recipe. In this case, the size of the second panel is maintained so that it looks like you are dragging it in from offscreen.

To accomplish this, the parameters in the SetProperty and SetStyle tags need to be updated when the application is resized so that the second panel is always offscreen until it's slid in. The code to handle this is in the onResize method.

When we first bring up the application, it's in out state, which means that the sliding content is offscreen. This is shown in Figure 2-8.

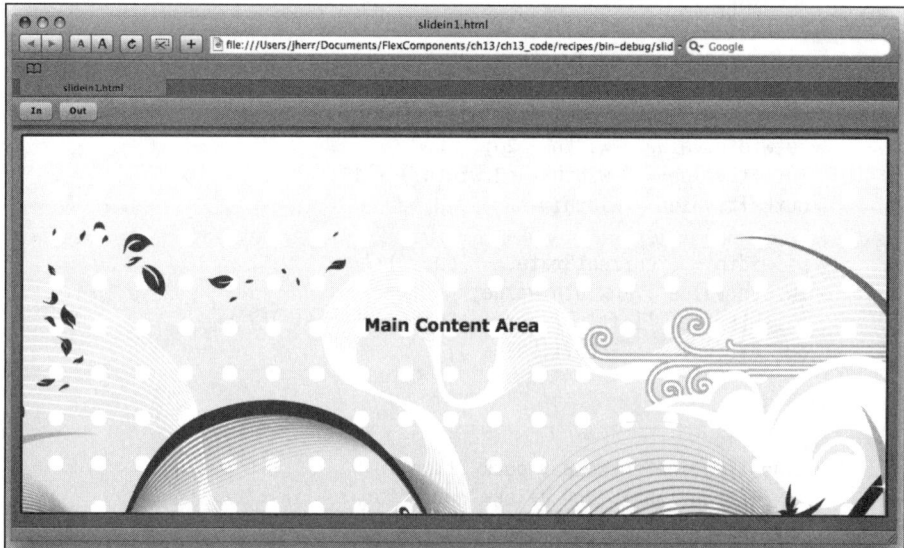

**Figure 2-8.** The application in out state

When we click the In button, the state of the application is changed to in, and the side panel is brought in. This is shown in Figure 2-9.

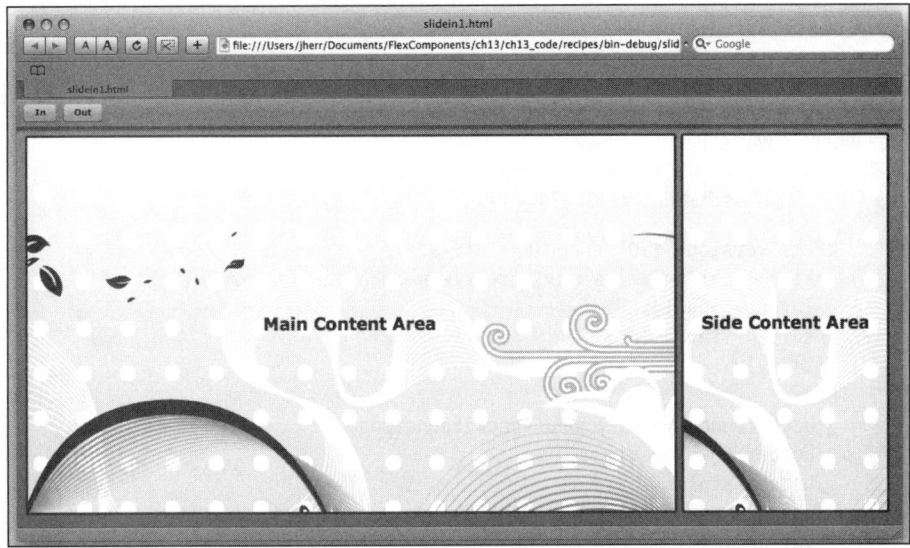

**Figure 2-9.** The application in in state

The slide is accomplished with the transitions code shown here:

```
<mx:transitions>
  <mx:Transition fromState="in" toState="out">
    <mx:Parallel duration="300">
    <mx:Resize target="{p1}" />
    <mx:Move target="{p2}" />
    </mx:Parallel>
  </mx:Transition>
  <mx:Transition fromState="out" toState="in">
    <mx:Parallel duration="300">
    <mx:Resize target="{p1}" />
    <mx:Move target="{p2}" />
    </mx:Parallel>
  </mx:Transition>
</mx:transitions>
```

The main panel is resized in parallel with the second panel being moved in from the right-hand side of the display. The application of these two animations simultaneously gives the illusion that the second panel is attached to the first and is being dragged in.

As with the previous recipes, you could place the second panel to the left, above, or below the main panel. Or even have multiple sliders that come in several different states.

## Pop-Out

Another popular state recipe is the "Pop-Out," which causes a panel to pop out from underneath a main panel. This was first seen on early versions of the Mac OS X user interface where it was called a "drawer."

The code to create a pop-out interface design using states is shown here:

```
<?xml version="1.0" encoding="utf-8"?>
<mx:Application xmlns:mx="http://www.adobe.com/2006/mxml"
  layout="absolute"
  currentState="in">
<mx:Style>
HBox {
  background-image: Embed('background.png');
  border-thickness: 3;
  border-style: solid;
  corner-radius: 3;
  vertical-align: middle;
  horizontal-align: center;
  border-color: #034EA2;
}
Label {
  font-weight: bold;
  font-size: 20;
}
.shelf {
  font-weight: normal;
  font-size: 15;
}
</mx:Style>
<mx:ApplicationControlBar dock="true">
  <mx:Button label="In" click="currentState='in';" />
  <mx:Button label="Out" click="currentState='out';" />
</mx:ApplicationControlBar>
<mx:states>
  <mx:State name="in">
    <mx:SetStyle target="{shelf}" name="left" value="50" />
  </mx:State>
  <mx:State name="out">
    <mx:SetStyle target="{shelf}" name="left"
  value="{topContent.width + topContent.x -3}" />
  </mx:State>
</mx:states>
<mx:HBox id="shelf" top="50" left="50" width="200" height="300">
  <mx:Label text="Shelf Content" styleName="shelf" />
```

```
    </mx:HBox>
    <mx:HBox top="10" left="10" width="300" height="400">
      <mx:Label text="Top Content" />
    </mx:HBox>
  </mx:Application>
```

This application doesn't use any ActionScript because the sizes of the individual elements are hard-coded in this absolutely positioned interface. The element that pops out is called the **shelf** and is located below the top content by defining its MXML content first.

When we bring this application up in Flex Builder 3, the application starts up in the in state. This is shown in Figure 2-10.

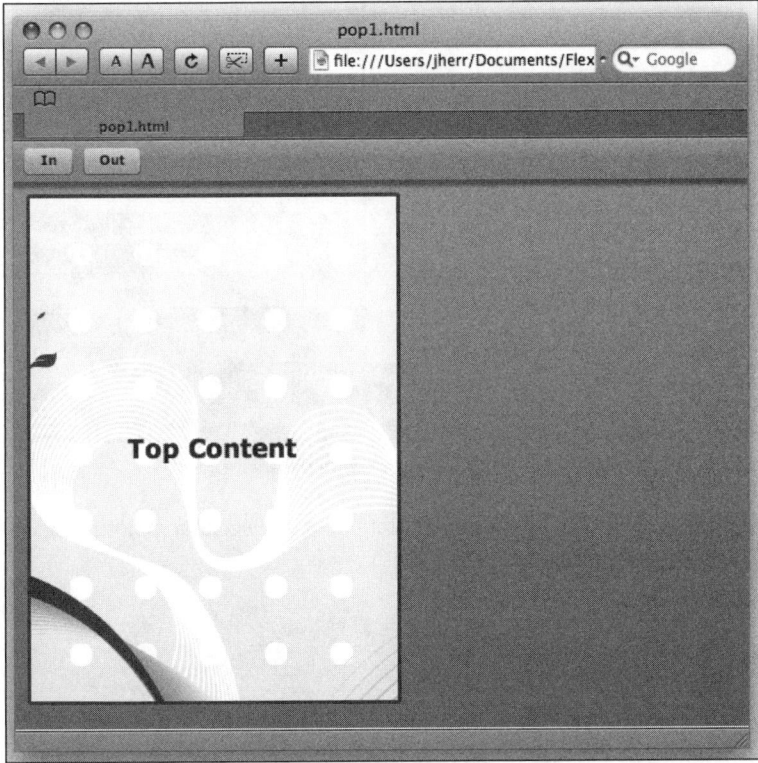

**Figure 2-10.** The in state of the application with the shelf hidden

From here, we press the Out button to show the shelf, which you can see in Figure 2-11.

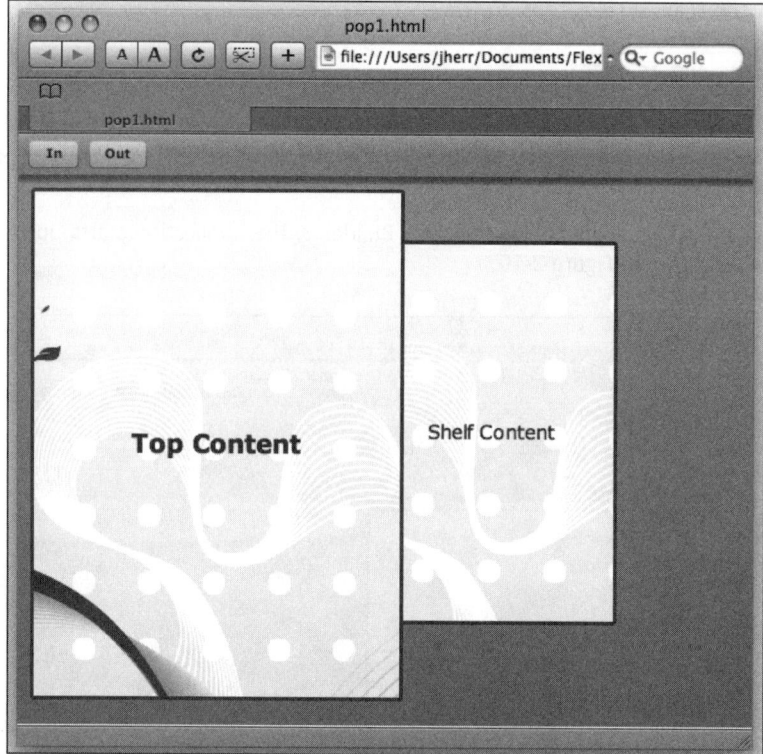

**Figure 2-11.** The out state of the application with the shelf shown

To give this transition from out state to in state (and vice versa) a smooth feel, we use the transitions code shown here:

```
<mx:transitions>
  <mx:Transition fromState="in" toState="out">
    <mx:Move duration="300" target="{shelf}" />
  </mx:Transition>
  <mx:Transition fromState="out" toState="in">
    <mx:Move duration="300" target="{shelf}" />
  </mx:Transition>
</mx:transitions>
```

This is an ideal candidate for using an easing parameter on the move to give the feeling of slowing as the shelf glides either in or out.

# Emerge

The "Emerge" recipe is something that's used a lot on television. The main content area is unobstructed until an overlay is faded in, or dragged up, to display additional information. That overlay is then faded or drawn back underneath to once again show the unobstructed main content.

Here's the Flex application code used to implement the "Emerge" recipe:

```
<mx:Application xmlns:mx="http://www.adobe.com/2006/mxml"
  layout="absolute"
  currentState="out"  horizontalScrollPolicy="off"
  verticalScrollPolicy="off">
<mx:Script>
<![CDATA[

]]>
</mx:Script>
<mx:Style>
HBox {
  background-color:#ccffcc;
  border-thickness: 3;
  border-style: solid;
  corner-radius: 3;
  vertical-align: middle;
  horizontal-align: center;
  border-color: #034EA2;
  background-alpha: 0.8;
}
Label {
  font-weight: bold;
  font-size: 50;
}
</mx:Style>
<mx:ApplicationControlBar dock="true">
  <mx:Button label="In" click="currentState='in';" />
  <mx:Button label="Out" click="currentState='out';" />
</mx:ApplicationControlBar>
<mx:states>
  <mx:State name="in">
    <mx:SetStyle target="{panel}" name="bottom" value="0"  />
  </mx:State>
  <mx:State name="out">
   <mx:SetStyle target="{panel}" name="bottom" value="-150"  />
  </mx:State>
```

```
</mx:states>
<mx:Label top="10" left="10" text="Content Area" fontSize="40" />
<mx:HBox id="panel" left="0" width="100%" height="150" >
<mx:Label text="Popup Area" />
</mx:HBox>
</mx:Application>
```

Because the overlay panel is coming up from the bottom, it needs to be located just off-screen on the bottom of the display. That means we need to track the resize of the window using ActionScript. This is done using the onResize method, which alters the parameters of the two SetStyle objects in the different states of the interface.

When the application first comes up, it's in the out mode, which means that the overlay panel is hidden offscreen. This is shown in Figure 2-12.

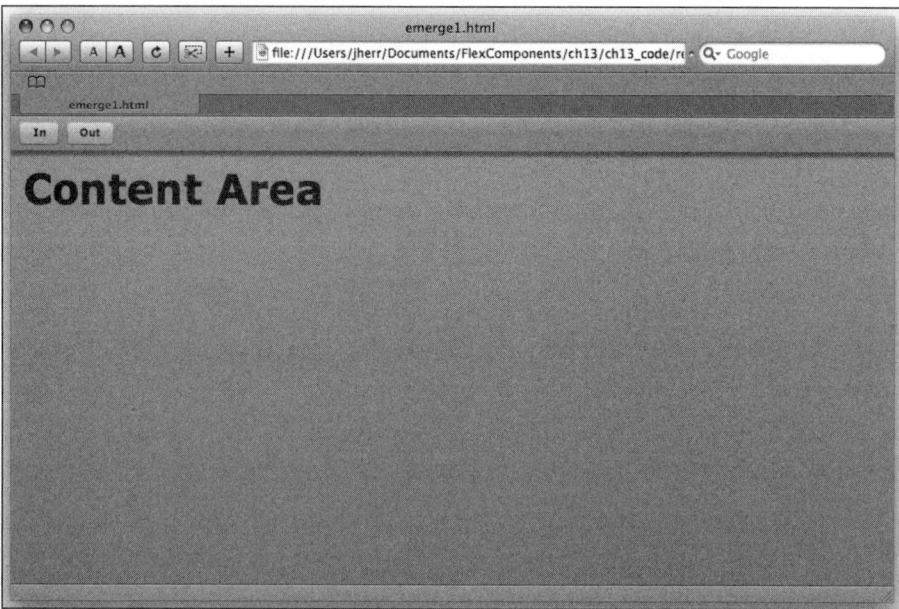

**Figure 2-12.** The out state of the application

Clicking the In button changes the state of the application to in, which brings in the overlay panel. This is shown in Figure 2-13.

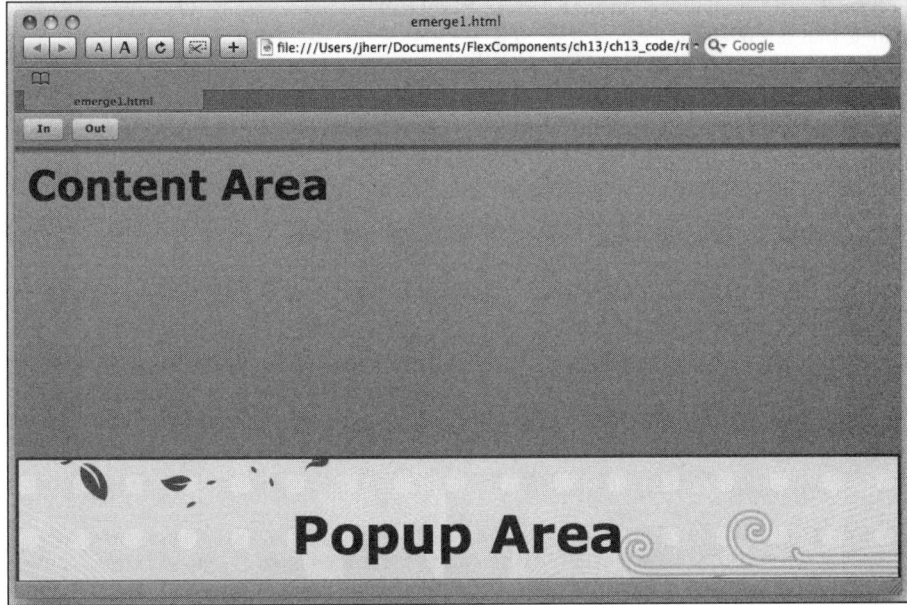

**Figure 2-13.** The in state of the application

To glide the overlay in, we use the transitions code shown here:

```
<mx:transitions>
  <mx:Transition fromState="in" toState="out">
    <mx:Move duration="300" target="{panel}" />
  </mx:Transition>
  <mx:Transition fromState="out" toState="in">
    <mx:Move duration="300" target="{panel}" />
  </mx:Transition>
</mx:transitions>
```

If gliding the overlay in doesn't work for you, you can do a Fade if you prefer to fade the overlay in and out.

# Flip

Card flipping is fast becoming a popular way of presenting the user with configuration options. The main interface has a configuration button on it which, when pressed, flips the item over to present a set of configuration controls. The user can then flip the interface back to the normal presentation by clicking OK or Cancel on the configuration interface.

Following is a Flex application that demonstrates using a flip to get between two different panels that are overlaid:

```xml
<?xml version="1.0" encoding="utf-8"?>
<mx:Application xmlns:mx="http://www.adobe.com/2006/mxml"
  layout="vertical"
  currentState="top">
<mx:Style>
Panel {
  background-image: Embed('background.png');
  vertical-align: middle;
  horizontal-align: center;
}
Label {
  font-weight: bold;
  font-size: 50;
}
</mx:Style>
<mx:ApplicationControlBar dock="true">
  <mx:Button label="Top" click="currentState='top';" />
  <mx:Button label="Bottom" click="currentState='bottom';" />
</mx:ApplicationControlBar>
<mx:states>
  <mx:State name="top">
    <mx:SetProperty target="{vs}" name="selectedChild"
    value="{ftile}" />
  </mx:State>
  <mx:State name="bottom">
    <mx:SetProperty target="{vs}" name="selectedChild"
    value="{btile}" />
  </mx:State>
</mx:states>
<mx:ViewStack id="vs" width="70%" height="90%">
  <mx:Panel id="ftile" title="Top" verticalAlign="middle"
  horizontalAlign="center" width="100%" height="100%">
    <mx:Label text="Top" fontSize="30" />
  </mx:Panel>
  <mx:Panel id="btile" title="Bottom" verticalAlign="middle"
  horizontalAlign="center" width="100%" height="100%">
    <mx:Label text="Bottom" fontSize="30" />
  </mx:Panel>
</mx:ViewStack>
</mx:Application>
```

In this case, we use a ViewStack container to overlay the two different tiles. The front tile is called ftile and is visible in top mode. The back tile is called btile and is visible in bottom mode. The states defined in the application flip between the top and bottom state to hide and show the ftile and btile appropriately.

The application, when first launched, is in the top state, shown in Figure 2-14.

**Figure 2-14.** The application in top state

From here we can click the Bottom button to flip the card over and expose the bottom tile, shown in Figure 2-15.

**Figure 2-15.** The application in bottom state

Unfortunately, the Flex framework does not have a flip effect built in. But the Distortion Effects library from Alex Uhlman (http://weblogs.macromedia.com/auhlmann/), which is included with the source code for this example, has the flip effect. The transitions code that uses it is shown here:

```
<mx:transitions>
  <mx:Transition fromState="top" toState="bottom">
    <mxeffects:Flip siblings="{[ftile]}" target="{btile}" />
  </mx:Transition>
  <mx:Transition fromState="bottom" toState="top">
    <mxeffects:Flip siblings="{[btile]}" target="{ftile}" />
  </mx:Transition>
</mx:transitions>
```

Not only does Alex's library do the flip effect, it also does cube rotates and other cool tricks.

# Grower

The "Grower" recipe is the final one that I will show. It's most useful when you have an individual object, a headshot of a person, that you can click, which will grow to show more content. Clicking it again will shrink it back to its normal size.

The Flex application code that demonstrates the grower state recipe is shown here:

```
<?xml version="1.0" encoding="utf-8"?>
<mx:Application xmlns:mx="http://www.adobe.com/2006/mxml"
  layout="vertical"
  currentState="small" horizontalAlign="left">
<mx:Style>
HBox {
  background-image: Embed('background.png');
  border-thickness: 3;
  border-style: solid;
  corner-radius: 3;
  vertical-align: middle;
  horizontal-align: center;
  border-color: #034EA2;
}
Label {
  font-weight: bold;
  font-size: 50;
}
```

```
    </mx:Style>
    <mx:ApplicationControlBar dock="true">
      <mx:Button label="Small" click="currentState='small';" />
      <mx:Button label="Big" click="currentState='big';" />
    </mx:ApplicationControlBar>
    <mx:states>
      <mx:State name="small">
        <mx:SetProperty name="width" target="{growbox}" value="300" />
      </mx:State>
      <mx:State name="big">
        <mx:SetProperty name="width" target="{growbox}" value="600" />
      </mx:State>
    </mx:states>
    <mx:HBox id="growbox" width="300" height="200">
      <mx:Label text="Grow box" />
    </mx:HBox>
    </mx:Application>
```

The code is fairly simple. The width property of the growbox window is set to something small, 300, in small mode, and set to something larger, 600, in large mode. The application starts out in small mode, shown in Figure 2-16.

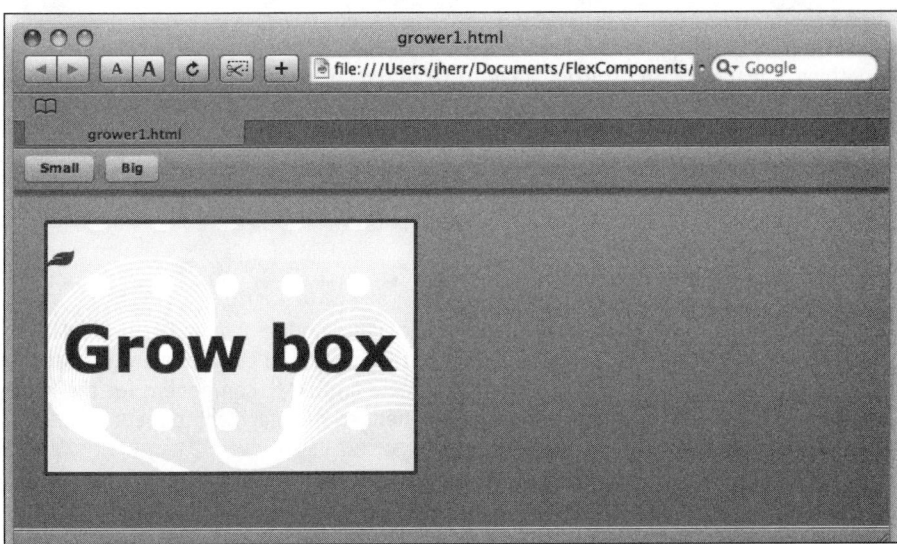

**Figure 2-16.** The small state of the grow box

From here, we can click the Big button to make the growbox larger. This is shown in Figure 2-17.

**Figure 2-17.** The large state of the grow box

Smoothing out the transition from small to large, or back again, is accomplished with a 300 millisecond Resize transition, shown in the following code:

```
<mx:transitions>
  <mx:Transition fromState="*" toState="*">
    <mx:Resize duration="300" target="{growbox}" />
  </mx:Transition>
</mx:transitions>
```

The "Grower" recipe often applies to multiple elements on the screen. For example, you have a display of various headshots, and you want to be able to click to open or close any that you choose. In this case, you will want to create an MXML component for the headshot and use the "Grower" recipe on that component so that each component handles its own growing and shrinking.

## Building your own state systems

Hopefully these recipes have whetted your appetite for creating cool state systems and transitions in your own application. Sometimes building state systems can be a pain because you are attempting to build everything: the interface components, the states and the transitions, all at the same time.

I recommend using a four-step approach to building your interface using states and transitions. Here are the "four steps to transition-y happiness":

**1.** Lay the controls out in the startup state. Test it.

**2.** Build the states and set the current state to the starting state. Test it.

**3.** Add the code required to flip between states. Test it.

**4.** Add the transitions to make everything change smoothly. Test it.

It starts with doing the layout of the interface at the starting point—in other words, what users will see when they first get into the application.

In the second step, you add additional controls that will be visible in the different states, and then build the states and test them, without transitions.

In the third step, you add the controls and code necessary to change between the different states of the application.

The final step is to finish it all off with transitions to make it glide. That being said, transitions can be overdone. You will find that anything over 300 milliseconds is a long time for a user to wait for an effect to finish. And while it might look sexy the first five or six times, it can be a pain later on as the user is more interested in getting to the functionality than he is in watching a sexy transition.

Here are a few common things that you should test at each step in developing your interface:

- Mouse over everything, making sure the right cursor comes up everywhere.
- If there are buttons to click, make sure you click them all.
- Use the Tab key to navigate around the interface.
- If you have resizable controls like HDividedBox or VDividedBox, make sure they work at the top, bottom, and middle.
- If the application can be resized, try it both very small and very large.

These should help you work the kinks out your interface.

Finally, I strongly recommend that you make liberal use of the CSS capability built into the Flex core. Not only will it make your code easier to read and easier to skin, but it also makes a clean separation between the properties that will stay constant and those that will change between states. Define the constant properties in CSS, and use the states tags to define the properties that are altered between states.

# Where we will go from here

As I present the components in the next few chapters, try to think of each one in the context of a larger interface design. For example, when we look at graphing, try and figure out how the user will get to the graph. Will there be one graph or multiple graphs? How will it all fit together into a single coherent application that the user can understand? This is where states come in very handy. Hopefully, this chapter will help you make the best use of the state mechanisms built into the Flex framework to develop applications that work well and look great.

Audio event: MP3, 16 kbps, Mono
- [ ] Override sound settings
- [ ] Export device sounds

- [x] Compress movie
- [x] Include hidden layers
- [x] Include XMP metadata
- [x] Export SWC

e and debug:
- [ ] Generate size report
- [ ] Protect from import
- [ ] Omit trace actions

| Companies | Employees | Payroll |
| --- | --- | --- |
| 18589 | 514046 | 2571858 |
| 162 | 4875 | 219348 |
| 39 | 392 | 15238 |
| 353 | 11389 | 435500 |
| 124 | 5976 | 294804 |
| 2808 | 76323 | 4319922 |
| 470 | 12681 | 644669 |
| 243 | 5512 | 223263 |
| 59 | 2686 | 193854 |
| 99 | 2297 | 123991 |

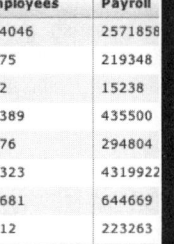

# Building a solid foundation

Installing Flex Builder 3 is only the starting point in the long road to getting the most out of the Flex framework. There are libraries and components to install in your application that you can reference in your code to build up your application quickly. And there is almost always a server component your application will reference.

This chapter starts by showing you how to install libraries in your application, as well as showing you how to turn Flash components into libraries that can be referenced in a Flex project. But that's just the first part; the second part of this chapter sets up your local web server with the data that the examples contained in the rest of the book will reference.

# Introducing components

There are several different ways that components are packaged, and you need to understand each of these and how to use them.

## Small components and skins

Smaller components, and skin sets, are usually packaged as a ZIP file that contains just the MXML or CSS files that are required. You can add these to your project by simply dragging and dropping them into the src directory of your Flex project in Flex Builder. Then reference them either by using a <local:ComponentName> reference to reference an MXML file or by using an <mx:style> to reference a CSS library.

If the components come along with any resources, like PNG files, audio, or other items, you will want to bring those in as well. You don't have to bring readme or installation text files into the project.

## MXP files

Flash components are shipped as MXP files. The icons for these files are little boxes that look like suitcases. These have to be installed with the Adobe Extension Manager and then converted using the Flash IDE. The full procedure is described in the "Creating SWC libraries from MXP components" section later in this chapter.

## Source code for libraries

Some libraries are shipped as source, or source and binaries. Usually, the source code will come in a directory called src with a subdirectory of com or org. You will want to drag the com or org directory into the src directory of your project in Flex Builder.

If the library ships with both source and a compiled SWC file, then you have a choice. If you think the library is in its early stages and you will be debugging it, you will probably want to include the source and forgo the compiled binary. For a well-established library like the AS3 Core Lib (AS3 CoreLib) or the Flex Library (FlexLib), both described in more detail later in the section "Installing AS3CoreLib and FlexLib," you can safely use the compiled SWC library. The only real difference between these two approaches is the clutter in your project file.

## SWC files

If the library is shipped as a SWC file, then drop this file into the libs directory of your project in Flex Builder to install it.

## Custom installers

Big packages like ILOG's Elixir data visualization package (described in more detail later in the section "Installing Elixir") or the yFiles FLEX graph visualization framework have their own custom installers or installation procedures that you have to follow. In both of these cases, you not only get Flex libraries that hold the components, but also documentation packages that integrate with Flex Builder 3.

## Canned components

Flash components that are delivered as SWF files are **canned components**, which are not the focus of this book. These components are meant to be adjusted at the HTML page level or by altering an XML output from the server. This book focuses on components that you can incorporate into your own SWF application. That being said, I might show one or two of the particularly excellent canned components that you can find out there to really blow away the visitors to your web site.

# Installing AS3CoreLib and FlexLib

There are two fundamental external libraries that almost all Flex developers use: AS3CoreLib (http://as3corelib.googlecode.com) and FlexLib (http://flexlib. googlecode.com/). Speaking broadly, AS3CoreLib focuses on extending the ActionScript toolkit, while FlexLib has new controls and containers to extend the framework.

Installing these libraries is as easy as downloading the most recent build and dragging the SWC file from the binary directory into the libs directory of your project. Alternatively, you can use the Project preferences to add the library SWC from a set location so that all of your projects can reference the same library file.

Following is a list of other good libraries that you should consider installing:

- **FlexUnit** (http://as3flexunit.googlecode.com): This is a port of the popular *Unit testing framework to Flex. You can use this to write unit tests for your application or library.

- **Degrafa** (http://degrafa.googlecode.com): Degrafa is an amazing graphics framework that makes it easy to create beautiful graphics in Flex using just tags.

- **Papervision3D** (http://papervision3d.googlecode.com): Papervision3D is a 3D rendering library built entirely in ActionScript. It can import models from applications like SketchUp, and then render them on a canvas.

- **WOW-Engine** (http://seraf.mediabox.fr/wow-engine/as3-3d-physics-engine-wow-engine/): This physics engine is used to apply real-world-style physics-based effects to 2D and 3D environments. This can come in really handy if you are looking to develop games.

- **AS3 Syndication Library** (http://as3syndicationlib.googlecode.com): This library makes parsing RSS feeds a snap.

- **Mappr** (http://as3mapprlib.googlecode.com): This library converts addresses to latitude and longitude values that you can use for mapping. The process is known is **geocoding**.

- **AS3 Flickr Library** (http://as3flickrlib.googlecode.com): This handy library gives you a clean AS3-feeling API that wraps the Flickr API. All you need is a free Flickr API key and the entire image repository is yours for the taking.

- **AS3 YouTube Library** (http://as3youtubelib.googlecode.com): This library opens up the world of YouTube for your video-consuming applications' pleasure.

- **AS3 AWS Library** (http://as3awss3lib.googlecode.com): If using Amazon Web Services (AWS) is critical to your application, this library will save you a lot of time. AWS provides data storage (S3), remote computing (EC2), and guaranteed messaging (SQS). This shouldn't be confused with the consumer side of the Amazon house that sells books and what not and has a completely different API.

- **AlivePDF** (http://alivepdf.bytearray.org/?page_id=2): This library gives you the ability to generate PDF files from within your Flex application.

- **ASTRA Web APIs** (http://developer.yahoo.com/flash/astra-webapis/): The APIs in this library give you easy access to Yahoo! services like Answers, Weather, and Search.

This is just a sampling of the available libraries out there for ActionScript 3 and Flex. If you are looking to connect to a popular web service, chances are there is an ActionScript library already out there that you can use instead of writing your own.

## Installing Elixir

The Elixir framework from ILOG (http://elixir.ilog.com) requires some special discussion here. The Flex framework provides a certain set of 2D charting classes. The Elixir framework extends those controls with additional 2D and 3D charts. I use the framework extensively throughout the book, so you will want to download and install the trial version to follow along.

You should install Flex Builder 3 before installing Elixir. The Elixir installer will automatically add itself to the Flex Builder 3 installation to provide additional help materials for the framework.

**3**

## Creating SWC libraries from MXP components

One issue you might run into with downloaded Flash components is that they are delivered in MXP format and not the SWC format that is most easily used by Flex. MXP files are component packages for the Flash IDE, and they are represented by little package icons as shown in Figure 3-1.

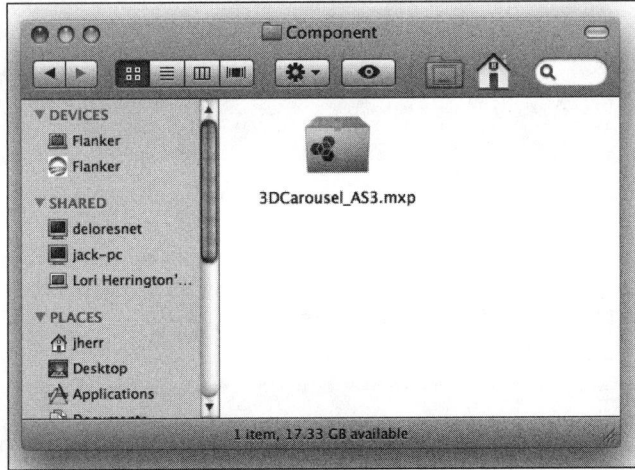

**Figure 3-1.** The 3D Carousel Flash component from Advanced Flash Components

In this case, the component is the 3D Carousel from Advanced Flash Components (http://afcomponents.com). If you don't see the icon as a box, you probably don't have the Flash IDE installed, or it isn't installed improperly. You will need to have the Flash IDE installed to make this recipe work.

The first step is to double-click the MXP box. This should launch the Adobe Extension Manager. It will then ask you if you want to install the extension as shown in Figure 3-2.

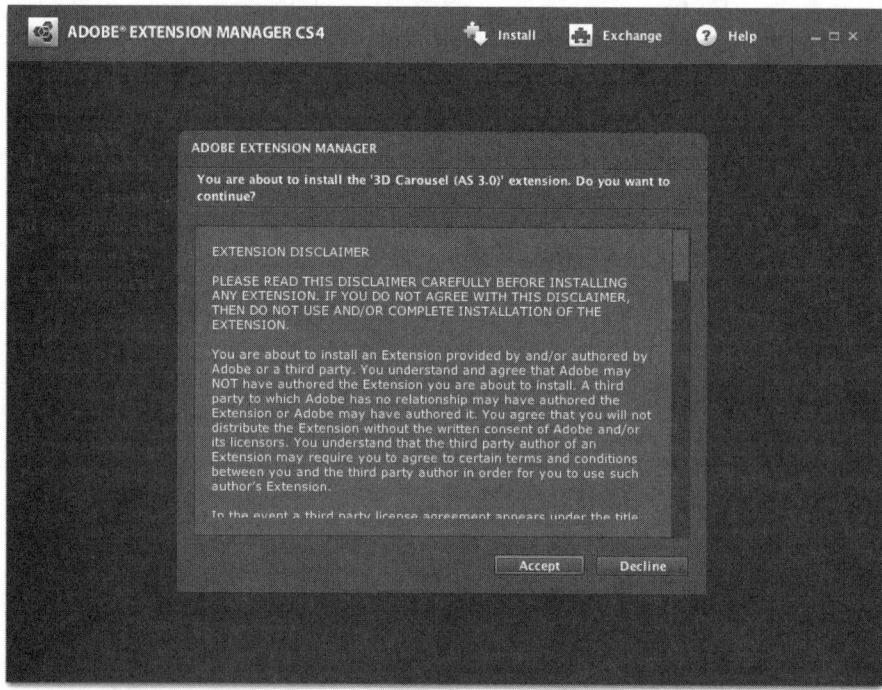

**Figure 3-2.** Installing the extension

The screenshot shows the Extension Manager CS4, but the other versions of the Extension Managers work exactly the same way. If the extension installs properly, you should see it in your list of Flash extensions, as shown in Figure 3-3.

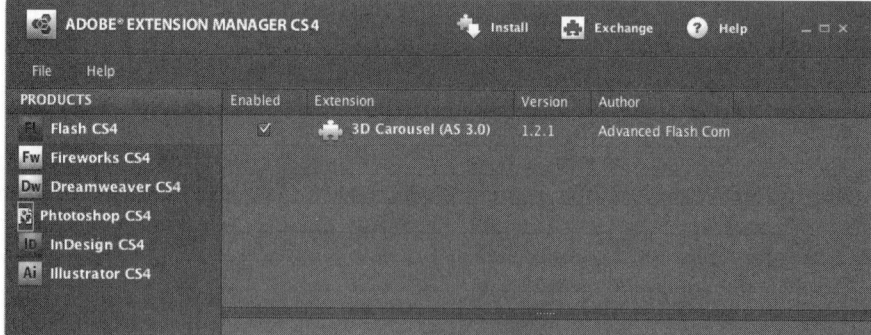

**Figure 3-3.** The installed Flash component

So far so good. At this point, you can close the Extension Manager and launch the Flash IDE. Once it comes up, click the Flash File (ActionScript 3.0) button under Create New menu on the splash screen. This option is shown highlighted in Figure 3-4.

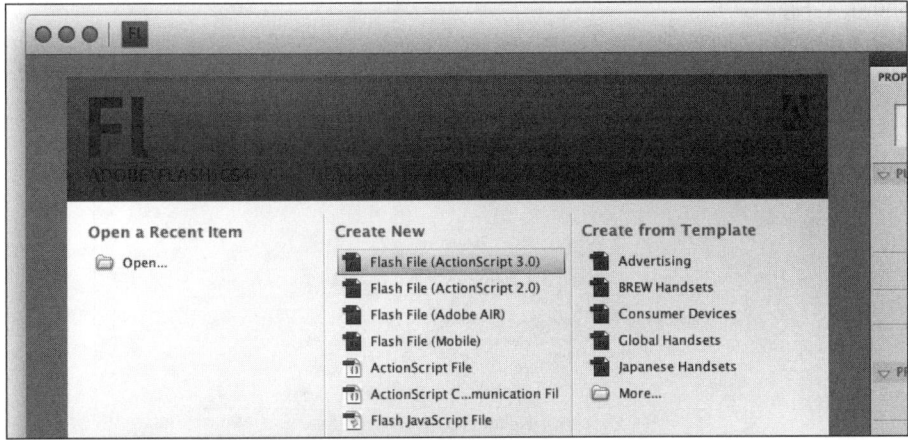

**Figure 3-4.** The Flash splash screen

Clicking the button will bring up an empty Flash application. From there, we select the Components item from the Window menu. This will bring up the Components palette from which you can select the component you installed. The selection of 3D Carousel is shown in Figure 3-5.

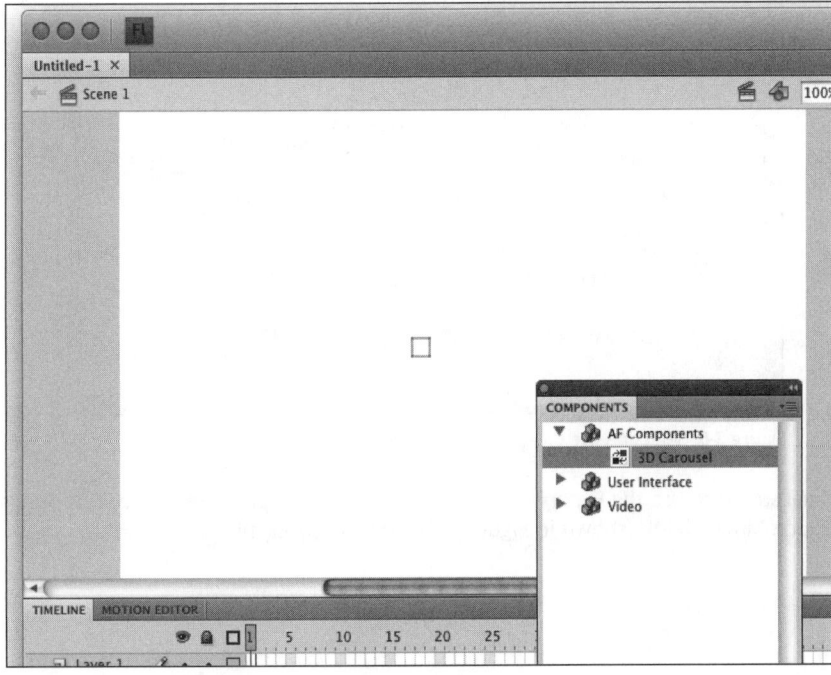

**Figure 3-5.** The 3D Carousel component selected

The next step is to drop a component of that type onto the stage. Anywhere is fine. The only thing that matters is that the SWF movie references the component. From there, we bring up the Publish Settings dialog and select the Flash panel. The important thing to do here is to select the Export SWC setting, since it's the SWC that we really want. This is shown in Figure 3-6.

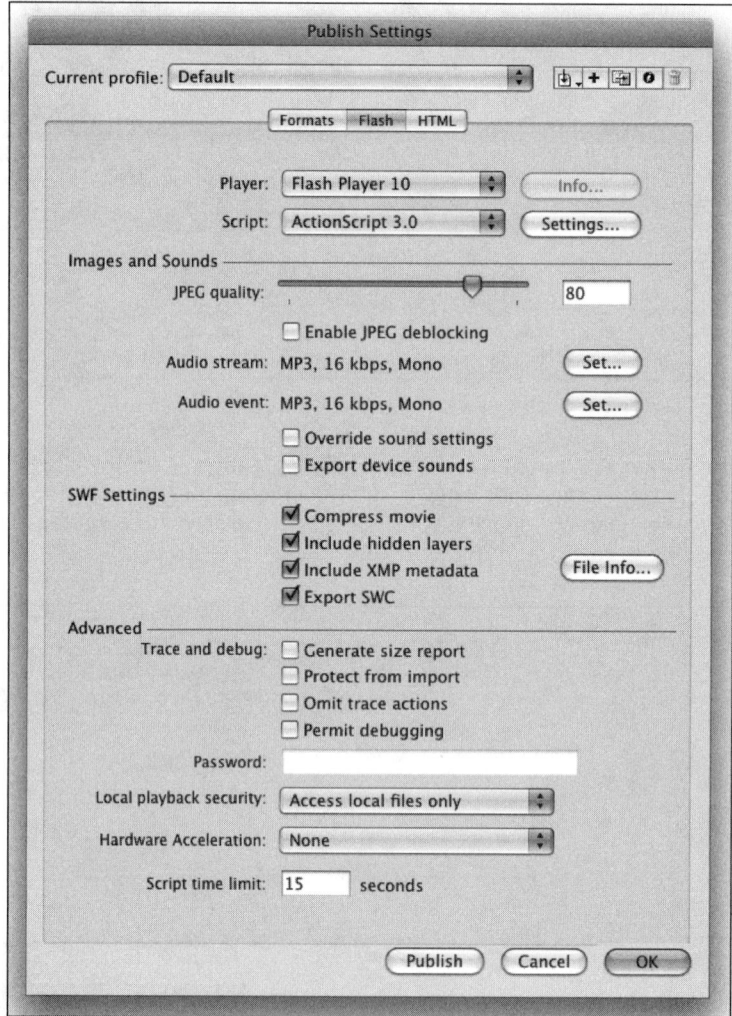

**Figure 3-6.** Selecting the Export SWC option

The final step is to use the Export item in the file menu to export the movie. This brings up the Export Movie dialog (shown in Figure 3-7) for saving your file.

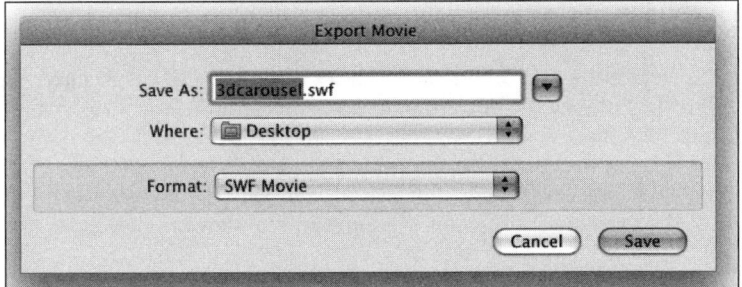

**Figure 3-7.** The Export Movie dialog

Select wherever you like to save the movie. The Flash IDE will write the SWC file into the same directory as the SWF. You can then take the SWF file and move it wherever you like. For example, you can put it into the same directory as the MXP file so that you remember where it is. This is shown in Figure 3-8.

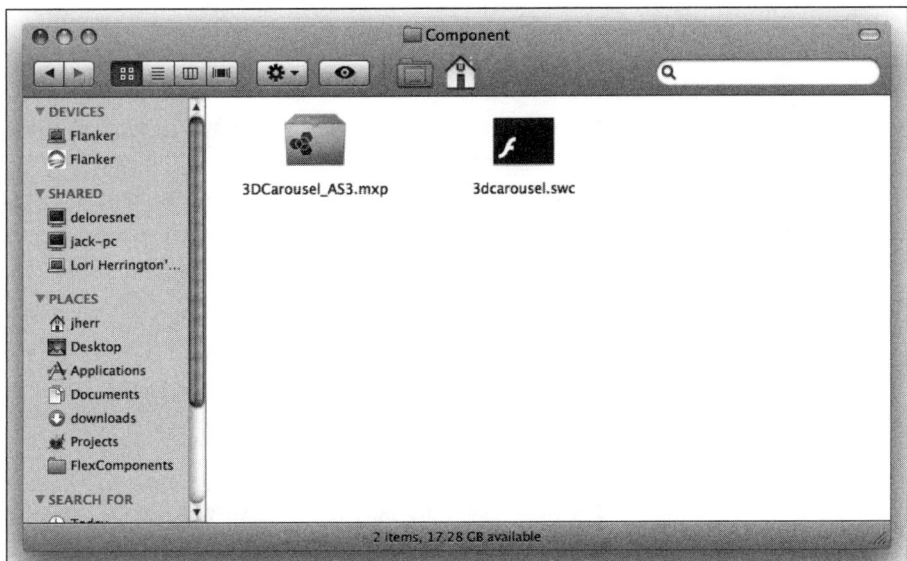

**Figure 3-8.** The exported SWC file

You can close the Flash IDE at this point, and delete the FLA or SWF files if you have either. Now that you have the SWC file, you can add it to your Flex project just as you would with any other SWC by adding it to the libs directory of your project or by referencing it in the Project dialog.

# Setting up the server

You might be wondering why a book about Flex components needs to cover server-side configuration. Most of these components can be demonstrated using data that is built into the application. But that's not the way they will likely be used. Most Flex applications use some type of web connection to get the data to display. To ensure that all of the components in this book are compatible with use of web services to retrieve the data they employ, all of the example applications use some type of network data access or dynamic data.

# Installing PHP

The easiest dynamic server technology to use, in my opinion, is PHP. This book uses PHP, and the AMFPHP project, to provide the data to the Flex applications I present. On the Macintosh platform, the PHP installation that comes with the operating system is sufficient to run the AMFPHP project and all of the services code. But there are a few things to set up first:

1. You need to install MySQL using the package from http://mysql.org.

2. You then need to start the MySQL server using either the control panel that comes with the installer or the command-line safe_mysqld script.

3. You need to change the httpd.conf file in /private/etc/apache2/ to enable PHP by removing the semicolon in front of this line:

   LoadModule php5_module        libexec/apache2/libphp5.so

4. You need to install PEAR for PHP if you haven't already. The script and all of the instructions to do that are at http://pear.php.net/go-pear.

5. You need to install MDB2_driver_MySQL using this PEAR command line:

   pear install MDB2_driver_MySQL

6. With all that set up, there is only one file left to tweak. You need to edit the /etc/php.ini file. Or copy /etc/php.ini.default to /etc/php.ini if it doesn't exist.

7. In the php.ini file, add the PEAR directory to the include_path variable if go-pear hasn't done it already.

8. In the php.ini file change the mysql.default_socket line to this:

   mysql.default_socket = /tmp/mysql.sock

It looks like a lot of work, but it's mostly about enabling PHP, installing MySQL, and getting the two to work together. If you've done that already on your Macintosh, then most of these steps will be unnecessary.

On Windows, I recommend installing the XAMPP (http://www.apachefriends.org/en/xampp.html) project, which installs PHP, MySQL, Apache, and everything you need with one easy installer.

# Installing AMFPHP

To make it easy to get to the data on the server, we will use AMF services. And to make it easy to create AMF services, we will use the AMFPHP (http://amfphp.org) project to create the services.

After you download the AMFPHP code, you can copy it directly to the Apache documents directory. From there, you can surf to the AMF browser that comes with the project in your web browser. This is shown in Figure 3-9.

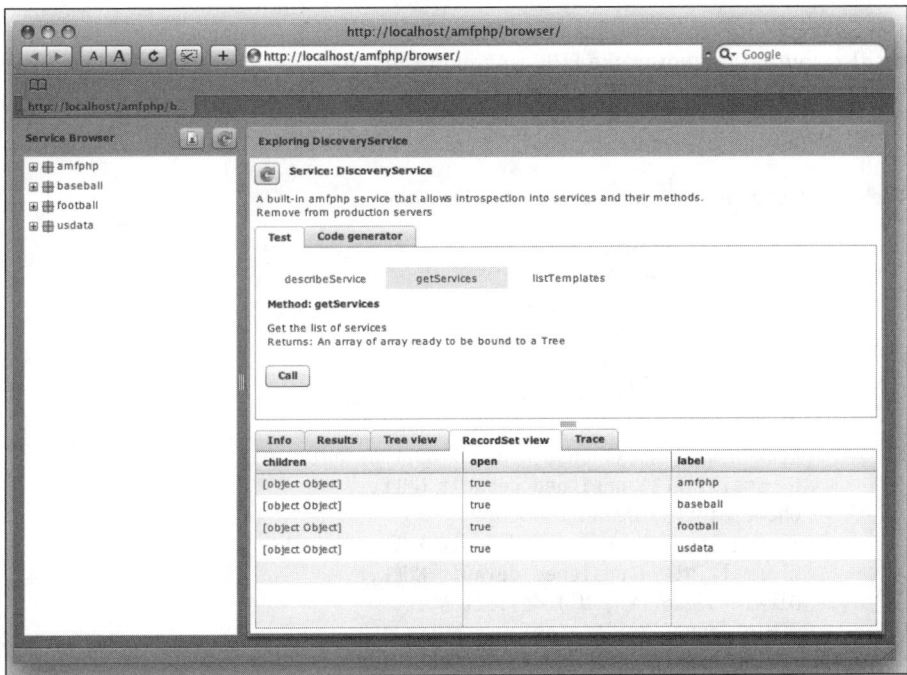

**Figure 3-9.** The AMFPHP browser

One service comes preinstalled with the AMFPHP system: the amfphp service that gives the AMFPHP browser the list of all of the services that have been installed. As you can see in Figure 3-9, there are several services already installed. I'll walk through how you can install and test each of these in the sections that follow.

# Installing the baseball data set

Most of the application examples in this book present some data to the user. To keep the examples both interesting and realistic, I have created a couple of example data sets and some corresponding AMFPHP services that access the data.

The first example data set consists of historical statistics for baseball teams. I found the data on the Internet, and I've included the data in the code download for this book so that you can install it yourself.

The first step is to create a MySQL database called baseball. To do this on the command line, use mysqladmin as shown here:

```
% mysqladmin --user=root create baseball
```

The user name and password will vary based on your MySQL installation.

The second step is to install this SQL schema and data in the database using either the mysql command prompt or the PHPMyAdmin restore function. The mysql command-line version looks like this:

```
% mysql --user=root baseball < teams.sql
```

The MySQL code for the teams database is shown here:

```
DROP TABLE IF EXISTS `Teams`;
CREATE TABLE `Teams` (
  `yearID` smallint(4) unsigned NOT NULL default '0',
  `lgID` char(2) NOT NULL default '',
  `teamID` char(3) NOT NULL default '',
  `franchID` char(3) NOT NULL default 'UNK',
  `divID` char(1) default NULL,
  `Rank` smallint(3) unsigned NOT NULL default '0',
  `G` smallint(3) unsigned default NULL,
  `Ghome` int(3) default NULL,
  `W` smallint(3) unsigned default NULL,
  `L` smallint(3) unsigned default NULL,
  `DivWin` enum('Y','N') default NULL,
  `WCWin` enum('Y','N') default NULL,
  `LgWin` enum('Y','N') default NULL,
  `WSWin` enum('Y','N') default NULL,
  `R` smallint(4) unsigned default NULL,
  `AB` smallint(4) unsigned default NULL,
  `H` smallint(4) unsigned default NULL,
  `2B` smallint(4) unsigned default NULL,
  `3B` smallint(3) unsigned default NULL,
  `HR` smallint(3) unsigned default NULL,
  `BB` smallint(4) unsigned default NULL,
  `SO` smallint(4) unsigned default NULL,
  `SB` smallint(3) unsigned default NULL,
```

```
`CS` smallint(3) unsigned default NULL,
`HBP` smallint(3) default NULL,
`SF` smallint(3) default NULL,
`RA` smallint(4) unsigned default NULL,
`ER` smallint(4) default NULL,
`ERA` decimal(4,2) default NULL,
`CG` smallint(3) unsigned default NULL,
`SHO` smallint(3) unsigned default NULL,
`SV` smallint(3) unsigned default NULL,
`IPouts` int(5) default NULL,
`HA` smallint(4) unsigned default NULL,
`HRA` smallint(4) unsigned default NULL,
`BBA` smallint(4) unsigned default NULL,
`SOA` smallint(4) unsigned default NULL,
`E` int(5) default NULL,
`DP` int(4) default NULL,
`FP` decimal(5,3) default NULL,
`name` varchar(50) NOT NULL default '',
`park` varchar(255) default NULL,
`attendance` int(7) default NULL,
`BPF` int(3) default NULL,
`PPF` int(3) default NULL,
`teamIDBR` char(3) default NULL,
`teamIDlahman45` char(3) default NULL,
`teamIDretro` char(3) default NULL,
PRIMARY KEY  (`yearID`,`lgID`,`teamID`),
KEY `team` (`teamID`,`yearID`,`lgID`)
) ENGINE=MyISAM DEFAULT CHARSET=latin1;

LOAD DATA LOCAL INFILE 'teams.csv' INTO TABLE teams ➡
FIELDS TERMINATED BY ',' OPTIONALLY ENCLOSED BY '"';
```

This SQL code creates a table called teams that contains one record for each year a team
played. That record stores the aggregate statistics for the year from that team. The data is
then loaded from a corresponding file called teams.csv, which is located in the same
directory as the SQL file.

To create the AMFPHP service to give Flex application access to this data, we first create a
baseball directory in the services directory of the AMFPHP installation. Then we add the
BaseballService.php file into the directory. Following is the code for the service:

```php
<?php
require_once("MDB2.php");
include_once(AMFPHP_BASE . "shared/util/MethodTable.php");
class BaseballService
{
  function getTeamList()
  {
    $dsn = 'mysql://root@localhost/baseball';
    $mdb2 =& MDB2::factory($dsn);
```

```php
$sth =& $mdb2->prepare( "SELECT teamid, name
    FROM teams GROUP BY name" );
$res = $sth->execute();
$rows = array();
while ($row = $res->fetchRow(MDB2_FETCHMODE_ASSOC))
{ $rows []= $row; }
return $rows;
}
function getTeams()
{
  $dsn = 'mysql://root@localhost/baseball';
  $mdb2 =& MDB2::factory($dsn);
  $sth =& $mdb2->prepare( "SELECT * FROM teams" );
  $res = $sth->execute();
  $rows = array();
  while ($row = $res->fetchRow(MDB2_FETCHMODE_ASSOC))
 { $rows []= $row; }
  return $rows;
}
function getTeamsByYear($year)
{
  $dsn = 'mysql://root@localhost/baseball';
  $mdb2 =& MDB2::factory($dsn);
  $sth =& $mdb2->prepare( "SELECT * FROM teams WHERE yearID=?" );
  $res = $sth->execute( $year );
  $rows = array();
  while ($row = $res->fetchRow(MDB2_FETCHMODE_ASSOC))
 { $rows []= $row; }
  return $rows;
}
function getYearsByTeam($teamid)
{
  $dsn = 'mysql://root@localhost/baseball';
  $mdb2 =& MDB2::factory($dsn);
  $sth =& $mdb2->prepare( "SELECT * FROM teams WHERE teamid=?" );
  $res = $sth->execute( $teamid );
  $rows = array();
  while ($row = $res->fetchRow(MDB2_FETCHMODE_ASSOC))
 { $rows []= $row; }
  return $rows;
  }
}
```

There are four methods in this service: getTeamList, getTeams, getTeamsByYear, and getYearsByTeam. The getTeamList method returns the list of all of the available teams in the database. The getTeams method simply returns all of the records in the database. The getTeamsByYear function returns all of the data for the individual teams from a given year. And the getYearsByTeam function takes a team ID and returns all of the records for that team in the database.

Most of the applications will first call the getTeamList to get the list of available teams, and then call the getYearsByTeam to get the statistical history of a specific selected team.

To test the service, we bring up the AMFPHP browser application, select the BaseballService, and run the getTeamList method. This should return the list of teams in the database. The correct result is show in Figure 3-10.

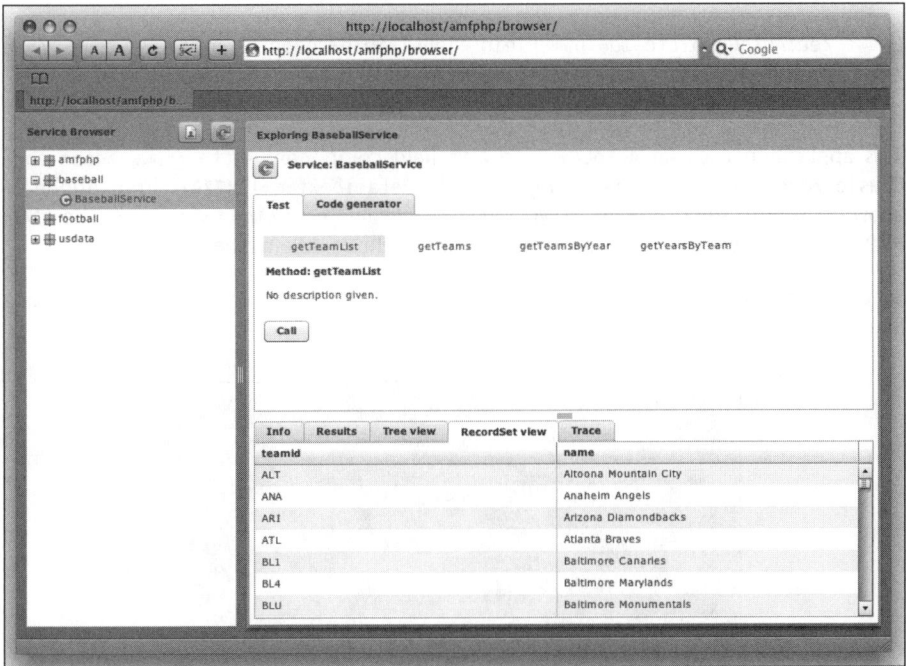

**Figure 3-10.** The AMFPHP browser showing the result of getTeamList

To go a little further and test this from Flex, we use the following code:

```
<?xml version="1.0" encoding="utf-8"?>
<mx:Application xmlns:mx="http://www.adobe.com/2006/mxml"
  layout="vertical"
  xmlns:ec="com.adobe.flex.extras.controls.*"
  creationComplete="baseballRO.getTeamList.send()">

<mx:Script>
<![CDATA[
private function onTeamsList() : void {
  nameField.dataProvider = baseballRO.getTeamList.lastResult;
}
]]>
</mx:Script>
```

```
<mx:RemoteObject id="baseballRO"
  endpoint="http://localhost/amfphp/gateway.php"
  source="baseball.BaseballService"
  destination="baseball.BaseballService"
  showBusyCursor="true">
<mx:method name="getTeamList" result="onTeamsList()" />
</mx:RemoteObject>

<ec:AutoComplete id="nameField" labelField="name" lookAhead="true" />

</mx:Application>
```

This application uses an AutoComplete text field component (http://www.adobe.com/cfusion/exchange/index.cfm?event=extensionDetail&extid=1047291) from Adobe to allow the user to select a team by typing in a few characters of the team name. The AMF-PHP service is specified in the RemoteObject tag in the middle of the file.

When we bring this up from the Flex Builder 3 IDE and type in cl, we should see something like Figure 3-11.

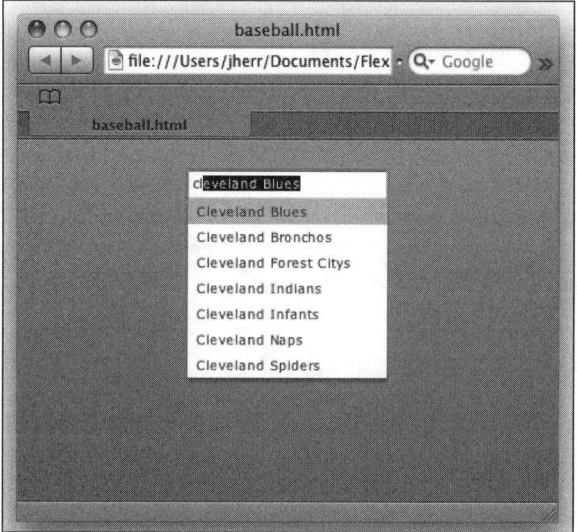

**Figure 3-11.** The teams that start with the letters "cl"

OK, now that we have some baseball data, it might be nice to have another data set that we can use when the data in the baseball service doesn't fit our needs. For that, we will often use the football data set that we install in the next section.

# Installing the football data set

Structurally, the football data set is much like the baseball data set. But instead of only a single table, there are now two tables, one for players and the other for individual games.

To install this data set, the first step is to create a MySQL database called football. The second step is to load the SQL shown here into the football database:

```
DROP TABLE IF EXISTS games;
CREATE TABLE games ( ID VARCHAR(64),
   year INTEGER, team VARCHAR(64), week INTEGER, opp VARCHAR(64),
   comp INTEGER, att INTEGER,
   passYD INTEGER, PassTD INTEGER, interceptions INTEGER,
   rush INTEGER, rushYD INTEGER,
   rec INTEGER, recYD INTEGER, tds INTEGER );

DROP TABLE IF EXISTS player;
CREATE TABLE player ( ID VARCHAR(64), last VARCHAR(64),
   first VARCHAR(64),
   position VARCHAR(64), birth INTEGER, debut INTEGER );

LOAD DATA LOCAL INFILE 'master.csv' INTO TABLE player
FIELDS TERMINATED BY ',' OPTIONALLY ENCLOSED BY '"';
LOAD DATA LOCAL INFILE 'games.csv' INTO TABLE games
FIELDS TERMINATED BY ',' OPTIONALLY ENCLOSED BY '"';
```

As with the baseball database, this SQL code reads data for the tables in from CSV files located in the same directory as the SQL file.

The AMFPHP service, in a file called FootballService.php, located in the football directory within the AMFPHP services directory, is shown here:

```php
<?php
require_once("MDB2.php");
include_once(AMFPHP_BASE . "shared/util/MethodTable.php");
class FootballService
{
  function findPlayer($name)
  {
    $dsn = 'mysql://root@localhost/football';
    $mdb2 =& MDB2::factory($dsn);
    $sth =& $mdb2->prepare(
      "SELECT * FROM player WHERE last LIKE ? OR first LIKE ?" );
    $res = $sth->execute( array( '%'.$name.'%', '%'.$name.'%' ) );
    $rows = array();
    while ($row = $res->fetchRow(MDB2_FETCHMODE_ASSOC))
  { $rows []= $row; }
    return $rows;
  }
  function getGamesByPlayer($player)
```

```
      {
        $dsn = 'mysql://root@localhost/football';
        $mdb2 =& MDB2::factory($dsn);
        $sth =& $mdb2->prepare(
        "SELECT * FROM games WHERE ID=? ORDER BY year,week" );
        $res = $sth->execute( $player );
        $rows = array();
        while ($row = $res->fetchRow(MDB2_FETCHMODE_ASSOC))
      { $rows []= $row; }
        return $rows;
      }
      function getGamesByOpponent($player)
      {
        $dsn = 'mysql://root@localhost/football';
        $mdb2 =& MDB2::factory($dsn);
        $sth =& $mdb2->prepare( "
SELECT
  opp, count(*) as games, sum(att) AS att,
  sum(comp) AS comp, sum(passyd) AS passyd,
  sum(tds) AS tds, sum(interceptions) AS interceptions
FROM
  games
WHERE ID=? AND opp != '' GROUP BY opp" );
        $res = $sth->execute( $player );
        $rows = array();
        while ($row = $res->fetchRow(MDB2_FETCHMODE_ASSOC))
      { $rows []= $row; }
        return $rows;
      }
    }
```

This service presents three methods to a potential Flex or Flash application. These three methods are findPlayer, which returns a list of matching players from a search string; getGamesByPlayer, which returns the data from all of the games a football player played; and finally getGamesByOpponent, which returns a report of how the player did against all of the teams he ever competed against.

The first step in testing this service is to bring it up in the AMFPHP browser and run the findPlayer method on it. This is shown in Figure 3-12.

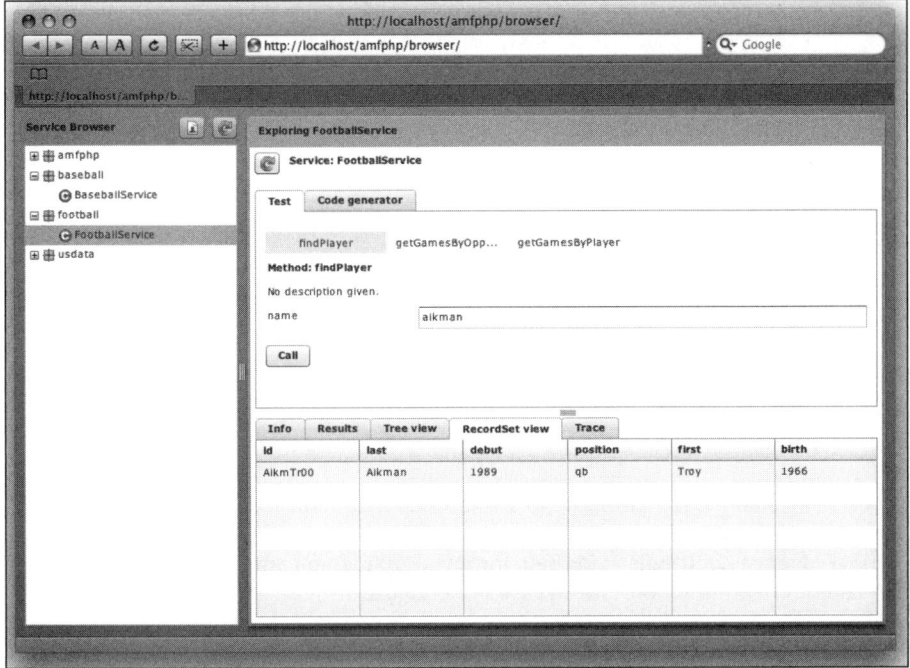

**Figure 3-12.** The FootballService and its return in the findPlayer function

In this case, we type aikman into the name field. This will return Troy Aikman, the Pro Football Hall of Fame quarterback from the Dallas Cowboys.

To test this service out in a Flex application, we use the following code to invoke the findPlayer service to update a list of players found after every keystroke into a search field:

```
<?xml version="1.0" encoding="utf-8"?>
<mx:Application xmlns:mx="http://www.adobe.com/2006/mxml"
  layout="horizontal">

<mx:Script>
<![CDATA[
private function onFindPlayer() : void {
  foundList.dataProvider = footballRO.findPlayer.lastResult;
}
private function onKeyUp() : void {
  footballRO.findPlayer.send( nameText.text );
}
private function myLabelFunc( item:Object ) : String {
  return item.first + " " + item.last;
}
]]>
</mx:Script>
```

```xml
<mx:RemoteObject id="footballRO"
  endpoint="http://localhost/amfphp/gateway.php"
  source="football.FootballService"
  destination="football.FootballService"
  showBusyCursor="true">
<mx:method name="findPlayer" result="onFindPlayer()">
<mx:arguments>
  <mx:name />
</mx:arguments>
</mx:method>
</mx:RemoteObject>

<mx:TextInput id="nameText" keyUp="onKeyUp()" width="20%" />
<mx:List id="foundList" labelFunction="myLabelFunc" width="80%" />

</mx:Application>
```

No custom components in this example. The TextInput control has an event listener on it that calls the web service on every keystroke through the onKeyUp method. The onFindPlayer result handler then sets the dataProvider for the list. The list text is then formatted for each item with the myLabelFunc callback.

The result of typing aik into this example Flex application is shown in Figure 3-13.

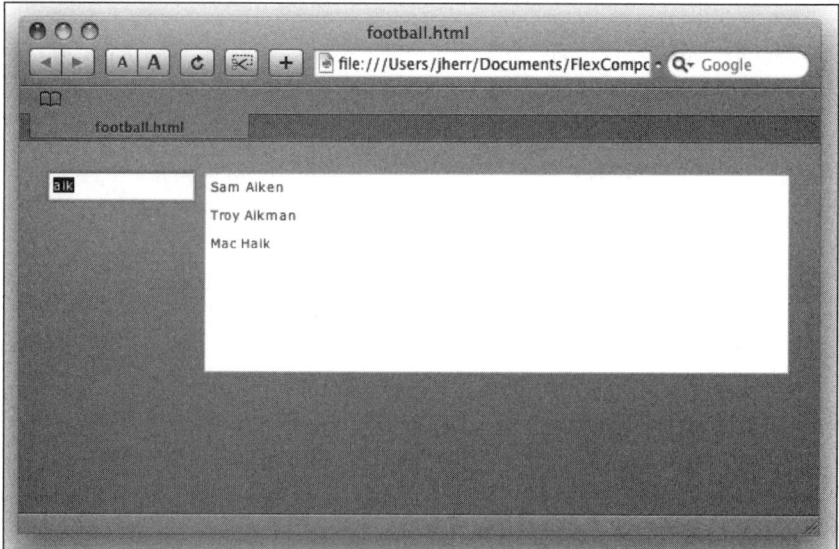

**Figure 3-13.** The football service returning a list of players

One final statistical database is some United State census data. We can use that data for charting applications that use maps.

# Installing the United States data (usdata) data set

As with the baseball and football data sets, the first step is to create a MySQL database that will store the data. This database is named usdata. And the SQL code to preload the database is shown here:

```
DROP TABLE IF EXISTS construction;
CREATE TABLE construction (
  state VARCHAR( 64 ),
  companies INT,
  employees INT,
  payroll INT,
  sales INT,
  statepopulation INT
);

LOAD DATA LOCAL INFILE 'construction.csv' INTO TABLE
construction FIELDS TERMINATED BY ',' OPTIONALLY ENCLOSED BY '"';

DROP TABLE IF EXISTS it;
CREATE TABLE it (
  state VARCHAR( 64 ),
  companies INT,
  employees INT,
  payroll INT,
  sales INT,
  statepopulation INT
);

LOAD DATA LOCAL INFILE 'it.csv' INTO TABLE
it FIELDS TERMINATED BY ',' OPTIONALLY ENCLOSED BY '"';

DROP TABLE IF EXISTS realestate;
CREATE TABLE realestate (
  state VARCHAR( 64 ),
  companies INT,
  employees INT,
  payroll INT,
  sales INT,
  statepopulation INT
);

LOAD DATA LOCAL INFILE 'realestate.csv' INTO TABLE
realestate FIELDS TERMINATED BY ',' OPTIONALLY ENCLOSED BY '"';
```

This database has three tables each with an identical structure but different data. The it table contains the financial data for the information technology sector in every state within the United States. The construction table does this for the construction sector, and the realestate table does this for the real estate sector.

Here is the service code to feed this data to a Flex or Flash application:

```php
<?php
require_once("MDB2.php");
include_once(AMFPHP_BASE . "shared/util/MethodTable.php");
class USDataService
{
  function getAll( $table )
  {
    $dsn = 'mysql://root@localhost/usdata';
    $mdb2 =& MDB2::factory($dsn);
    $sth =& $mdb2->prepare( "SELECT * FROM ".$table );
    $res = $sth->execute();
    $rows = array();
    while ($row = $res->fetchRow(MDB2_FETCHMODE_ASSOC))
    { $rows []= $row; }
    return $rows;
  }
}
```

It's a pretty simple service. It simply returns the data from the specified table to the client. If the application passes it, realestate, or construction, it will get a valid set of rows returned. Otherwise, it will get an error message because there is no table named the same as the input.

To test the service, we first bring it up in the AMFPHP browser, as shown in Figure 3-14.

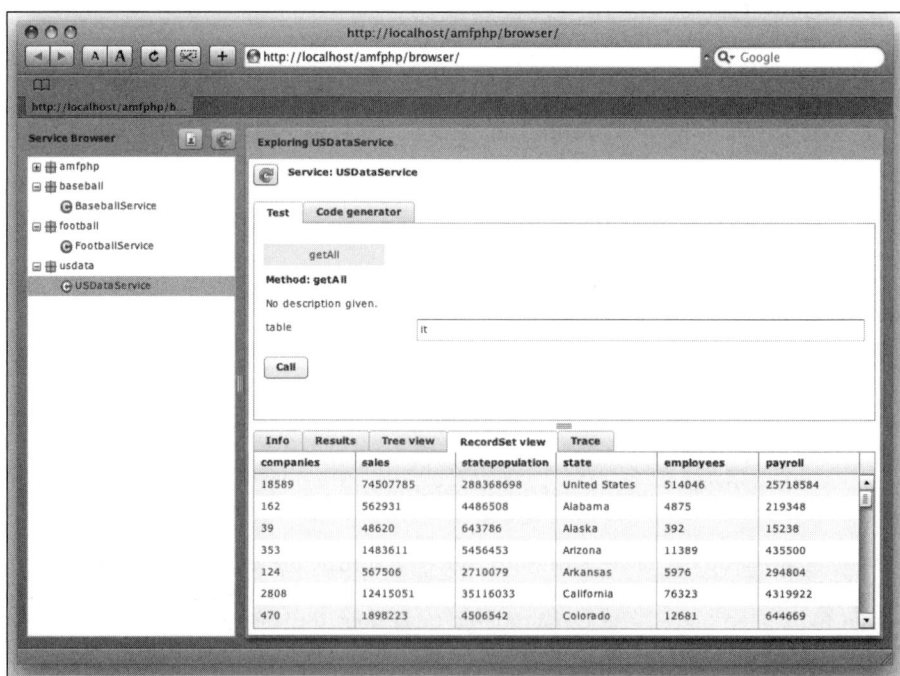

**Figure 3-14.** The data for the information technology sector in the United States

A sample Flex application that displays the data from the IT sector is shown in the following code sample:

```xml
<?xml version="1.0" encoding="utf-8"?>
<mx:Application xmlns:mx="http://www.adobe.com/2006/mxml"
  layout="vertical"
  creationComplete="usdataRO.getAll.send('it');">

<mx:RemoteObject id="usdataRO"
  endpoint="http://localhost/amfphp/gateway.php"
  source="usdata.USDataService" destination="usdata.USDataService"
  showBusyCursor="true">
<mx:method name="getAll">
<mx:arguments>
  <mx:table />
</mx:arguments>
</mx:method>
</mx:RemoteObject>

<mx:DataGrid dataProvider="{usdataRO.getAll.lastResult}"
  width="100%" height="100%" sortableColumns="true">
<mx:columns>
  <mx:DataGridColumn dataField="state"
    headerText="State" sortable="true" />
  <mx:DataGridColumn dataField="statepopulation"
    headerText="Population" />
  <mx:DataGridColumn dataField="companies" headerText="Companies" />
  <mx:DataGridColumn dataField="employees" headerText="Employees" />
  <mx:DataGridColumn dataField="payroll" headerText="Payroll" />
  <mx:DataGridColumn dataField="sales" headerText="Sales" />
</mx:columns>
</mx:DataGrid>

</mx:Application>
```

This application first calls the getAll method on the service and specifies the it table. The DataTable automatically shows the data returned from the service because of the data binding in the dataProvider attribute. The DataGridColumn objects then specify the different columns. You don't need to specify those, but it makes for a nicer display.

The result of running this application is shown in Figure 3-15.

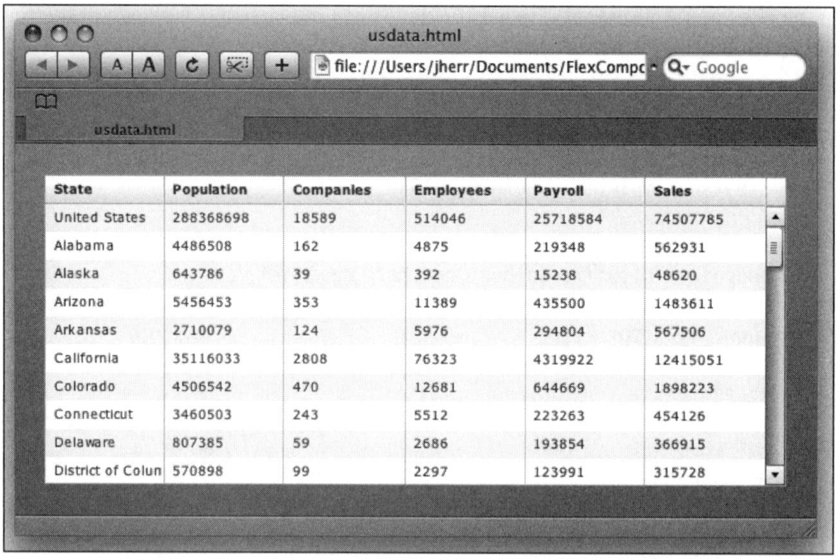


| State | Population | Companies | Employees | Payroll | Sales |
|---|---|---|---|---|---|
| United States | 288368698 | 18589 | 514046 | 25718584 | 74507785 |
| Alabama | 4486508 | 162 | 4875 | 219348 | 562931 |
| Alaska | 643786 | 39 | 392 | 15238 | 48620 |
| Arizona | 5456453 | 353 | 11389 | 435500 | 1483611 |
| Arkansas | 2710079 | 124 | 5976 | 294804 | 567506 |
| California | 35116033 | 2808 | 76323 | 4319922 | 12415051 |
| Colorado | 4506542 | 470 | 12681 | 644669 | 1898223 |
| Connecticut | 3460503 | 243 | 5512 | 223263 | 454126 |
| Delaware | 807385 | 59 | 2686 | 193854 | 366915 |
| District of Colun | 570898 | 99 | 2297 | 123991 | 315728 |

**Figure 3-15.** The information technology data for each state from the US Census

The next sample data set is nothing like the previous data sets. It's a music database that we will use when we have components that display images or require hierarchic data.

# The static content

The source code package that is included on the Apress web site for this book includes several sources of static content that the example applications use. These include the `music`, `videos`, and `pics` directories. These should be installed in the root directory of your `localhost` server so that you can play with the applications yourself. If you install them somewhere else, then all you need to do is change the URL in the `HTTPService` objects within each application to match the new location.

To test this out, let's first have a look at the `music.xml` file in the `music` folder.

```
<genres>
  <genre name="Rock">
    <band name="AC/DC" image="acdc.png" founded="1973" status="Active">
      <member>Angus Young</member>
      <member>Malcolm Young</member>
      <member>Brian Johnson</member>
      <member>Cliff Williams</member>
      <member>Phil Rudd</member>
    </band>
    <band name="Aerosmith" image="aerosmith.png" founded="1970"
     status="Active">
      <member>Steven Tyler</member>
```

```
      <member>Joe Perry</member>
      <member>Tom Hamilton</member>
      <member>Brad Whitford</member>
      <member>Joey Kramer</member>
    </band>
    ...
  </genre>
  ...
</genres>
```

This is a small database of bands and their members that we can use to test components that display images as well as displaying tree structures since the data is hierarchic.

A test application for this data set is shown in the code that follows:

```
<?xml version="1.0" encoding="utf-8"?>
<mx:Application xmlns:mx="http://www.adobe.com/2006/mxml"
    layout="vertical"
  creationComplete="musicData.send()">
<mx:HTTPService url="http://localhost/music/music.xml" id="musicData"
    resultFormat="e4x" />
<mx:TileList dataProvider="{musicData.lastResult..band}" width="100%"
  height="100%">
<mx:itemRenderer>
  <mx:Component>
    <mx:Canvas width="110" height="110">
      <mx:Image top="1" left="1"
      source=http://localhost/music/{data.@image}
      height="100" width="100"
        toolTip="{data.@name}">
        <mx:filters>
          <mx:DropShadowFilter />
        </mx:filters>
      </mx:Image>
    </mx:Canvas>
  </mx:Component>
</mx:itemRenderer>
</mx:TileList>
</mx:Application>
```

This application uses an HTTPService object to request the XML data from the static XML file located on the localhost server. The TileList object watches that object for changes, and when new data arrives, it updates its list. The list is rendered using an itemRenderer that displays the image for each band.

The result is shown in Figure 3-16.

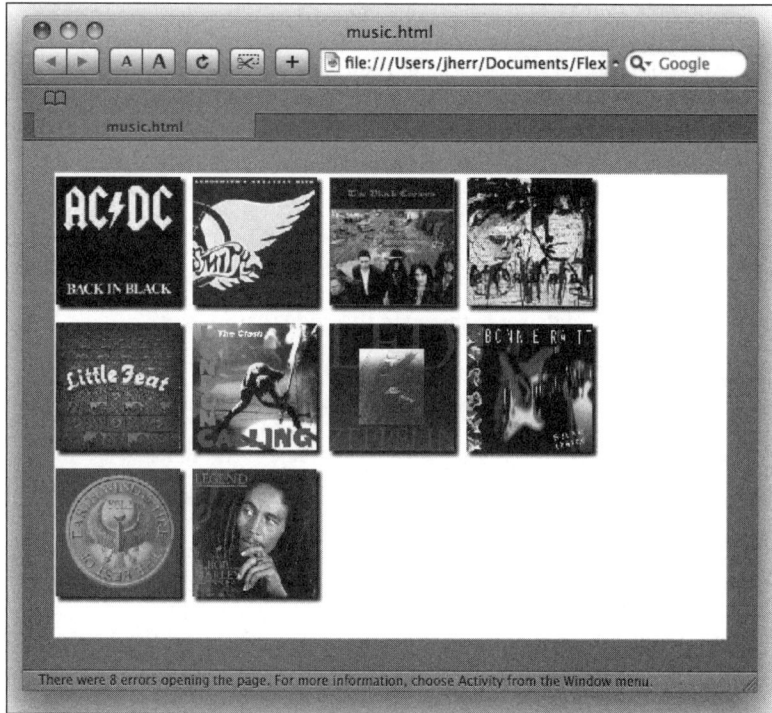

**Figure 3-16.** The display of band images

This shows that the music database is installed properly and that the images are coming back in response to our queries.

# Where we will go from here

So, all is well and good at this point. With everything installed, we have to think about the cool ways that we can use it. In the chapters that follow, we will make use of all of this data, and data from services like Flickr and others. This will demonstrate all of the cool things that you can do with Flex with only a little coding on your part.

# 4 UPGRADING YOUR CONTAINERS

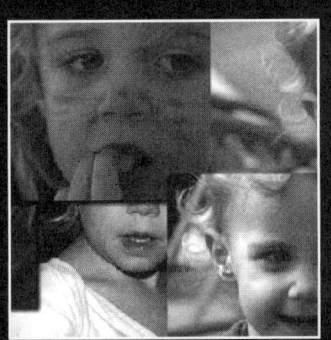
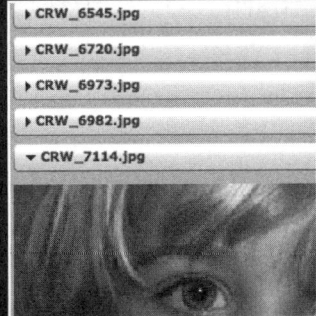
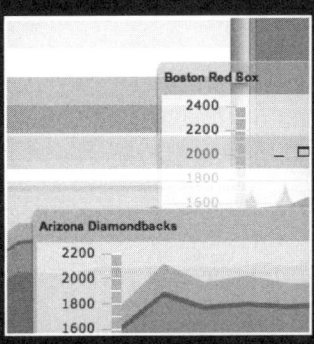

Updated: 7/3/08

# New styles of containers

I'm lazy, I'll admit it. I hate to do gruntwork, and to me, laying out controls and handling scrollbars is the ultimate in gruntwork. To me, the fact that I can drop a few controls into an HBox or a Form and have it laid out nicely for me is fantastic.

While the Flex framework has a bunch of containers that work very well, there are some great open source and commercial Flex containers that you can use in your own projects.

This chapter will show you how to use better canvas controls, forms, toolbars, and more. There are new containers that automatically flow elements depending on their unique width and height parameters, one that allows the user to position and resize individual elements, and ones that extend the existing containers with new effects like blur scrolling or roll-up windows. There is even a Multiple Document Interface (MDI) component that gives you a complete windowing solution for your Flex application.

# Flow container

The TileList container from the Flex framework has a fixed width and height that is applied to every component. One container type that is left out from the original set of controls is a container that stacks interface elements horizontally based on their width. So each element can have a unique width and height, and the container will lay them out without gaps.

The FlexLib (http://flexlib.googlecode.com) has several new container types, one of which is the FlowBox, which handles a flow-style layout.

Following is application code that uses the FlowBox to lay out a set of images from the server where every image has a different size. The images and XML used by this application need to be installed in the Apache directory per the installation instructions in Chapter 3.

```
<?xml version="1.0" encoding="utf-8"?>
<mx:Application xmlns:mx="http://www.adobe.com/2006/mxml"
  layout="absolute"
  xmlns:cntnr="flexlib.containers.*"
  creationComplete="picDataWide.send()" horizontalScrollPolicy="off"
  verticalScrollPolicy="on">
<mx:Script>
<![CDATA[
import mx.rpc.events.ResultEvent;

private function onPicResultWide( event:ResultEvent ) : void {
  picDataTall.send();
}
```

```
    private function onPicResultTall( event:ResultEvent ) : void {
      var images:Array = [];
      for each( var wpic:XML in picDataWide.lastResult..image )
        images.push( wpic.@name.toString() );
      for each( var tpic:XML in picDataTall.lastResult..image )
        images.push( tpic.@name.toString() );

      for each( var pic:String in images ) {
        var img:ImageRenderer = new ImageRenderer();
        img.data = pic;
        fb.addChild( img );
      }
    }
  }
  ]]>
</mx:Script>
<mx:HTTPService url="http://localhost/pics/wide.xml" id="picDataWide"
  resultFormat="e4x"
  result="onPicResultWide( event )" />
<mx:HTTPService url="http://localhost/pics/tall.xml" id="picDataTall"
  resultFormat="e4x"
  result="onPicResultTall( event )" />
<cntnr:FlowBox id="fb" width="100%" height="100%"
  horizontalScrollPolicy="off" />
</mx:Application>
```

The application starts off by using the picDataWide and picDataTall services to get a list of images. It then creates an ImageRenderer object for each of the images and adds it to the FlowBox container, just as you would with an HBox.

The code for the ImageRenderer component is shown here:

```
<?xml version="1.0" encoding="utf-8"?>
<mx:Canvas xmlns:mx="http://www.adobe.com/2006/mxml" height="200"
  horizontalScrollPolicy="off" verticalScrollPolicy="off">
  <mx:Image top="1" left="1" source="http://localhost/pics/{data}"
    height="195"
    toolTip="{data}">
    <mx:filters>
      <mx:DropShadowFilter />
    </mx:filters>
  </mx:Image>
</mx:Canvas>
```

This module just puts a little space around the image and adds a drop shadow to make everything look pretty.

When we bring the layout up in Flex Builder 3, it looks something like Figure 4-1.

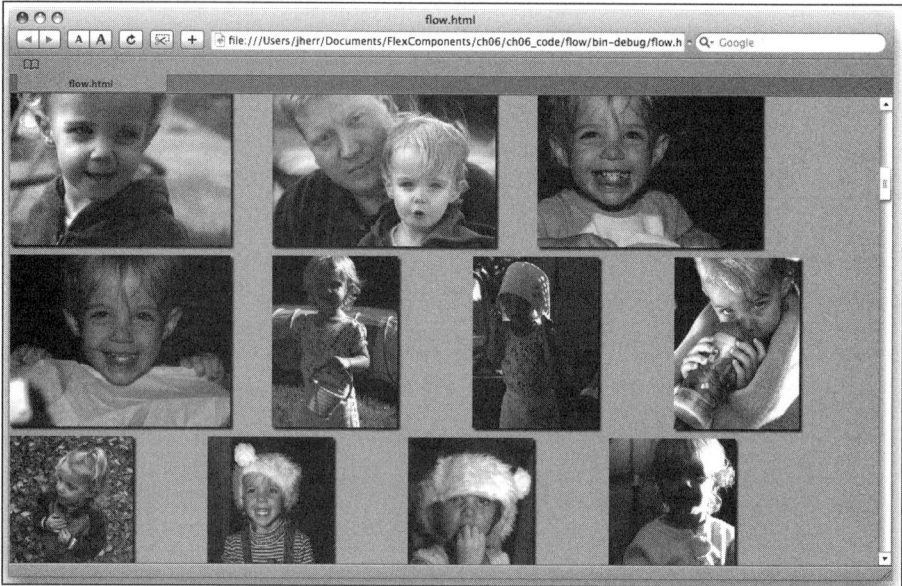

**Figure 4-1.** The images in a flow box

As you can see, the FlowBox handles laying out the images in each row in a way that adjusts to the size of each image.

## Drag scrolling

When Google Maps (http://maps.google.com) first came out, the thing that impressed me about it the most was the fact that you could click anywhere on the map and scroll the map just by dragging the mouse. The FlexLib includes the DragScrollingCanvas that brings this drag scrolling functionality to your Flex application.

The application code shown here puts up some server images on a drag-scrolling canvas:

```
<?xml version="1.0" encoding="utf-8"?>
<mx:Application xmlns:mx="http://www.adobe.com/2006/mxml"
  layout="absolute"
  width="100%" height="100%"
  horizontalScrollPolicy="off" verticalScrollPolicy="off"
  creationComplete="picData.send()"
  xmlns:flexlib="flexlib.containers.*">
<mx:Script>
<![CDATA[
import mx.rpc.events.ResultEvent;
```

```
    private function onPicResult( event:ResultEvent ) : void {
      for each( var pic:XML in event.result..image ) {
        var img:ImageRenderer = new ImageRenderer();
        img.data = pic.@name.toString();
        img.setStyle( 'top', Math.random() * 1000 );
        img.setStyle( 'left', Math.random() * 1000 );
        cnvs.addChild( img );
      }
    }
  ]]>
  </mx:Script>
  <mx:HTTPService url="http://localhost/pics/wide.xml" id="picData"
    resultFormat="e4x"
    result="onPicResult( event )" />
  <flexlib:DragScrollingCanvas id="cnvs" width="100%" height="100%" />
</mx:Application>
```

The code starts by requesting the list of images with the picData request. When the XML is returned, the application adds the image to a random location within the DragScrollingCanvas container. The result is shown in Figure 4-2.

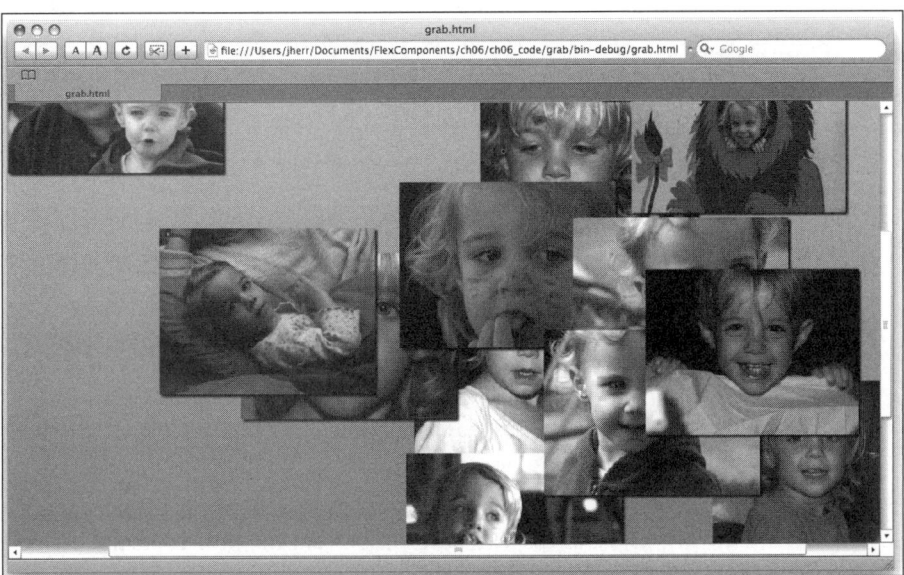

**Figure 4-2.** The DragScrollingCanvas example

Anywhere you click the canvas, you can simply hold down the mouse button and scroll it by flicking left, right, up, or down.

## Smooth HBox and VBox

Flex Componentor has released two free smooth scrolling replacements for HBox and VBox called HSmoothBox and VSmoothBox in a library called containerEx (http://strawberrypixel.com/blog/downloads/).

The application code shown here loads a set of images into the HSmoothBox container:

```
<?xml version="1.0" encoding="utf-8"?>
<mx:Application xmlns:mx="http://www.adobe.com/2006/mxml"
  layout="absolute"
  xmlns:containerEx="containerEx.*" width="600" height="220"
  horizontalScrollPolicy="off" verticalScrollPolicy="off"
  creationComplete="picData.send()">
<mx:Script>
<![CDATA[
import mx.rpc.events.ResultEvent;
import mx.collections.ArrayCollection;

[Bindable]
private var images:ArrayCollection = new ArrayCollection();

private function onPicResult( event:ResultEvent ) : void {
  for each( var pic:XML in event.result..image )
    images.addItem( pic.@name.toString() );
  vsb.dataProvider = images;
}
]]>
</mx:Script>
<mx:HTTPService url="http://localhost/pics/wide.xml" id="picData"
  resultFormat="e4x"
  result="onPicResult( event )" />
<containerEx:HSmoothBox blurEnabled="true" width="600" height="220"
  backgroundColor="white" backgroundAlpha="1"
  id="vsb" itemRenderer="ImageRenderer" itemHeight="200"
  itemWidth="280" horizontalScrollPolicy="on" />
</mx:Application>
```

The first thing this application does is get the list of images from the server using the picData service. It then uses the ImageRenderer class from the flow container example code to render some images into the HSmoothBox container.

The result is shown in Figure 4-3.

**Figure 4-3.** The HSmoothBox blurring while it's scrolling

The application code that does the same thing with the VSmoothBox control is shown here:

```
<?xml version="1.0" encoding="utf-8"?>
<mx:Application xmlns:mx="http://www.adobe.com/2006/mxml"
  layout="absolute"
  xmlns:containerEx="containerEx.*" width="300" height="400"
  horizontalScrollPolicy="off" verticalScrollPolicy="off"
  creationComplete="picData.send()">
<mx:Script>
<![CDATA[
import mx.rpc.events.ResultEvent;
import mx.collections.ArrayCollection;

[Bindable]
private var images:ArrayCollection = new ArrayCollection();

private function onPicResult( event:ResultEvent ) : void {
  for each( var pic:XML in event.result..image )
    images.addItem( pic.@name.toString() );
  vsb.dataProvider = images;
}
]]>
</mx:Script>
<mx:HTTPService url="http://localhost/pics/wide.xml" id="picData"
  resultFormat="e4x"
  result="onPicResult( event )" />
<containerEx:VSmoothBox blurEnabled="true" width="300" height="400"
  backgroundColor="white" backgroundAlpha="1"
  id="vsb" itemRenderer="ImageRenderer" itemHeight="200"
  itemWidth="280" verticalScrollPolicy="on" />
</mx:Application>
```

Here the application uses the ImageRenderer component to add images into containerEx's VSmoothBox.

After bringing that up from Flex Builder 3, the result looks like Figure 4-4 when it's in the process of scrolling.

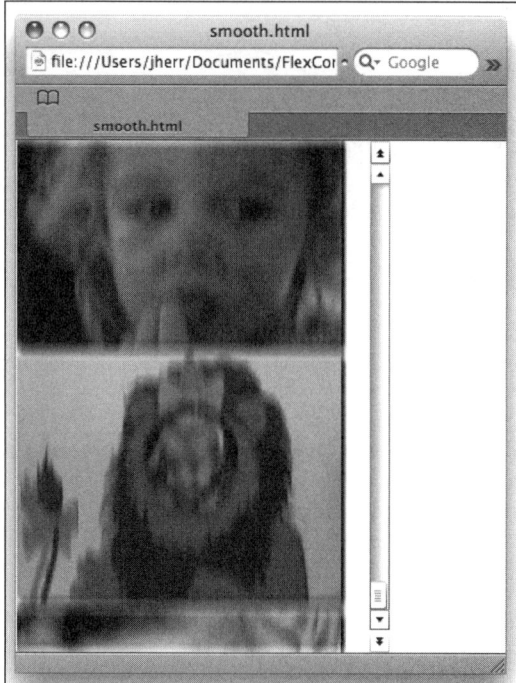

**Figure 4-4.** The vertical smooth scrolling box

This smooth effect is fun to play with and gives you a real sense of movement as you scroll around the images.

# Button scrolling

FlexLib contains another container type that presents an alternative to scrollbars, the ButtonScrollingCanvas. This container puts up four big buttons on the left, right, top, and bottom of the area that you can use to scroll around the canvas.

The application code that follows loads images into a ButtonScrollingCanvas:

```
<?xml version="1.0" encoding="utf-8"?>
<mx:Application xmlns:mx="http://www.adobe.com/2006/mxml"
  layout="absolute"
  width="100%" height="100%"
```

```
  horizontalScrollPolicy="off" verticalScrollPolicy="off"
  creationComplete="picData.send()"
  xmlns:flexlib="flexlib.containers.*">
<mx:Script>
<![CDATA[
import mx.rpc.events.ResultEvent;

private function onPicResult( event:ResultEvent ) : void {
  for each( var pic:XML in event.result..image ) {
    var img:ImageRenderer = new ImageRenderer();
    img.data = pic.@name.toString();
    img.setStyle( 'top', Math.random() * 1000 );
    img.setStyle( 'left', Math.random() * 1000 );
    cnvs.addChild( img );
  }
}
]]>
</mx:Script>
<mx:HTTPService url="http://localhost/pics/wide.xml" id="picData"
  resultFormat="e4x"
  result="onPicResult( event )" />
<flexlib:ButtonScrollingCanvas id="cnvs" width="100%" height="100%" />
</mx:Application>
```

Just as with the other image canvas examples, this application first loads the list of images, and then uses the ImageRenderer class to put images into the ButtonScrollingCanvas.

When this example is launched from Flex Builder 3, it looks something like Figure 4-5.

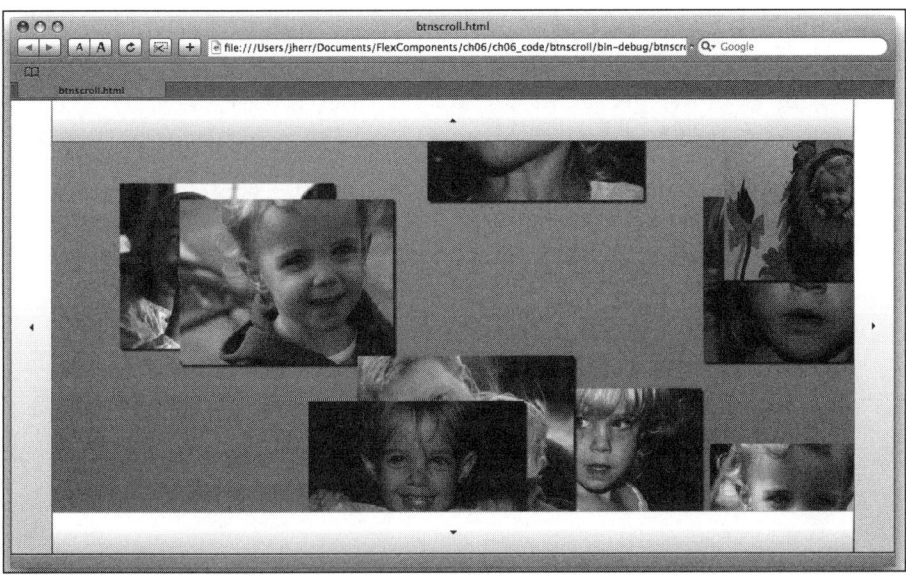

**Figure 4-5.** The images in the ButtonScrollingCanvas

You can now scroll around the canvas by using the oversized buttons located on the left, right, top, and bottom of the display.

# Resizable and movable objects

I get a lot of requests for interfaces where the user can organize things like images by dragging them around and resizing them. It's a lot of work to put that together. Which makes the Teoti Graphix (http://www.teotigraphix.com/) ResizeManagerFX component all the more valuable.

The following application code shows just how easy it is to use this commercial component to add image moving and resizing to a Flex application:

```
<?xml version="1.0" encoding="utf-8"?>
<mx:Application xmlns:mx="http://www.adobe.com/2006/mxml"
  creationComplete="picData.send();" layout="vertical">
<mx:HTTPService url="http://localhost/pics/wide.xml" id="picData"
  resultFormat="e4x"
  result="onPicResult( event )" />
<mx:Script>
<![CDATA[
import mx.rpc.events.ResultEvent;
import mx.controls.Image;

import com.teotiGraphix.managers.ResizePosition;
import com.teotiGraphix.managers.ResizeManagerFX;
import com.teotiGraphix.managers.MoveManagerFX;

private function onPicResult( event:ResultEvent ) : void {
  var count:int = 0;
  for each( var pic:XML in picData.lastResult..image ) {
    if ( count++ > 5 ) break;

    var ratio:Number = ( Math.random() * 0.5 ) + 0.5;
    var img:Image = new Image();
    img.data = 'http://localhost/pics/'+pic.@name.toString();
    img.height = 225 * ratio;
    img.width = 300 * ratio;
    img.move( Math.random() * ( width - 300 ),
      Math.random() * ( height - 225 ) );
```

```
      parentCanvas.addChild( img );
    }
    MoveManagerFX.addParentClient(parentCanvas);
    ResizeManagerFX.addParentClient(parentCanvas);
  }
]]>
</mx:Script>
<mx:Style>
.masterStyle {
  moveManagerStyleName:"moveStyle";
  resizeManagerStyleName:"resizeStyle";
  moveClientOverlayAlpha:0.5;
  resizeClientOverlayAlpha:0.8;
  lockAspectRatio:true;
}
.moveStyle {
  overlayBorderThickness:5;
  overlayBorderOffset:"outside";
}
.resizeStyle {
  overlayButtonOffset:"inside";
  overlayButtonThickness:10;
  overlayButtonWidth:10;
  overlayFillColor:#FF0000;
}
</mx:Style>
<mx:Canvas id="parentCanvas"
  styleName="masterStyle"
  backgroundColor="#FFFFFF" backgroundAlpha="0.3"
  width="100%" height="100%" />
</mx:Application>
```

The ResizeManagerFX component uses the standard Flex Canvas component to create a playing field where you can move and resize all of the child elements. This example application starts up and fetches the image list from the server. It then adds all of the images to the canvas and tells the ResizeManagerFX to make them all resizable.

The result of the simple addition of the ResizeManagerFX code to this application is shown in Figure 4-6.

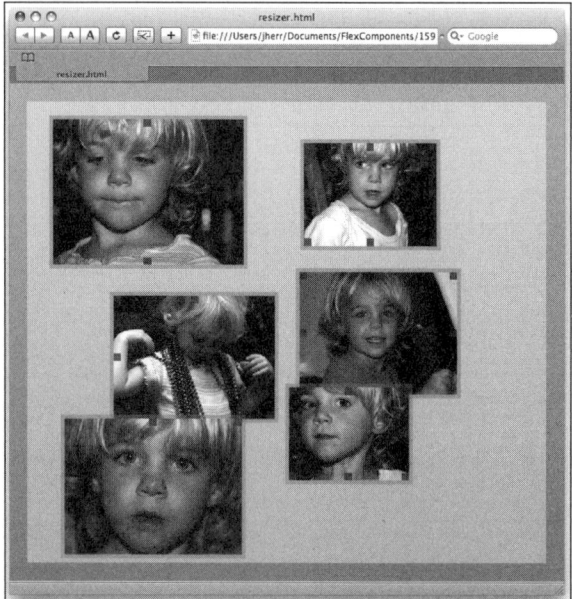

**Figure 4-6.** When the application first starts up

From here, we can click one of the resize controls and start dragging the image to resize it. That's shown in progress in Figure 4-7.

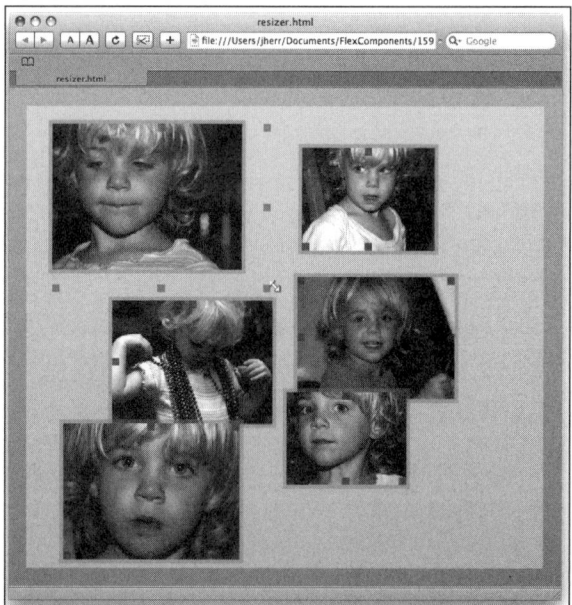

**Figure 4-7.** What it looks like when you are resizing

We can move an image around just by clicking its blue border and then dragging the image to where you want it to be located. You can see this happening in Figure 4-8.

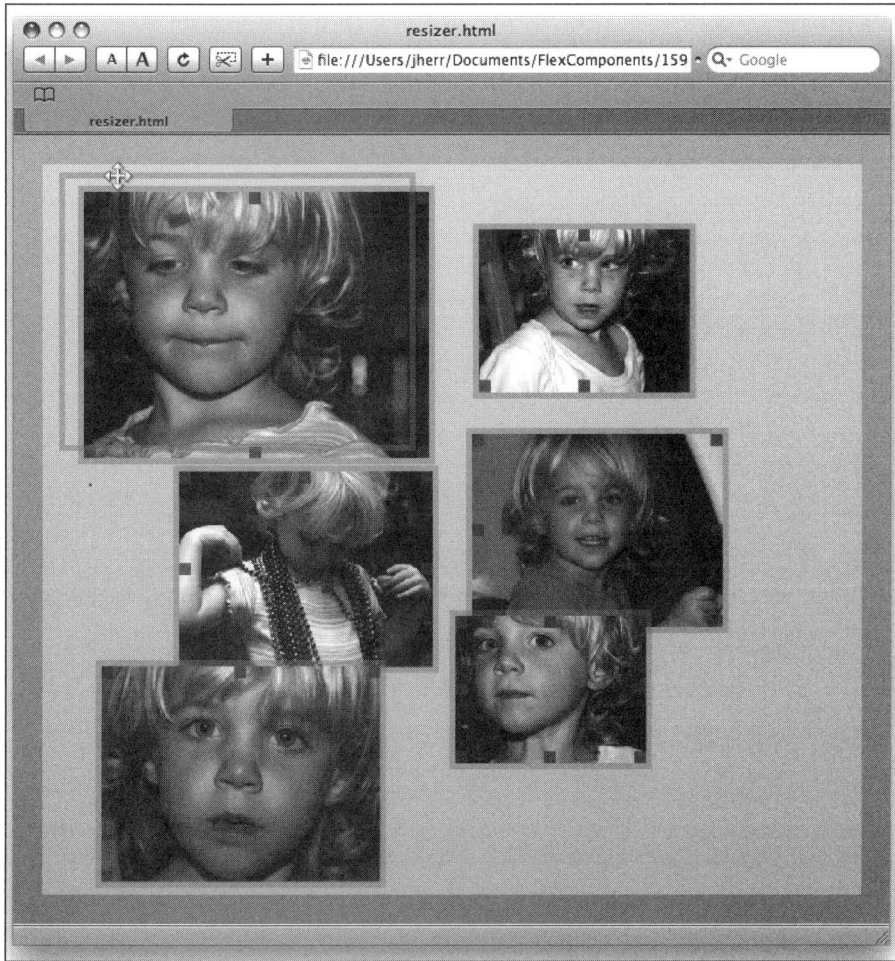

**Figure 4-8.** The image moving shown in progress

The objects you're moving around don't have to be images, they can be any type of Flex components: graphs, data grids, buttons, you name it.

## Window shades

FlexLib provides another missing component from the Flex framework with the WindowShade container. This container puts up a title bar that is the width of the contained components. The title bar also includes an arrow control that you can use to expand or collapse the window.

The following application code loads the image into WindowShade containers and adds them into a vertical layout:

```
<?xml version="1.0" encoding="utf-8"?>
<mx:Application xmlns:mx="http://www.adobe.com/2006/mxml"
  layout="vertical"
  width="100%" height="100%"
  verticalScrollPolicy="on"
  creationComplete="picData.send()"
  xmlns:flexlib="flexlib.containers.*">
<mx:Script>
<![CDATA[
import flexlib.containers.WindowShade;
import mx.controls.Image;
import mx.rpc.events.ResultEvent;

private function onPicResult( event:ResultEvent ) : void {
  for each( var pic:XML in event.result..image ) {
    var ws:WindowShade = new WindowShade();
    ws.label = pic.@name.toString();

    var img:Image = new Image();
    img.data = 'http://localhost/pics/'+pic.@name.toString();
    img.width = 400;
    img.height = 300;
    ws.addChild( img );

    addChild( ws );
  }
}
]]>
</mx:Script>
<mx:HTTPService url="http://localhost/pics/wide.xml"
  id="picData" resultFormat="e4x"
  result="onPicResult( event )" />
</mx:Application>
```

The application starts up by getting the list of images from the server. It then creates a `WindowShade` container for each image and adds an image into it. That `WindowShade` control is then added to the application window, which uses a vertical layout to organize it.

You can see the result in Figure 4-9.

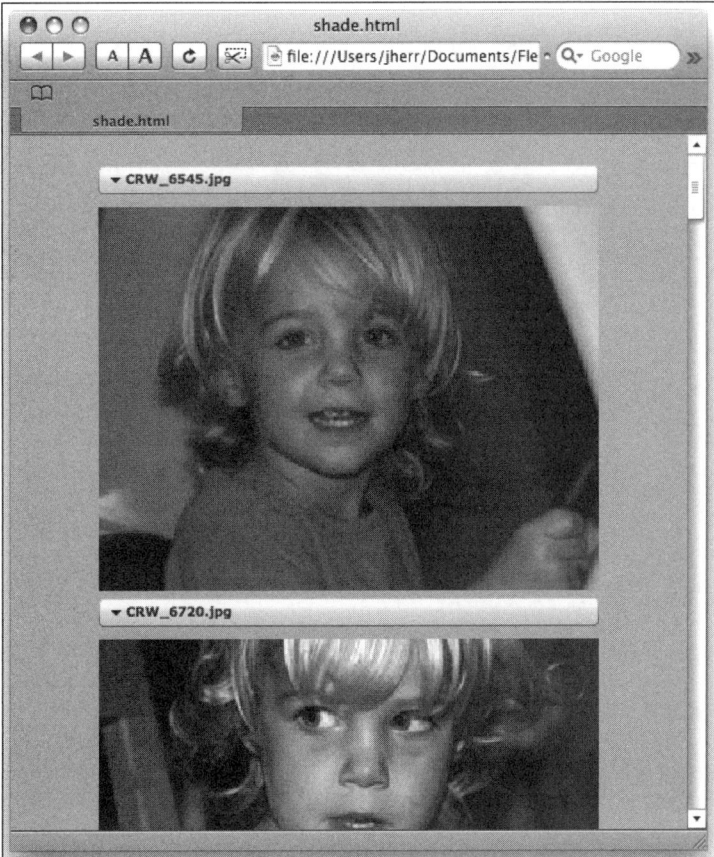

**Figure 4-9.** The application after startup with the images in `WindowShade` containers

You can then use the arrow controls to show or hide some of the images as you can see in Figure 4-10.

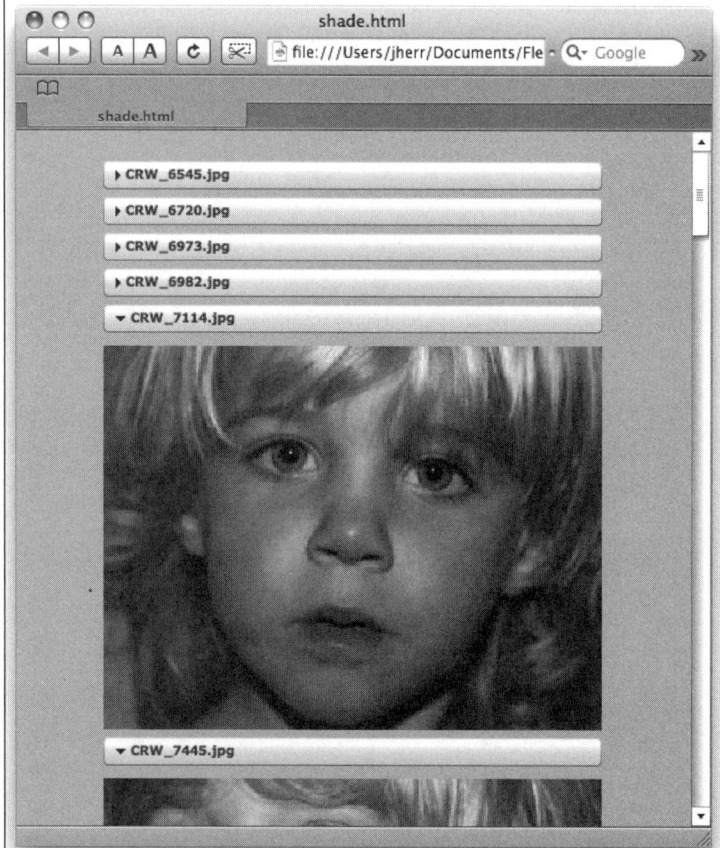

**Figure 4-10.** The application after a few of the windows have been collapsed

The result is kind of like an accordion container where you can have more than one item open at a time.

## Horizontal accordion

Speaking of accordions, the FlexLib contains an extra set of horizontal and vertical accordions. To demonstrate the original vertical accordion and the new horizontal accordion, I've included an example application shown here:

```
<?xml version="1.0" encoding="utf-8"?>
<mx:Application xmlns:mx="http://www.adobe.com/2006/mxml"
  layout="horizontal"
  width="100%" height="100%"
  creationComplete="picData.send()"
  xmlns:flexlib="flexlib.containers.*">
```

```
<mx:Style>
Application { font-family: MyArial; font-size: 14pt; }
Button { font-family: MyArial; }
AccordionHeader { font-size: 18pt; font-weight: bold; }
@font-face { src:local("Arial Narrow"); font-family:
  MyArial; font-weight:bold; }
@font-face { src:local("Arial Narrow"); font-family: MyArial; }
</mx:Style>
<mx:Script>
<![CDATA[
import mx.core.UIComponent;
import mx.containers.HBox;
import mx.controls.Image;
import mx.rpc.events.ResultEvent;

private function addImagesTo( cntnr:UIComponent ) : void {
  var count:int = 0;
  for each( var pic:XML in picData.lastResult..image ) {
    if ( count > 3 ) break;

    var cnv:HBox = new HBox();
    cnv.label = pic.@name.toString();
    cnv.setStyle( 'paddingTop', 5 );
    cnv.setStyle( 'paddingLeft', 5 );
    var img:Image = new Image();
    img.data = 'http://localhost/pics/'+pic.@name.toString();
    img.height = 280;
    cnv.addChild( img );

    cntnr.addChild( cnv );
    count++;
  }
}
private function onPicResult( event:ResultEvent ) : void {
  addImagesTo( vert );
  addImagesTo( horz );
}
]]>
</mx:Script>
<mx:HTTPService url="http://localhost/pics/wide.xml" id="picData"
  resultFormat="e4x"
  result="onPicResult( event )" />
<mx:Accordion height="100%" width="30%" id="vert" />
<flexlib:HAccordion height="300" width="70%" id="horz"
  headerLocation="left" />
</mx:Application>
```

The first thing the application does is get the image list. It then adds the first four images to both of the accordions using the addImagesTo function. One critical thing to note in this example is that we have had to use a custom embedded font (Arial) so that the names can be rotated in the horizontal accordion.

The compiled and executed application is shown in Figure 4-11.

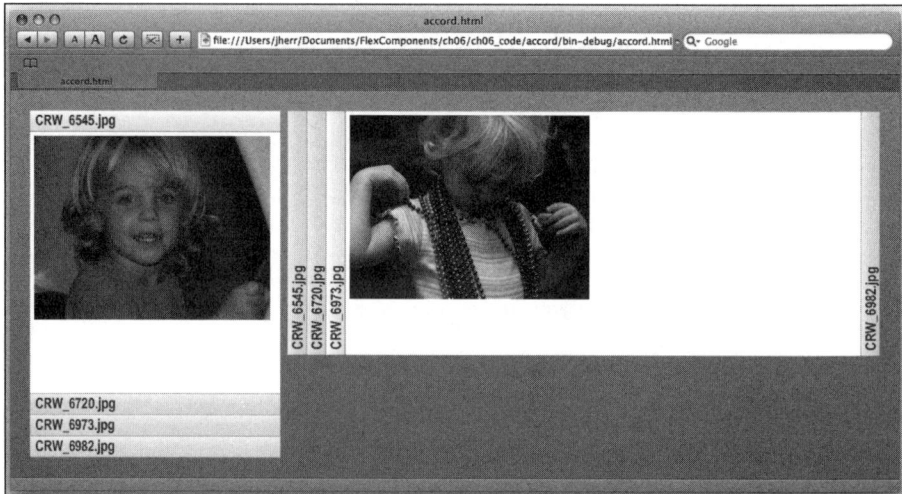

**Figure 4-11.** The vertical and horizontal accordions

The horizontal accordion works just like its vertical cousin. It's a nice choice when you have a lot of horizontal room but are limited vertically.

# Super tabs

The tab navigator built into the Flex framework is great, but FlexLib provides a SuperTabBar control that goes above and beyond. The user can close tabs using a close button, or rearrange tabs by dragging and dropping them.

Some application code that shows how the SuperTabBar works is shown here:

```
<?xml version="1.0" encoding="utf-8"?>
<mx:Application xmlns:mx="http://www.adobe.com/2006/mxml"
  layout="vertical"
  xmlns:flexlib="flexlib.controls.*">
<mx:Panel width="100%" height="100%" title="Super Tab Nav"
  paddingBottom="5" paddingLeft="5" paddingRight="5" paddingTop="5"
  verticalGap="0">
<flexlib:SuperTabBar width="100%" dataProvider="{stack}"
  closePolicy="always" editableTabLabels="true">
</flexlib:SuperTabBar>
<mx:ViewStack id="stack" width="100%" height="100%"
  borderColor="#cccccc" borderStyle="solid" borderThickness="1">
```

```
<mx:HBox label="Megan 1" height="100%" paddingBottom="5"
  paddingLeft="5" paddingRight="5" paddingTop="5">
  <mx:Image source="@Embed('assets/megan1.jpg')" height="300" />
</mx:HBox>
<mx:HBox label="Megan 2" height="100%" paddingBottom="5"
  paddingLeft="5" paddingRight="5" paddingTop="5">
  <mx:Image source="@Embed('assets/megan2.jpg')" height="300" />
</mx:HBox>
<mx:HBox label="Megan 3" height="100%" paddingBottom="5"
  paddingLeft="5" paddingRight="5" paddingTop="5">
  <mx:Image source="@Embed('assets/megan3.jpg')" height="300" />
</mx:HBox>
</mx:ViewStack>
</mx:Panel>
</mx:Application>
```

The SuperTabBar control is linked to the ViewStack that contains the actual tabs. In this example, the application just uses a set of embedded images. You can see the application when it first comes up in Figure 4-12.

**Figure 4-12.** The SuperTabNav example on startup

You can then close a tab using the close button on the left-hand side of the tab. When we close the first tab, you can see the result in Figure 4-13.

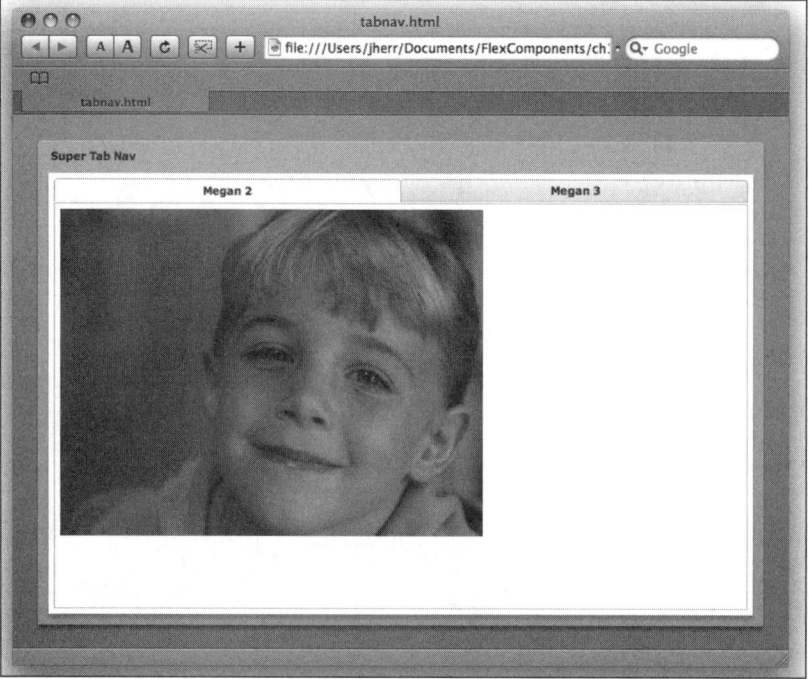

**Figure 4-13.** After closing the first tab

The user can even edit the name of a tab by double-clicking the title and editing the text. The result is shown in Figure 4-14.

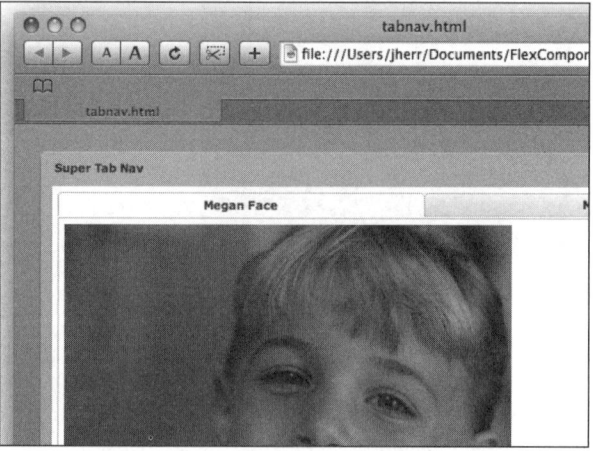

**Figure 4-14.** Changing the name of a tab

With this tab control, you could build a tab system as elaborate as the ones currently in use in browsers like Safari, or the most recent versions of Internet Explorer.

# Toolbars

There are two Flex toolbars that should be of interest to you. The first is in the FlexLib library, and the second is a commercial toolbar library from Teoti Graphix (http://www.teotigraphix.com/). Either one will save you a lot of time if you are thinking about building your own.

The first application shows an example use of the DockableToolbar and Docker controls from FlexLib:

```
<?xml version="1.0" encoding="utf-8"?>
<mx:Application xmlns:mx="http://www.adobe.com/2006/mxml"
  layout="absolute"
  xmlns:flexlib="flexlib.containers.*">
<flexlib:Docker>
<flexlib:DockableToolBar draggable="true" initialPosition="top">
  <mx:Button label="Google" />
  <mx:Button label="Yahoo" />
  <mx:Button label="Microsoft" />
</flexlib:DockableToolBar>
<flexlib:DockableToolBar draggable="true" initialPosition="top">
  <mx:TextInput />
  <mx:Button label="Search" />
</flexlib:DockableToolBar>
<flexlib:DockableToolBar draggable="true" initialPosition="top">
  <mx:CheckBox label="Live update" />
  <mx:CheckBox label="Send messages" />
</flexlib:DockableToolBar>
</flexlib:Docker>
</mx:Application>
```

The toolbars are very easy to use. You simply add a Docker object where you want a dock for the toolbars, and then add several child DockableToolBar objects that contain the controls for each toolbar.

When we run this code from Flex Builder 3, the result is as shown in Figure 4-15.

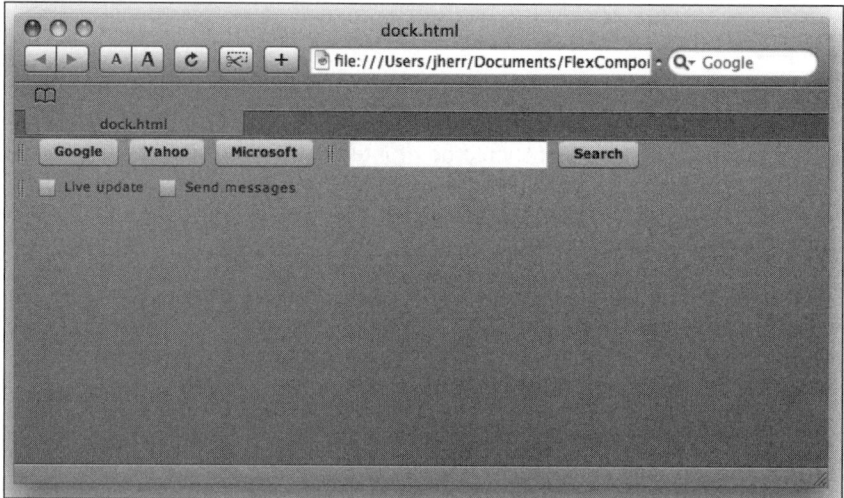

**Figure 4-15.** The FlexLib toolbars

You can then pick up and drag a toolbar as shown in Figure 4-16.

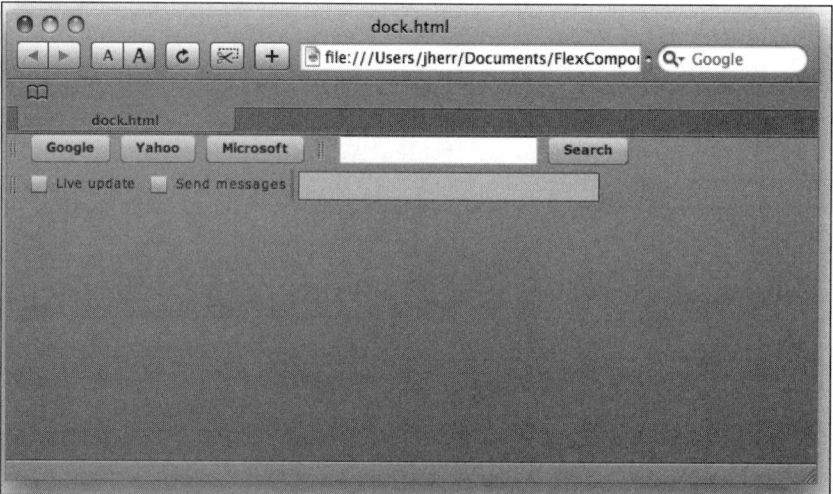

**Figure 4-16.** A toolbar drag in progress

When you release it on another line of the toolbar, the Docker class handles rearranging the toolbars as you can see in Figure 4-17.

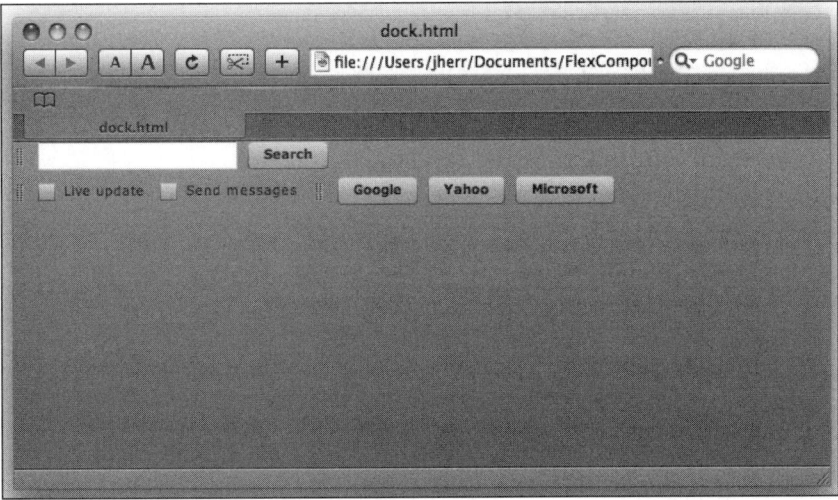

**Figure 4-17.** The toolbar after it's been moved

The DockAreaFX package from Teoti Graphix is like the FlexLib toolbars on steroids. You can have docking regions anywhere you want them. Toolbars can float around. Any control can be hosted. And you have complete control over the skinning of all of the toolbar elements.

Some example code that uses the DockAreaFX package is shown here:

```
<?xml version="1.0" encoding="utf-8"?>
<mx:Application xmlns:mx="http://www.adobe.com/2006/mxml"
  xmlns:containers="com.teotiGraphix.containers.*"
  xmlns:dockPanes="components.dockPanes.*"
  xmlns:dockLists="components.dockLists.*"
  xmlns:baseExample="components.baseExample.*"
  creationComplete="onStartup();" paddingTop="0"
  paddingLeft="0" paddingRight="0" paddingBottom="0"
  verticalGap="0" layout="vertical">

<mx:Move duration="250" id="DockerMove"/>
<mx:Fade duration="250" id="DockPaneFade"/>

<mx:Script>
<![CDATA[
import com.teotiGraphix.managers.events.ResizeManagerEvent;
import mx.core.UIComponent;
import com.teotiGraphix.containers.events.DockEvent;

private function onStartup() : void
{
  vPaneDockArea.addEventListener(
  ResizeManagerEvent.RESIZE_MANAGER_END,
```

```
      resizeManagerEndHandler);
    vToolDockArea.addEventListener(
    ResizeManagerEvent.RESIZE_MANAGER_END,
      resizeManagerEndHandler);
    hBottomToolBar.addEventListener(
    ResizeManagerEvent.RESIZE_MANAGER_END,
      resizeManagerEndHandler);
  }
  private function resizeManagerEndHandler(
    event:ResizeManagerEvent ) : void {
    vPaneDockArea.percentHeight = 100;
    vToolDockArea.percentHeight = 100;
    hBottomToolBar.percentWidth = 100;
  }
  private function panelDockHandler( event:DockEvent ) : void {
    UIComponent(event.dockInitiator).percentWidth = 100;
  }
]]>
</mx:Script>

<mx:Style>
.verticalToggleDockStyles {
}
.horizontalToggleDockStyles {
}
DockAreaFX {
  cornerRadius:0;
  backgroundAlpha:1;
  borderStyle:"none";
  boundingBoxColor:#FFFFFF;
  boundsCheckEnabled:false;
  overlayButtonOffset:"center";
  resizeType:"realtime";
  overlayButtonThickness:7;
  overlayFillColor:#242424;
  resizeBarGap:0;

}
DockPaneFX {
  addedEffect:"DockPaneFade";
  resizeClientOverlayAlpha:0;
  overlayButtonOffset:"inside";
  overlayButtonThickness:5;

}
.verticalResizeBarStyles {
  borderSkin:Embed(source='/assets/vertical_bar_skin.png');
}
.horizontalResizeBarStyles {
```

```
      borderSkin:Embed(source='/assets/horizontal_bar_skin.png');
   }
</mx:Style>

<containers:ResizeDockAreaFX layout="flow"
   showResizeBar="true" resizeEnabled="false"
   resizeBarThickness="7" resizeBarPlacement="bottom"
   horizontalResizeBarStyleName="horizontalResizeBarStyles"
   width="100%" minHeight="50">

<baseExample:HToolBar floatTitleBarPlacement="bottom" title="Tool One">
<mx:Button label="Open" />
<mx:Label text="Size" />
<mx:NumericStepper value="12"/>
<mx:ComboBox selectedIndex="0">
   <mx:dataProvider>
      <mx:Array>
         <mx:String>Times New Roman</mx:String>
         <mx:String>Arial</mx:String>
      </mx:Array>
   </mx:dataProvider>
</mx:ComboBox>
</baseExample:HToolBar>

</containers:ResizeDockAreaFX>

<mx:HBox width="100%" height="100%">

<containers:ResizeDockAreaFX id="vPaneDockArea"
   dock="panelDockHandler(event)" showResizeBar="true"
   resizeBarThickness="7" resizeBarPlacement="right"
   verticalResizeBarStyleName="verticalResizeBarStyles"
   height="100%" minHeight="0" minWidth="200" maxWidth="420">

<dockPanes:DockPanelPane id="paneTwo" title="Panel Two">
   <mx:DateChooser/>
</dockPanes:DockPanelPane>

</containers:ResizeDockAreaFX>

<mx:HBox width="100%" height="100%" />
<containers:ResizeDockAreaFX id="vToolDockArea" horizontalAlign="right"
   showResizeBar="true" resizeEnabled="false" resizeBarThickness="7"
   resizeBarPlacement="left"
   verticalResizeBarStyleName="verticalResizeBarStyles"
   height="100%" minWidth="7" maxWidth="200" />

</mx:HBox>
```

```
<containers:ResizeDockAreaFX layout="horizontal" id="hBottomToolBar"
  showResizeBar="true" resizeBarThickness="7" resizeBarPlacement="top"
  horizontalResizeBarStyleName="horizontalResizeBarStyles"
  width="100%" />

</mx:Application>
```

This code creates two toolbars. The first is a horizontal toolbar with a button, a label, a numeric stepper, and a combo box. The second is a much better toolbar with a calendar control embedded in it.

When the application is first launched, it looks like Figure 4-18.

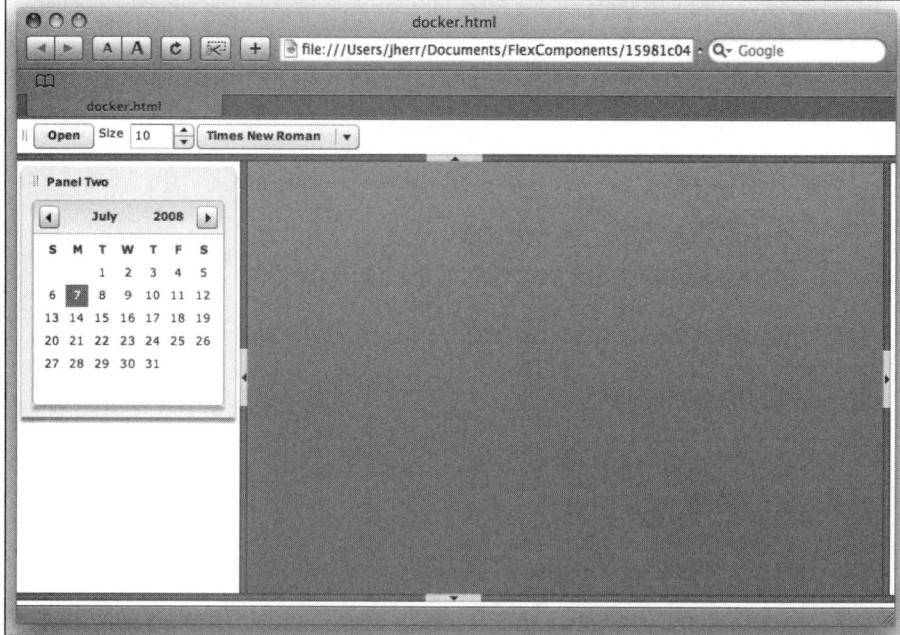

**Figure 4-18.** When the application first starts up

You can then drag a toolbar and move it to another docking area. The toolbar dragging in progress is shown in Figure 4-19.

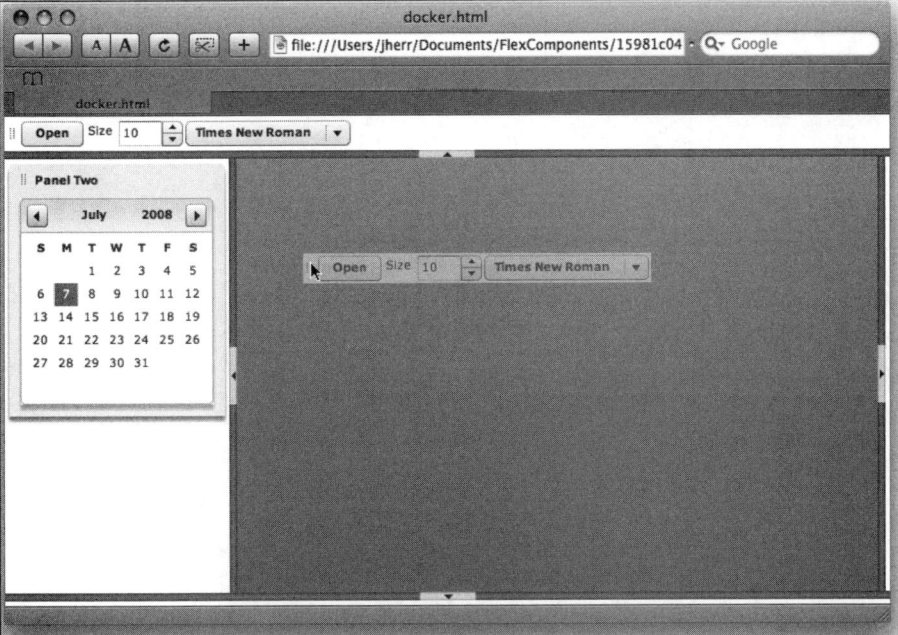

**Figure 4-19.** The dragging of the toolbar caught in progress

If you release it without docking it on one of the sides of the application space, it will just float in the middle of the application area as shown in Figure 4-20.

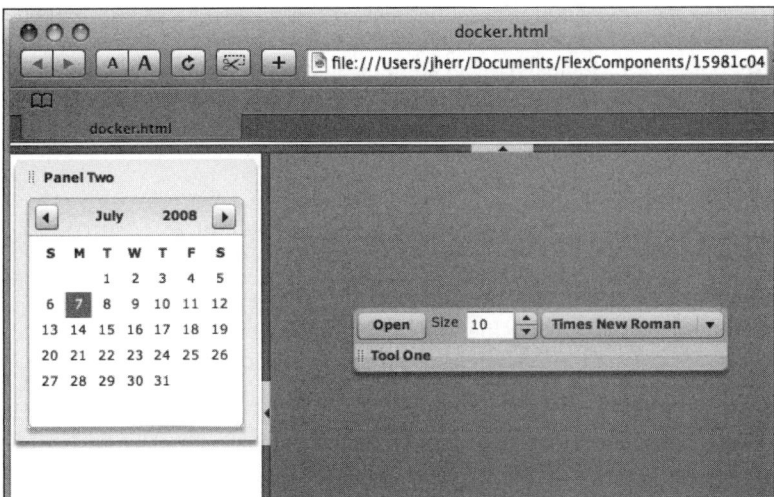

**Figure 4-20.** The toolbar in the middle of the window

You can even move around the big toolbar components like the calendar, as you can see in Figure 4-21.

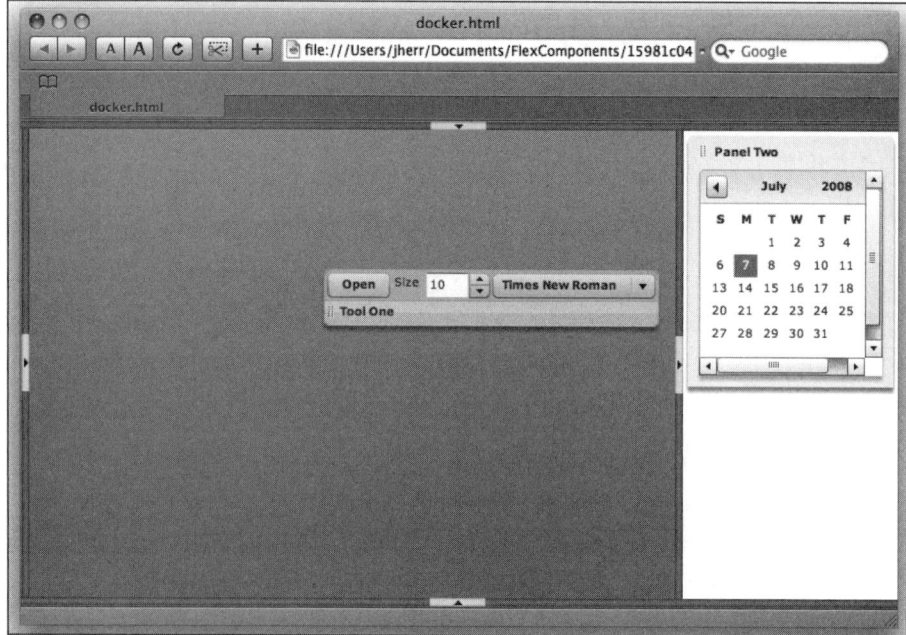

**Figure 4-21.** The calendar docked on the left-hand side of the window

Both the FlexLib and the Teoti Graphix package can save you a lot of time and effort. The decision between the two really depends on the extent to which your application is going to make serious use of toolbars. If you are looking for something industrial strength, you are going to want to use the Teoti Graphix toolbar. But if you just need an upgrade to the ApplicationControlBar, you can easily get by with the FlexLib toolbars.

# Multiple Document Interface

Microsoft coined the term MDI, for Multiple Document Interface, to describe their user interface for applications where the application hosted several windows within a larger window. You can do the same thing for your Flex application using the MDI container and windows that are built into the FlexLib.

The following application shown uses the baseball database interface to put up graphs for each of the teams you select in separate windows:

```
<?xml version="1.0" encoding="utf-8"?>
<mx:Application xmlns:mx="http://www.adobe.com/2006/mxml"
  layout="absolute"
  xmlns:flexlib="http://code.google.com/p/flexlib/"
  creationComplete="baseballRO.getTeamList.send()">
```

```
<mx:Script>
<![CDATA[
import mx.rpc.events.ResultEvent;
import mx.charts.series.AreaSeries;
import mx.charts.LinearAxis;
import mx.charts.CategoryAxis;
import mx.charts.AreaChart;
import flexlib.mdi.containers.MDIWindow;

private var requestedTeam:String = null;

private function onDoubleClick() : void {
  requestedTeam = teamList.selectedItem.name;
  baseballRO.getYearsByTeam.send( teamList.selectedItem.teamid );
}

private function onReportResult( event:ResultEvent ) : void {
  var win:MDIWindow = new MDIWindow();
  win.setStyle('top',100);
  win.setStyle('left',100);
  win.width = 400;
  win.height = 300;
  win.title = requestedTeam;
  win.setStyle( 'backgroundAlpha', 0.8 );

  var data:Array = [];
  for each ( var row:Object in event.result )
    data.push( row );

  var vertAxis:LinearAxis = new LinearAxis();
  vertAxis.title = 'Count';
  var horzAxis:CategoryAxis = new CategoryAxis();
  horzAxis.title = 'Year';
  horzAxis.categoryField = 'yearid';

  var series1:AreaSeries = new AreaSeries();
  series1.xField = 'yearid';
  series1.yField = 'h';
  series1.dataProvider = data;
  var series2:AreaSeries = new AreaSeries();
  series2.xField = 'yearid';
  series2.yField = '2b';
  series2.dataProvider = data;
  var series3:AreaSeries = new AreaSeries();
  series3.xField = 'yearid';
  series3.yField = '3b';
  series3.dataProvider = data;
  var series4:AreaSeries = new AreaSeries();
  series4.xField = 'yearid';
```

4

```
        series4.yField = 'hr';
        series4.dataProvider = data;

        var ac:AreaChart = new AreaChart();
        ac.percentHeight = 100;
        ac.percentWidth = 100;
        ac.type = 'stacked';
        ac.verticalAxis = vertAxis;
        ac.horizontalAxis = horzAxis;
        ac.dataProvider = data;
        ac.series = [ series1, series2, series3, series4 ];
        win.addChild( ac );

        mdiCanvas.windowManager.add( win );
    }
]]>
</mx:Script>

<mx:RemoteObject id="baseballRO"
  endpoint="http://localhost/amfphp/gateway.php"
  source="baseball.BaseballService"
  destination="baseball.BaseballService"
  showBusyCursor="true">
<mx:method name="getTeamList" />
<mx:method name="getYearsByTeam" result="onReportResult( event )">
<mx:arguments>
        <mx:teamid />
</mx:arguments>
</mx:method>
</mx:RemoteObject>

<flexlib:MDICanvas id="mdiCanvas" horizontalScrollPolicy="off"
  verticalScrollPolicy="off"
  width="100%" height="100%" backgroundColor="#FFFFFF"
  backgroundAlpha="0">
<flexlib:MDIWindow
  title="Teams" x="20" y="20" width="400" height="200">
<mx:DataGrid width="100%" height="100%"
  dataProvider="{baseballRO.getTeamList.lastResult}"
  doubleClickEnabled="true" doubleClick="onDoubleClick()"
  id="teamList">
<mx:columns>
  <mx:DataGridColumn dataField="name" headerText="Team" />
</mx:columns>
</mx:DataGrid>
</flexlib:MDIWindow>
</flexlib:MDICanvas>

</mx:Application>
```

The application starts up by getting the list of teams. The Teams window, defined at the bottom of the file by the MDIWindow tag enclosed in the MDICanvas tag, displays the list of teams once the data is received from the server. When the user double-clicks a team name, the onDoubleClick method is called. This method creates a new MDIWindow and an AreaChart within that window to display the data for the team that is retrieved from the server.

When we first launch the application, the Teams window comes up with the list of teams. This is shown in Figure 4-22.

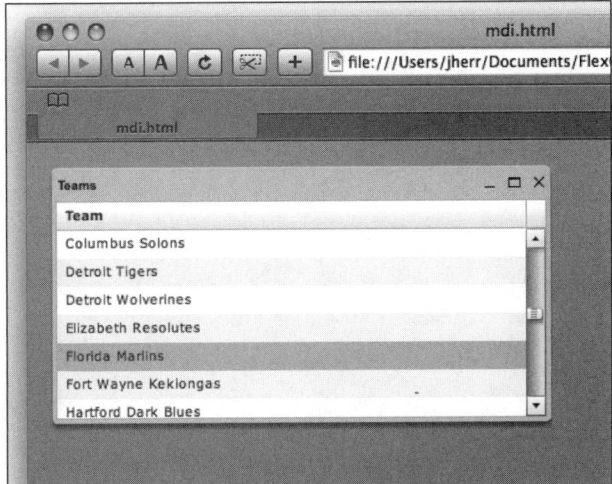

**Figure 4-22.** The startup window showing the baseball teams

When you double-click the team names, new windows are launched with the area charts that show the single, double, triple, and homer production for every year the team played.

An example of the data for the Florida Marlins, Arizona Diamondbacks, and Boston Red Sox is shown in Figure 4-23.

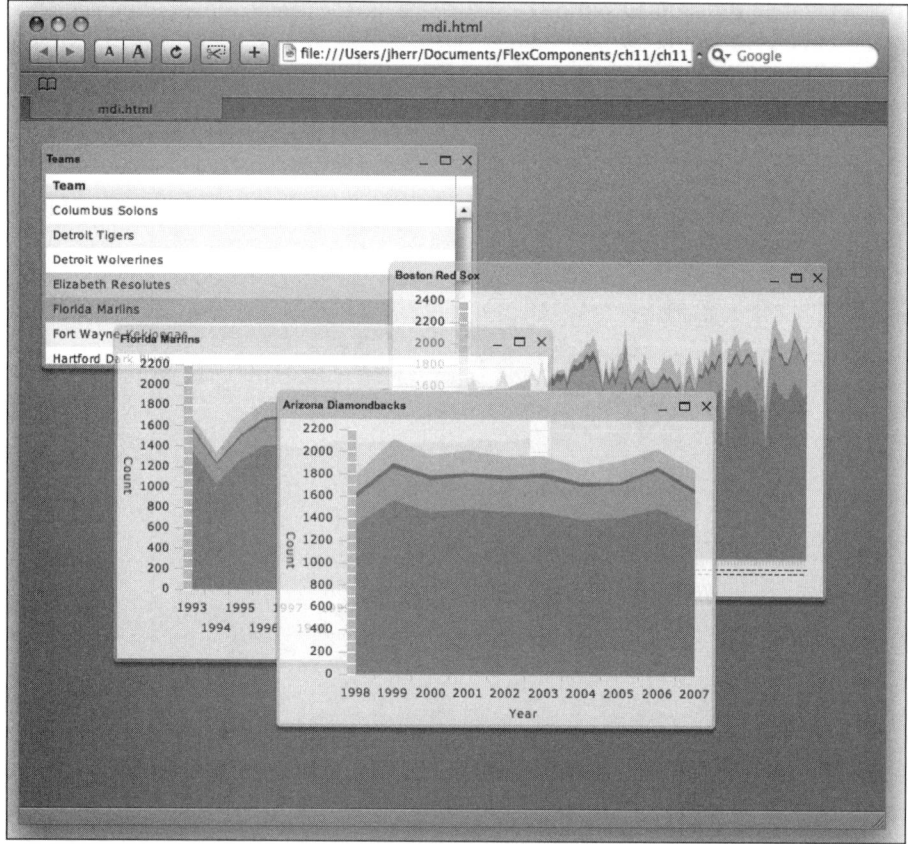

**Figure 4-23.** Four windows to show the list of teams and some team results

If you are looking for a windowing framework that works on the client, I think you have found it in the MDI classes within the FlexLib. It's a very easy-to-use API that works remarkably well.

## Upgraded forms

Flex comes with Form and FormItem containers built in, but these have been extended by two different libraries. The first is the AdvancedForm in the FlexLib. This class adds support for undo, as well as resetting the form. The MultiColumnForm upgrades the visual containment aspects of the form by allowing for multiple columns.

This first application shows how to use the AdvancedForm from the FlexLib:

```
<?xml version="1.0" encoding="utf-8"?>
<mx:Application xmlns:mx="http://www.adobe.com/2006/mxml"
  layout="vertical"
  xmlns:flexlib="http://code.google.com/p/flexlib/">
<flexlib:AdvancedForm id="myForm" undoHistorySize="15">
  <mx:FormItem label="First name">
    <mx:TextInput />
  </mx:FormItem>
  <mx:FormItem label="Last name">
    <mx:TextInput />
  </mx:FormItem>
  <mx:FormItem label="Email">
    <mx:TextInput />
  </mx:FormItem>
</flexlib:AdvancedForm>
<mx:Button click="myForm.resetForm()" label="Reset" />
</mx:Application>
```

The AdvancedForm works just like a Form, but adds support for undo and reset. The size of the undo stack is set by the undoHistorySize attribute on the tag. And the reset function is handled by calling the reset method on the form object.

When we bring this example up in Flex Builder 3, it looks like Figure 4-24.

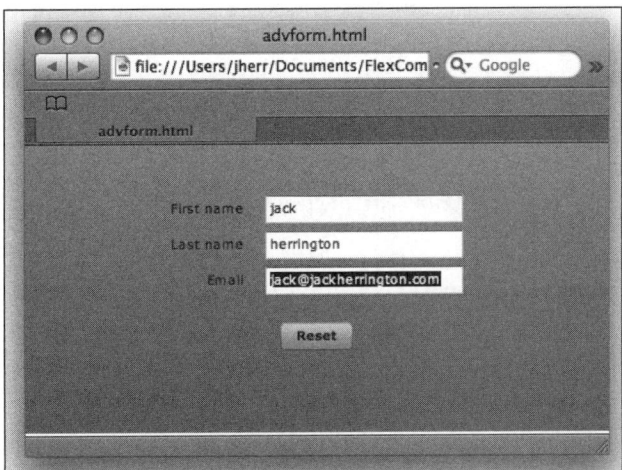

**Figure 4-24.** The advanced form with the Reset button

When we click the Reset button, all of the fields in the form are reset. This is shown in Figure 4-25.

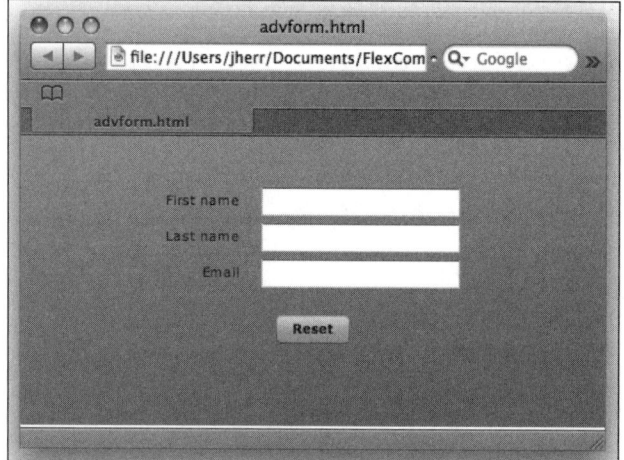

**Figure 4-25.** The reset form

The AdvancedForm component is a very good example of how to extend the Flex framework while respecting the design of the framework itself.

The MultiColumnForm is another replacement for the Form tag. But in this case, you also need to use MultiColumnFormItem tags instead of the original FormItem tags. These MultiColumnFormItem tags provide support for the colSpan attribute, which tells the MultiColumnForm the number of columns that this particular item will span.

The example application that demonstrates the MultiColumnForm is shown here:

```
<?xml version="1.0" encoding="utf-8"?>
<mx:Application xmlns:mx="http://www.adobe.com/2006/mxml"
  layout="vertical"
  xmlns:mc="nz.co.codec.flex.multicolumnform.*"
  defaultButton="{submit}">

<mx:Panel title="Your Information" width="600"
  paddingBottom="5" paddingLeft="5" paddingRight="5"
  paddingTop="5" layout="vertical"
  horizontalAlign="center">
<mc:MultiColumnForm numColumns="2">
  <mc:MultiColumnFormItem label="First">
    <mx:TextInput id="first" width="200" />
  </mc:MultiColumnFormItem>
```

```
      <mc:MultiColumnFormItem label="Last">
        <mx:TextInput id="last" width="200" />
      </mc:MultiColumnFormItem>
      <mc:MultiColumnFormItem label="Address" colspan="2" width="100%">
        <mx:TextInput id="address1" width="100%" />
      </mc:MultiColumnFormItem>
      <mc:MultiColumnFormItem label="" colspan="2" width="100%">
        <mx:TextInput id="address2" width="100%" />
      </mc:MultiColumnFormItem>
      <mc:MultiColumnFormItem label="Email" colspan="2" width="100%">
        <mx:TextInput id="email" width="100%" />
      </mc:MultiColumnFormItem>
    </mc:MultiColumnForm>
    <mx:Button label="Submit" id="submit" />
  </mx:Panel>

</mx:Application>
```

You can see the result of this layout in Figure 4-26.

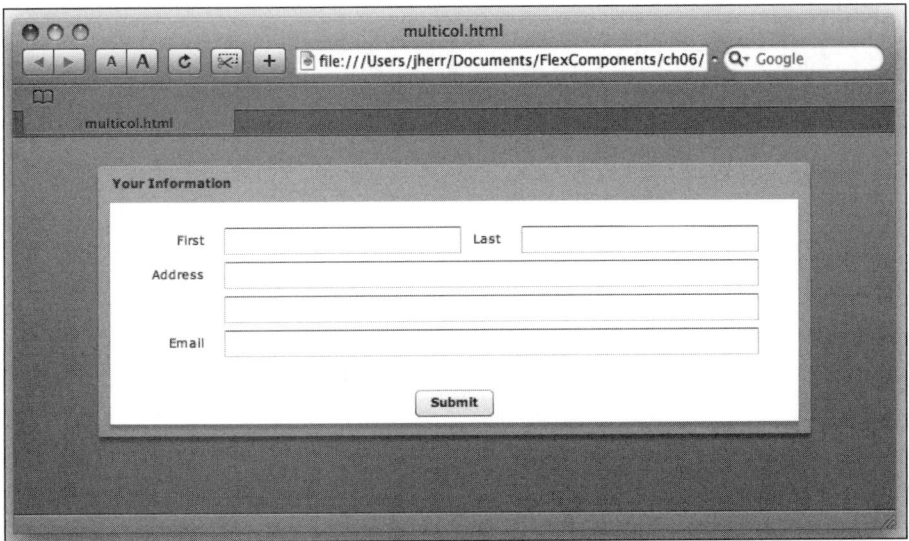

**Figure 4-26.** The multicolumn form

This is a nice way to get high-quality form style layout without having to forgo the niceties of a Form tag.

# Where we will go from here

The container classes supplied by the Flex framework provide a great starting point. Many GUI toolkits don't even have basic containment systems such as the HBox or VBox. But the Flex framework still leaves a lot of room for new types of containers like the ones I've demonstrated in this chapter. With these tools in hand, building applications that show large amounts of data, or include all resizing and reordering elements, or need expanding and collapsing segments, are just a drop-in component away.

Using the right containers and layout is critical to building a user interface that scales and skins well. These new containers give you a lot of layout tools to go in your tool bag. In the next chapter, we upgrade the basic control types.

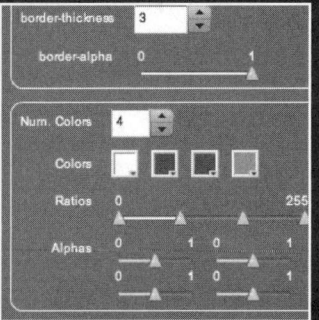
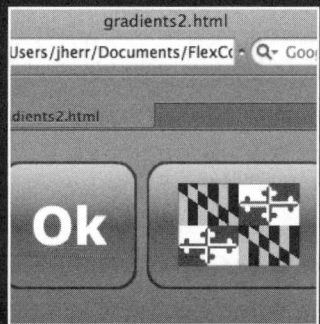
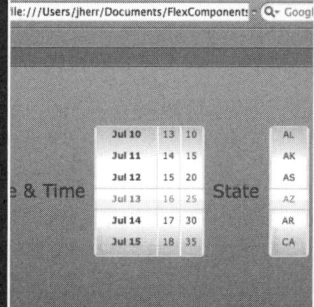

# New types of controls

The Flex framework provides a nice set of the standard controls: buttons, scrollbars, combo boxes, lists, data grids, and more. But there is some room for extra controls, and that's made up by the bevy of new controls I'll show you in this chapter. These controls work just as well as those in the original framework and make up for a lot of the gaps in the original control set.

# Canvas buttons

The first control we will look at is the CanvasButton available in the framework. This control, contained in the FlexLib (http://flexlib.googlecode.com) library, is built on the button class. It provides a Canvas-style container within a button frame.

The following example code shows two buttons, each of which uses the CanvasButton in a different way:

```
<?xml version="1.0" encoding="utf-8"?>
<mx:Application xmlns:mx="http://www.adobe.com/2006/mxml"
  layout="horizontal"
 xmlns:flexlib="flexlib.controls.*">
<flexlib:CanvasButton width="150">
   <mx:VBox height="100%" width="100%" verticalGap="0"
     paddingBottom="10" paddingTop="10">
     <mx:Label text="Please" textAlign="center" width="100%" />
     <mx:Label text="Click" textAlign="center" width="100%"
      fontSize="20" fontWeight="bold" />
     <mx:Label text="here!" textAlign="center" width="100%" />
   </mx:VBox>
</flexlib:CanvasButton>
<flexlib:CanvasButton width="150">
  <mx:VBox height="100%" width="100%" verticalGap="0" paddingBottom="10"
   paddingTop="10" horizontalAlign="center">
   <mx:Image source="http://localhost/states/Maryland.gif" height="65"
      width="100" />
  </mx:VBox>
</flexlib:CanvasButton>
</mx:Application>
```

To get this example to work, you will first need to install the images on your local server per the instructions in Chapter 3.

The first CanvasButton uses a VBox container to place some Label items. The second CanvasButton shows a VBox containing an Image. The resulting application is shown in Figure 5-1.

**Figure 5-1.** The cool new CanvasButtons

The content inside the image works just like a Canvas container, and the outside wrapper works just like a Button. It's even skinnable!

# Enhanced button skin

EnhancedButtonSkin, in the FlexLib, is not a control but an easy way to upgrade the existing button control with a multigradient look. The most common use for that is to create the Aqua-style glossy buttons seen in Mac OS X. To make it easy to build the CSS for the EnhancedButtonSkin programmatic skin, you can use the Flex EnhancedButtonSkin Explorer, available on the Wabysabi site (http://www.wabysabi.com/flex/enhancedbuttonskin/). This explorer is shown in Figure 5-2.

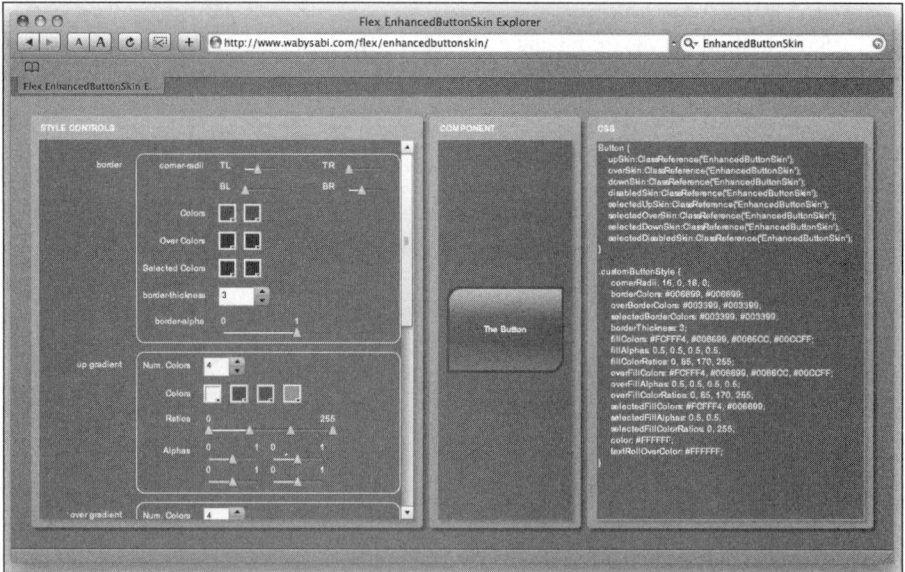

**Figure 5-2.** The EnhancedButtonSkin Explorer

From here you can change the parameters to alter the colors, the gradients, and so on. Then when you have what you want, you can copy the CSS code in the right-hand panel and paste it into your Flex application to make use of the EnhancedButtonSkin code.

An example application that uses the EnhancedButtonSkin is shown here:

```
<?xml version="1.0" encoding="utf-8"?>
<mx:Application xmlns:mx="http://www.adobe.com/2006/mxml"
 layout="horizontal"
  xmlns:flexlib="http://code.google.com/p/flexlib/">
<mx:Script>
<![CDATA[
import flexlib.skins.*;
]]>
</mx:Script>
<mx:Style>
Button {
  upSkin:ClassReference('flexlib.skins.EnhancedButtonSkin');
  overSkin:ClassReference('flexlib.skins.EnhancedButtonSkin');
  downSkin:ClassReference('flexlib.skins.EnhancedButtonSkin');
  disabledSkin:ClassReference('flexlib.skins.EnhancedButtonSkin');
  selectedUpSkin:ClassReference('flexlib.skins.EnhancedButtonSkin');
  selectedOverSkin:ClassReference('flexlib.skins.EnhancedButtonSkin');
  selectedDownSkin:ClassReference('flexlib.skins.EnhancedButtonSkin');
  selectedDisabledSkin:ClassReference(➥
'flexlib.skins.EnhancedButtonSkin');
```

```
}
.customButtonStyle {
   cornerRadii: 16, 16, 16, 16;
   borderColors: #FF0000, #990033;
   overBorderColors: #003399, #003399;
   selectedBorderColors: #990066, #9933CC;
   borderThickness: 2;
   fillColors: #FCFFF4, #FF0000, #FF6666;
   fillAlphas: 0.5, 0.5, 0.5;
   fillColorRatios: 0, 128, 255;
   overFillColors: #FCFFF4, #006699, #0066CC, #00CCFF;
   overFillAlphas: 0.5, 0.5, 0.5, 0.5;
   overFillColorRatios: 0, 85, 170, 255;
   selectedFillColors: #FCFFF4, #006699;
   selectedFillAlphas: 0.5, 0.5;
   selectedFillColorRatios: 0, 255;
   color: #FFFFFF;
   textRollOverColor: #FFFFFF;
   fontSize: 40;
}
</mx:Style>
<mx:Button label="Ok" styleName="customButtonStyle" height="100"
  width="150" />
</mx:Application>
```

To make this example, I simply used the explorer to create the CSS code and pasted it into my application to make the gradient effect shown in Figure 5-3. You can also use the CSS designer in Flex Builder 3 to try different CSS variations.

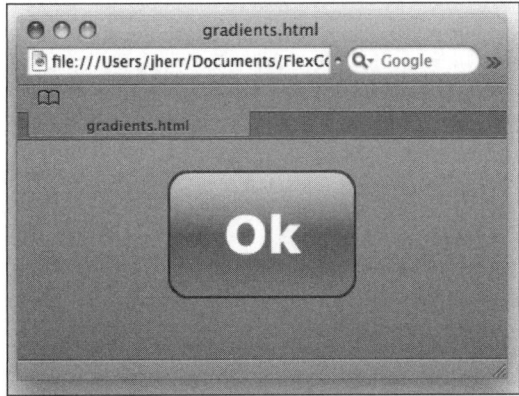

**Figure 5-3.** A glossy button using the EnhancedButtonSkin

In this next application, I'll use the EnhancedButtonSkin and apply it to both a regular Button and a CanvasButton. The code for this is shown here:

```
<?xml version="1.0" encoding="utf-8"?>
<mx:Application xmlns:mx="http://www.adobe.com/2006/mxml"
  layout="horizontal"
  xmlns:flexlib="http://code.google.com/p/flexlib/">
<mx:Script>
<![CDATA[
import flexlib.skins.*;
]]>
</mx:Script>
<mx:Style>
Button {
  upSkin:ClassReference('flexlib.skins.EnhancedButtonSkin');
  overSkin:ClassReference('flexlib.skins.EnhancedButtonSkin');
  downSkin:ClassReference('flexlib.skins.EnhancedButtonSkin');
  disabledSkin:ClassReference('flexlib.skins.EnhancedButtonSkin');
  selectedUpSkin:ClassReference('flexlib.skins.EnhancedButtonSkin');
  selectedOverSkin:ClassReference('flexlib.skins.EnhancedButtonSkin');
  selectedDownSkin:ClassReference('flexlib.skins.EnhancedButtonSkin');
  selectedDisabledSkin:ClassReference(➥
'flexlib.skins.EnhancedButtonSkin');
}
.customButtonStyle {
    cornerRadii: 16, 16, 16, 16;
    borderColors: #FF0000, #990033;
    overBorderColors: #003399, #003399;
    selectedBorderColors: #990066, #9933CC;
    borderThickness: 2;
    fillColors: #FCFFF4, #FF0000, #FF6666;
    fillAlphas: 0.5, 0.5, 0.5;
    fillColorRatios: 0, 128, 255;
    overFillColors: #FCFFF4, #006699, #0066CC, #00CCFF;
    overFillAlphas: 0.5, 0.5, 0.5, 0.5;
    overFillColorRatios: 0, 85, 170, 255;
    selectedFillColors: #FCFFF4, #006699;
    selectedFillAlphas: 0.5, 0.5;
    selectedFillColorRatios: 0, 255;
    color: #FFFFFF;
    textRollOverColor: #FFFFFF;
    fontSize: 40;
}
</mx:Style>
<mx:Button label="Ok" styleName="customButtonStyle" height="100"
  width="110" />
<flexlib:CanvasButton width="150" styleName="customButtonStyle"
  height="100">
```

```
<mx:VBox height="100%" width="100%" verticalGap="0" paddingBottom="10"
  paddingTop="10"
    horizontalAlign="center" verticalAlign="middle">
  <mx:Image source="http://localhost/states/Maryland.gif" height="65"
  width="100" />
</mx:VBox>
</flexlib:CanvasButton>
</mx:Application>
```

Because CanvasButton is based on Button, it uses all of the CSS properties of the Button class. So the same red glossy CSS EnhancedButtonSkin works on both the Button and CanvasButton controls. This is shown when we run this application and see the result in Figure 5-4.

**Figure 5-4.** The EnhancedButtonSkin applied to a Button and a CanvasButton

Now you can get the Aqua glossy look, or any other gradient look you dream up, any time you want by using the EnhancedButtonSkin from the FlexLib.

# Korax ColorPicker

If you are looking for a control that gives your application a more precise color picker, you should check out the Korax ColorPicker (http://kss.korax.ru/flex/cp/index.html). The following application code is a simple demonstration of the color picker:

```
<?xml version="1.0" encoding="utf-8"?>
<mx:Application xmlns:mx="http://www.adobe.com/2006/mxml"
  layout="vertical" creationComplete="onStartup()">
<mx:Script>
<![CDATA[
import korax.controls.ColorPicker.*;
```

```
    private function onStartup() : void {
      addEventListener("apply",  onColorSelect);
    }
    private function onColorSelect( event:ColorPickerEvent ) : void {
      colorPanel.setStyle( 'backgroundColor', event.color )
    }
    private function onColorClick() : void {
      ColorPickerWindow.show_window( this, colorPanel.getStyle(
        'backgroundColor' ), true );
    }
  ]]>
  </mx:Script>
  <mx:Panel title="Color picker" paddingBottom="15" paddingLeft="15"
    paddingRight="15" paddingTop="15" layout="horizontal">
  <mx:Label text="Color" fontSize="14" />
  <mx:Canvas id="colorPanel" backgroundColor="#00ff00" width="20"
    height="20" click="onColorClick()" />
  </mx:Panel>
  </mx:Application>
```

The Korax ColorPicker comes as source code. You can download the source code by using the right-click menu on the example and selecting View Source. Once you have it installed in your application, you use it by importing the ColorPickerWindow class, and then invoke it using the show_window method. Take a look in the code and notice that we never call addEventListener on the ColorPickerWindow. That's because the ColorPickerWindow always calls back to the apply event on the parent window. So, in the case of this code, we map that to the onColorSelect method.

When we start this up in Flex Builder, we see something like Figure 5-5.

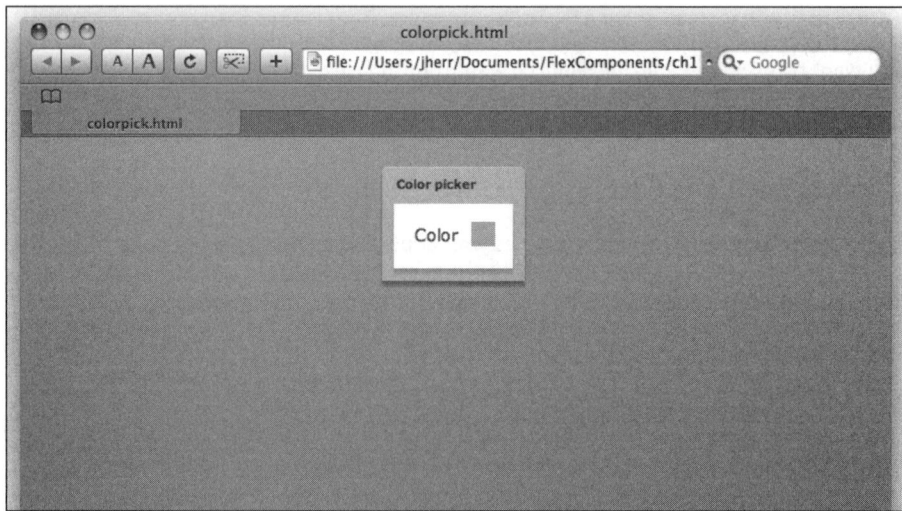

**Figure 5-5.** The window with the color control

From here, we click the little green square, which is just a Canvas control with a backgroundColor of green. That brings up the ColorSelectorWindow shown in Figure 5-6.

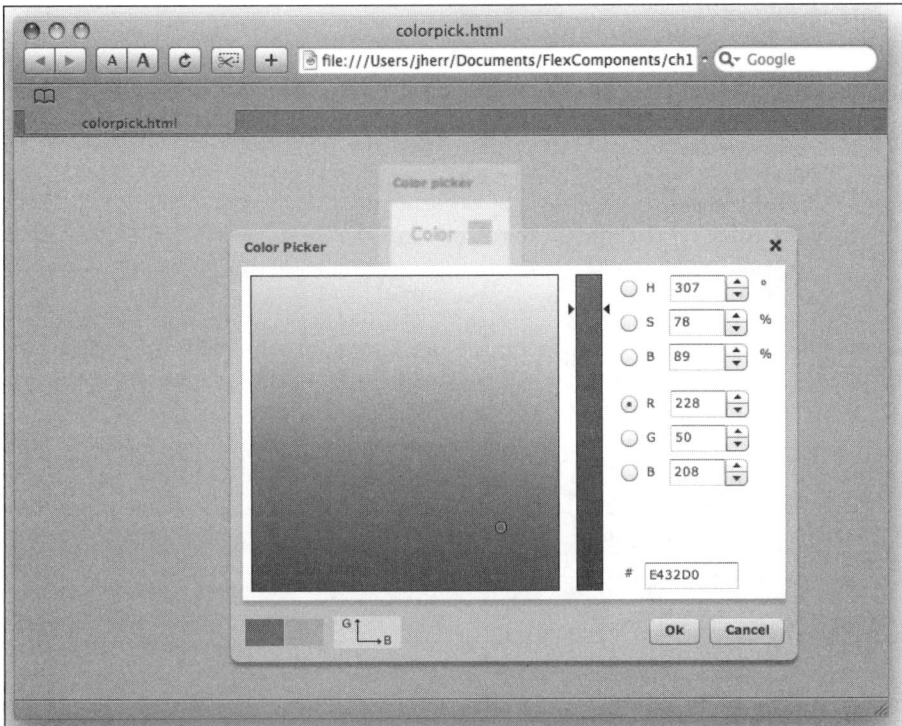

**Figure 5-6.** The Korax color selector window

With this window, we can specify the RGB value or the HSB value, or select from the color spectrum on the right. Once we click OK, the parent window gets the apply event, and it sets the backgroundColor of the Canvas object to the selected color.

# Wheels

The iPhone was a marvel on its release for many reasons. One of them was Apple's development of some new control types that made it easier to put data into the phone through the touch screen interface. Among these advancements was a wheel interface you use by flicking your thumb up and down to select from multiple preset values. The FlexWheel controls (http://strawberrypixel.com/blog/flexwheel-component-page/) bring this functionality to your Flex application.

The example application code shown here puts up just a sampling of the preset wheel types available:

```xml
<?xml version="1.0" encoding="utf-8"?>
<mx:Application xmlns:mx="http://www.adobe.com/2006/mxml"
  layout="horizontal" verticalAlign="middle"
  xmlns:wheel="flexWheel.components.*">
  <mx:Label text="Amount" fontSize="20" />
  <wheel:NumericWheel minVal="10" maxVal="100" />
  <mx:Label text="Date &amp; Time" fontSize="20" />
  <wheel:AppointmentWheel />
  <mx:Label text="State" fontSize="20" />
  <wheel:USStateWheel />
</mx:Application>
```

Because these are true Flex components, we can declare them in MXML by specifying the custom namespace xmlns:wheel, and then adding the NumericWheel, AppointmentWheel, and USStateWheel anywhere we want in the interface.

You can see the result in Figure 5-7.

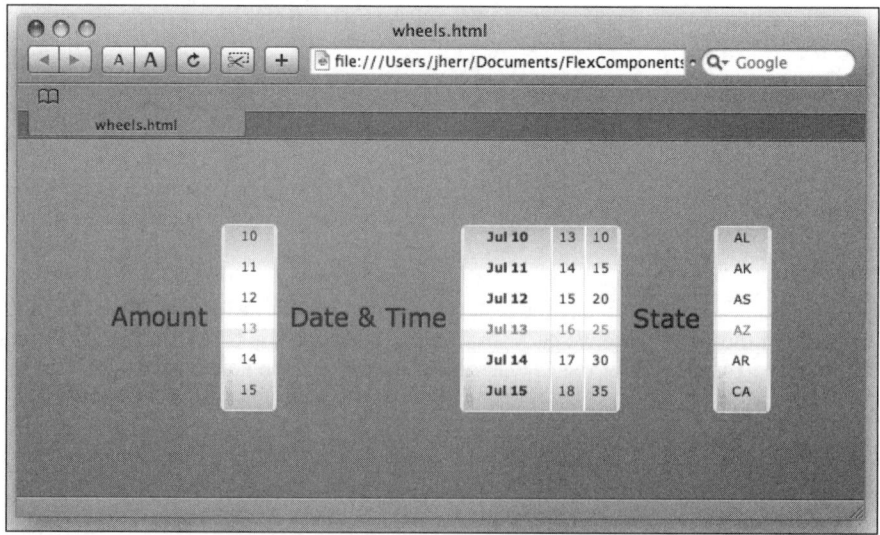

**Figure 5-7.** Three example wheel controls

To change the values, you simply click and drag up or down on the wheel until the value you want is in the middle highlighted area.

These controls are very well designed. You can provide data to them to put in your own values, or subclass the controls to make all new custom controls based on the wheel platform.

# Dual slider

Brendan Meutzner has developed a handy "dual slider" control (http://www.visualconcepts.ca/flex2/dualslider2/DualSlideTest.html) that makes it easy to specify a range of values and then move that range up and down along the slider scale. You can download the source by selecting View Source when looking at the demo.

The following application code demonstrates Brendan's dual slider:

```
<?xml version="1.0"?>
<mx:Application xmlns:mx="http://www.adobe.com/2006/mxml" xmlns:ds="*"
  creationComplete="pageComplete()" layout="vertical"
  horizontalAlign="left">

<mx:Script>
<![CDATA[
private function pageComplete() : void {
  mySlider.setComponent()
}
private function getSliderLabels( amount:Number,
  numberOfLabels:Number ) : Array {
  var interval:Number = amount / (numberOfLabels - 1);
  var labelCounter:Number = mySlider.minimum;
  var loopCounter:Number = 0;

  var tmpArray:Array = new Array();
  while(loopCounter <= amount) {
    tmpArray.push(Math.round(labelCounter));
    labelCounter += interval;
    loopCounter += interval;
  }
  return tmpArray;
}
private function tmpDataTipFunction( value:String ) : String {
  return "The Value = " + value;
}
private function catchSliderChangeEvent( event:Event ) : void {
  text1.text = "Left Value = " + event.target.values[0];
  text2.text = "Right Value = " + event.target.values[1];
}
]]>
</mx:Script>

<ds:DualDragSlider id="mySlider" width="600" values="[50, 150]"
  numberOfLabels="5" showDataTip="true" dragSliderColor="0x0033CC"
  minimum="0" maximum="200"
  dataTipFormatFunction="{tmpDataTipFunction}"
  sliderLabels="{getSliderLabels(Math.abs(mySlider.maximum -
```

5

```
        mySlider.minimum), mySlider.numberOfLabels)}"
    sliderChange="catchSliderChangeEvent(event)" />

  <mx:Text id="text1" text="No Value Set" />
  <mx:Text id="text2" text="No Value Set" />
  </mx:Application>
```

The DualDragSlider works much like the HSlider it's based on, but it just takes a few more values. The sliderLabels function, which is mapped to the getSliderLabels method, returns the labels that are placed along the horizontal axis. The catchSliderChangeEvent method is called when the slider changes, and it updates the two text items that hold the low and high values of the slider.

You can see the resulting application in Figure 5-8.

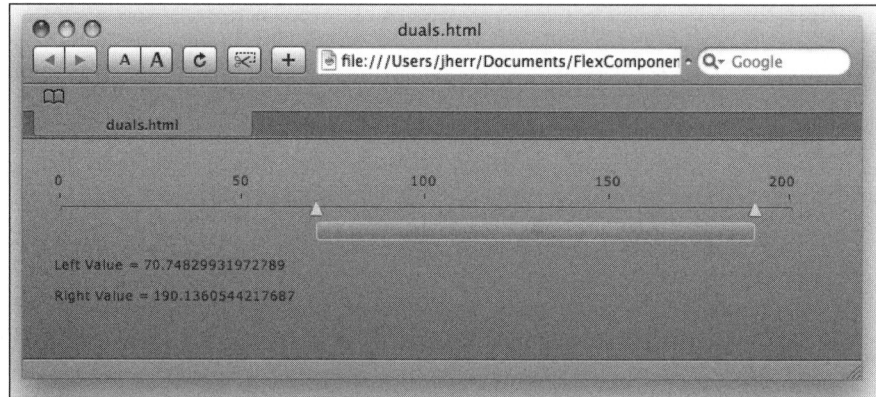

**Figure 5-8.** Brendan's dual slider in action

You can adjust both the low and high values by clicking the grip that's held between the two slider values and dragging it back and forth.

There are several dual slider controls out there that you can try out in addition to Brendan's control. You should also check out Doug McCune's dual slider control (http://dougmccune.com/blog/2007/01/21/draggable-slider-component-for-flex/).

# Loading spinners

I'm not sure why the Flex framework doesn't come with a loading spinner control built into it. Eventually, every application is going to have to put up a little "just wait a little longer" graphic to keep users from throwing their laptops out the window in frustration.

The spinner control (http://grakl.com/flex/SpinnerApp/SpinnerApp.html) is handy because it's both the source for a spinner and a demo application that provides an explorer that helps you set the attributes of the spinner all in one.

The example application shown here uses the spinner:

```xml
<?xml version="1.0" encoding="utf-8"?>
<mx:Application xmlns:mx="http://www.adobe.com/2006/mxml"
  xmlns:controls="controls.*" width="100%" height="100%"
  layout="vertical">

<mx:Panel width="100%" height="100%" horizontalAlign="center"
  verticalAlign="middle"
  layout="vertical">
  <controls:Spinner tickColor="#ff0000" size="38" numTicks="14"
    tickWidth="3" />
  <mx:Label text="Loading..." fontSize="20" fontWeight="bold" />
</mx:Panel>

</mx:Application>
```

You can change the color of the spinner item, the size of the spinner, the number of ticks, and the size of them. In this case, I've also added the loading text to provide a little more information to the user. You can see the result in Figure 5-9.

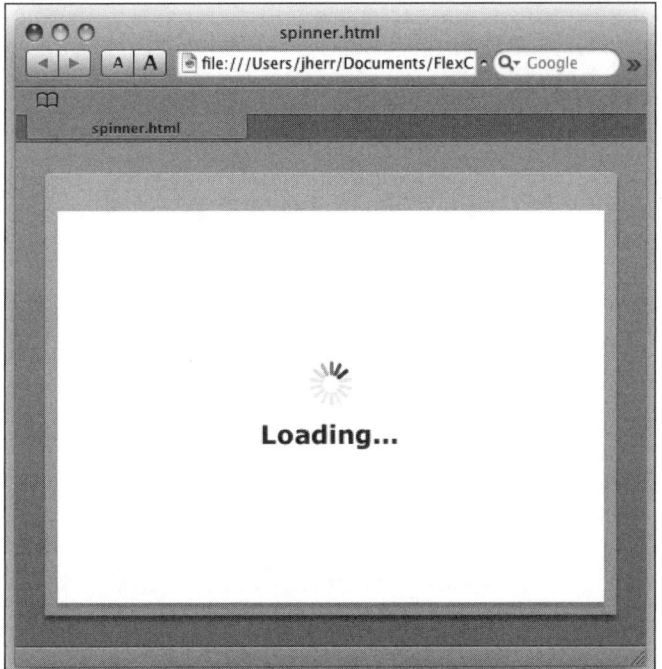

**Figure 5-9.** A red loading spinner

This component doesn't require any assets (images, CSS, etc.), so it's very lightweight and easy to use.

# Prompts, description panes, and tooltips

There are several ways to present more information to users about the fields they are typing into in subtle ways. The first is the PromptingTextInput control provided in the FlexLib.

```
<?xml version="1.0" encoding="utf-8"?>
<mx:Application xmlns:mx="http://www.adobe.com/2006/mxml"
  layout="horizontal"
 xmlns:flexlib="flexlib.controls.*">
<mx:Panel width="100%" height="100%" title="Form">
  <mx:Form>
  <mx:FormItem label="First name">
    <flexlib:PromptingTextInput prompt="Jack" />
  </mx:FormItem>
  <mx:FormItem label="Last name">
    <flexlib:PromptingTextInput prompt="Herrington" />
  </mx:FormItem>
  </mx:Form>
</mx:Panel>
</mx:Application>
```

The PromptingTextInput is just a simple replacement for the TextInput control that takes an additional prompt parameter. That parameter is the text that is put in light gray and italicized when the current contents of the field is empty. You can see the result in Figure 5-10.

**Figure 5-10.** The PromptingTextInput control

Another alternative is a tooltip that comes up very close to the control with a tail to drop down to the control. For that, I'll use the AS3 Tooltip component from the folks at Advanced Flash Components (http://afcomponents.com). The code for this is shown here:

```
<?xml version="1.0" encoding="utf-8"?>
<mx:Application xmlns:mx="http://www.adobe.com/2006/mxml"
  layout="absolute"
  xmlns:afcomponents="http://www.afcomponents.com/" >
<mx:Form left="10" top="20">
  <mx:FormItem label="User ID">
    <mx:TextInput id="userName" mouseOver="myTooltip.show()"
      mouseOut="myTooltip.hide()" />
  </mx:FormItem>
  <mx:FormItem label="First name">
    <mx:TextInput />
  </mx:FormItem>
  <mx:FormItem label="Last name">
    <mx:TextInput />
  </mx:FormItem>
</mx:Form>
<afcomponents:Tooltip x="135" y="8" shapeStrokeEnabled="false"
  content="Your user name"
  contentType="text" id="myTooltip" autoShow="false"
  shapeCornerRadius="5"
  shapeFillColor="0xFFFFFFCC" shapeFillEnabled="true"
  shapeStrokeColor="black"
  shapeStrokeThickness="1" contentAutoSize="false"
  contentHorizonalPadding="2"
  contentMaintainAspectRatio="true" contentScaleContent="false"
  contentVerticalPadding="2"
  tailEnabled="true" tailHeight="12" tailOffset="0"
  tailPosition="bottom" tailWidth="10"/>
</mx:Application>
```

The tooltip is shown and hidden using the show and hide methods invoked by the mouseOver and mouseOut events. You can adjust almost any aspect of the display of this tooltip using the attributes on the MXML. You can see the resulting tooltip in Figure 5-11.

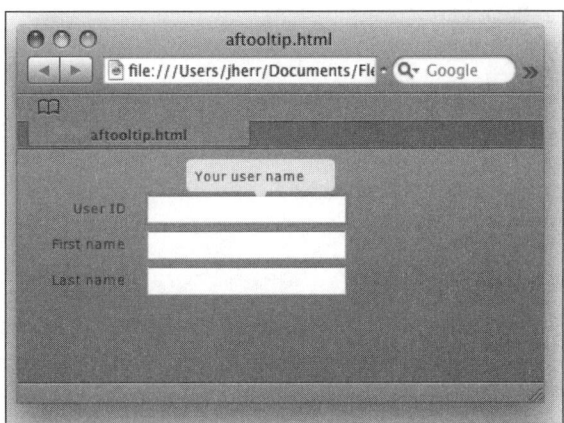

**Figure 5-11.** The Advanced Flash Components Tooltip

The third option is the DescriptionPane, also from Advanced Flash Components (http://afcomponents.com). This control is better when you have some text that would be a little too long for a tooltip, as shown in the following application code:

```
<?xml version="1.0" encoding="utf-8"?>
<mx:Application xmlns:mx="http://www.adobe.com/2006/mxml"
  layout="absolute"
  creationComplete="onStartup()">
<mx:Script>
<![CDATA[
import com.afcomponents.descriptionpane.*;
import mx.core.UIComponent;
import fl.transitions.*;
import fl.transitions.easing.*;

private function onStartup() : void {
  var uic:UIComponent = new UIComponent();
  txtComp.addChild( uic );

  var myDescrPane:DescriptionPane = new DescriptionPane();
  myDescrPane.content = "Picking the right user ID is important! ➡
It's the one decision you can't take back.";
  myDescrPane.transition = {type:Fade, direction:Transition.IN,
  duration:1, easing:Strong.easeOut, startPoint:2};
  myDescrPane.visibility = DescriptionPaneVisibility.AUTOHIDE;
  myDescrPane.setOwner( {owner:userName,
  align:DescriptionPanePosition.BOTTOM_CENTER, w:0.9, h:0.2} );
  uic.addChild( myDescrPane );
}
]]>
</mx:Script>
<mx:Form left="10" top="20">
  <mx:FormItem label="User ID">
    <mx:HBox id="txtComp">
    <mx:TextInput id="userName" />
    </mx:HBox>
  </mx:FormItem>
  <mx:FormItem label="First name">
    <mx:TextInput />
  </mx:FormItem>
  <mx:FormItem label="Last name">
    <mx:TextInput />
  </mx:FormItem>
</mx:Form>
</mx:Application>
```

The DescriptionPane is built on the Sprite class. This means it needs to be hosted in a UIComponent class. That's all created and set up in the onStartup method. The setOwner call to the DescriptionPane sets up the connection between the description pane and its related control. And that linkage means that when the focus shifts to the owner control, the DescriptionPane is automatically shown as seen in Figure 5-12.

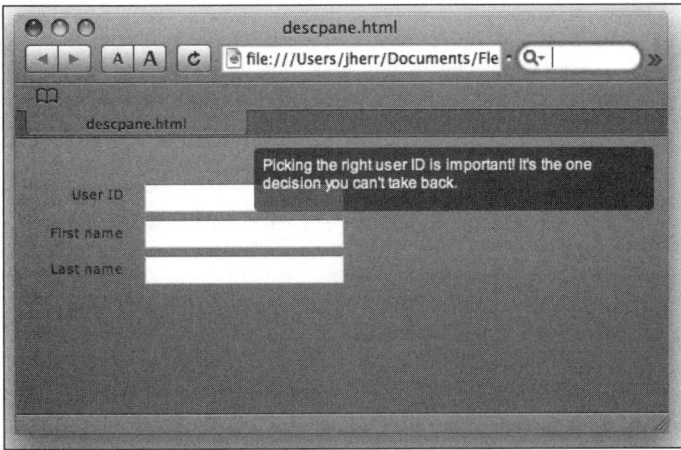

**Figure 5-12.** The DescriptionPane in action

The nice thing about all of these controls is that they provide more information without overly obstructing the interface. They give the user the information she needs, when she needs it, and then leave when the user's focus changes to a different portion of the form.

# Masked inputs

Another way to make it easier to get the right data from the user is to be more explicit about how the data should be formatted. Probably the best way to do this is to have a masked text input. The Adobe Exchange has a MaskedTextInput control (http://www.adobe.com/cfusion/exchange/index.cfm?event=extensionDetail&loc=en_us&extid=1049969) that I use in the application code shown here:

```
<?xml version="1.0" encoding="utf-8"?>
<mx:Application xmlns:mx="http://www.adobe.com/2006/mxml"
  layout="vertical"
  xmlns:fc="com.adobe.flex.extras.controls.*">
  <mx:Form>
    <mx:FormItem label="First name">
      <mx:TextInput />
    </mx:FormItem>
    <mx:FormItem label="Last name">
      <mx:TextInput />
    </mx:FormItem>
    <mx:FormItem label="Phone number">
      <fc:MaskedTextInput inputMask="(###)###-####" required="true"
        autoAdvance="true" defaultCharacter=""/>
    </mx:FormItem>
```

```
        <mx:FormItem label="Amount">
          <fc:MaskedTextInput id="amt" inputMask="$#####/.##"
            required="false" defaultCharacter=""/>
        </mx:FormItem>
        <mx:FormItem label="Date">
          <fc:MaskedTextInput inputMask="MM/DD/YYYY"
            required="true" autoAdvance="true"/>
        </mx:FormItem>
        <mx:FormItem label="Credit Card">
          <fc:MaskedTextInput inputMask="####-####-####-####"
            required="true" autoAdvance="true"/>
        </mx:FormItem>
        <mx:FormItem label="SSN">
          <fc:MaskedTextInput inputMask="###-##-####"
            required="true" autoAdvance="true" />
        </mx:FormItem>
      </mx:Form>
    </mx:Application>
```

I've tried to put in as many relevant examples as I could. The phone number mask corresponds to standard U.S. phone numbers. The amount mask has five optional digits. The date mask requires dates to be in the format MM/DD/YYYY. The credit card mask has four required four-digit values. And the social security mask does the same kind of thing for a standard U.S. Social Security number.

You can see the result in Figure 5-13.

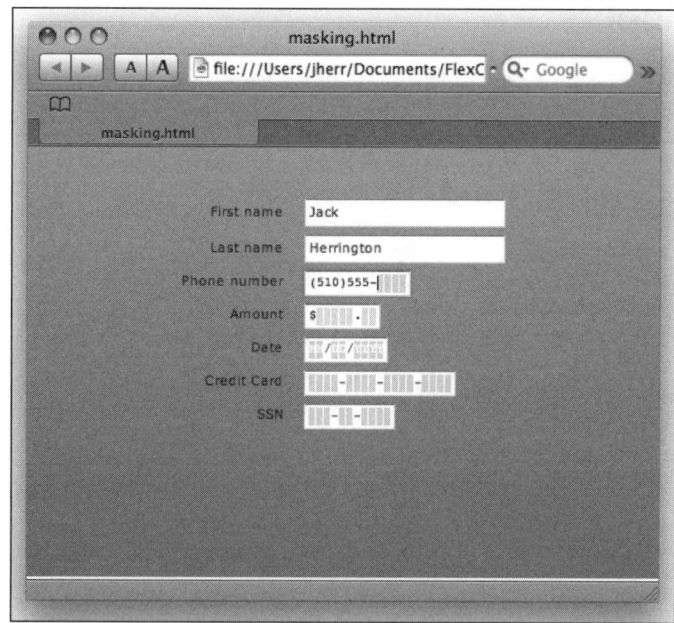

**Figure 5-13.** A set of masked text inputs

As the user types, the individual characters are filled in, and the cursor moves forward to the next item, and so on.

# Auto-completion

Auto-completing text fields are also another way to make it easy for the user to get the right data into the text field. The Adobe Exchange also includes an AutoComplete component (http://www.adobe.com/cfusion/exchange/index.cfm?event=extensionDetail& extid=1047291) that adds onto the original TextInput control. An example of this is shown in the following application code:

```
<?xml version="1.0" encoding="utf-8"?>
<mx:Application xmlns:mx="http://www.adobe.com/2006/mxml"
  layout="vertical" xmlns:fc="http://www.adobe.com/2006/fc">
<mx:Script>
<![CDATA[
import mx.collections.ArrayCollection;

[Bindable]
private var names:ArrayCollection = new ArrayCollection( [
  { name: 'Jack Herrington' },
  { name: 'Megan Herrington' },
  { name: 'Lori Herrington' },
  { name: 'Oso Herrington' }
] );
]]>
</mx:Script>
<mx:Panel title="Auto Complete" height="100%" width="100%"
  layout="horizontal"
  paddingTop="10" paddingBottom="10" paddingLeft="10"
  paddingRight="10">
<mx:Label text="Name" />
<fc:AutoComplete dataProvider="{names}" labelField="name"/>
</mx:Panel>
</mx:Application>
```

The data for the auto-complete is just an array of ActionScript 3 objects. The field to be placed into the input is specified by the labelField attribute on the AutoComplete control. In this case, we just specify a set of hard-coded values, but in the real world, we would likely get these from a web service. You can see the control in action in Figure 5-14.

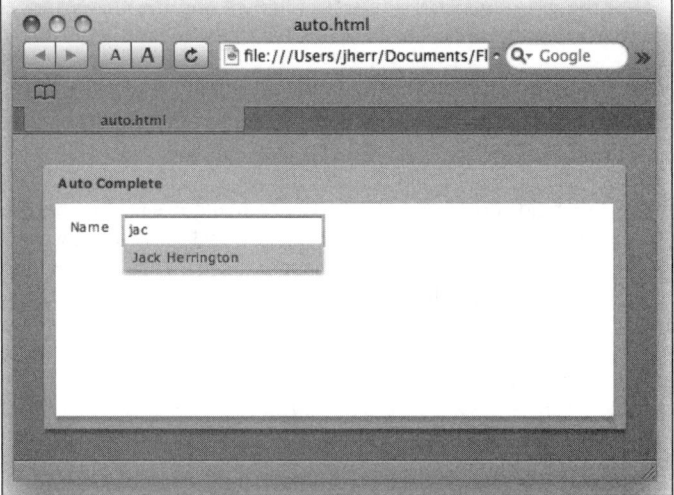

**Figure 5-14.** The AutoComplete control in action

This is a great way to make it very easy for users to contextually get the value they want for the field.

## Time entry

To make it easy to get time entry right, the TimeSelector control (http://www.adobe.com/cfusion/exchange/index.cfm?event=extensionDetail&extid=1144469) puts a set of numeric values for hours, minutes, and seconds, as well as an AM/PM selector into one large field. An example application that uses the control is shown in the following code:

```
<?xml version="1.0" encoding="utf-8"?>
<mx:Application xmlns:mx="http://www.adobe.com/2006/mxml"
  layout="horizontal" xmlns:local="*">
  <mx:Label text="Time" />
  <local:TimeSelector />
</mx:Application>
```

There really isn't a lot to it, of course. You can see the result in Figure 5-15.

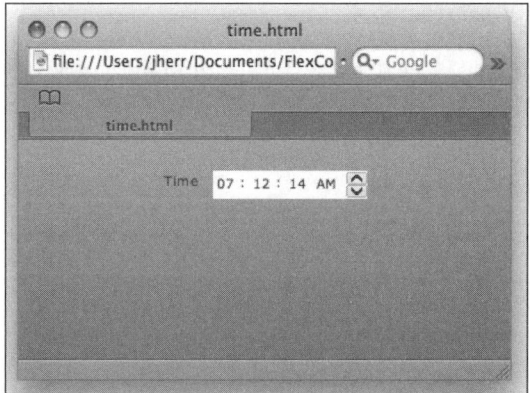

**Figure 5-15.** The TimeSelector control in action

Setting the time is easy: if you want to change the minutes, you click the minutes text and either type in the value or use the spinner. The same applies to the hours, seconds, and the AM/PM selector.

# Vertical menus

Another cool control variant is the vertical menus from Doug McCune (http:// dougmccune.com/blog/2007/01/25/vertical-menubar-component). An example application that uses these vertical menus is shown here:

```
<?xml version="1.0"?>
<mx:Application xmlns:mx="http://www.adobe.com/2006/mxml"
  xmlns:mccune="com.dougmccune.controls.*">

<mx:XMLListCollection id="menuBarCollection">
<mx:XMLList>
<menuitem label="File">
<menuitem label="New" />
<menuitem label="Open" />
<menuitem type="separator" />
<menuitem label="Save" />
<menuitem type="separator" />
<menuitem label="Quit" />
</menuitem>
<menuitem label="Edit">
<menuitem label="Cut" />
<menuitem label="Copy" />
<menuitem label="Paste" />
</menuitem>
<menuitem label="View">
<menuitem label="Special items" type="check" />
```

**5**

```
<menuitem type="separator" />
<menuitem label="Views" >
  <menuitem label="Real data" type="radio" groupName="views" />
  <menuitem label="Generated data " type="radio" groupName="views" />
</menuitem>
</menuitem>
</mx:XMLList>
</mx:XMLListCollection>

<mx:HBox width="100%" height="100%">
<mccune:VerticalMenuBar height="100%" direction="right"
  labelField="@label"
  dataProvider="{menuBarCollection}"  />
<mx:Spacer width="100%" />
<mccune:VerticalMenuBar height="100%" direction="left"
  labelField="@label"
  dataProvider="{menuBarCollection}"  />
</mx:HBox>
</mx:Application>
```

The VerticalMenuBar component takes an XMLListCollection as input in a
dataProvider. It also takes the XML path to use in the label as the labelField. This example shows the same menu in both the left and right sides of the window. Figure 5-16 shows
the menu when it's clicked from the left-hand side of the panel.

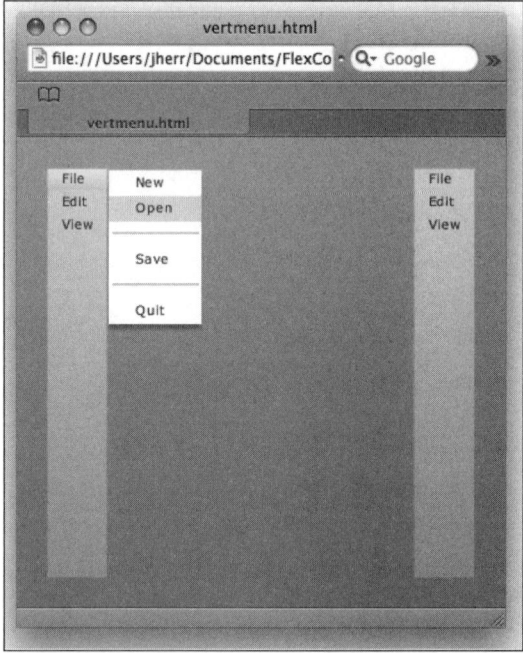

**Figure 5-16.** The vertical menu bar in action

The menu system supports a radio button type menu, check box menus, the whole deal. Doug McCune has done a great job with this component.

# Where we will go from here

This chapter should just whet your appetite for looking into enhanced controls like these. Most of the component libraries, sites, vendors, and authors have a few more components for you to take a look at and play with. For example, FlexLib (http://flexlib. googlecode.com) is filled with useful controls and containers that I've just touched on here. And almost all of them are as easy to use as the ones that I have shown here.

In the next chapter, I show you the amazing things that you can do with image compo- nents in Flex applications.

5

# 6 **FUN WITH IMAGES**

# Introducing image components

I had a problem writing this chapter. I found some of the components so mesmerizing that I would just stop working on the example and play with the image component just because it was fun to do. Images are incredibly engaging, and these interactive image components make images sing and dance.

There are some amazing Flex and Flash components to play with here: carousels that show a circular spinning band of images, cover flow–style layouts similar to iTunes, animated image menus, even a 3D wall of images. Come along with me on a journey through these incredible image components, and maybe you will be mesmerized too.

# 3D Carousel

Advanced Flash Components have a few very cool components for display images of people, products, pets, whatever you want. One of these is the 3D Carousel control that I make use of in the application code shown here:

```
<?xml version="1.0" encoding="utf-8"?>
<mx:Application xmlns:mx=http://www.adobe.com/2006/mxml
  layout="absolute" creationComplete="picsData.send()"
  backgroundColor="white" backgroundAlpha="1"
  backgroundGradientColors="[#000000,#000066]"
  backgroundGradientAlphas="[1,1]">
<mx:Script>
<![CDATA[
import mx.rpc.events.ResultEvent;
import fl.data.DataProvider;
import mx.core.UIComponent;
import com.afcomponents.carousel3d.*;

private var car:Carousel = new Carousel();

public function onImageData( event:ResultEvent ) : void {
  var uic:UIComponent = new UIComponent();
  addChild( uic );

  var dp:DataProvider = new DataProvider();
  for each ( var pic:XML in event.result..image ) {
    var imgObj:Object = {};
    imgObj.path = "http://localhost/pics/flowers/"+
      pic.@name.toString();
    imgObj.type = "image";
    dp.addItem( imgObj );
  }
  car.content = dp;
```

```
        car.animationStyle = {easing:"easeOut", enabled:true,
          duration:1500, type:"Strong"};
        car.displayStyle = {autoSize:false, maintainAspectRatio:true,
         scaleContent:true};
        car.carouselStyle = {direction:'auto', distance:2000, radius:2000,
         type:'outside'};
        car.width = width;
        car.height = width * 0.2;
        car.move( 0, width * 0.1 );
        car.camera3D.zoom = 8;
        uic.addChild( car );
      }
    ]]>
    </mx:Script>
    <mx:HTTPService url="http://localhost/pics/flowers/images.xml"
      id="picsData" resultFormat="e4x"
      result="onImageData(event)" />
    </mx:Application>
```

In this example, the application gets the list of images from the server. The onImageData method is called when the XML data comes back from the server, and it's this method that sets up the carousel control. The first step is to create the UIComponent that will hold the Carousel object because it's based on Sprite and can't be directly added to a Flex container.

The next step is to build the data provider for the Carousel. This is just a list of objects added to the Advanced Flash Components proprietary DataProvider object. The third step is to set up all of the visual aspects of the control. This includes the animation style that will be used when the user clicks parts of the control to scroll between images. It specifies how the images should be scaled in the displayStyle, and how the images should be positioned in the carouselStyle.

With all that done, we can now launch the application and see what it looks like. It should appear something like Figure 6-1.

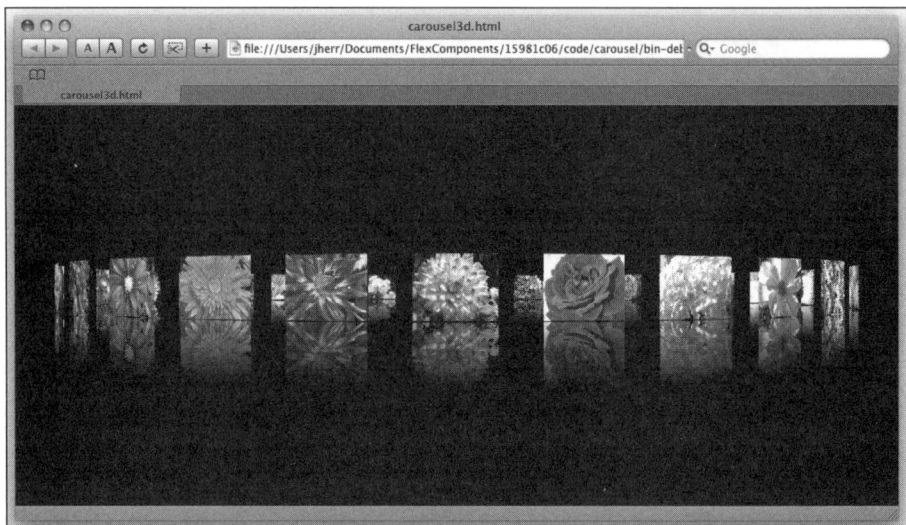

**Figure 6-1.** The initial state of the carousel

From here, we can click images to the left or right and scroll the spinner around. You can adjust the spinning effect by changing the parameters in the animationStyle property.

By tweaking some of the rotation parameters on the carouselStyle object, you can get some neat effects. One example is when you look down into the carousel by changing the rotationX value. This is shown in Figure 6-2.

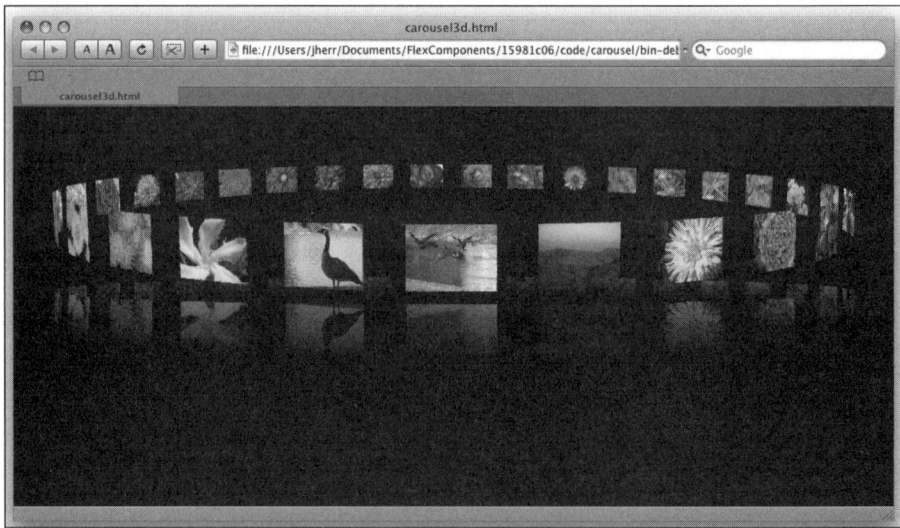

**Figure 6-2.** Looking down into the carousel

This control was built with Papervision3D (http://blog.papervision3d.org/), as are many of the controls in this chapter. If you like what you see here but want to build your own control, then you should check out the Papervision3D library for a good starting point.

# Cover flow

Cover flow is an image display technique that was popularized by Apple's iTunes application. Instead of looking at a list of album covers tiled vertically or horizontally, the cover flow technique shows the selected image in the middle of the display, and the rest of the images stacked on their sides like old album stacks we used to have on shelves separated by cinder blocks.

In this section, I'll demonstrate two different cover flow components. The first one is the 3D Flow List component from Advanced Flash Components. The first version of the cover flow example for this component is in the following Flex code:

```
<?xml version="1.0" encoding="utf-8"?>
<mx:Application xmlns:mx="http://www.adobe.com/2006/mxml"
  layout="vertical"
  creationComplete="imageData.send()" backgroundColor="white"
  backgroundAlpha="1"
  backgroundGradientColors="[#000000,#002200]"
  backgroundGradientAlphas="[1,1]">
<mx:Script>
<![CDATA[
import mx.rpc.events.ResultEvent;
import fl.data.DataProvider;
import mx.core.UIComponent;
import com.afcomponents.flowlist3d.*;

private var flow:FlowList3D = new FlowList3D();

public function onImageData( event:ResultEvent ) : void {
  var uic:UIComponent = new UIComponent();

  var dp:DataProvider = new DataProvider();
  for each ( var image:XML in event.result..image ) {
    var imgObj:Object = {};
    imgObj.path = "http://localhost/pics/"+image.@name.toString();
    imgObj.type = "image";
    imgObj.data = "http://localhost/pics";
    dp.addItem( imgObj );
  }
  flow.content = dp;
  flow.flowListStyle = {angleH:15, angleV:0, displayedItemCount:5,
    forceRotationY:true, forceRotationZ:true, itemAlpha:0,
    itemDistance:50, itemRotationY:70, itemRotationZ:-1,
```

6

```
            itemScale:1, selectedPaddingX:70, selectedPaddingY:0,
            selectedPaddingZ:100, useFlatAngleV:false,
            useFlatAngleH:false};
        flow.itemDefaultStyle = { cornerRadius:10, fill:true, fillAlpha:0.4,
            fillColor:0xFFFFFF, stroke:false, strokeAlpha:1,
            strokeColor:0xFFFFFF,
            strokeWidth:1, horizontalPadding:0, verticalPadding:3 };

        uic.addChild( flow );
        addChild( uic );
    }
    ]]>
    </mx:Script>
    <mx:HTTPService url="http://localhost/pics/tall.xml" id="imageData"
      resultFormat="e4x"
      result="onImageData(event)" />
</mx:Application>
```

The application starts up by going to the server to get the list of images. When the onImageData method is called, it then creates a container for the 3D Flow List component, creates a data provider with all of the images in it, sets up the control, and adds it to the display. The critical portion is in the setting of the flowListStyle object, which has the parameters for the display of the list. You can start out by simply not setting that value and see how it works. But you will likely want to tweak some of the parameters to get a result that appeals to you.

The defaultItemStyle code brackets the image in a little off-white box to give each image a visual separation. This is another parameter that you can tweak or simply not set to get various different effects.

When we run this application, it looks like Figure 6-3.

**Figure 6-3.** The 3D Flow List from Advanced Flash Components

The next example application also uses the 3D Flow List component, but with some slightly different settings to get a much different result. This new code is shown here:

```
<?xml version="1.0" encoding="utf-8"?>
<mx:Application xmlns:mx="http://www.adobe.com/2006/mxml"
  layout="vertical"
  creationComplete="imageData.send()" backgroundColor="white"
  backgroundAlpha="1"
  backgroundGradientColors="[#000000,#220000]"
  backgroundGradientAlphas="[1,1]">
<mx:Script>
<![CDATA[
...
public function onImageData( event:ResultEvent ) : void {
  ...
  flow.content = dp;
  flow.flowListStyle = { displayedItemCount:5,
    forceRotationY:false, forceRotationZ:false, itemAlpha:0,
   itemDistance:60,
    itemRotationY:60, itemRotationZ:10, itemScale:1,
    selectedPaddingX:100,
    selectedPaddingY:0, selectedPaddingZ:800, useFlatAngleV:false,
    useFlatAngleH:false};

  uic.addChild( flow );
  addChild( uic );
}
]]>
</mx:Script>
...
</mx:Application>
```

All of the code remains the same with the exception of the setting of the `flowListStyle` and the omission of the setting of the `itemDefaultStyle`. As you can see in Figure 6-4, you tweak a few parameters, and you can get a really different look and feel as a result.

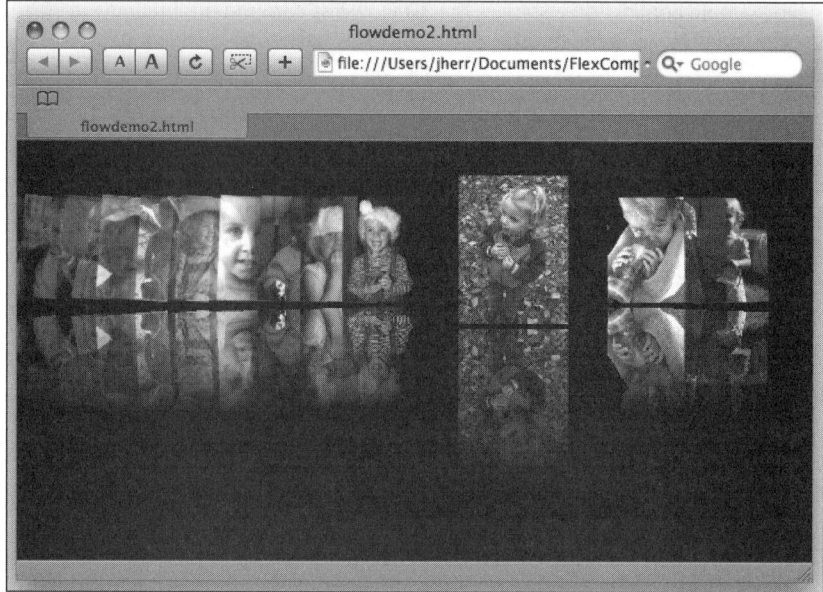

**Figure 6-4.** Another variation on the Advanced Flash Components 3D Flow List component

As you can see, as the images go on to the right and left, they slowly fade away and start to twist. It's a nice little effect.

The other cover flow component I want to demonstrate is from Digicrafts, and it's called the photoFlip (http://www.digicrafts.com.hk/components/photo-flip). Using this control is fairly similar to the Advanced Flash Components control. You can see an example use of the photoFlip control here:

```
<?xml version="1.0" encoding="utf-8"?>
<mx:Application xmlns:mx="http://www.adobe.com/2006/mxml"
  layout="absolute"
  creationComplete="picData.send()"
  horizontalScrollPolicy="off" verticalScrollPolicy="off">
<mx:Style>
Application {
  background-alpha: 1;
  background-color: #000000;
  background-gradient-colors: #000000, #330000;
  padding-left: 0;
  padding-top: 0;
  padding-right: 0;
  padding-bottom: 0;
}
</mx:Style>
<mx:Script>
<![CDATA[
import mx.rpc.events.ResultEvent;
```

```
import mx.core.UIComponent;
import com.digicrafts.controls.PhotoFlip;

private var pf:PhotoFlip = new PhotoFlip();

public function onPicData( event:ResultEvent ) : void {
  var uic:UIComponent = new UIComponent();
  addChild( uic );

  pf.setSize( width, height );

  for each ( var pic:XML in event.result..image ) {
    var imgObj:Object = {};
    imgObj.source = "http://localhost/pics/harold/"+➥
pic.@name.toString();
    imgObj.type = 'image';
    pf.addItem( imgObj );
  }

  uic.addChild( pf );
}
]]>
</mx:Script>
<mx:HTTPService url="http://localhost/pics/harold/images.xml"
  id="picData" resultFormat="e4x"
  result="onPicData(event)" />
</mx:Application>
```

Much of the code between the two examples is similar. The application fetches the list of images from the server and then loads up the control. In this case, adding images is as simple as calling the addItem method. The only alteration I make is to set the mirror attribute to 0.75, which strengthens the reflection a little.

The result of running this application can be seen in Figure 6-5.

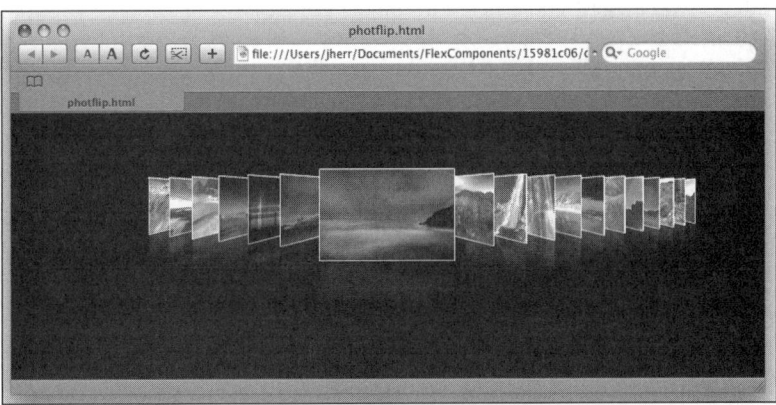

**Figure 6-5.** The Digicrafts photoFlip control in its default state

By default, you can see that the images are given a nice little border, and the effect is very similar to the iTunes cover flow effect.

In the next version of the application, I will do a little tweaking of the control to get a somewhat different effect.

```
<?xml version="1.0" encoding="utf-8"?>
<mx:Application xmlns:mx="http://www.adobe.com/2006/mxml"
  layout="absolute"
  creationComplete="picData.send()"
  horizontalScrollPolicy="off" verticalScrollPolicy="off">
...
<mx:Script>
<![CDATA[
...

public function onPicData( event:ResultEvent ) : void {
...

  pf.vPerspective = 1;
  pf.hPerspective = 1;
  pf.itemScaleRatio = 0.9;
  pf.mouseEnabled = true;
  pf.popItemScale = 3.5;
  pf.popupItemDistance = 250;
  pf.maxDimension = 100;

...
}
]]>
</mx:Script>
...
</mx:Application>
```

In this next example, I set some of the member variables to new values to get some different effects. The biggest changes are in the popItemScale and popupItemDistance values, which affect the selected (pop-up) image. These values are set much higher than they are by default, and you can see the result in Figure 6-6.

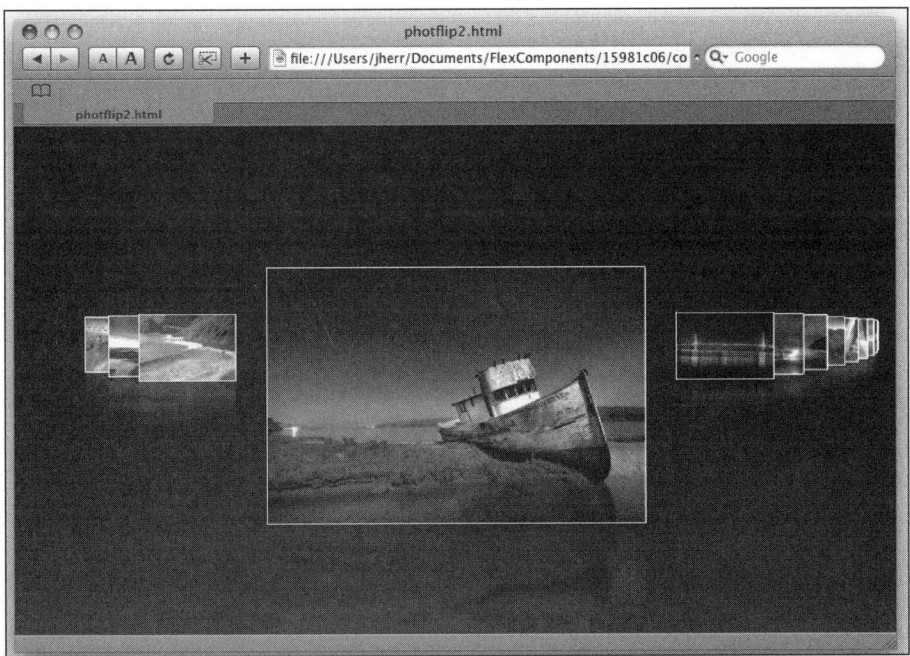

**Figure 6-6.** The selected image popped out

Now it's very clear which is the selected image. And the images that are off to the left and the right aren't twisted in the same way because of the changes to the hPerspective and vPerspective.

One final twist on this control is to view the arc of images from the middle of a circle, which you can do by making a few changes to the photoFlip member values. The code for this is shown here:

```
<?xml version="1.0" encoding="utf-8"?>
<mx:Application xmlns:mx="http://www.adobe.com/2006/mxml"
  layout="absolute"
  creationComplete="picData.send()"
  horizontalScrollPolicy="off" verticalScrollPolicy="off">
...
<mx:Script>
<![CDATA[
...
public function onPicData( event:ResultEvent ) : void {
...
  pf.vPerspective = 0.69;
  pf.hPerspective = 0.79;
  pf.itemScaleRatio = 1.3;
  pf.mouseEnabled = true;
  pf.popItemScale = 1;
  pf.popupItemDistance = 100;
```

```
    pf.itemDistance = 70;
    pf.maxDimension = 80;
  ...
  }
  ]]>
  </mx:Script>
  ...
  </mx:Application>
```

Having played around with the variable effect, you can simulate being in the middle of a circle of images as shown in Figure 6-7.

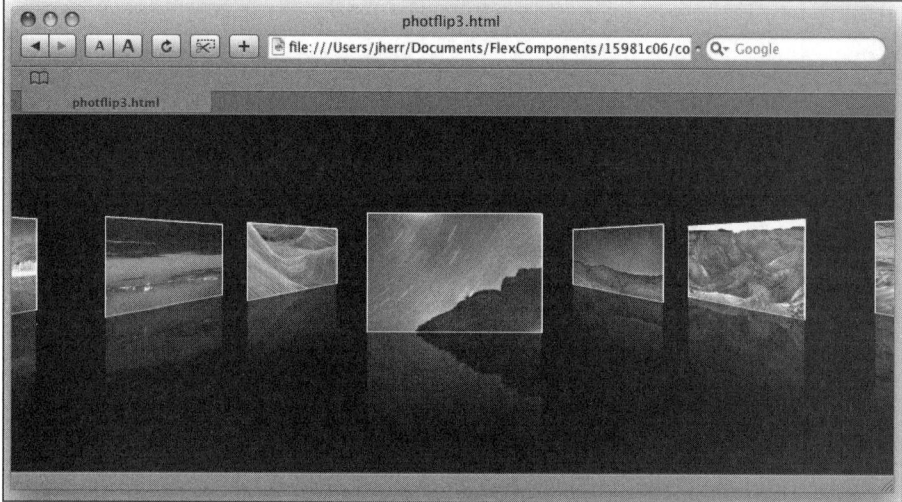

**Figure 6-7.** Viewing the images from within a circle of images

Clicking the images on the left or right really scrolls the view in such a way as to give you the illusion you're in the middle of a circle of images. It's a very fun effect.

# Rotating menus

Another component from Digicrafts is the RotationMenu CS component (http://www.digicrafts.com.hk/components/rt-menu-cs). This component once again takes a list of thumbnail images, but this time it presents them in a three-dimensional circular menu.

The following application code adds a set of images into a horizontal RotationMenu:

```
<?xml version="1.0" encoding="utf-8"?>
<mx:Application xmlns:mx="http://www.adobe.com/2006/mxml"
  layout="absolute"
  creationComplete="picData.send()" backgroundColor="black"
  backgroundAlpha="1"
```

```
      backgroundGradientColors="[#000000,#000000]"
      backgroundGradientAlphas="[1,1]">
<mx:Script>
<![CDATA[
import mx.rpc.events.ResultEvent;
import mx.core.UIComponent;
import com.digicrafts.controls.RotationMenu;

private var rm:RotationMenu = new RotationMenu();

public function onPicData( event:ResultEvent ) : void {
  var uic:UIComponent = new UIComponent();

  rm.perspectiveScaling = true;
  rm.perspectiveTransform = true;
  rm.mouseEnabled = true;
  rm.globalScale = 0.3;
  rm.x = 0;
  rm.y = 0;
  rm.autoStart = true;
  rm.mouseScroll = true;
  rm.move( 0, height - 100 );
  rm.setSize( width, 100 );
  rm.rotationY = 0;
  rm.rotationX = -8;
  rm.blur = 50;
  rm.alpha = 15;

  for each ( var pic:XML in event.result..image ) {
    var imgObj:Object = {};
    imgObj.name = "http://localhost/pics/food/"+pic.@name.toString();
    rm.addItem( imgObj );
  }

  uic.addChild( rm );
  addChild( uic );
}
]]>
</mx:Script>
<mx:HTTPService url="http://localhost/pics/food/images.xml"
    id="picData" resultFormat="e4x"
    result="onPicData(event)" />
</mx:Application>
```

There are a few key attributes of this control. The rotationX rotates the menu down a little bit so that it feels as if we are looking at it from a little bit of an elevation. The
globalScale attribute just sets the image scaling for all of the images. The
perspectiveScaling and perspectiveTransform parameters set the three-dimensional
effect. And the blur parameter sets the amount of blur on the images in the distance.

When we bring this application up from Flex Builder 3, it looks like Figure 6-8.

**Figure 6-8.** The horizontal RotationMenu

The effect of this control is slightly similar to the Dock in Mac OS X, or the thumbnails of related movies after the end of a YouTube video. One nice thing is that the menu scrolls to the left or right without clicking, which gives a nice spinning effect.

The vertical version of the RotationMenu is also pretty interesting. The code for that is shown here:

```
<?xml version="1.0" encoding="utf-8"?>
<mx:Application xmlns:mx="http://www.adobe.com/2006/mxml"
  layout="vertical"
  creationComplete="picData.send()" backgroundColor="white"
  backgroundAlpha="1"
  backgroundGradientColors="[#ffffff,#ffffff]"
  backgroundGradientAlphas="[1,1]">
<mx:Script>
<![CDATA[
import mx.rpc.events.ResultEvent;
...

public function onPicData( event:ResultEvent ) : void {
  var uic:UIComponent = new UIComponent();

  rm.perspectiveScaling = true;
  rm.perspectiveTransform = true;
```

```
    rm.mouseEnabled = true;
    rm.globalScale = 0.3;
    rm.x = 0;
    rm.y = 0;
    rm.autoStart = true;
    rm.mouseScroll = true;
    rm.move( ( width / 2 ) * -1, 0 );
    rm.setSize( width, rm.width );
    rm.rotationY = -90;
    rm.rotationX = 8;
    rm.blur = 50;
    rm.alpha = 15;
    rm.menuOrientation = 'vertical';
    ...
  }
]]>
</mx:Script>
<mx:HTTPService url="http://localhost/pics/wide.xml"
  id="picData" resultFormat="e4x"
  result="onPicData(event)" />
</mx:Application>
```

The menuOrientation is the most important parameter. It sets the rotation on the images from horizontal to vertical. The rotationY then sets the orientation of the whole menu from top to bottom instead of from left to right. You can see the result of these changes in Figure 6-9.

**Figure 6-9.** The vertical version of the RotationMenu

This is a really fun and engaging way to make menu selections using thumbnails. You shouldn't only think of using this control with images. You can use it with transparent PNGs as well to present a button-style control.

# Image grids

An image grid is a component that presents a paginated set of images organized into rows and columns. It's not an earth-shattering novel interface technique, but it can be a pretty attractive look.

The following application uses the Digicrafts Grid control (http://www.digicrafts.com.hk) to display a set of images loaded from the localhost server:

```
<?xml version="1.0" encoding="utf-8"?>
<mx:Application xmlns:mx="http://www.adobe.com/2006/mxml"
  xmlns:degrafa="com.degrafa.*" xmlns:paint="com.degrafa.paint.*"
  xmlns:geometry="com.degrafa.geometry.*" layout="absolute"
  creationComplete="onStartup( event )" backgroundColor="black"
  backgroundAlpha="1"
  backgroundGradientColors="[#000000,#000000]"
  backgroundGradientAlphas="[1,1]">
<mx:Script>
<![CDATA[
import com.afcomponents.events.GridEvent;
import mx.rpc.events.ResultEvent;
import mx.core.UIComponent;
import com.afcomponents.grid.Grid;

private var myGrid:Grid;

public function onInitialize( event:GridEvent ) : void {
  picData.send();
}

public function onPicData( event:ResultEvent ) : void {
  for each ( var img:XML in picData.lastResult..image ) {
    var imgObj:Object = {};
    imgObj.path = "http://localhost/pics/family/"+img.@name.toString();
    imgObj.type = "image";
    myGrid.addItem( imgObj );
  }
}

public function onStartup( event:Event ) : void {
  var uic:UIComponent = new UIComponent();
  myGrid = new Grid();
  myGrid.move( 30, 40 );
  myGrid.width = width;
```

```
        myGrid.addEventListener(GridEvent.INITIALIZE, onInitialize);
        myGrid.contentStyle = {width:100, height:78,
        maintainAspectRatio:true, scaleContent:true, autoSize: false};
        myGrid.scrollAnimation = {enabled: true,duration: 500,
        easing: "easeIn",scrollDirection: "horizontal"};
        myGrid.scrollLoop = true;
        myGrid.gridStyle = {rowCount: 2, rowCountAuto:false,
        colCount:5, colCountAuto:false, rowSpacing:10, colSpacing:10};
        uic.addChild( myGrid );
        addChild( uic );
    }
]]>
</mx:Script>
<mx:HBox top="10" left="10">
    <mx:Button label="&lt;&lt;" click="myGrid.displayPreviousPage();" />
    <mx:Button label="&gt;&gt;" click="myGrid.displayNextPage();" />
</mx:HBox>

<degrafa:Surface x="0" y="190">
<degrafa:fills>
<paint:LinearGradientFill id="blueGradient" angle="270">
<paint:GradientStop alpha=".3" color="#62ABCD"/>
<paint:GradientStop alpha=".8" color="#FFFFFF"/>
</paint:LinearGradientFill>
</degrafa:fills>
<degrafa:GeometryGroup>
    <geometry:RegularRectangle fill="{blueGradient}"
    width="1500" height="200" />
</degrafa:GeometryGroup>
</degrafa:Surface>
<mx:HTTPService url="http://localhost/pics/family/wide.xml"
    id="picData" resultFormat="e4x"
    result="onPicData(event)" />
</mx:Application>
```

This application combines the Grid control to display the image, with Degrafa to put a nice beveled background behind the grid. The Grid control is set up in the onStartup function and then populated in the onPicData method. The Degrafa background is at the bottom of the file. It creates a surface located a little ways down on the stage that is filled with a linear gradient fill.

The result is shown in Figure 6-10.

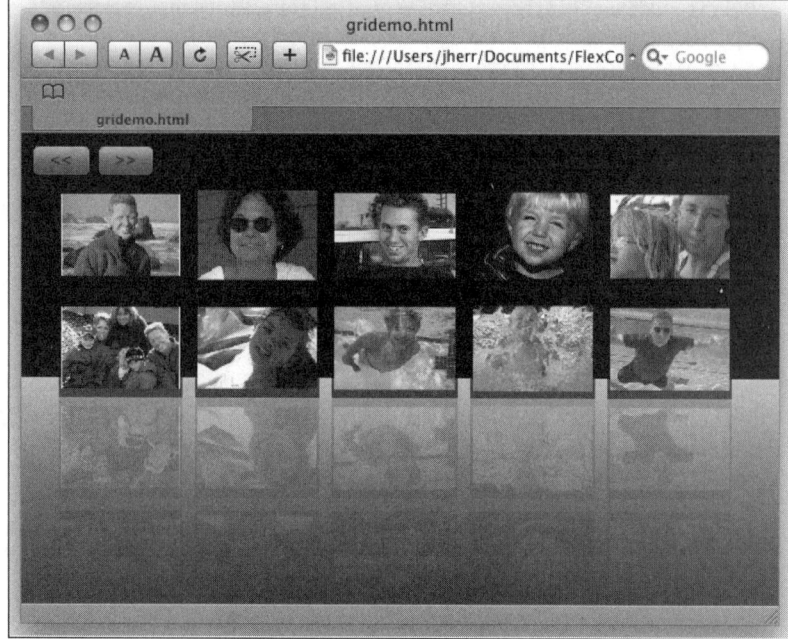

**Figure 6-10.** The startup state of the image grid

Clicking the left or right buttons scrolls the grid to the left or right to reveal more images as shown in Figure 6-11.

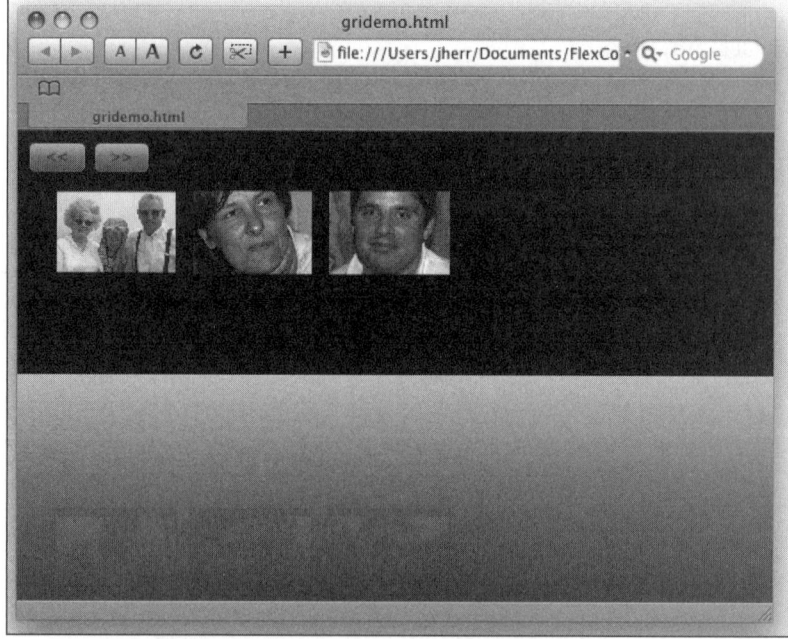

**Figure 6-11.** The image grid after clicking the right button

This control is an elegant way of showing large volumes of pictures in a very manageable and user-friendly manner.

# Slideshows

The FX Components site (http://www.fxcomponents.com/?p=27) has a solid and elegant slideshow component that is fairly easy to integrate with. The FX SlideShow component comes as code, so you add the contents of the download to your project. From there, you use the SlideShow component to display a list of images as shown in the following application code:

```
<?xml version="1.0" encoding="utf-8"?>
<mx:Application xmlns:mx="http://www.adobe.com/2006/mxml"
  xmlns:controls="com.fxcomponents.controls.*"
  backgroundColor="black" verticalAlign="middle"
  width="400" height="300"
  creationComplete="picData.send();"
  backgroundGradientColors="[#000000,#662266]"
  backgroundGradientAlphas="[1,1]">
<mx:Style source="stylesheet.css" />
<mx:Script>
<![CDATA[
import mx.rpc.events.ResultEvent;

public function onPicData( event:ResultEvent ) : void {
  var pics:Array = [];
  for each( var pic:XML in picData.lastResult..image ) {
    pics.push( { image: pic.@name, caption: 'Megan',
      details:'A nice Megan picture.' } );
  }
  sls.dataProvider = pics;
}
]]>
</mx:Script>
<mx:HTTPService url="http://localhost/pics/wide.xml"
  id="picData" resultFormat="e4x"
  result="onPicData(event)" />
  <controls:SlideShow id="sls" width="300" height="225"
   imageField="image" captionField="caption" detailsField="details"
   imagePath="http://localhost/pics/" />
</mx:Application>
```

The SlideShow component is located at the bottom of the file. To populate the slide show, you give it an array of objects in the dataProvider. Fields for the file name, caption, and description are specified by the imageField, captionField, and detailsField in the SlideShow declaration.

When we bring this up in Flex Builder 3, we see something like Figure 6-12.

**Figure 6-12.** The startup state of the Flex SlideShow component

Clicking the Show Details area brings up the description in a nice little pop-up screen. This is shown in Figure 6-13.

**Figure 6-13.** The description of the image

It's great to see elegant components like this that do a solid job solving a real-world problem.

# Degrafa

Degrafa (http://www.degrafa.com/) is not an image component per se. It's an entire graphics toolkit that makes it easy to use assets, like images, in unique and novel ways. One particularly cool demo for Degrafa is the masking example. The following code shows a simplified version of the example from the web site:

```
<?xml version="1.0" encoding="utf-8"?>
<mx:Application xmlns:mx="http://www.adobe.com/2006/mxml"
  layout="absolute"
  backgroundGradientColors="[#333333, #222222]"
  xmlns="http://www.degrafa.com/2007"
  xmlns:flash.filters="flash.filters.*">

<mx:Image alpha=".3" source="http://localhost/pics/IMG_1558.jpg"
  autoLoad="true" maintainAspectRatio="true" scaleContent="false"
  top="150" left="50">
  <mx:filters><flash.filters:BlurFilter blurX="20" blurY="20"/>
  </mx:filters>
</mx:Image>
<mx:Image mask="{topMask}" source="http://localhost/pics/IMG_1558.jpg"
  autoLoad="true" maintainAspectRatio="true" scaleContent="false"
  top="150" left="50" />

<Surface>
<GeometryGroup id="topMask" x="{xSlider.value}" y="{ySlider.value}"
  rotation="{rotationSlider.value}">
  <fills><SolidFill color="#FFF" alpha="1" id="fill1"/></fills>
  <RegularRectangle width="{widthSlider.value}"
    height="{heightSlider.value}"
      fill="{fill1}" stroke="{stroke1}"/>
</GeometryGroup>
<GeometryGroup x="{xSlider.value}" y="{ySlider.value}"
  rotation="{rotationSlider.value}">
  <stroke><SolidStroke color="#000" weight="2" id="stroke1"/></stroke>
  <RegularRectangle width="{widthSlider.value}"
    height="{heightSlider.value}"
      stroke="{stroke1}"/>
</GeometryGroup>
</Surface>

<mx:VBox top="10" backgroundColor="#666666"
  borderStyle="solid" borderColor="#111111"
  cornerRadius="8" paddingBottom="5" paddingLeft="5"
```

```
                        paddingRight="5" paddingTop="5" left="5">
                  <mx:Form>
                    <mx:FormItem label="Width">
                      <mx:HSlider id="widthSlider" minimum="0" maximum="600"
                        liveDragging="true" value="300"/>
                    </mx:FormItem>
                    <mx:FormItem label="Height">
                      <mx:HSlider id="heightSlider" minimum="0" maximum="600"
                        liveDragging="true" value="140"/>
                    </mx:FormItem>
                    <mx:FormItem label="X">
                      <mx:HSlider id="xSlider" minimum="0" maximum="1000"
                        liveDragging="true" value="220"/>
                    </mx:FormItem>
                    <mx:FormItem label="Y">
                      <mx:HSlider id="ySlider" minimum="0" maximum="1000"
                        liveDragging="true" value="220"/>
                    </mx:FormItem>
                    <mx:FormItem label="Rotation">
                      <mx:HSlider id="rotationSlider" minimum="0" maximum="360"
                        liveDragging="true" value="0"/>
                    </mx:FormItem>
                  </mx:Form>
                </mx:VBox>

              </mx:Application>
```

The application is broken into three portions. At the top are two overlaid images that are included using a standard mx:Image control. The first one is blurred, and the second one, which sits exactly on top of the first, is masked based on the topMask, which is specified by the Degrafa code in the middle of the file.

The Degrafa code creates two rectangles. The first is the mask rectangle for the nonblurry image. And the second is a nice border rectangle that sits around the mask.

The location, size, and rotation of the mask and the border rectangles are controlled by the HSlider controls located at the bottom of the file.

When we bring this up from Flex Builder 3 and play with the controls a little, we get something like Figure 6-14.

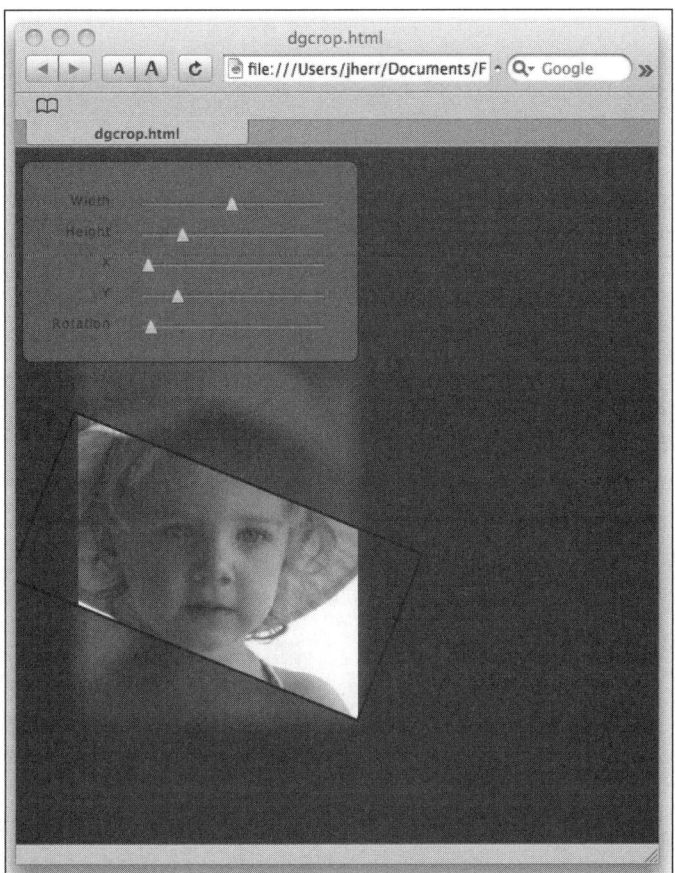

**Figure 6-14.** The Degrafa dynamic masking example

This is a really fun example of the power of the Degrafa framework to implement declarative graphics and to do it in a high-performance way. This example is remarkably snappy.

## 3D Wall

The final example I will show is not a Flex component at all but a Flash component that works off of XML on the server. I bring it up here because it's just so cool that you might want to use it on your site anyway. The component is the 3D Wall from Flashloaded (http://flashloaded.com). We can see the component when we are viewing a portion of the wall shown in Figure 6-15.

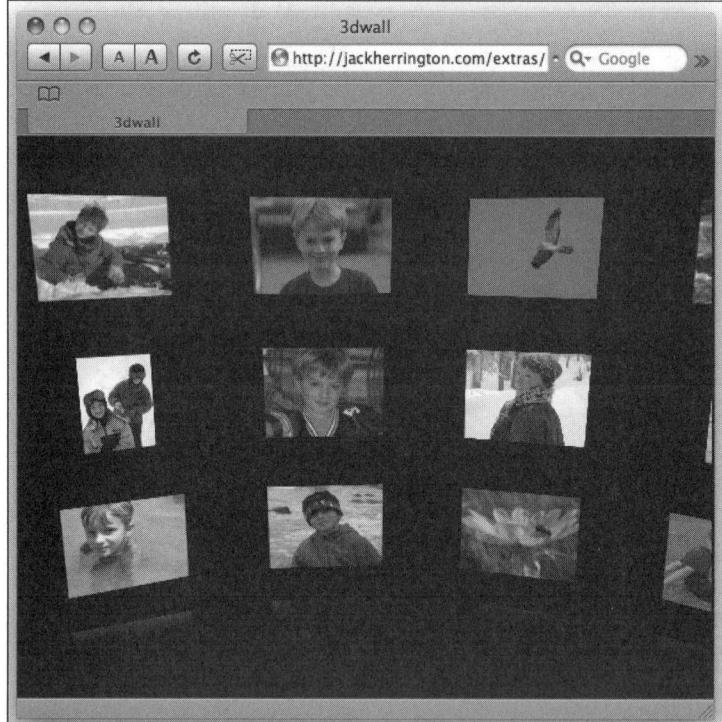

**Figure 6-15.** The 3D Wall from Flashloaded

Double-clicking zooms in on an image as shown in Figure 6-16.

**Figure 6-16.** The zoomed-in image

The 3D Wall component supports several different variations of wall geometries. You can go for a circular wall that is similar to the 3D carousel or a semicircular wall where your viewing point starts in the middle of the wall. There is a twisty wall option as well. This is a remarkable piece of work that I hope Flashloaded will port to Flex soon.

## Where we will go from here

This chapter provides a wide variety of ways to view your images. Remember that images can be anything. They can be controls. You can generate the images on the fly if you like. You can use Degrafa to build bitmaps and blend multiple images. With these tools in hand, the only limitation is your own creativity.

The next stop on the component express is components that make it much easier to support using audio and video sources in your application.

# 7 AUDIO AND VIDEO COMPONENTS

Updated 7/8/08

I'd argue that audio and video, especially video, made the Flash platform what it is today. It wasn't until the advent of YouTube and viral video that everyone had to have Flash installed on their computers.

It's no wonder that YouTube went with Flash because it makes doing multimedia so easy, or does it? Yes, you can play a sound, and yes, you can put up a video display, but if you want all of the playback controls, well, as RuPaul says, "You gotta work!" Of course, in my case, I'd rather let some off-the-shelf components do the work for me.

In this chapter, I'll show a set of components that make it very easy to put fully featured audio and video players in your Flex application.

# XML MP3 Player project

For any entertainment site, you are going to have a little music to go along with whatever other material you are presenting. You can either just play the songs and have a mute button, or you can give your customers a better experience by providing a nice player that allows them to pick the songs and control the playback.

The open source XML MP3 Player project (http://xmlmp3player.googlecode.com) is the first of a set of players I'll demonstrate here. This one provides a set of source code and a couple of example wrapper Flex applications.

The Flex application shown here uses the ControlsSmall version of the XML MP3 Player component:

```
<?xml version="1.0" encoding="utf-8"?>
<mx:Application xmlns:mx="http://www.adobe.com/2006/mxml"
  xmlns:vp="views.player.*" layout="absolute"
  creationComplete="onStartup()" backgroundColor="#757A80"
  width="320" horizontalScrollPolicy="off" verticalScrollPolicy="off">

<mx:HTTPService id="album" url="http://localhost/music/album.xml"
  resultFormat="e4x"
  result="onAlbumResult(event);" />

<mx:Script>
<![CDATA[
import mx.rpc.events.ResultEvent;
import vo.MP3Player;
import vo.TrackVO;

[Bindable]
private var mp3Player:MP3Player = MP3Player.getInstance();
```

```
    private function onStartup():void {
      album.send();
      mp3Player.addEventListener("onDelayError",onDelayError);
    }
    private function onAlbumResult( event:ResultEvent ) : void {
      var aTracks:Array = new Array();
      for each( var track:XML in event.result..track ) {
        aTracks.push(new TrackVO( '', '', '', '', '',
            '', '', 'http://localhost/music/'+track.@file.toString(),
          0, 0, track.@name.toString(), '' ) );
      }
      mp3Player.dataProvider.source = aTracks;
      mp3Player.play();
    }
    private function onDelayError(event:Event):void{
      mp3Player.isPaused = false;
      mp3Player.getNextTrack();
    }
    ]]>
    </mx:Script>

    <mx:Style source="style.css"/>
    <mx:Image source="@Embed('headshot.jpg')" width="100%" />
    <mx:HBox backgroundColor="white" top="350" width="100%"
      horizontalScrollPolicy="off" verticalScrollPolicy="off"
      paddingTop="10" paddingBottom="10" horizontalAlign="center"
      borderSides="top,bottom" borderColor="#757A80" borderThickness="2"
      borderStyle="solid">
    <vp:ControlsSmall horizontalAlign="center" verticalAlign="middle"
      borderStyle="none" />
    </mx:HBox>
    </mx:Application>
```

The application uses the dataProvider in the ControlsSmall object to set the playlist. The application builds the playlist by reading an XML file from the server that has a list of tracks in a particular album. I wrote the code that way to demonstrate how you can load the playlist from ActionScript. If you want an easier solution, you can just point the XML MP3 Player at an XSPF-formatted XML playlist, and it will load it up and play it for you.

When we load this application from Flex Builder 3, it looks like Figure 7-1.

**Figure 7-1.** The XML MP3 Player
(photo courtesy of Bo Boswell [http://blue-wire.com])

This is one of the two possible user interface variants for this control. There is a larger version that presents a little more information about each track but overall has the same look and feel.

## Advanced Flash Components MP3 player

The Sound object in the Flash API is great, but it can be a little complex to use. To get play, pause, stop, volume control, and scrubber functionality, you have to manage three different objects: Sound, SoundChannel, and SoundTransform. To make it a little easier on us, the team at Advanced Flash Components (http://afcomponents.com) created a single headless MP3Player object on which you can wrap any user interface.

This first example application provides basic controls like Play, Pause, Mute, and a volume control while playing a single song:

```
<?xml version="1.0" encoding="utf-8"?>
<mx:Application xmlns:mx="http://www.adobe.com/2006/mxml"
  creationComplete="onCreation()" layout="absolute"
  width="585" height="393" horizontalScrollPolicy="off"
  verticalScrollPolicy="off">
<mx:Style>
.boundingBox {
  padding-bottom: 10; padding-left: 10;
  padding-right: 10; padding-top: 10;
  corner-radius: 15; border-style: solid;
  border-color: #cccccc; border-thickness: 1;
  background-color: #eeeeee;
  background-alpha: 0.5;
}
</mx:Style>
<mx:Script>
<![CDATA[
import com.afcomponents.mp3player.MP3Player;
import com.afcomponents.mp3player.events.MP3PlayerEvent;

public var player:MP3Player = new MP3Player();

private function onCreation():void
{
  player.volume = 0.7;
  volumeSlider.value = 0.7;

  player.load("http://localhost/music/01 A Reminiscent Drive - ➥
Ambrosia.mp3");

  mp3Progress.source = player;

  player.addEventListener(MP3PlayerEvent.BUFFERING_STATE_ENDED,
  onPlayerBuffered);
  player.addEventListener(MP3PlayerEvent.PLAYHEAD_UPDATE,
  onPlayerUpdate);
}

private function onPlayerBuffered( event:Event ) : void {
  player.play(); }

private function onPlayerUpdate( event:Event ) : void {
  var dspTime:String  = "";
  var time:Number = Math.round( player.playheadTime );
  if(Math.floor(time/60) < 10)
    dspTime = "0" + String(Math.floor(time/60)) + ":"
  else
    dspTime = String(Math.floor(time/60)) + ":"
```

7

```
      var seconds:Number = time;
      if(Math.floor(time/60) > 0)
        seconds = time - (Math.floor(time/60) * 60);

      if(seconds < 10)
        dspTime += "0" + String(seconds);
      else
        dspTime += String(seconds);
      lblTime.text = dspTime;
    }

    private function onPlay(event:MouseEvent) : void {
      if(player.state != "playing") player.play();
    }

    private function onMute( event:MouseEvent ) : void {
      if( player.mute ) {
        player.mute = false;
        btnMute.label = "Mute";
      } else {
        player.mute = true;
        btnMute.label = "Unmute";
      }
    }
  ]]>
</mx:Script>
<mx:Image source="@Embed('band.png')" />
<mx:VBox styleName="boundingBox" top="267" left="10"
 horizontalAlign="center">
<mx:ProgressBar id="mp3Progress" width="242" labelPlacement="center"
  barColor="#FF4342"/>
<mx:HBox verticalAlign="middle">
<mx:Button label="Play" click="onPlay(event)"/>
<mx:Button label="Pause" click="player.pause()"/>
<mx:Button label="Stop" click="player.seek(0);player.stop();"/>
<mx:Label text="00:00" textAlign="right" id="lblTime"/>
</mx:HBox>
<mx:HBox>
<mx:HSlider width="80" id="volumeSlider" minimum="0" maximum="1"
  snapInterval="0.1" liveDragging="true"
  change="player.volume=volumeSlider.value"/>
<mx:Button label="Mute" id="btnMute" click="onMute(event)"/>
</mx:HBox>
</mx:VBox>
</mx:Application>
```

This application is split into three sections. At the top is the CSS code that puts a nice little wrapper around the interface. In the middle are the ActionScript event handlers that handle all of the buttons on the interface, as well as the progress bar that indicates how much of the sound has been loaded. The MXML interface code at the bottom of the file is a no-thrills set of standard Flex buttons, a slider, a label, and a progress bar.

When we bring this application up from Flex Builder, it looks like Figure 7-2.

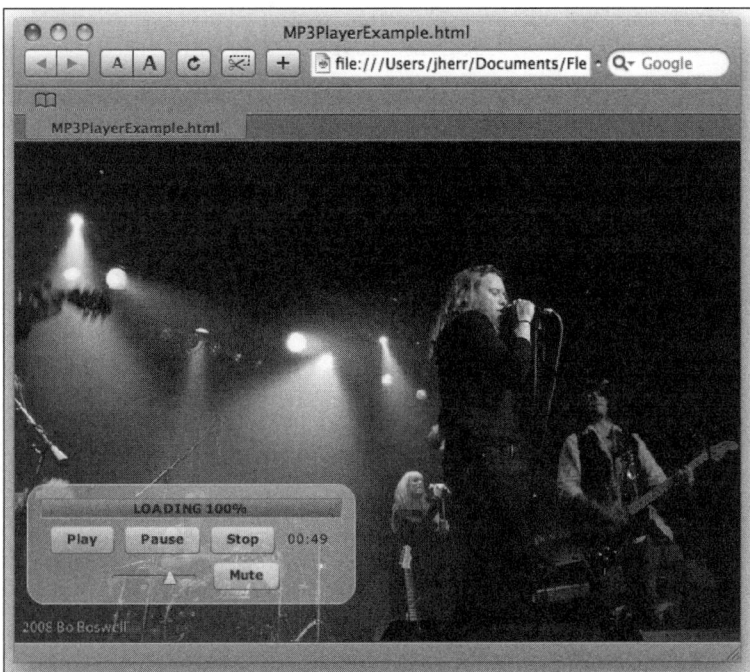

**Figure 7-2.** A simple MP3 player application that uses the MP3Player object

To put a different spin on the interface, the next application uses Degrafa to build a single big progress bar with the name of the currently playing MP3 in it. As the song plays, the progress bar rolls along underneath the name. The code for this is derived from the Capacity Indicator example in the Degrafa samples collection.

Following is the code for this application:

```
<?xml version="1.0" encoding="utf-8"?>
<mx:Application xmlns:mx="http://www.adobe.com/2006/mxml"
  layout="absolute"
  xmlns="http://www.degrafa.com/2007"
  xmlns:reflector="com.rictus.reflector.*"
  xmlns:filters="flash.filters.*"
  backgroundGradientColors="[ #000000, #222222 ]"
  color="#FFFFFF" creationComplete="onStartup()">

<mx:Script>
<![CDATA[
import com.afcomponents.mp3player.MP3Player;
import com.afcomponents.mp3player.events.MP3PlayerEvent;
```

```
public var player:MP3Player = new MP3Player();

[Bindable]
public var capacityWidth:Number = 570;

private function onStartup() : void {
  player.load("http://localhost/music/01 A Reminiscent Drive - ➥
Ambrosia.mp3");
  player.addEventListener(MP3PlayerEvent.BUFFERING_STATE_ENDED,
  onPlayerBuffered);
  player.addEventListener(MP3PlayerEvent.PLAYHEAD_UPDATE,
  onPlayheadUpdate);
}

private function initChange( event:Event ) : void {
  if ( theReflection ) theReflection.invalidateDisplayList();
}

private function onPlayheadUpdate( event:MP3PlayerEvent ) : void {
  firstRect.width = ( player.playheadTime / player.totalTime ) *
  capacityWidth;
}

private function onPlayerBuffered( event:Event ) : void {
  player.play(); }

private function onPlay( ) : void {
  player.pause();
}
]]>
</mx:Script>

<GeometryComposition graphicsTarget="{[capacitySurface]}"
  propertyChange="initChange(event);">

<fills>
<LinearGradientFill id="colorOne" angle="0">
  <GradientStop color="#62ABCD" alpha="0.6"/>
  <GradientStop color="#62ABCD" alpha="1"/>
</LinearGradientFill>
<LinearGradientFill id="highlight" angle="90">
  <GradientStop color="#FFF" alpha=".3"/>
  <GradientStop color="#FFF" alpha=".05"/>
</LinearGradientFill>
<LinearGradientFill id="shadow" angle="90" blendMode="multiply">
  <GradientStop color="#000" alpha=".01"/>
  <GradientStop color="#000" alpha=".5"/>
</LinearGradientFill>
<LinearGradientFill id="inset" angle="90">
```

```
    <GradientStop color="#CCC" alpha=".2" ratio="0" ratioUnit="pixels"/>
    <GradientStop color="#FFF" alpha=".3" ratio="16" ratioUnit="pixels"/>
  </LinearGradientFill>
</fills>

<strokes>
  <SolidStroke id="whiteStroke" color="#FFF" weight="1" alpha=".15"/>
  <SolidStroke id="darkStroke" color="#000" weight="1" alpha=".2"/>
</strokes>

<RegularRectangle id="insetRect" width="{capacityWidth}"
  height="{capacitySurface.height}" fill="{inset}"/>
<RegularRectangle id="firstRect" width="100"
  height="{capacitySurface.height}" fill="{colorOne}"/>
<RegularRectangle id="shadowRect" width="{capacityWidth}"
  height="{capacitySurface.height}" fill="{shadow}"/>
<RoundedRectangleComplex id="highlightRect" bottomLeftRadius="10"
  bottomRightRadius="10" width="{capacityWidth}"
  height="{capacitySurface.height/2}"
  fill="{highlight}"/>

</GeometryComposition>

<mx:Image source="@Embed('band.png')" />
<mx:Canvas top="294" left="0" width="591" height="70"
  backgroundColor="#222222">

<mx:Canvas id="pill" click="onPlay()" top="10" left="10">
<Surface id="capacitySurface" verticalCenter="0" horizontalCenter="0"
  width="{capacityWidth}" height="40" mask="{roundMask}">
<GeometryGroup id="roundMask">
<RoundedRectangle width="{capacityWidth}"
  height="{capacitySurface.height}"
  cornerRadius="20" fill="{colorOne}"/>
</GeometryGroup>
<filters>
<filters:GlowFilter color="#000000" alpha=".1" blurX="4" blurY="4"
  inner="true" quality="6"/>
</filters>
</Surface>
<mx:Label top="4" left="20" fontWeight="bold"
  fontSize="20" text="Ambrosia" />
</mx:Canvas>
<reflector:Reflector id="theReflection" target="{pill}" alpha=".8"
  falloff=".5" blurAmount=".1"/>

</mx:Canvas>

</mx:Application>
```

7

Most of the application code is in the Degrafa portion at the bottom of the page. The Degrafa code sets up the different fills and shapes, and then the GeometryComposition and GeometryGroup objects bring it all together into a complete interface. At the very bottom is the Reflector object that puts that great Web 2.0 reflection on the bottom of the control. The small bit of ActionScript at the top sets up the event handlers on the MP3 control and sets the URL of the MP3 itself.

When we bring this up from Flex Builder, it looks like Figure 7-3.

**Figure 7-3.** The MP3 pill player example

I really like the aqua pill effect in this example. If you are looking to use that aqua effect in your own applications, this is some good Degrafa code to copy. The progress bar interface here is actually surprisingly effective as well.

# Yet another audio player example

Chapter 15, which covers building your own component, builds an example MP3 audio player. You are free to use the code in that chapter as a legitimate MP3 player component in its own right.

# Video

Playing video is a big step up from playing audio. The Flex framework provides a VideoDisplay, but that only gives you basic playback. You still need to get video into the FLV format required for the Flash Player, and you need to put some controls on the player so that people can start the movie, stop it, rewind, fast forward, and so on.

There are several ways to get movies into FLV format. If you like the command line, you should look at the FFMpeg converter (http://ffmpeg.mplayerhq.hu/). It's an open source application that can take almost any video format and turn it into any other video format. If you have bought a suite of design software from Adobe, then you will likely have their Media Encoder application, which you can use to encode one or more movies from any video format into FLV. You can also use the Pro version of Apple's QuickTime Player to export movies as FLV files.

FLV movies don't just come in one shape and size. You will want to experiment with different FLV conversion settings, for example, the dimensions of the movie (such as 320×240 or 640×480) as well as the quality and sound settings, to find what works best for you and your customers.

# FX movie player

The first video player we will have a look at is the Flex Video Player (http://www.fxcomponents.com/?p=29) from FX Components. This is an incredibly easy-to-use video player that takes a height, width, and FLV source as attributes and rewards you with a full-featured video player with all of the required controls.

The first example application that uses the FX Player is shown here:

```
<?xml version="1.0" encoding="utf-8"?>
<mx:Application xmlns:mx="http://www.adobe.com/2006/mxml"
  layout="absolute"
  xmlns:controls="com.fxcomponents.controls.*"
  xmlns:ext="nl.wv.extenders.panel.*"
  backgroundGradientColors="[#000000,#000000]"
  horizontalScrollPolicy="off" verticalScrollPolicy="off">
<mx:Image source="@Embed('coaster.jpg')" width="800" />
<mx:Canvas backgroundColor="black" backgroundAlpha="0.6" x="0"
  y="263" width="800" height="310"
  borderStyle="none">
<controls:FXVideo width="480" height="270" top="10" left="10"
  source="http://localhost/videos/Coaster1.flv" autoPlay="false"
  bufferTime="10" />
</mx:Canvas>
</mx:Application>
```

This is really just a wrapper around the FXVideo player control. The rest of the MXML code is the image and the canvas that goes around the video player. When we bring this application up from Flex Builder, it looks like Figure 7-4.

**Figure 7-4.** Going for a ride on the roller coaster player

As you can see, the player has play and stop buttons, as well as a scrubber to move the playback of the movie around. It provides the current play position as well as the complete movie length. And at the end of the toolbar, it provides a mute button and a volume controller.

The second application that uses the FX Player allows the user to select which movie to play from a list of movies provided by the server. Here's the code for this example:

```
<?xml version="1.0" encoding="utf-8"?>
<mx:Application xmlns:mx="http://www.adobe.com/2006/mxml"
  layout="absolute"
  xmlns:controls="com.fxcomponents.controls.*"
  creationComplete="videos.send()"
  horizontalScrollPolicy="off" verticalScrollPolicy="off">
<mx:Script>
<![CDATA[
public function onListClick() : void {
  var newSource:String = 'http://localhost/videos/'+➥
videoList.selectedItem.@src;
  player.source = newSource;
  player.load();
}
]]>
</mx:Script>
<mx:HTTPService id="videos" url="http://localhost/videos/moto.xml"
  resultFormat="e4x" />
<mx:Image source="@Embed('motorcycle.jpg')" width="1400" top="-100">
  <mx:filters>
    <mx:BlurFilter blurX="15" blurY="5" />
  </mx:filters>
</mx:Image>
<mx:HBox id="vidPnl" paddingBottom="45" paddingLeft="15"
  paddingRight="15" paddingTop="15" top="20" left="20"
  backgroundAlpha="0.4" backgroundColor="white" cornerRadius="10"
  borderStyle="solid"
  borderColor="#666666" borderThickness="2">
  <mx:filters>
    <mx:DropShadowFilter />
  </mx:filters>
<controls:FXVideo width="480" height="360" id="player"
  source="http://localhost/videos/moto1.flv"
  autoPlay="false" bufferTime="10" />
<mx:List height="100%" width="200" borderThickness="1"
  borderStyle="solid" borderColor="#cccccc"
  dataProvider="{videos.lastResult..video}"
  labelField="@name" id="videoList"
  click="onListClick()" alpha="0.4" fontWeight="bold" fontSize="16" />
</mx:HBox>
</mx:Application>
```

The application starts up by loading the list of videos from the server. The videoList control then updates itself once the server returns the XML list of videos. You can change videos by clicking the list, which is handled by the onListClick method. The rest of the MXML in the application sets up the somewhat elaborate motorcycle-themed interface shown in Figure 7-5.

**Figure 7-5.** The motorcycle-themed video player with multiple movies

This Flex Video Player is a solid and reliable piece of work. Since you download it as source code, you can use it as a template for your own video player even if you don't use it as your video playing component.

## FLVPlayer

The Flash IDE comes with a complete video player called FLVPlayer with all of the playback controls. This player is also skinnable so that you can change the look and feel of the playback controls. Unfortunately, the FLVPlayer and its related skins are all ActionScript 2 components, and there are issues with interoperating ActionScript 2 and 3 code simultaneously.

To solve this problem, the Advanced Flash Components guys built an AS3 version of the playback control and its related skins. Following is the first of three example applications that show how to use the FLVPlayer:

```
<?xml version="1.0" encoding="utf-8"?>
<mx:Application xmlns:mx="http://www.adobe.com/2006/mxml"
  layout="absolute"
  creationComplete="onStartup()" backgroundAlpha="0"
  horizontalScrollPolicy="off"
  verticalScrollPolicy="off">
<mx:Script>
<![CDATA[
```

```
import mx.core.UIComponent;
import fl.video.FLVPlayback;

private var player:FLVPlayback = new FLVPlayback();

private function onStartup() : void {
  Security.allowDomain( 'localhost' );

  var uic:UIComponent = new UIComponent();
  uic.width = 480;
  uic.height = 360;
  uic.setStyle('top',0);
  uic.setStyle('left',0);
  vidPnl.addChild( uic );

  player.addEventListener('skinLoaded',onSkinLoaded);
  uic.addChild( player );

  player.x = 0;
  player.y = 0;
  player.width = 480;
  player.height = 360;
  player.skinBackgroundColor = 0x333333;
  player.skinBackgroundAlpha = 0.6;
  player.skin = "http://localhost/videos/AFComponents_ClassicSkin.swf";
  player.skinAutoHide = false;
  player.autoPlay = true;
  player.scaleMode = "maintainAspectRatio";
}
private function onSkinLoaded( event:Object ) : void {
  player.source = 'http://localhost/videos/MVI_3412.FLV';
}
]]>
</mx:Script>
<mx:Image source="@Embed('flower1.jpg')" width="680">
  <mx:filters>
    <mx:BlurFilter blurX="5" blurY="5" />
  </mx:filters>
</mx:Image>
<mx:HBox id="vidPnl" paddingBottom="45" paddingLeft="15"
  paddingRight="15" paddingTop="15" top="20" left="80"
  backgroundAlpha="0.4" backgroundColor="white" cornerRadius="10"
  borderStyle="solid"
  borderColor="#666666" borderThickness="2" rotation="5">
  <mx:filters>
    <mx:DropShadowFilter />
  </mx:filters>
</mx:HBox>
</mx:Application>
```

7

As with other Flash components, the control, which is based on the Sprite class, needs to be hosted by a Flex UIComponent. The onStartup method handles adding the video player to the stage as well as setting up the parameters of the control itself. These parameters include the height, the width, the location of the movie, as well as the skin parameters.

The MXML code at the bottom of the page adds the background image as well as a nice rotated box container for the movie player. You can see the result in Figure 7-6.

**Figure 7-6.** The first FLVPlayer example

It's always amazing to me that Flash and Flex components work even when rotated. In this case, you can still click all of the video playback controls in their rotated alignment. It even looks pretty good slightly rotated.

In the second application, we use another skin for the playback controls as well as applying a mask to the control using Degrafa. The code for this is shown here:

```
<?xml version="1.0" encoding="utf-8"?>
<mx:Application xmlns:mx="http://www.adobe.com/2006/mxml"
  layout="absolute"
  creationComplete="onStartup()" xmlns="http://www.degrafa.com/2007"
```

```
    horizontalScrollPolicy="off" verticalScrollPolicy="off">
<mx:Script>
<![CDATA[
import mx.core.UIComponent;
import fl.video.FLVPlayback;

private var player:FLVPlayback = new FLVPlayback();

private function onStartup() : void {
  Security.allowDomain( 'localhost' );

  var uic:UIComponent = new UIComponent();
  uic.width = 480;
  uic.height = 360;
  uic.setStyle('top',0);
  uic.setStyle('left',0);
  vidPnl.addChild( uic );

  player.addEventListener('skinLoaded',onSkinLoaded);
  uic.addChild( player );

  player.mask = topMask;
  player.x = 0;
  player.y = 0;
  player.width = 500;
  player.height = 400;
  player.skinBackgroundColor = 0x333333;
  player.skinBackgroundAlpha = 0.6;
  player.skin = "http://localhost/videos/➥
AFComponents_PixelOverlaySkin.swf";
  player.skinAutoHide = false;
  player.autoPlay = true;
  player.scaleMode = "maintainAspectRatio";
}
private function onSkinLoaded( event:Object ) : void {
  player.source = 'http://localhost/videos/dance.flv';
}
]]>
</mx:Script>
<Surface>
<GeometryGroup id="topMask" x="95" y="50">
  <fills><SolidFill color="#FFF" alpha="1" id="fill1"/></fills>
  <stroke><SolidStroke color="#000" weight="2" id="stroke1"/></stroke>
  <RoundedRectangle width="495" height="368" cornerRadius="10"
      fill="{fill1}" stroke="{stroke1}"/>
</GeometryGroup>
</Surface>
<mx:Image source="@Embed('lifecycle.jpg')" width="680">
  <mx:filters>
```

```
      <mx:BlurFilter blurX="3" blurY="3" />
    </mx:filters>
  </mx:Image>
  <mx:HBox id="vidPnl" paddingBottom="10" paddingLeft="10"
    paddingRight="10" paddingTop="10" top="20" left="80"
    backgroundAlpha="0">
    <mx:filters>
      <mx:DropShadowFilter distance="10" alpha="0.5" />
    </mx:filters>
  </mx:HBox>
</mx:Application>
```

You will notice that in some of these examples, we set the Security.allowDomain to allow for access to localhost. This is because player security will often prevent us from showing FLV videos from any domain. You can get around that restriction by making the call to Security.addDomain with the domain you wish to access.

Much of the code remains the same as with the first example, though the URL of the skin has changed to reference another sleeker video controls skin. The Degrafa code at the bottom sets up a mask named topMask, which is applied to the video player to give it some rounded edges. You can see the results in Figure 7-7.

**Figure 7-7.** The FLVPlayer with overlaid controls and rounded edges

The masking technique can do a lot more than just round the edges. You could use a raggedy black-and-white image to give the movie a cut-out look. Or you could use a gradient fill in the mask to selectively accentuate portions of the video display.

In the final version of the application, I demonstrate how to watch the events from the FLVPlayback control to cycle through a set of movies specified in an XML file downloaded from the server. The application code is shown here:

```
<?xml version="1.0" encoding="utf-8"?>
<mx:Application xmlns:mx="http://www.adobe.com/2006/mxml"
  layout="absolute"
  creationComplete="onStartup()" horizontalScrollPolicy="off"
  verticalScrollPolicy="off">
<mx:Script>
<![CDATA[
import mx.events.VideoEvent;
import mx.core.UIComponent;
import fl.video.FLVPlayback;

private var player:FLVPlayback = new FLVPlayback();
private var videoList:Array = [];

private function onStartup() : void {
  Security.allowDomain( 'localhost' );

  var uic:UIComponent = new UIComponent();
  uic.width = 480;
  uic.height = 360;
  uic.setStyle('top',0);
  uic.setStyle('left',0);
  vidPnl.addChild( uic );

  player.addEventListener('skinLoaded',onSkinLoaded);
  player.addEventListener(VideoEvent.COMPLETE,gotoNextMovie);
  uic.addChild( player );

  player.x = 0;
  player.y = 0;
  player.width = 480;
  player.height = 360;
  player.skinBackgroundColor = 0x333333;
  player.skinBackgroundAlpha = 0.6;
  player.skin = "http://localhost/videos/➥
AFComponents_PixelOverlaySkin.swf";
  player.skinAutoHide = false;
  player.autoPlay = true;
  player.scaleMode = "maintainAspectRatio";
}
private function onSkinLoaded( event:Object ) : void {
```

7

```
        videos.send();
      }
      private function onVideoListLoad() : void {
        for each( var vid:XML in videos.lastResult..video )
          videoList.push( 'http://localhost/videos/'+vid.@src );
        gotoNextMovie();
      }
      private function gotoNextMovie( event:Event = null ) : void {
        if ( videoList.length > 0 )
          player.source = videoList.pop();
      }
    ]]>
    </mx:Script>
    <mx:HTTPService id="videos" url="http://localhost/videos/videos.xml"
      resultFormat="e4x"
      result="onVideoListLoad()" />
    <mx:Image source="@Embed('flower_bottom.png')" />
    <mx:Panel id="vidPnl" title="Video Player" paddingBottom="5"
      paddingLeft="5"
      paddingRight="5" paddingTop="5" top="50" left="50" />
    <mx:Image source="@Embed('flower_top.png')" mouseEnabled="false" />
    </mx:Application>
```

The big change from the previous example comes in the use of an HTTPService to download the list of movies as XML from the server. It's the onVideoListLoad method that takes the XML and creates an array of movies in the videoList object. When the application sets up the movie player, it adds an event listener for the VideoEvent.COMPLETED event. This event signals the end of a movie playback. The gotoNextMovie method handles this event and loads the next movie in the sequence.

The other difference with this application is that it has both a background and a foreground image. You can see the result in Figure 7-8.

To build the foreground and background images, I started with a flower picture and a screenshot of the application without either image. I brought both images into Fireworks and overlaid the screenshot on top of the flowers on a single canvas. From there, I set the alpha of the screenshot to 50% so that I could see the flowers through the screenshot. I then duplicated the flowers and overlaid it on top of the screenshot. From there, I cut away everything from the top layer that I didn't need. With that done, I saved the top layer as the foreground image and the bottom layer as the background image.

**Figure 7-8.** The video player with both foreground and background graphics

# Where we will go from here

Audio and video are two of the most powerful aspects of the Flash platform. The components in this chapter should help you build Flex applications that provide a complete audio or video experience very quickly. The example applications also give you a set of ideas as to how to integrate video and audio playback into your application in unique ways. Enjoy playing with the code and trying out some of these neat techniques in your own work.

In the next chapter, we dig into how to visualize data that your application loads from a database in two dimensions.

# 8 2D GRAPHING COMPONENTS: INTRODUCING CHARTING

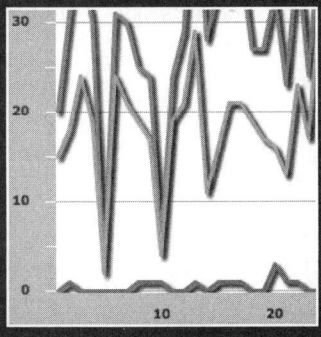
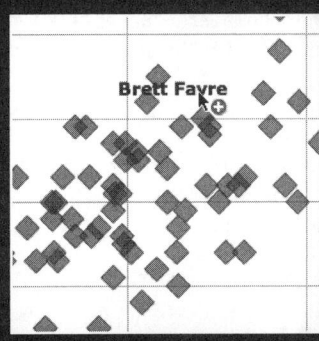
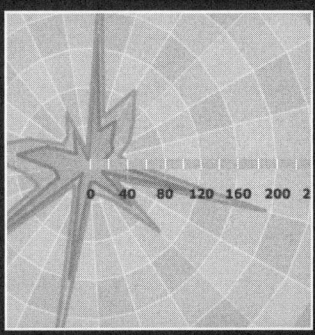

Updated 6/22/08

One of the best components that you can use with Flex is baked right into the framework. Charting has always been a pain on the Web. You can use open source frameworks like GD (http://www.boutell.com/gd/) to draw graphics on the server, but the results often leave a lot to be desired, and there is little or no interactivity in the charts. Because of Flex's initial focus on the business market, Adobe put a data visualization framework right into the base set of controls.

What a framework it is! The controls are designed to support almost any type of data and at the same time be graphically extensible. For example, effects can be applied to the charts so that as changes are made to the display, the charting elements glide gently to their new positions.

In this chapter, I'll cover a number of example Flex applications that show off both the visualization and interactivity elements of the framework. I'll use the baseball and football data sets that we installed in Chapter 2 to drive the visualizations. Feel free to use any of these examples as a starting point for building your own visualizations.

# Bubble charts

Bubble charts provide three dimensions of data in a two-dimensional chart. There is the horizontal and vertical axis, as well as the size of the bubble to which you can attach any value. You can also alter the fill color of any bubble to provide a fourth data axis.

In this first application, we use the baseball database to plot home runs on the horizontal axis and the earned run average (ERA) on the vertical axis. We then size the bubble based on the average attendance. The application also changes the color of the bubble dynamically depending on whether the team is in the National League or the American League.

```
<?xml version="1.0" encoding="utf-8"?>
<mx:Application xmlns:mx="http://www.adobe.com/2006/mxml"
  layout="vertical"
  creationComplete="baseballRO.getTeamsByYear.send( 2006 )"
  xmlns:degrafa="http://www.degrafa.com/2007">

<mx:Style>
Application {
  background-gradient-colors: #9999FF, #eeeeff;
  font-weight: bold;
  font-size: 14;
}
</mx:Style>

<mx:Script>
<![CDATA[
import com.degrafa.paint.GradientStop;
import mx.graphics.RadialGradient;
import com.degrafa.paint.RadialGradientFill;
```

```
import mx.charts.series.items.BubbleSeriesItem;
import mx.graphics.SolidColor;
import mx.charts.series.items.PlotSeriesItem;
import mx.graphics.IFill;
import mx.charts.ChartItem;
import mx.charts.HitData;

private function onTeamsByYear() : void {
  var teams:Array = baseballRO.getTeamsByYear.lastResult;
  for each( var team:Object in teams ) {
    team.hr = parseInt( team.hr );
    team.era = parseFloat( team.era );
    team.w = parseInt( team.w );
    team.attendance = parseInt( team.attendance );
  }
  chart.dataProvider = teams;
}

private function makeDataTip( hd:HitData ):String {
  return "<b>"+hd.item.name+"</b><br/>Wins <b>"+hd.item.w+
  "</b> Losses <b>"+hd.item.l+"</b>";
}

public function myFillFunction(item:ChartItem, index:Number):IFill {
  var curItem:BubbleSeriesItem = BubbleSeriesItem(item);
  var rgf:RadialGradientFill = new RadialGradientFill();
  var color:uint = (curItem.item.lgid == 'AL' ) ? 0xFF0000 : 0x0000FF;
  rgf.gradientStops = [ new GradientStop( color, 1, 0.5 ),
  new GradientStop( color, 0.2, 1 ) ];
  return rgf;
}
]]>
</mx:Script>

<mx:RemoteObject id="baseballRO"
  endpoint="http://localhost/amfphp/gateway.php"
  source="baseball.BaseballService"
  destination="baseball.BaseballService"
  showBusyCursor="true">
<mx:method name="getTeamsByYear" result="onTeamsByYear()">
<mx:arguments>
  <mx:Year />
</mx:arguments>
</mx:method>
</mx:RemoteObject>

<mx:VBox paddingBottom="10" paddingLeft="10"
  paddingRight="10" paddingTop="10" backgroundColor="white"
  backgroundAlpha="0.4" borderColor="#cccccc"
```

8

```
cornerRadius="15" borderThickness="3" borderStyle="solid"
width="100%" height="100%">

<mx:BubbleChart width="100%" height="100%" id="chart"
 showDataTips="true" maxRadius="30" dataTipFunction="makeDataTip">

<mx:backgroundElements>
<degrafa:Surface>
  <degrafa:fills>
    <degrafa:SolidFill id="whiteFill" color="white" alpha="0.6" />
  </degrafa:fills>
  <degrafa:GeometryGroup>
    <degrafa:RegularRectangle x="0" y="0"
      width="{chart.width}" height="{chart.height}"
       fill="{whiteFill}" />
  </degrafa:GeometryGroup>
</degrafa:Surface>
<mx:GridLines direction="both">
  <mx:horizontalStroke>
    <mx:Stroke color="#bbbbbb" />
  </mx:horizontalStroke>
  <mx:verticalStroke>
    <mx:Stroke color="#bbbbbb" />
  </mx:verticalStroke>
</mx:GridLines>
</mx:backgroundElements>

<mx:horizontalAxis>
<mx:LinearAxis title="Home Runs" minimum="100" maximum="250" />
</mx:horizontalAxis>
<mx:verticalAxis>
<mx:LinearAxis title="ERA" minimum="3" maximum="6" />
</mx:verticalAxis>
<mx:series>
<mx:BubbleSeries xField="hr" yField="era" radiusField="attendance"
  fillFunction="myFillFunction">
  <mx:stroke>
    <mx:Stroke alpha="0" />
  </mx:stroke>
</mx:BubbleSeries>
</mx:series>
</mx:BubbleChart>

</mx:VBox>

</mx:Application>
```

The code for this application is divided into three parts. The first is the ActionScript that sets the data in the graph, as well as provides custom data types with the makeDataTip method and custom bubble coloring with the myFillFunction method.

The second part of the code is in the definition of the `RemoteObject` protocol with the server. This time we are using the baseball AMF service.

The third part of the code is the definition of the bubble chart itself. As you can see, it works just like any other Flex control. You can define the height and width of the control, assign it an id, and set any charting parameters like `showDataTips`, which means that a tooltip will pop up as you mouse over an item.

The MXML also sets the horizontal and vertical axis objects to linear axes. You can choose a logarithmic axis if you like. Or if your axis contains discrete categories, you can specify a category axis.

The final element in the `BubbleChart` MXML definition is the series array, which defines each data series. In this case, there is only one series, where the x axis (defined by the `xField` attribute) is the number of home runs, the y axis is the ERA, the radius of the bubble is gleaned from the attendance field, and the fill color of the bubble is defined dynamically by `myFillFunction`.

When we launch this from Flex Builder 3, we see something like Figure 8-1.

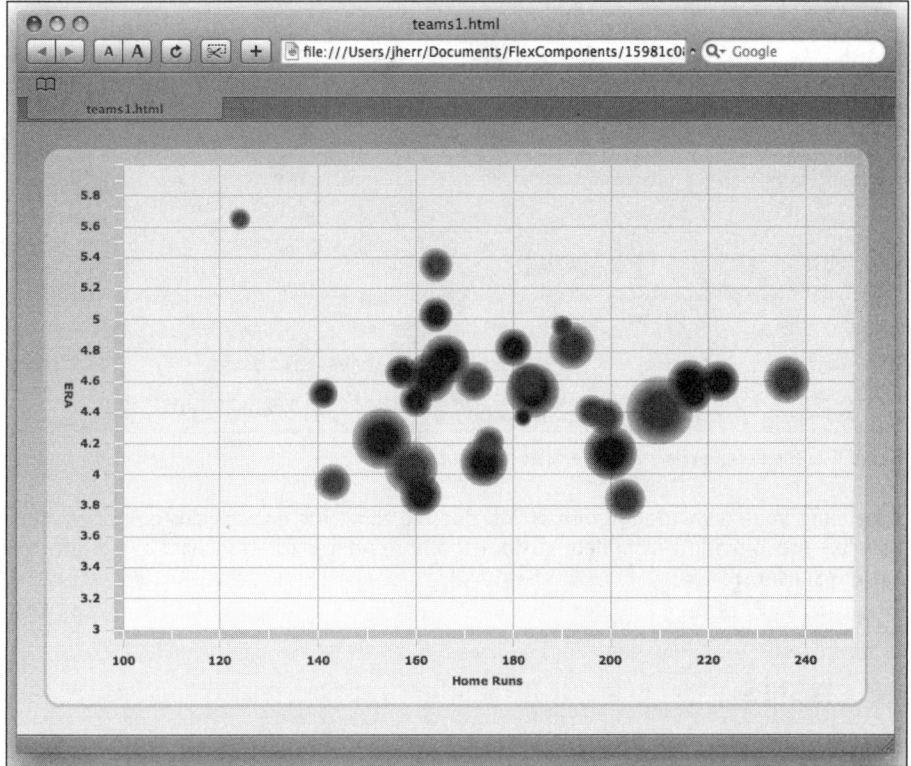

**Figure 8-1.** The baseball bubble chart

The Flex charting controls do a pretty good job of formatting the tooltips for the bubbles by default. But if you want something custom, you can specify a method to call using the dataTipFunction attribute on the BubbleChart object. That function needs to return an HTML string that should be used to tell the customer something about the bubble.

You can see the custom tooltip that comes from the data tip function in this Flex application in Figure 8-2.

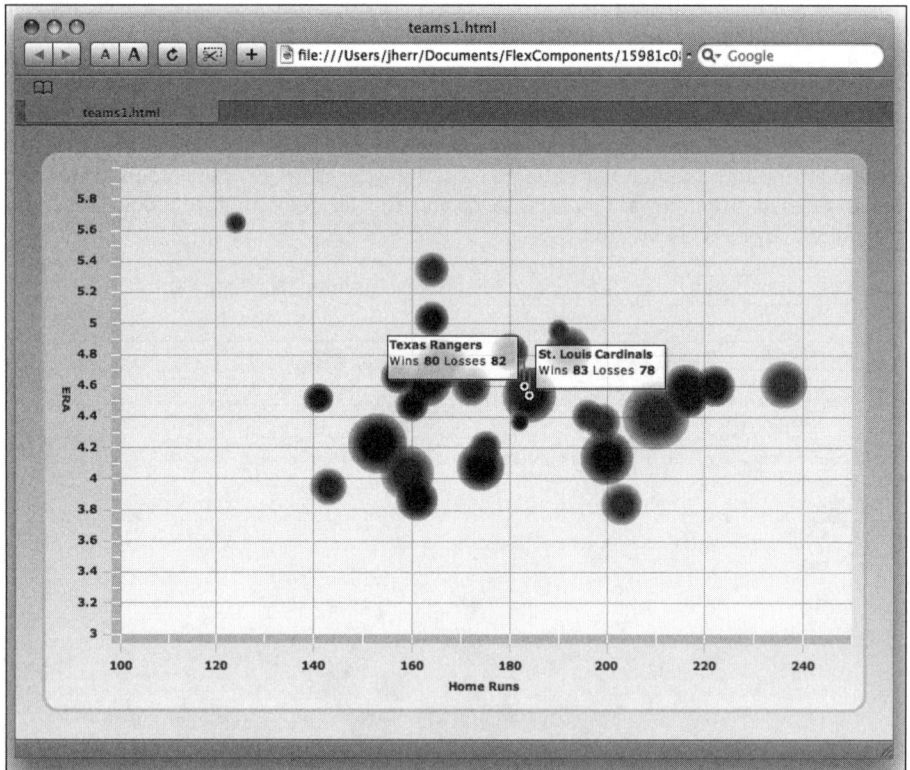

**Figure 8-2.** The bubble chart with the custom tooltips

If defining your own tooltip with HTML doesn't allow for enough customization, then you can also provide a complete custom tooltip renderer for the chart by specifying a dataTipRenderer.

## Line charts

The next example will show how to combine a chart control with search functionality to create an interactive application that easily allows customers to contrast and compare different data sets. In this case, I'll use the football data set and allow customers to view the performance of different quarterbacks over the years.

On the left-hand side of the application will be the search area where a customer can enter a name and see a list of potential matching players. Double-clicking a player will bring up his performance metrics in the line chart. The line chart will show three different data elements that are very relevant to quarterbacks: passing attempts, completions, and interceptions—in other words, how often a quarterback threw the football, how many times it got caught by one of his own players, and how often it got caught by a player on the opposing team.

The code for this example is shown here:

```
<?xml version="1.0" encoding="utf-8"?>
<mx:Application xmlns:mx="http://www.adobe.com/2006/mxml"
  layout="absolute"
  creationComplete="searchPlayers()"
  xmlns:degrafa="http://www.degrafa.com/2007">

<mx:Style>
Application {
  background-gradient-colors: #66FF66, #eeffee;
  font-weight: bold;
  font-size: 14;
}
</mx:Style>

<mx:Script>
<![CDATA[
import mx.charts.HitData;

private function searchPlayers() : void {
  footballRO.findPlayer.send( srchText.text );
}

private function onFindPlayer() : void {
  var players:Array = footballRO.findPlayer.lastResult;
  for each( var player:Object in players ) {
    player.name = player.first + " " + player.last;
  }
  playerList.dataProvider = players;
}

private function onPlayerDblClick() : void {
  footballRO.getGamesByPlayer.send( playerList.selectedItem.id );
}

private function onGamesByPlayer() : void {
  var games:Array = footballRO.getGamesByPlayer.lastResult;
  var gameind:int = 1;
  for each( var game:Object in games ) {
    game.game = gameind;
```

```
        gameind++;
      }
      lineChart.dataProvider = games;
    }

    private function makeDataTip( hd:HitData ) : String {
      return "<b>"+hd.item.team+"</b> "+hd.item.year+" week "+hd.item.week;
    }
  ]]>
</mx:Script>

<mx:RemoteObject id="footballRO"
  endpoint="http://localhost/amfphp/gateway.php"
  source="football.FootballService"
  destination="football.FootballService"
  showBusyCursor="true">
<mx:method name="findPlayer" result="onFindPlayer()">
<mx:arguments>
  <mx:Name />
</mx:arguments>
</mx:method>
<mx:method name="getGamesByPlayer" result="onGamesByPlayer()">
<mx:arguments>
  <mx:Player />
</mx:arguments>
</mx:method>
</mx:RemoteObject>

<mx:VBox paddingBottom="15" paddingLeft="15"
  paddingRight="15" paddingTop="15" backgroundColor="#cccccc"
  borderColor="#eeeeee" cornerRadius="15"
  borderThickness="3" borderStyle="solid"
  width="90%" height="90%" top="30" left="30">
<mx:filters>
  <mx:DropShadowFilter distance="10" alpha="0.7" />
</mx:filters>

<mx:LineChart width="100%" height="100%" id="lineChart"
 showDataTips="true" dataTipFunction="makeDataTip">

<mx:backgroundElements>
<degrafa:Surface>
  <degrafa:fills>
    <degrafa:SolidFill id="whiteFill" color="white" />
  </degrafa:fills>
  <degrafa:GeometryGroup>
    <degrafa:RegularRectangle x="0" y="0" width="{lineChart.width}"
     height="{lineChart.height}"
       fill="{whiteFill}" />
```

```
    </degrafa:GeometryGroup>
  </degrafa:Surface>
  <mx:GridLines>
    <mx:horizontalStroke>
      <mx:Stroke color="#bbbbbb" />
    </mx:horizontalStroke>
  </mx:GridLines>
</mx:backgroundElements>

<mx:series>
  <mx:LineSeries yField="att" xField="game" displayName="Attempts" />
  <mx:LineSeries yField="comp" xField="game"
   displayName="Completions" />
  <mx:LineSeries yField="interceptions" xField="game"
   displayName="Interceptions" />
</mx:series>
</mx:LineChart>
<mx:Legend dataProvider="{lineChart}" direction="horizontal" />

</mx:VBox>

<mx:Panel title="Search" width="200" height="150" paddingBottom="5"
  paddingLeft="5"
  paddingRight="5" paddingTop="5" layout="vertical" left="600" top="10"
  borderAlpha="0.8">
  <mx:TextInput width="100%" id="srchText" text="Aikman"
  keyUp="searchPlayers()" />
  <mx:List id="playerList" width="100%" height="100%" labelField="name"
  doubleClickEnabled="true" doubleClick="onPlayerDblClick()" />
</mx:Panel>

</mx:Application>
```

As with all of the example applications in this chapter, this application is broken into three major components. The ActionScript at the top performs the search, sets the list box, and responds to a double-click by setting the dataProvider on the graph.

The RemoteObject definition specifies the methods that we will be calling on the server to get the data.

The user interface section, at the bottom of the file, has two Panel containers. The first one, which is positioned on the left, contains the search text input, the search button, and the results list. The second Panel, positioned on the right, contains the LineChart object that will display the data.

In this case, we specify three data series objects in the LineChart object. Each is defined via a LineSeries object. All of the series share the same x axis field, game, but have a different y axis data source. They also specify a display name that is used in the Legend control, which is located below the graph.

When we launch this application from Flex Builder 3, we see something like Figure 8-3.

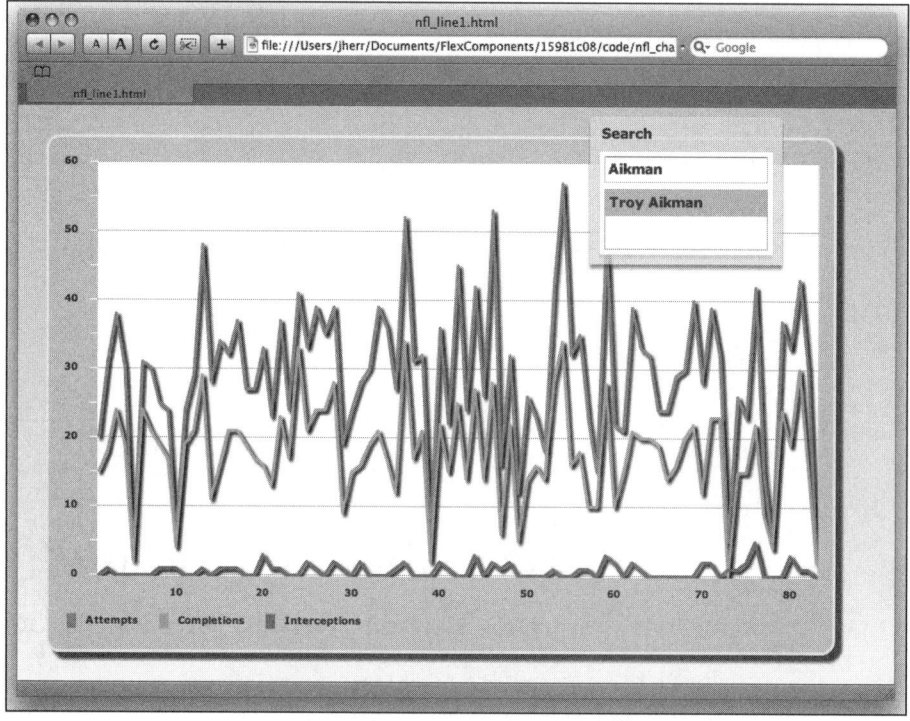

**Figure 8-3.** Troy Aikman's attempts, completions, and interceptions over his career

The application is set to initially search on Aikman. That search returns Troy Aikman, a quarterback for the Dallas Cowboys. Double-clicking his name brings up the graph that you see here.

As you can see, the Flex charting controls do a nice job of representing the data attractively right out of the box. To refine the look further, we can specify colors, change the fonts, add labels, provide custom tooltips, and so on.

## Area charts

Area charts are a good way to represent the changing percentages of the various components of a system as they change over time. In this next example, I'll show how the count of singles, doubles, triples, and home runs changes over time within a given baseball team.

Following is the code for this application:

```xml
<?xml version="1.0" encoding="utf-8"?>
<mx:Application xmlns:mx="http://www.adobe.com/2006/mxml"
  layout="vertical"
  creationComplete="baseballRO.getTeamList.send()"
  xmlns:degrafa="http://www.degrafa.com/2007">

<mx:Style>
Application {
  background-gradient-colors: #9999FF, #eeeeff;
  font-weight: bold;
  font-size: 14;
}
</mx:Style>
<mx:Script>
<![CDATA[
import mx.charts.series.items.BubbleSeriesItem;
import mx.graphics.SolidColor;
import mx.charts.series.items.PlotSeriesItem;
import mx.graphics.IFill;
import mx.charts.ChartItem;
import mx.charts.HitData;

private function onYearsResult() : void {
  areaChart.dataProvider = baseballRO.getYearsByTeam.lastResult;
}

private function onTeamsList() : void {
  teamSelector.dataProvider = baseballRO.getTeamList.lastResult;
  teamSelector.selectedIndex = 0;
}

private function onTeamChange() : void {
  if ( teamSelector.selectedItem != null &&
    teamSelector.selectedItem.teamid != null )
      baseballRO.getYearsByTeam.send( teamSelector.selectedItem.teamid );
}

private function makeDataTip( hd:HitData ):String {
  return "Hits <b>"+hd.item.h+"</b><br/>Doubles <b>"+
    hd.item['2b']+"</b>";
}
]]>
</mx:Script>
```

8

```
<mx:RemoteObject id="baseballRO"
  endpoint="http://localhost/amfphp/gateway.php"
  source="baseball.BaseballService"
  destination="baseball.BaseballService"
  showBusyCursor="true">
<mx:method name="getYearsByTeam" result="onYearsResult()">
<mx:arguments>
  <mx:Team />
</mx:arguments>
</mx:method>
<mx:method name="getTeamList" result="onTeamsList()" />
</mx:RemoteObject>

<mx:VBox paddingBottom="10" paddingLeft="10"
  paddingRight="10" paddingTop="10" backgroundColor="white"
  backgroundAlpha="0.4" borderColor="#cccccc"
  cornerRadius="15" borderThickness="3" borderStyle="solid"
  width="100%" height="100%">

<mx:HBox>
<mx:ComboBox id="teamSelector" labelField="name"
  change="onTeamChange()" />
<mx:Legend dataProvider="{areaChart}" direction="horizontal" />
</mx:HBox>

<mx:AreaChart id="areaChart" dataTipFunction="makeDataTip"
   type="stacked" width="100%" height="100%">

<mx:backgroundElements>
<degrafa:Surface>
  <degrafa:fills>
    <degrafa:SolidFill id="whiteFill" color="white" alpha="0.6" />
  </degrafa:fills>
  <degrafa:GeometryGroup>
    <degrafa:RegularRectangle x="0" y="0" width="{areaChart.width}"
     height="{areaChart.height}"
        fill="{whiteFill}" />
  </degrafa:GeometryGroup>
</degrafa:Surface>
<mx:GridLines>
  <mx:horizontalStroke>
    <mx:Stroke color="#bbbbbb" />
  </mx:horizontalStroke>
</mx:GridLines>
</mx:backgroundElements>
```

```
      <mx:verticalAxis>
        <mx:LinearAxis title="Count" />
      </mx:verticalAxis>

      <mx:horizontalAxis>
        <mx:CategoryAxis title="Year" categoryField="yearid" />
      </mx:horizontalAxis>

      <mx:series>
        <mx:AreaSeries xField="yearid" yField="h" displayName="Hits">
          <mx:areaFill><mx:SolidColor color="#99ff99" /></mx:areaFill>
          <mx:areaStroke><mx:Stroke color="#00ff00" weight="3" />
          </mx:areaStroke>
        </mx:AreaSeries>
        <mx:AreaSeries xField="yearid" yField="2b" displayName="Doubles">
          <mx:areaFill><mx:SolidColor color="#ff9999" /></mx:areaFill>
          <mx:areaStroke><mx:Stroke color="#ff0000" weight="3" />
          </mx:areaStroke>
        </mx:AreaSeries>
        <mx:AreaSeries xField="yearid" yField="3b" displayName="Triples">
          <mx:areaFill><mx:SolidColor color="#9999ff" /></mx:areaFill>
          <mx:areaStroke><mx:Stroke color="#0000ff" weight="3" />
          </mx:areaStroke>
        </mx:AreaSeries>
        <mx:AreaSeries xField="yearid" yField="hr" displayName="Home runs">
          <mx:areaFill><mx:SolidColor color="#ff99ff" /></mx:areaFill>
          <mx:areaStroke><mx:Stroke color="#ff00ff" weight="3" />
          </mx:areaStroke>
        </mx:AreaSeries>
      </mx:series>
    </mx:AreaChart>
  </mx:VBox>

</mx:Application>
```

This application allows the customer to select one of the many different baseball teams in the data set. It then displays the chart for that particular team. The ActionScript code, located at the top of the file, sets the dataProvider of the teamSelector combo box object. It also responds to a selection change by setting the dataProvider of the graph in the onTeamChange method.

The RemoteObject tag, located in the center of the file, defines the two methods that we will use when we access the baseball data set. These are getTeamList, which returns a list of the team names, and getYearsByTeam, which returns a record set where each row is a year for the specified team and contains aggregate statistics for that year.

The user interface for the application, which is specified with the tags at the bottom of the file, consists of a Panel that contains all of the controls, along with a combo box to select the team. The majority of the tags are used to define the AreaChart itself, which defines a linear axis for the vertical element, and a category axis for the years along the horizontal. It then defines a series array with four AreaSeries objects, one for each single (hit), double (2b), triple (3b), and home run (hr).

The Legend control, located at the bottom of the file, gives the customer some sense of what all of the colors mean.

When we bring this up in Flex Builder 3, we should see something like Figure 8-4.

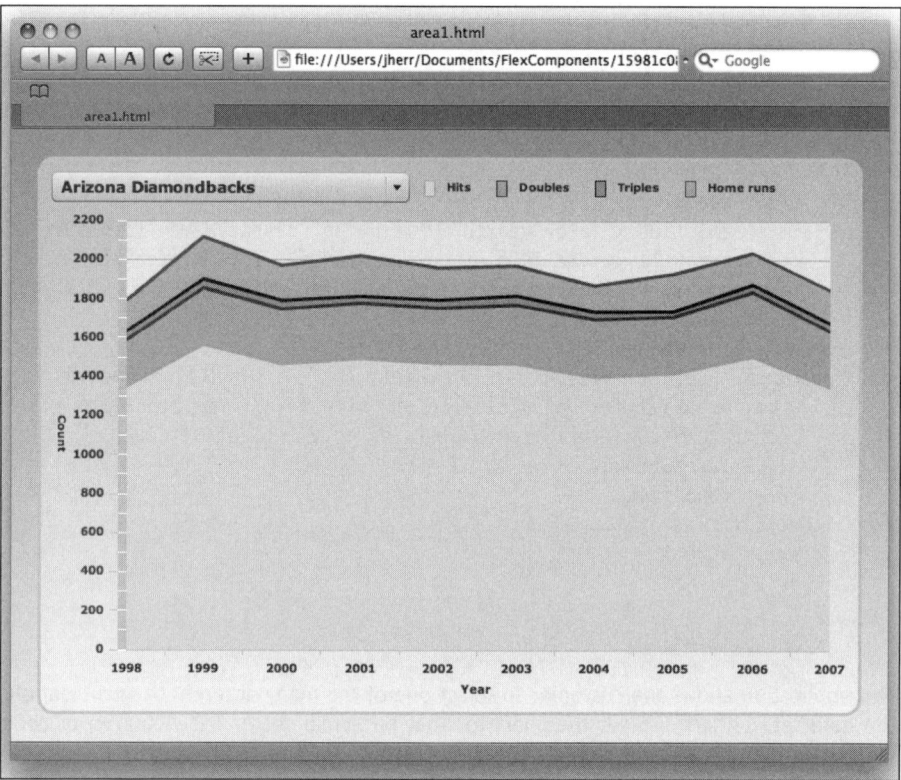

**Figure 8-4.** The batting counts for the Arizona Diamondbacks

This is actually a remarkable fun little application to play with if you are a baseball stats buff.

# Interactive scatter plotting

Flex presents you with a real opportunity to go above and beyond what users expect from a web application. For example, Flex makes it easy to add drag and drop, which is a real benefit to the feel of the application.

In this example, I'll use the football database along with drag-and-drop capability to allow users to compare quarterbacks using a scatter chart.

The code for this application is shown here:

```
<?xml version="1.0" encoding="utf-8"?>
<mx:Application xmlns:mx="http://www.adobe.com/2006/mxml"
  layout="absolute"
  creationComplete="searchPlayers()"
  xmlns:degrafa="http://www.degrafa.com/2007">

<mx:Style>
Application {
  background-gradient-colors: #66FF66, #eeffee;
  font-weight: bold;
  font-size: 14;
}
</mx:Style>

<mx:Script>
<![CDATA[
import mx.graphics.SolidColor;
import mx.graphics.Stroke;
import mx.charts.series.PlotSeries;
import mx.core.UIComponent;
import mx.managers.DragManager;
import mx.events.DragEvent;
import mx.charts.HitData;

private var requestPlayer:Object = null;

private function searchPlayers() : void {
  footballRO.findPlayer.send( srchText.text );
}

private function onFindPlayer() : void {
  var players:Array = footballRO.findPlayer.lastResult;
  for each( var player:Object in players ) {
    player.name = player.first + " " + player.last;
  }
  playerList.dataProvider = players;
}
```

```
private function onPlayerDblClick() : void {
  requestPlayer = playerList.selectedItem;
  footballRO.getGamesByPlayer.send( playerList.selectedItem.id );
}

private var dataSeriesList:Array = [];

private var fills:Array = [ 0xFF0000, 0x00FF00, 0x0000FF ];

private function onGamesByPlayer() : void {
  var ls:PlotSeries = new PlotSeries();
  ls.displayName = requestPlayer.first + " " + requestPlayer.last;
  ls.xField = "passyd";
  ls.yField = "att";
  ls.setStyle( 'stroke', new Stroke( fills[ dataSeriesList.length ], ➥
1 ) );
  ls.setStyle( 'fill', new SolidColor( fills[ ➥
dataSeriesList.length ], 0.5 ) );
  ls.setStyle( 'radius', 10 );
  ls.dataProvider = footballRO.getGamesByPlayer.lastResult;

  dataSeriesList.push( ls );

  lineChart.series = dataSeriesList;
}

private function makeDataTip( hd:HitData ) : String {
  return "<b>"+hd.item.team+"</b> "+hd.item.year+" week "+hd.item.week;
}

private function onDragDrop( event:DragEvent ) : void {
  var items:Array = event.dragSource.dataForFormat("items") as Array;
  for each( var player:Object in items ) {
    requestPlayer = player;
    footballRO.getGamesByPlayer.send( player.id );
  }
}

private function onDragEnter( event:DragEvent ) : void {
  var dragInitiator:UIComponent = UIComponent(event.currentTarget);
  DragManager.acceptDragDrop( dragInitiator );
}

private function onDragOver( event:DragEvent ) : void {
  DragManager.showFeedback( DragManager.COPY );
}
]]>
</mx:Script>
```

```
<mx:RemoteObject id="footballRO"
  endpoint="http://localhost/amfphp/gateway.php"
  source="football.FootballService"
  destination="football.FootballService"
  showBusyCursor="true">
<mx:method name="findPlayer" result="onFindPlayer()">
<mx:arguments>
  <mx:Name />
</mx:arguments>
</mx:method>
<mx:method name="getGamesByPlayer" result="onGamesByPlayer()">
<mx:arguments>
  <mx:Player />
</mx:arguments>
</mx:method>
</mx:RemoteObject>

<mx:VBox paddingBottom="15" paddingLeft="15"
  paddingRight="15" paddingTop="15" backgroundColor="#cccccc"
  borderColor="#eeeeee" cornerRadius="15" borderThickness="3"
  borderStyle="solid"
  width="90%" height="90%" top="30" left="30"
  dragEnter="onDragEnter(event)" dragOver="onDragOver(event)"
  dragDrop="onDragDrop(event)">
<mx:filters>
  <mx:DropShadowFilter distance="10" alpha="0.7" />
</mx:filters>

<mx:PlotChart width="100%" height="100%" id="lineChart"
  showDataTips="true" dataTipFunction="makeDataTip">

<mx:backgroundElements>
<degrafa:Surface>
  <degrafa:fills>
   <degrafa:SolidFill id="whiteFill" color="white" />
  </degrafa:fills>
  <degrafa:GeometryGroup>
    <degrafa:RegularRectangle x="0" y="0" width="{lineChart.width}"
    height="{lineChart.height}"
      fill="{whiteFill}" />
  </degrafa:GeometryGroup>
</degrafa:Surface>
<mx:GridLines direction="both">
  <mx:horizontalStroke>
   <mx:Stroke color="#bbbbbb" />
  </mx:horizontalStroke>
  <mx:verticalStroke>
   <mx:Stroke color="#bbbbbb" />
  </mx:verticalStroke>
```

8

```
        </mx:GridLines>
      </mx:backgroundElements>

      <mx:verticalAxis>
        <mx:LinearAxis title="Attempts" />
      </mx:verticalAxis>
      <mx:horizontalAxis>
        <mx:LinearAxis title="Yards" />
      </mx:horizontalAxis>
    </mx:PlotChart>
    <mx:Legend dataProvider="{lineChart}" direction="horizontal" />

  </mx:VBox>

  <mx:Panel title="Search" width="200" height="150" paddingBottom="5"
    paddingLeft="5"
    paddingRight="5" paddingTop="5" layout="vertical" left="600" top="10"
    borderAlpha="0.8">
    <mx:TextInput width="100%" id="srchText" text="Aikman"
     keyUp="searchPlayers()" />
    <mx:List id="playerList" width="100%" height="100%" labelField="name"
      doubleClickEnabled="true" doubleClick="onPlayerDblClick()"
      dragEnabled="true" />
  </mx:Panel>

</mx:Application>
```

At the top of the application file is the ActionScript code that handles not only the search functionality we have seen in previous NFL data-set applications, but also some new methods, onDragEnter, onDragDrop, and onDragOver, that allow you to drag players right from the list box and onto the line chart. These methods make use of the DragManager, which is built into the Flex framework.

The RemoteObject code is the same as the previous NFL example, so I have omitted it from this code listing. You can download the complete source code from the downloads area of the friends of ED web site (http://www.friendsofed.com).

The user interface code at the bottom is structurally the same as in the previous NFL example. But in this new code, the list box has dragEnabled set to true.

The PlotChart control is what the Flex framework calls a **scatter plot**. In this case, there are no series arrays defined because the onGamesByPlayer method in the ActionScript section adds a series to the chart dynamically.

When we bring this example up in Flex Builder, it starts out with an empty scatter plot. From there, I drag Troy Aikman onto the chart, and that plots his passing attempts versus total yards on the chart. This is shown in Figure 8-5.

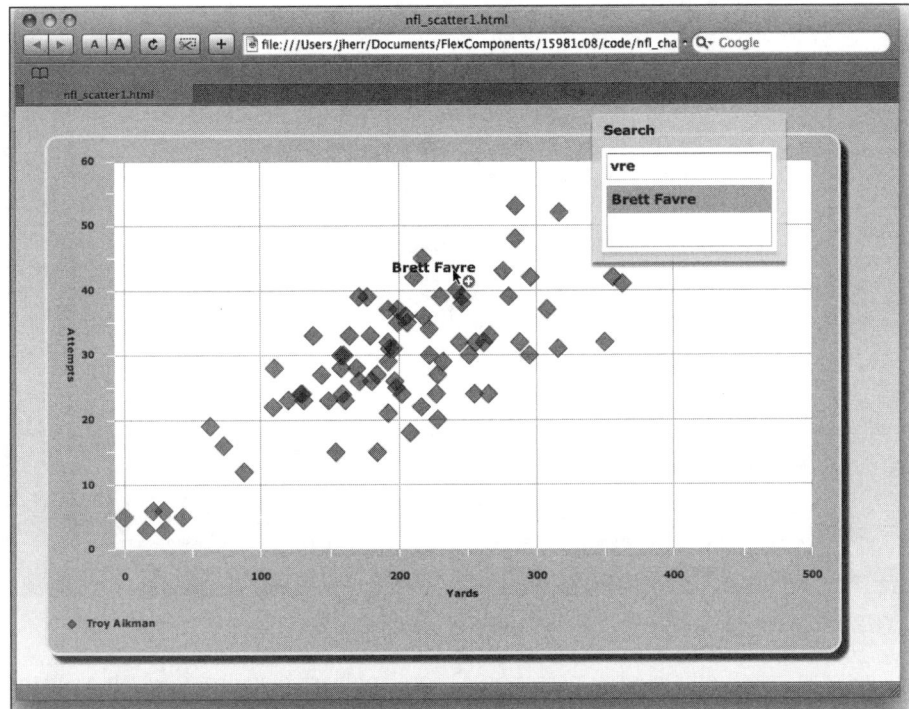

**Figure 8-5.** Troy Aikman's scatter plot

From there, you can search for Brett Favre, the quarterback of the Green Bay Packers, and drag his name onto the graph. This will result in the graph that you see in Figure 8-6.

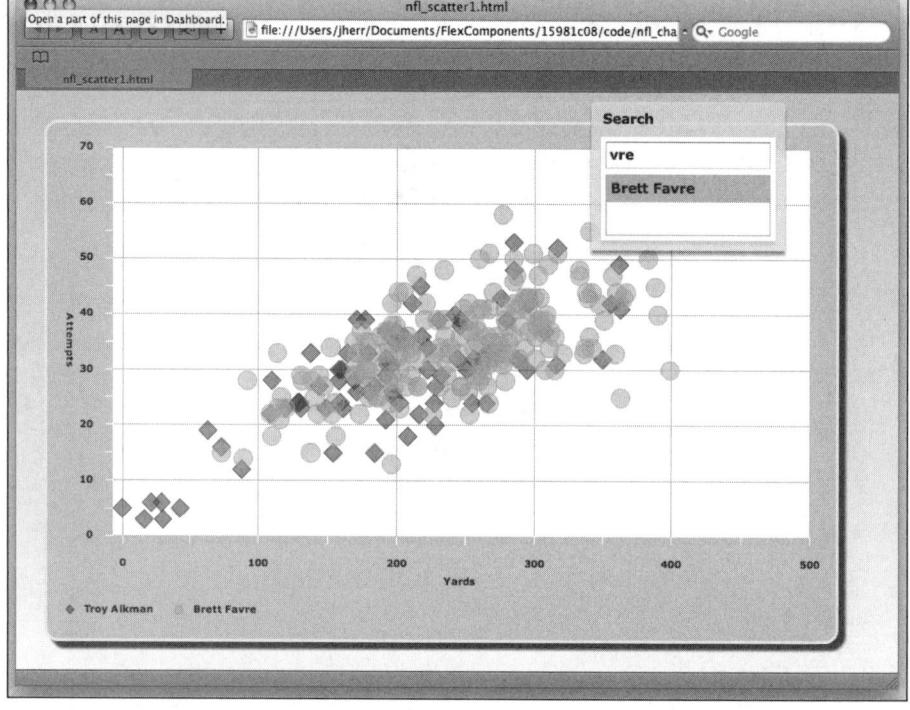

**Figure 8-6.** After adding Brett Favre to the graph

As you can see, Brett's numbers are a little more compact than Troy's, which gives the impression that his performance is a bit more consistent.

## Radar charts

Radar charts are a popular way of comparing metrics between categories without implying importance based upon position on a horizontal or vertical axis. Because all of the elements radiate out from the center of a circle, no particular element is given extra weight.

Radar charts are not built into the framework like the other graphs. To get radar charts, you need to download the Elixir package from ILOG. I show you how to install Elixir in Chapter 3, which uses it almost exclusively to present 3D graphs.

In this example, I'll use the radar chart to show the number of attempts and completions for a given quarterback versus each team he competes against. The code for the application is shown here:

```
<?xml version="1.0" encoding="utf-8"?>
<mx:Application xmlns:mx="http://www.adobe.com/2006/mxml"
  layout="absolute" creationComplete="searchPlayers()"
  xmlns:ilog="http://www.ilog.com/2007/ilog/flex">
```

```
<mx:Style>
...
</mx:Style>

<mx:Script>
...
</mx:Script>

<mx:RemoteObject ...>
...
</mx:RemoteObject>

<mx:VBox paddingBottom="15" paddingLeft="15" paddingRight="15"
  paddingTop="15" backgroundColor="#cccccc"
  borderColor="#eeeeee" cornerRadius="15" borderThickness="3"
  borderStyle="solid"
  width="90%" height="90%" top="30" left="30">
<mx:filters>
  <mx:DropShadowFilter distance="10" alpha="0.7" />
</mx:filters>

<ilog:RadarChart width="100%" height="100%" id="radarChart">
<ilog:angularAxis>
  <ilog:AngularAxis categoryField="opp" displayName="Opponent" />
</ilog:angularAxis>
<ilog:radialAxis>
  <mx:LinearAxis displayName="Completions" />
</ilog:radialAxis>
  <ilog:series>
    <ilog:RadarLineSeries dataField="comp" displayName="Completions" />
    <ilog:RadarLineSeries dataField="att" displayName="Attempts" />
  </ilog:series>
</ilog:RadarChart>
<mx:Legend dataProvider="{radarChart}" direction="horizontal" />

</mx:VBox>

<mx:Panel title="Search" width="200" height="150" paddingBottom="5"
  paddingLeft="5"
  paddingRight="5" paddingTop="5" layout="vertical" left="500" top="10"
  borderAlpha="0.8">
  <mx:TextInput width="100%" id="srchText" text="Aikman"
  keyUp="searchPlayers()" />
  <mx:List id="playerList" width="100%" height="100%" labelField="name"
      doubleClickEnabled="true" doubleClick="onPlayerDblClick()"
          dragEnabled="true" />
</mx:Panel>

</mx:Application>
```

8

I've omitted the ActionScript section, the RemoteObject section, and the search box code because that's exactly the same as with the other NFL examples. The big change comes at the bottom with the use of the ilog:RadarChart control.

As you can see, the RadarChart works exactly the same as the other built-in Flex charting controls. As with the other charts, you define a series array that in this case contains two RadarLineSeries objects, one for completions and one for attempts.

You can see the result of running this application in Figure 8-7.

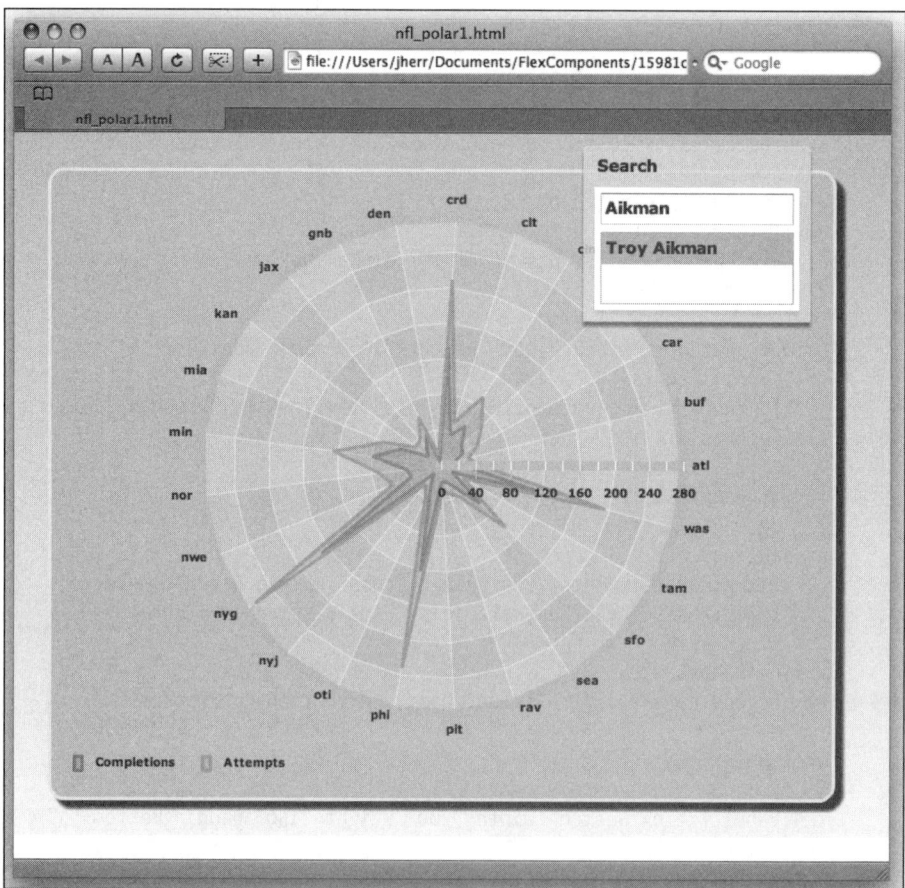

**Figure 8-7.** The radar line chart for Aikman against the other teams

From this, you can see that Aikman does really well against teams like the New York Giants, but not so well against other teams like the Green Bay Packers.

Another option with radar charts is to use columns instead of lines. I've updated the application to use columns in the following code:

```xml
<?xml version="1.0" encoding="utf-8"?>
<mx:Application xmlns:mx="http://www.adobe.com/2006/mxml"
  layout="absolute" creationComplete="searchPlayers()"
  xmlns:ilog="http://www.ilog.com/2007/ilog/flex">

 <mx:Style>
...
</mx:Style>

<mx:Script>
...
</mx:Script>

<mx:RemoteObject ...>
...
</mx:RemoteObject>

<mx:VBox paddingBottom="15" paddingLeft="15"
  paddingRight="15" paddingTop="15" backgroundColor="#cccccc"
  borderColor="#eeeeee" cornerRadius="15" borderThickness="3"
  borderStyle="solid"
  width="90%" height="90%" top="30" left="30">
<mx:filters>
  <mx:DropShadowFilter distance="10" alpha="0.7" />
</mx:filters>

<ilog:RadarChart width="100%" height="100%" id="radarChart">
<ilog:angularAxis>
  <ilog:AngularAxis categoryField="opp" displayName="Opponent" />
</ilog:angularAxis>
<ilog:radialAxis>
  <mx:LinearAxis displayName="Completions" />
</ilog:radialAxis>
  <ilog:series>
    <ilog:RadarColumnSeries dataField="comp"
    displayName="Completions" />
    <ilog:RadarColumnSeries dataField="att"
    displayName="Attempts" />
  </ilog:series>
</ilog:RadarChart>
<mx:Legend dataProvider="{radarChart}" direction="horizontal" />

</mx:VBox>

<mx:Panel title="Search" width="200" height="150" paddingBottom="5"
  paddingLeft="5"
  paddingRight="5" paddingTop="5" layout="vertical" left="500" top="10"
  borderAlpha="0.8">
  <mx:TextInput width="100%" id="srchText" text="Aikman"
```

8

```
            keyUp="searchPlayers()" />
      <mx:List id="playerList" width="100%" height="100%" labelField="name"
        doubleClickEnabled="true" doubleClick="onPlayerDblClick()"
                dragEnabled="true" />
    </mx:Panel>

    </mx:Application>
```

The code is almost exactly the same but for the change from using RadarLineSeries to RadarColumnSeries objects. You can see the difference in Figure 8-8.

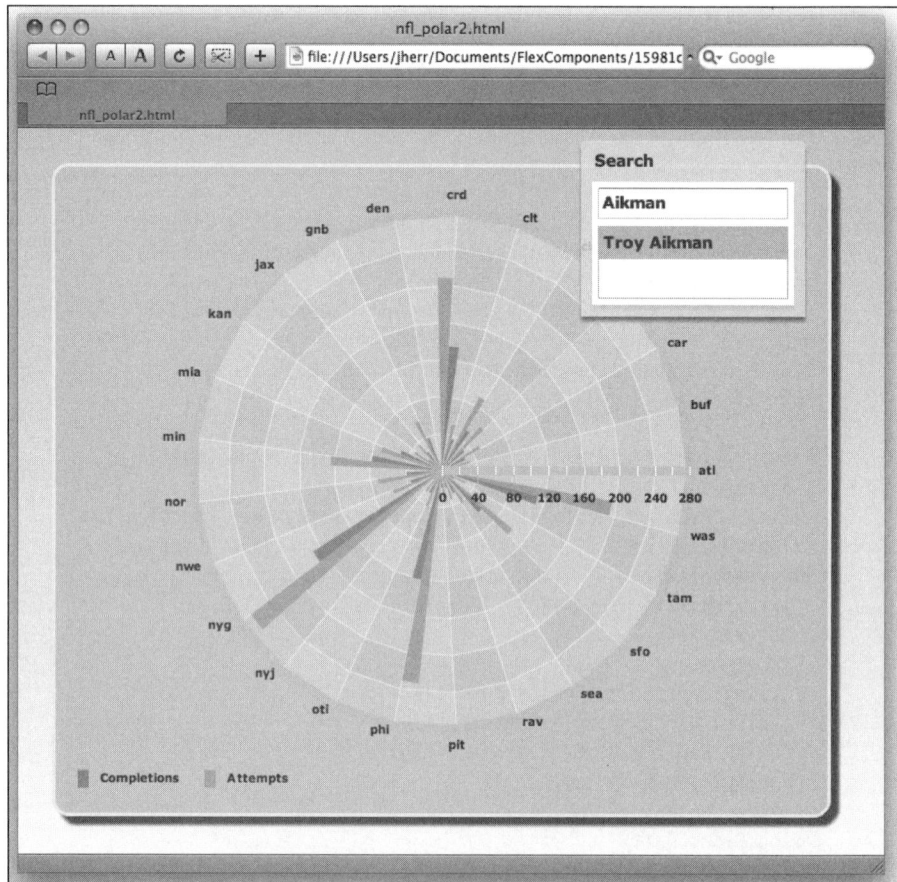

**Figure 8-8.** The radar column control

If you want to mix and match the line and column series in a single radar chart, Elixir is flexible enough to do that. You just use both RadarColumnSeries objects as well as RadarLineSeries objects attached to the same chart.

# Pie charts

My last example data visualization for this chapter is a pie chart. Pie charts are a common, if almost too common, way to contrast elements within a data set. In this example, I'll use the football data set to show how a player stacks up against various teams.

Here's the code for this application:

```
<?xml version="1.0" encoding="utf-8"?>
<mx:Application xmlns:mx="http://www.adobe.com/2006/mxml"
  layout="absolute"
  creationComplete="searchPlayers()"
  xmlns:degrafa="http://www.degrafa.com/2007">

<mx:Style>
...
</mx:Style>

<mx:Script>
...
</mx:Script>

<mx:RemoteObject ...>
...
</mx:RemoteObject>

<mx:VBox paddingBottom="15" paddingLeft="15" paddingRight="15"
  paddingTop="15" backgroundColor="#cccccc"
  borderColor="#eeeeee" cornerRadius="15" borderThickness="3"
  borderStyle="solid"
  width="90%" height="90%" top="30" left="30">
<mx:filters>
  <mx:DropShadowFilter distance="10" alpha="0.7" />
</mx:filters>

<mx:PieChart width="100%" height="100%" id="pieChart"
  showDataTips="true" dataTipFunction="makeOpponentTip">
<mx:series>
  <mx:PieSeries field="comp" explodeRadius="0.1" />
</mx:series>
</mx:PieChart>

</mx:VBox>

<mx:Panel title="Search" width="200" height="150" paddingBottom="5"
  paddingLeft="5"
  paddingRight="5" paddingTop="5" layout="vertical" left="400" top="10"
  borderAlpha="0.8">
  <mx:TextInput width="100%" id="srchText" text="Aikman"
```

8

```
        keyUp="searchPlayers()" />
      <mx:List id="playerList" width="100%" height="100%" labelField="name"
        doubleClickEnabled="true" doubleClick="onPlayerDblClick()"
        dragEnabled="true" />
    </mx:Panel>

  </mx:Application>
```

I shortened this code because most of it is the same as that for the previous NFL examples. The difference comes at the bottom where I use a PieChart to represent the data. In this case, we are comparing the number of completions (caught passes) between each of the opponents that the quarterback has faced.

When we bring this up from Flex Builder 3, we see something like Figure 8-9.

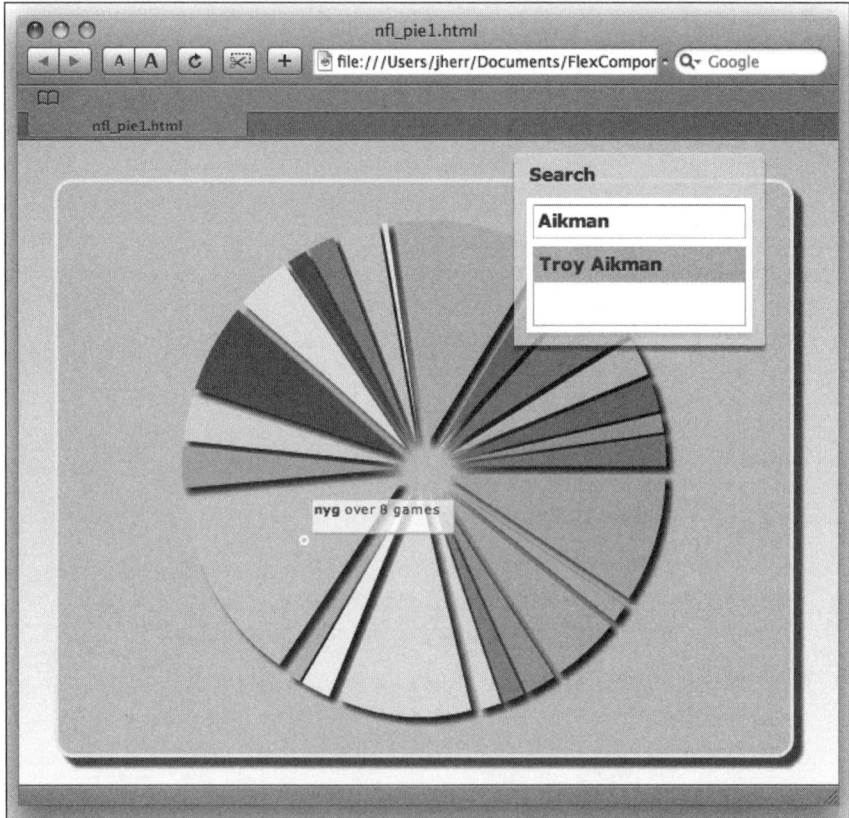

**Figure 8-9.** Troy Aikman's completions against various teams

To make it look a little prettier, I've set the exploded radius, which moves the wedges out from the center a little. The pie chart control allows you to change the exploded radius of individual elements if you want.

I've also chosen to display tooltips all the time by setting showAllDataTips to true. You can set that to false to remove visual clutter if you want. You can then use a legend to link the colors to a name. But with this many opponents, that might be a problem for the user.

# Sparklines

Sparklines are an effective way to put a lot of data into a small amount of space. They are graphs without axis markings used to connote general trends in the data. In this example application, we are going to use a Degrafa-based Sparkline component (http://www.insideria.com/2008/04/degrafa-data-part-2-the-sparkl.html) to render the winning lines for each of the teams shown in a ComboBox.

The demonstration code that shows sparklines in a combo box is as follows:

```
<?xml version="1.0" encoding="utf-8"?>
<mx:Application xmlns:mx="http://www.adobe.com/2006/mxml"
  layout="vertical"
  creationComplete="baseballRO.getTeamList.send()">

<mx:RemoteObject id="baseballRO"
  endpoint="http://localhost/amfphp/gateway.php"
  source="baseball.BaseballService"
  destination="baseball.BaseballService"
  showBusyCursor="true">
<mx:method name="getTeamList" />
</mx:RemoteObject>

<mx:Panel title="Team Stats" paddingBottom="5" paddingLeft="5"
  paddingRight="5" paddingTop="5" width="100%" height="100%">
<mx:ComboBox dataProvider="{baseballRO.getTeamList.lastResult}"
  itemRenderer="SparkRenderer"
  labelField="name" width="400">
</mx:ComboBox>
</mx:Panel>

</mx:Application>
```

This application gets the list of baseball teams and feeds that to the ComboBox. It's the itemRenderer, which is assigned to the SparkRenderer, that does the majority of the work. The code for the SparkRenderer is shown here:

```
<?xml version="1.0" encoding="utf-8"?>
<mx:HBox xmlns:mx="http://www.adobe.com/2006/mxml" width="300"
    height="50"
  dataChange="onDataChange()" creationComplete="onDataChange()"
  xmlns:sparkline="sparkline.*"
```

```
    xmlns:degrafa="http://www.degrafa.com/2007"
    horizontalScrollPolicy="off" verticalScrollPolicy="off">

<mx:Script>
<![CDATA[
import mx.collections.ArrayCollection;

private function onDataResult() : void {
  if ( baseballRO.getYearsByTeam.lastResult.length == 0 ||
       baseballRO.getYearsByTeam.lastResult[0].teamid != data.teamid )
    return;

  var sparkData:ArrayCollection = new ArrayCollection();
  var min:Number = Number.MAX_VALUE;
  var max:Number = Number.MIN_VALUE;
  for each ( var res:Object in baseballRO.getYearsByTeam.lastResult ) {
    var wins:Number = Number( res.w );
    min = Math.min( wins, min );
    max = Math.max( wins, max );
    sparkData.addItem( { wins: wins } );
  }
  spark.minimum = min;
  spark.maximum = max;
  spark.dataProvider = sparkData;
}
private function onDataChange() : void {
  if ( data != null && initialized )
    baseballRO.getYearsByTeam.send( data.teamid );
}
]]>
</mx:Script>

<mx:RemoteObject id="baseballRO"
  endpoint="http://localhost/amfphp/gateway.php"
  source="baseball.BaseballService"
  destination="baseball.BaseballService"
  showBusyCursor="true">
<mx:method name="getYearsByTeam" result="onDataResult()">
<mx:arguments>
  <mx:Team />
</mx:arguments>
</mx:method>
</mx:RemoteObject>

<sparkline:Sparkline width="150" height="30" id="spark"
  dataField="wins">
<sparkline:lineStroke>
<degrafa:LinearGradientStroke angle="0" weight="3">
<degrafa:gradientStops>
```

```
          <degrafa:GradientStop color="#330000" ratio="0" />
          <degrafa:GradientStop color="#FF0000" ratio="1" />
        </degrafa:gradientStops>
      </degrafa:LinearGradientStroke>
    </sparkline:lineStroke>
  </sparkline:Sparkline>
  <mx:Label text="{data.name}" fontSize="14" fontWeight="bold" />

</mx:HBox>
```

This code runs the getYearsByTeam query with the current teamid. It then gets the results and sets the Sparkline data provider to it. The Sparkline component then does all of the work of rendering the minigraph. You can see the result in Figure 8-10.

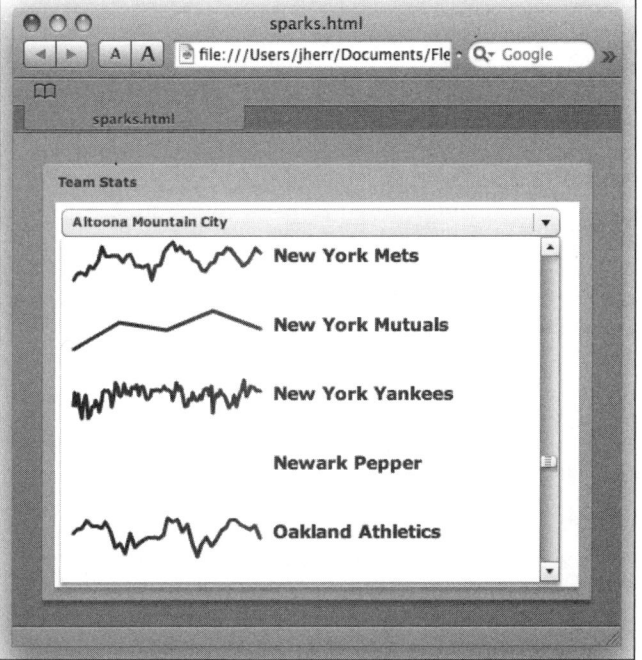

**Figure 8-10.** The sparkline combo box

Sparklines were popularized by Edward Tufte, who has several excellent books out on data visualization. If this component intrigues you, I think you should look into those books as well as perhaps attending one of Tufte's excellent lectures.

# Scientific plotting

There is an open source scientific plotting component (http://www.flashandmath.com/advanced/art/overview.html) that you can use to parse equations and show the result on a two-dimensional chart.

The simple application that follows shows how to use these custom scientific plotting components:

```
<?xml version="1.0" encoding="utf-8"?>
<mx:Application xmlns:mx="http://www.adobe.com/2006/mxml"
  layout="vertical" creationComplete="onStartup()">
<mx:Script>
<![CDATA[
import bkde.as3.boards.GraphingBoard;
import bkde.as3.parsers.MathParser;
import bkde.as3.parsers.CompiledObject;

private var gboard:GraphingBoard;

private function onStartup() : void {
  gboard = new GraphingBoard( plotHost.width, plotHost.height );
  plotHost.addChild( gboard );

  gboard.changeBorderColorAndThick(0,0);
  gboard.setAxesColorAndThick( 0xCCCCCC, 1 );

  runPlot();
}

private function runPlot() : void
{
  var procFun:MathParser = new MathParser(['x']);
  var co:CompiledObject = procFun.doCompile( funcText.text );

  var xDiffs:Array = [
    { diff:1, color: 0xFF0000 },
    { diff:2, color: 0x00FF00 },
    { diff:4, color: 0x0000FF },
    { diff:8, color: 0xFFFF00 }  ];

  gboard.cleanBoard();
  gboard.setVarsRanges(-10,10,-10,10);
  gboard.setMaxNumGraphs( xDiffs.length );
  gboard.drawAxes();
```

```
    for( var i:String in xDiffs )
    {
      var output:Array = new Array();
      for( var x:Number = -10; x < 10; x += 0.1 )
        output.push( [ x, procFun.doEval( co.PolishArray,
        [x / Number( xDiffs[i].diff ) ] ) ] );
      gboard.drawGraph( int(i) + 1, ( xDiffs.length + 1 ) - int(i),
      output, xDiffs[i].color );
    }
  }

  private function onResize() : void {
    if ( initialized == false ) return;
    gboard.width = plotHost.width;
    gboard.height = plotHost.height;
  }
  ]]>
  </mx:Script>
  <mx:Panel width="100%" height="100%" title="Math Plotter"
    paddingBottom="5" paddingLeft="5" paddingRight="5" paddingTop="5">
  <mx:HBox>
    <mx:TextInput id="funcText" text="sin(x*2)*10" />
    <mx:Button label="Plot" click="runPlot()" />
  </mx:HBox>
    <mx:UIComponent id="plotHost" width="100%" height="100%"
      resize="onResize()" />
  </mx:Panel>
  </mx:Application>
```

The onStartup method creates the GraphingBoard that will display the results of the equation. The runPlot function then parses the equation in the text input field with MathParser. It then uses a for loop to create four different traces, one for each of four different x multipliers. It's pretty bogus scientifically, but it sure makes for a pretty graph with the four different colors of traces.

The results of this are shown in Figure 8-11.

8

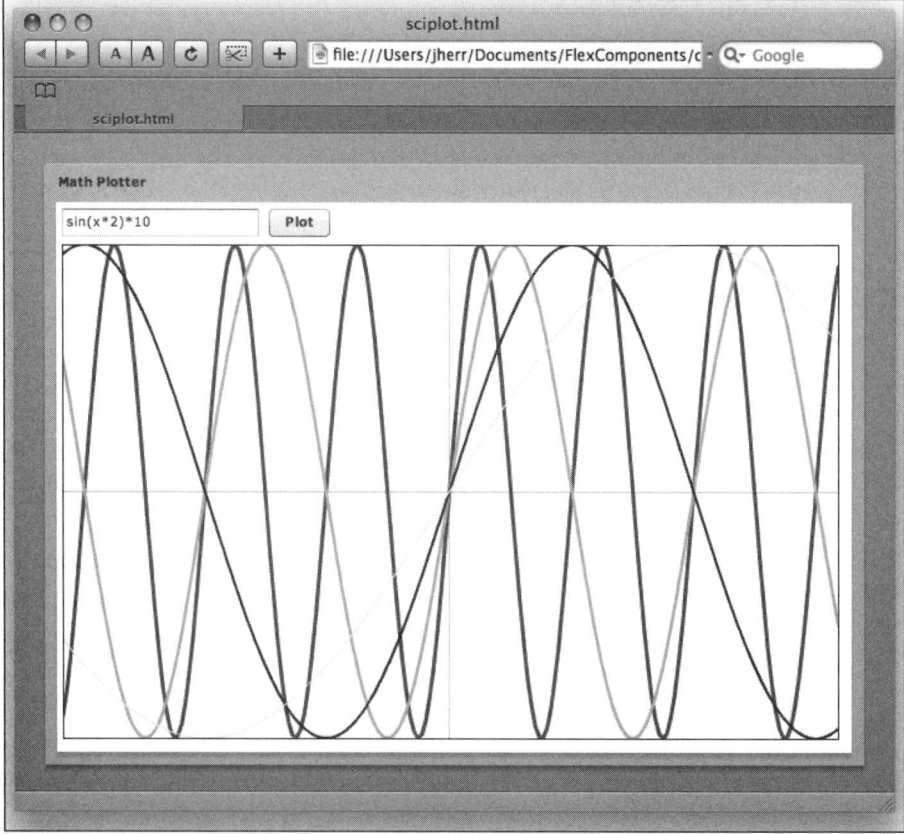

**Figure 8-11.** A scientific example showing the plot of a user-entered function. A simple equation is plotted with four different x multipliers and each trace is given an individual color.

This particular component also allows for users to draw on the graph and make annotations. I think the original intention was to use this as a math teaching tool, and it seems to do a pretty good job with that.

## Where we will go from here

The next stop on the data visualization express is to move from 2D to 3D. But before we go, let's consider the toolkit that Adobe and Elixir has given us here. It's very powerful, but more importantly, it makes it easy to adjust rapidly to the response of the customer. The best data visualizations aren't designed on a blackboard perfectly, and then implemented and passed to an immediately happy customer. Sometimes you may think the best way to go is with a radar chart, only to find that what made for the most effective visualization was a simple line chart with a few controls. The power of this framework is that you can make the necessary changes quickly, and you should avail yourself of the opportunities that provides.

# 9  3D GRAPHING COMPONENTS

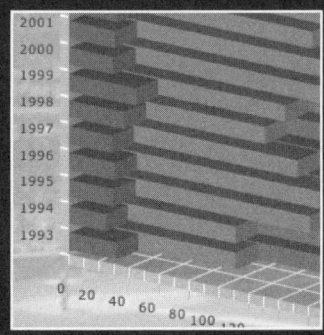 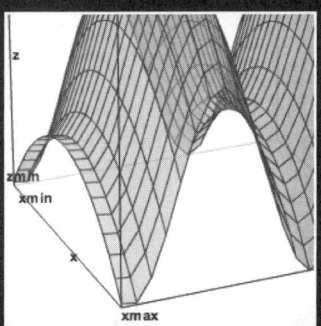 

Updated 6/22/08

Where the charting controls built into the Flex framework leave off is where component frameworks like the Elixir library from ILOG kick in. These frameworks provide additional 2D graphing components, like the Radar Chart and Tree Map (among others), but also provide 3D versions of some of the charts in the original Flex framework.

In this chapter, I'll demonstrate a few of these 3D charting components. To use these examples, you will need to install the data sources as well as the Elixir components. Instructions for installing all of these are in Chapter 2.

# Introducing 3D charts

Before I begin, a word of warning about 3D. While three dimensions can look sexier than two dimensions, it's important to realize that the third dimension ideally should have some meaning or add some value to the presentation. In some of these examples, the third dimension clearly adds value, but in others, for example the pie chart, it's strictly for looks. It's up to you to make the judgment call for your application. But I recommend taking a little bit of time trying to work the 2D version before jumping into 3D, because you might not gain any additional data in the third dimension.

## 3D area charts

What most people consider a 3D chart is a 2D bar chart where the bars have an artificial depth that implies a third dimension. Elixir provides that functionality, as well as bars or lines that are stacked in three dimensions, as a **3D area chart**.

An example use of the 3D area chart is shown in the application code that follows. This application uses the baseball data source and allows you to select a team. The doubles, triples, and home runs are then charted in the vertical axis against seasons in the horizontal axis. Adding the number of singles just blew the chart out.

```
<?xml version="1.0" encoding="utf-8"?>
<mx:Application xmlns:mx="http://www.adobe.com/2006/mxml"
  layout="absolute"
  creationComplete="baseballRO.getTeamList.send()"
  xmlns:ilog="http://www.ilog.com/2007/ilog/flex"
  xmlns:reflector="com.rictus.reflector.*"
  backgroundGradientColors="[#000000,#336666]">

<mx:Style>
.chartStyle {
  color: white;
}
</mx:Style>

<mx:Script>
<![CDATA[
import mx.charts.series.items.BubbleSeriesItem;
```

```
import mx.graphics.SolidColor;
import mx.charts.series.items.PlotSeriesItem;
import mx.graphics.IFill;
import mx.charts.ChartItem;
import mx.charts.HitData;

private function onYearsResult() : void {
  chart.dataProvider = baseballRO.getYearsByTeam.lastResult;
}

private function onTeamsList() : void {
  teamSelector.dataProvider = baseballRO.getTeamList.lastResult;
  teamSelector.selectedIndex = 0;
}

private function onTeamChange() : void {
  if ( teamSelector.selectedItem != null && teamSelector.➡
selectedItem.teamid != null )
    baseballRO.getYearsByTeam.send( teamSelector.selectedItem.teamid );
}

private function makeDataTip( hd:HitData ):String {
  return "Hits <b>"+hd.item.h+➡
"</b><br/>Doubles <b>"+hd.item['2b']+"</b>";
}

private var lastPt:Point = null;

private function onMouseDown( event:MouseEvent ) : void {
  lastPt = new Point( event.localX, event.localY );
}
private function onMouseUp( event:MouseEvent ) : void {
  lastPt = null;
}
private function onMouseMove( event:MouseEvent ) : void {
  if ( lastPt == null ) return;
  chart.rotationAngle += ( event.localX - lastPt.x ) * 0.2;
  chart.elevationAngle += ( event.localY - lastPt.y ) * 0.2;
  lastPt = new Point( event.localX, event.localY );
}
]]>
</mx:Script>

<mx:RemoteObject id="baseballRO"
  endpoint="http://localhost/amfphp/gateway.php"
  source="baseball.BaseballService"
  destination="baseball.BaseballService"
  showBusyCursor="true">
<mx:method name="getYearsByTeam" result="onYearsResult()">
```

9

```
<mx:arguments>
  <mx:Team />
</mx:arguments>
</mx:method>
<mx:method name="getTeamList" result="onTeamsList()" />
</mx:RemoteObject>

<ilog:AreaChart3D id="chart" type="overlaid" width="100%" height="70%"
  top="50"
  depthGap="10" dataTipFunction="makeDataTip" showDataTips="true"
  mouseDown="onMouseDown(event)" mouseUp="onMouseUp(event)"
  mouseMove="onMouseMove(event)"
  styleName="chartStyle">
<ilog:wallsFill>
  <mx:SolidColor color="0x666666" alpha="0.5"/>
</ilog:wallsFill>
 <ilog:horizontalAxis>
  <mx:CategoryAxis categoryField="yearid" />
</ilog:horizontalAxis>
<ilog:series>
  <ilog:AreaSeries3D xField="yearid" yField="2b"
  displayName="Doubles" />
  <ilog:AreaSeries3D xField="yearid" yField="hr"
  displayName="Homers" />
  <ilog:AreaSeries3D xField="yearid" yField="3b"
  displayName="Triples" />
</ilog:series>
</ilog:AreaChart3D>

<reflector:Reflector target="{chart}" alpha=".6"
  falloff=".3" blurAmount=".1"/>

<mx:Panel title="Teams" top="20" left="20" borderAlpha="0.4"
  backgroundAlpha="0.4">
<mx:ComboBox id="teamSelector" labelField="name"
  change="onTeamChange()" />
</mx:Panel>

</mx:Application>
```

The ActionScript code at the top of the application is split into two pieces. The onTeamChange, onTeamList, and onYearsResult are all related to getting the data from the server from the RemoteObject interface that is defined in the middle of the file. The application first requests the list of teams and uses that to populate the teamSelector combo box. It then makes the request to the server for the statistics for every season for the selected team when the user changes the team in the combo box. The onYearsResult is called when the statistics come back. Its job is to update the chart.

The makeDataTip method is used by the graph to present a data tip that is formatted correctly for the baseball data. The onMouseDown, onMouseUp, and onMouseMove methods allow the user to spin the graph by clicking it.

The interface itself is defined within a panel that tidies up the presentation. At the top of the panel is a combo box to select the team. Then within that is the AreaChart3D control from the Elixir framework. It contains a series array with three AreaSeries3D objects, one each for doubles, triples, and home runs.

When we bring this application up from Flex Builder 3 and select the Florida Marlins as the team, we see something like Figure 9-1.

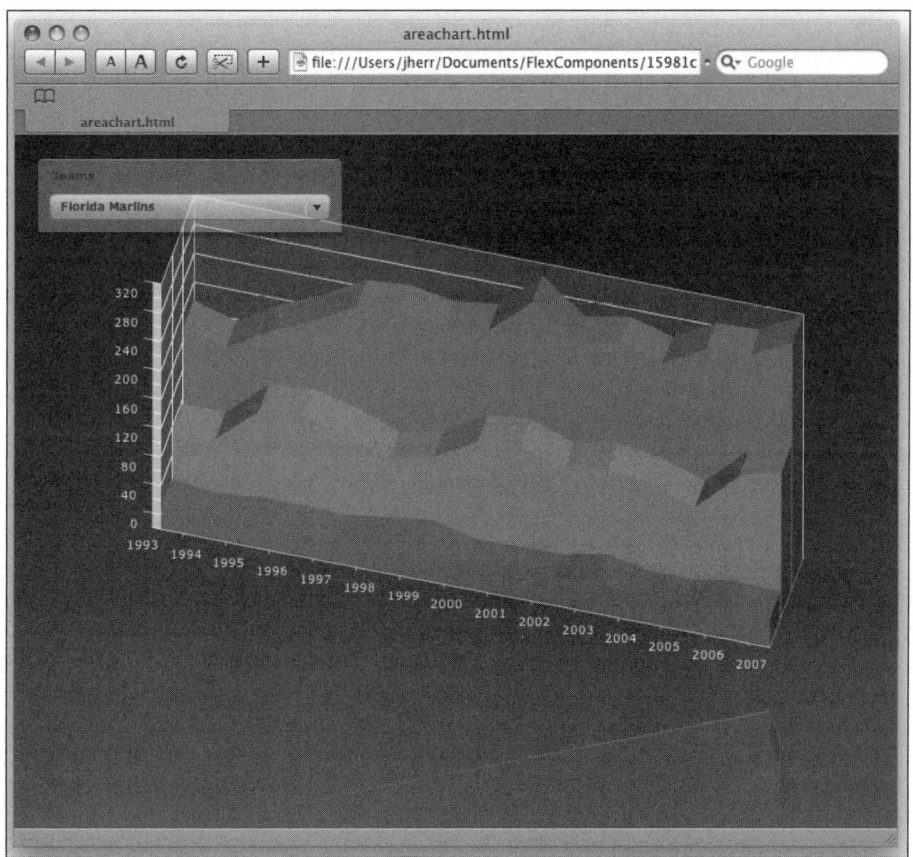

**Figure 9-1.** The Florida Marlins batting averages

We can click and drag on the graph to change the rotation in both the x and y axes.

## Stepped area chart

Stepped area charts are pretty common, so I want to give you a few more options. Shown here is the same application, but in this case I'm using a "step" type format to show the individual seasons as bars:

```
<?xml version="1.0" encoding="utf-8"?>
<mx:Application xmlns:mx="http://www.adobe.com/2006/mxml"
  layout="absolute"
  creationComplete="baseballRO.getTeamList.send()"
  xmlns:ilog="http://www.ilog.com/2007/ilog/flex"
  xmlns:reflector="com.rictus.reflector.*"
  backgroundGradientColors="[#000000,#336666]">

<mx:Script>
<![CDATA[
...
]]>
</mx:Script>

<mx:RemoteObject id="baseballRO" ...>
...
</mx:RemoteObject>

<ilog:AreaChart3D id="chart" type="overlaid" width="100%"
  height="70%" top="50"
  depthGap="10" dataTipFunction="makeDataTip" showDataTips="true"
  mouseDown="onMouseDown(event)" mouseUp="onMouseUp(event)"
  mouseMove="onMouseMove(event)"
  styleName="chartStyle">
<ilog:wallsFill>
  <mx:SolidColor color="0x666666" alpha="0.5"/>
</ilog:wallsFill>
<ilog:horizontalAxis>
  <mx:CategoryAxis categoryField="yearid" />
</ilog:horizontalAxis>
<ilog:series>
  <ilog:AreaSeries3D xField="yearid" yField="2b"
  displayName="Doubles" form="step">
    <ilog:stroke>
      <mx:Stroke color="#ff0000" weight="2" />
    </ilog:stroke>
    <ilog:fill>
      <mx:SolidColor color="#ff3333" />
    </ilog:fill>
  </ilog:AreaSeries3D>
  <ilog:AreaSeries3D xField="yearid" yField="hr"
  displayName="Homers" form="step">
    <ilog:stroke>
      <mx:Stroke color="#00ff00" weight="2" />
```

```
        </ilog:stroke>
        <ilog:fill>
          <mx:SolidColor color="#33ff33" />
        </ilog:fill>
      </ilog:AreaSeries3D>
      <ilog:AreaSeries3D xField="yearid" yField="3b"
      displayName="Triples" form="step">
        <ilog:stroke>
          <mx:Stroke color="#0000ff" weight="2" />
        </ilog:stroke>
        <ilog:fill>
          <mx:SolidColor color="#3333ff" />
        </ilog:fill>
      </ilog:AreaSeries3D>
    </ilog:series>
  </ilog:AreaChart3D>

  <reflector:Reflector target="{chart}" alpha=".6"
    falloff=".3" blurAmount=".1"/>

  <mx:Panel title="Teams" top="20" left="20" borderAlpha="0.4"
    backgroundAlpha="0.4">
  <mx:ComboBox id="teamSelector" labelField="name"
    change="onTeamChange()" />
  </mx:Panel>


  </mx:Application>
```

The only alteration in the code is the change in the series objects to use the "step" form and to specify the stroke and the color of each series. The result of these changes is shown in Figure 9-2.

**9**

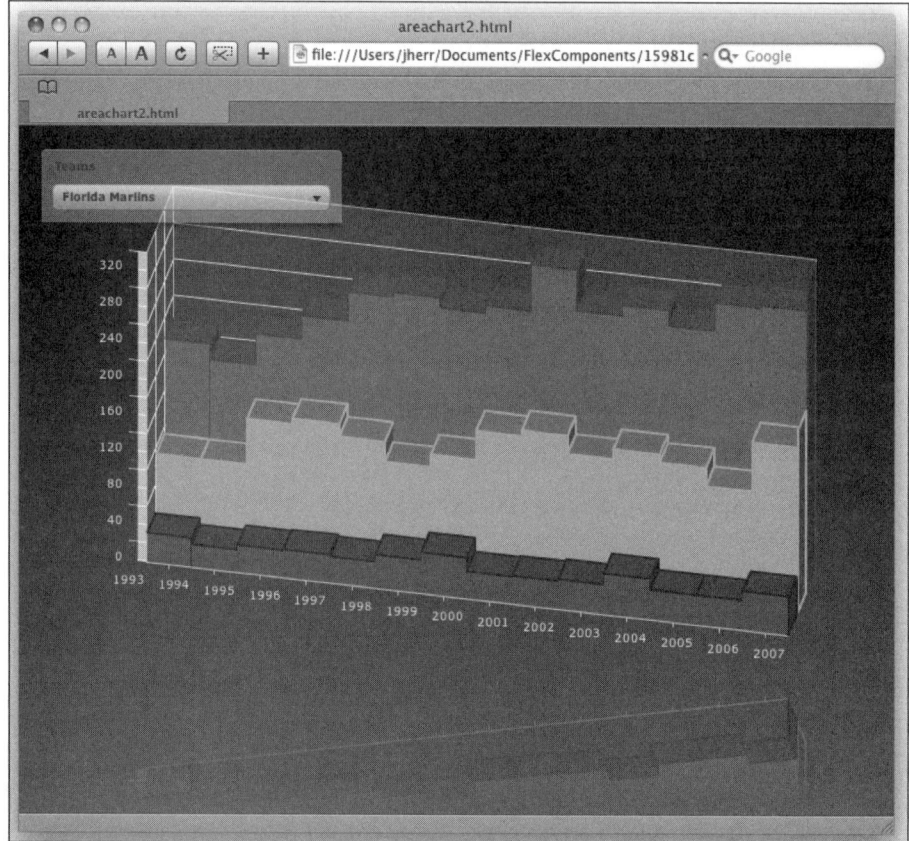

**Figure 9-2.** The updated area chart with bars instead of lines

## Stacked area chart

Another very popular option is the stacked model of the area chart. This is where the individual series are "stacked" on top of each other. This allows the user to see the total amount in any given category, and then see the contribution of each series.

Following is the area chart application, updated one final time to show the stacked display:

```
<?xml version="1.0" encoding="utf-8"?>
<mx:Application xmlns:mx="http://www.adobe.com/2006/mxml"
  layout="absolute"
  creationComplete="baseballRO.getTeamList.send()"
  xmlns:ilog="http://www.ilog.com/2007/ilog/flex"
  xmlns:reflector="com.rictus.reflector.*"
  backgroundGradientColors="[#000000,#336666]">

<mx:Script>
<![CDATA[
```

```
...
]]>
</mx:Script>

<mx:RemoteObject ...>
...
</mx:RemoteObject>

<ilog:AreaChart3D id="chart" type="stacked" width="100%"
  height="70%" top="50"
  depthGap="10" dataTipFunction="makeDataTip" showDataTips="true"
  mouseDown="onMouseDown(event)" mouseUp="onMouseUp(event)"
  mouseMove="onMouseMove(event)"
  styleName="chartStyle">
<ilog:wallsFill>
  <mx:SolidColor color="0x666666" alpha="0.5"/>
</ilog:wallsFill>
<ilog:horizontalAxis>
  <mx:CategoryAxis categoryField="yearid"
  labelFunction="myLabelFunc" />
</ilog:horizontalAxis>
<ilog:series>
  <ilog:AreaSeries3D xField="yearid" yField="2b"
  displayName="Doubles" />
  <ilog:AreaSeries3D xField="yearid" yField="hr"
  displayName="Homers" />
  <ilog:AreaSeries3D xField="yearid" yField="3b"
  displayName="Triples" />
</ilog:series>
</ilog:AreaChart3D>

<reflector:Reflector target="{chart}" alpha=".6"
  falloff=".3" blurAmount=".1"/>

<mx:Panel title="Teams" top="20" left="20" borderAlpha="0.4"
  backgroundAlpha="0.4">
<mx:ComboBox id="teamSelector" labelField="name"
  change="onTeamChange()" />
</mx:Panel>

</mx:Application>
```

I've removed the adjustments to each of the AreaSeries3D objects and added a type attribute to the AreaChart3D object that is set to stacked. You can see the result in Figure 9-3.

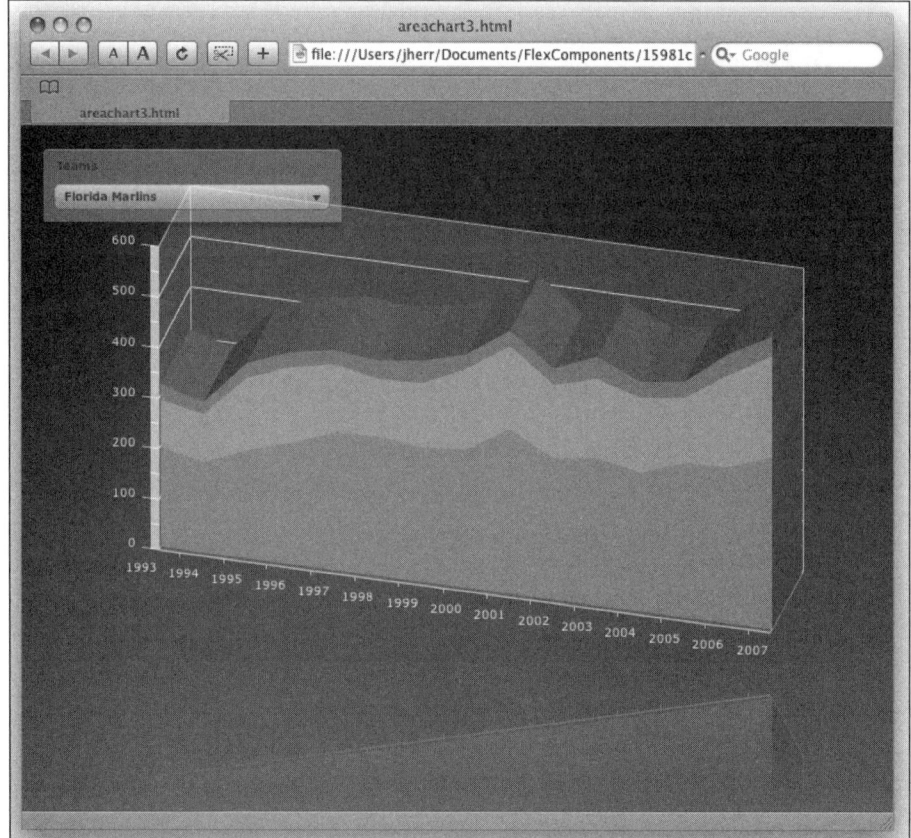

**Figure 9-3.** The stacked chart

In my own opinion, I think this is the best choice for this particular visualization. You can see the relative strength of the season along the ridge line. And then get a feel for the remarkably consistent contributions of the consistent parts by looking at the individual colors.

## 3D bar charts

Another alternative is the **bar chart**, which lays the bars out horizontally instead of vertically. The following application shows how a BarChart3D control can be applied to the baseball statistics example:

```
<?xml version="1.0" encoding="utf-8"?>
<mx:Application xmlns:mx="http://www.adobe.com/2006/mxml"
  layout="absolute"
  creationComplete="baseballRO.getTeamList.send()"
  xmlns:ilog="http://www.ilog.com/2007/ilog/flex"
  horizontalScrollPolicy="off" verticalScrollPolicy="off">
```

```
<mx:Script>
<![CDATA[
import mx.charts.series.items.BubbleSeriesItem;
import mx.graphics.SolidColor;
import mx.charts.series.items.PlotSeriesItem;
import mx.graphics.IFill;
import mx.charts.ChartItem;
import mx.charts.HitData;

private function onYearsResult() : void {
  chart.dataProvider = baseballRO.getYearsByTeam.lastResult;
}

private function onTeamsList() : void {
  teamSelector.dataProvider = baseballRO.getTeamList.lastResult;
  teamSelector.selectedIndex = 0;
}

private function onTeamChange() : void {
  if ( teamSelector.selectedItem != null &&
  teamSelector.selectedItem.teamid != null )
    baseballRO.getYearsByTeam.send( teamSelector.selectedItem.teamid );
}

private function makeDataTip( hd:HitData ):String {
  return "Hits <b>"+hd.item.h+"</b><br/>Doubles <b>"+➥
hd.item['2b']+"</b>";
}

private var lastPt:Point = null;

private function onMouseDown( event:MouseEvent ) : void {
  lastPt = new Point( event.localX, event.localY );
}
private function onMouseUp( event:MouseEvent ) : void {
  lastPt = null;
}
private function onMouseMove( event:MouseEvent ) : void {
  if ( lastPt == null ) return;
  chart.rotationAngle += ( event.localX - lastPt.x ) * 0.2;
  chart.elevationAngle += ( event.localY - lastPt.y );
  lastPt = new Point( event.localX, event.localY );
}
]]>
</mx:Script>

<mx:RemoteObject id="baseballRO"
  endpoint="http://localhost/amfphp/gateway.php"
  source="baseball.BaseballService"
```

9

```
            destination="baseball.BaseballService"
            showBusyCursor="true">
        <mx:method name="getYearsByTeam" result="onYearsResult()">
        <mx:arguments>
          <mx:Team />
        </mx:arguments>
        </mx:method>
        <mx:method name="getTeamList" result="onTeamsList()" />
        </mx:RemoteObject>

        <mx:Image width="1000" source="@Embed('background.jpg')">
          <mx:filters>
            <mx:BlurFilter blurX="4" blurY="4" />
          </mx:filters>
        </mx:Image>

        <mx:VBox paddingBottom="10" paddingLeft="10" paddingRight="19"
          paddingTop="10" verticalGap="10" width="85%" height="85%"
          top="50" left="50" borderThickness="4" borderColor="#dddddd"
          backgroundColor="white" backgroundAlpha="0.7"
          cornerRadius="15" borderStyle="solid"
          mouseDown="onMouseDown(event)" mouseUp="onMouseUp(event)"
          mouseMove="onMouseMove(event)">
        <mx:ComboBox id="teamSelector" labelField="name"
          change="onTeamChange()" />
        <ilog:BarChart3D id="chart" type="overlaid" width="100%" height="100%"
          depthGap="10" dataTipFunction="makeDataTip" showDataTips="true">
        <ilog:wallsFill>
          <mx:SolidColor color="0x226666" alpha="0.5"/>
        </ilog:wallsFill>
        <ilog:verticalAxis>
          <mx:CategoryAxis categoryField="yearid" />
        </ilog:verticalAxis>
        <ilog:series>
          <ilog:BarSeries3D yField="yearid" xField="2b" displayName="Doubles"/>
          <ilog:BarSeries3D yField="yearid" xField="hr" displayName="Homers"/>
          <ilog:BarSeries3D yField="yearid" xField="3b" displayName="Triples"/>
        </ilog:series>
        </ilog:BarChart3D>
        <mx:Legend dataProvider="{chart}" direction="horizontal" />
        </mx:VBox>

        </mx:Application>
```

Most of the code here remains the same as with the previous area chart examples. The difference is that the AreaChart3D control has been replaced by a BarChart3D control, and the series objects have been changed to BarSeries3D objects.

The result can be seen in Figure 9-4.

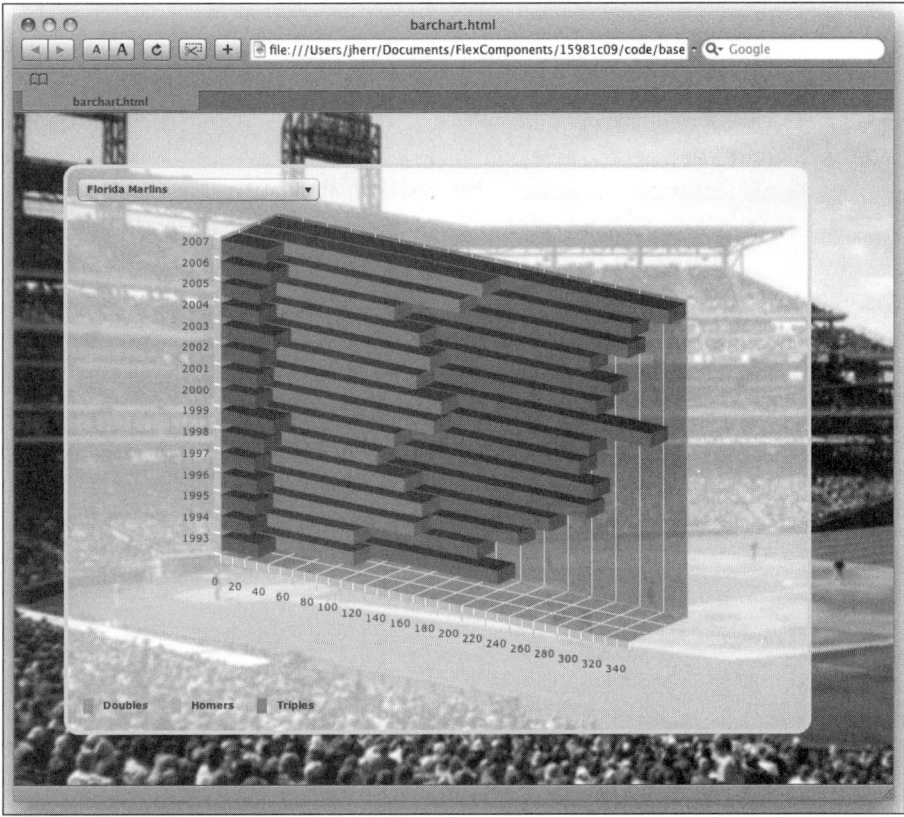

**Figure 9-4.** The bar chart example

As with the AreaChart3D control, you can change the format of the chart as well as the individual series objects.

## 3D pie charts

To illustrate 3D pie charts, I'm going to change the example application to use a more interesting rendering technique. We will still pick a baseball team, but in this case the application will render a list where each cell is a season and contains its own pie chart and bar chart.

This starts by creating the host application code, shown here:

```
<?xml version="1.0" encoding="utf-8"?>
<mx:Application xmlns:mx="http://www.adobe.com/2006/mxml"
  layout="vertical"
  creationComplete="baseballRO.getTeamList.send()"
  backgroundGradientColors="[#000000,#339933]">
```

```
<mx:Script>
<![CDATA[
private function onYearsResult() : void {
  chartList.dataProvider = baseballRO.getYearsByTeam.lastResult;
}
private function onTeamsList() : void {
  teamSelector.dataProvider = baseballRO.getTeamList.lastResult;
  teamSelector.selectedIndex = 0;
  for each ( var team:Object in baseballRO.getTeamList.lastResult )
    if ( team.teamid == 'FLO' )
    {
      teamSelector.selectedItem = team;
      onTeamChange();
    }
}
private function onTeamChange() : void {
  if ( teamSelector.selectedItem != null &&
  teamSelector.selectedItem.teamid != null )
    baseballRO.getYearsByTeam.send( teamSelector.selectedItem.teamid );
}
]]>
</mx:Script>

<mx:RemoteObject id="baseballRO"
  endpoint="http://localhost/amfphp/gateway.php"
  source="baseball.BaseballService"
  destination="baseball.BaseballService"
  showBusyCursor="true">
<mx:method name="getYearsByTeam" result="onYearsResult()">
<mx:arguments>
  <mx:Team />
</mx:arguments>
</mx:method>
<mx:method name="getTeamList" result="onTeamsList()" />
</mx:RemoteObject>

<mx:VBox paddingBottom="10" paddingLeft="10" paddingRight="10"
  paddingTop="10" verticalGap="5"
  width="100%" height="100%" backgroundAlpha="0.6"
  borderColor="white" borderThickness="3"
  borderStyle="solid" cornerRadius="15" backgroundColor="white">
<mx:ComboBox id="teamSelector" labelField="name"
  change="onTeamChange()" />
<mx:List id="chartList" itemRenderer="PieRenderer1" width="100%"
  height="100%" backgroundAlpha="0.1">
</mx:List>
</mx:VBox>

</mx:Application>
```

The application handles all of the work of selecting the team, getting the data from the server, and then updating the list control to show the individual years.

The majority of the work in this example application is done in the PieRenderer1 class, which is shown here:

```
<?xml version="1.0" encoding="utf-8"?>
<mx:Canvas xmlns:mx="http://www.adobe.com/2006/mxml" width="100%"
height="160" xmlns:ilog="http://www.ilog.com/2007/ilog/flex"
  xmlns="http://www.degrafa.com/2007"
  dataChange="onDataChange()" creationComplete="onDataChange()"
 verticalScrollPolicy="off" horizontalScrollPolicy="off"
  paddingBottom="0" paddingLeft="0" paddingRight="0" paddingTop="0">
<mx:Script>
<![CDATA[
import mx.graphics.SolidColor;
import mx.graphics.IFill;
import mx.charts.ChartItem;
import mx.collections.ArrayCollection;
import mx.controls.List;
import mx.charts.HitData;

private function onDataChange() : void {
  if ( pieChart == null || !initialized || data == null )
    return;
  pieChart.dataProvider = [
    { name:'Hits', hits:data.h },
    { name:'Doubles', hits:data['2b'] },
    { name:'Triples', hits:data['3b'] },
    { name:'Homers', hits:data.hr }
  ];
  var list:List = parent.parent as List;
  yearChart.dataProvider = list.dataProvider as ArrayCollection;
}
private function winFill( item:ChartItem, index:Number ) : IFill {
  return new SolidColor( 0x00FF00,
    ( item.item.yearid == data.yearid ) ? 1 : 0.2 );
}
private function lossFill( item:ChartItem, index:Number ) : IFill {
  return new SolidColor( 0xFF0000,
    ( item.item.yearid == data.yearid ) ? 1 : 0.2 );
}
]]>
</mx:Script>

<Surface>
<fills>
<LinearGradientFill id="backColor" angle="0">
  <GradientStop color="#62ABCD" alpha="0.6"/>
```

9

```
      <GradientStop color="#62ABCD" alpha="1"/>
    </LinearGradientFill>
  </fills>
  <strokes>
    <SolidStroke id="whiteStroke" color="#FFF" weight="1" alpha=".15"/>
  </strokes>
  <GeometryGroup>
  <RoundedRectangle cornerRadius="12" x="20" y="20" width="800"
    height="120" fill="{backColor}" stroke="{whiteStroke}" />
  </GeometryGroup>
</Surface>

<ilog:PieChart3D id="pieChart" height="160" width="200"
  zoom="1.2" left="30">
<ilog:filters>
  <mx:DropShadowFilter distance="10" alpha="0.5" />
</ilog:filters>
<ilog:series>
  <ilog:PieSeries3D displayName="Hits" field="hits"
  nameField="name" explodeRadius="0.1" />
</ilog:series>
</ilog:PieChart3D>

<mx:ColumnChart id="yearChart" height="120" width="580"
  type="100%" left="230" top="18" >
<mx:horizontalAxis>
  <mx:CategoryAxis categoryField="yearid"  />
</mx:horizontalAxis>
<mx:series>
  <mx:ColumnSeries xField="yearid" yField="w" displayName="Wins"
  fillFunction="winFill" />
  <mx:ColumnSeries xField="yearid" yField="l" displayName="Losses"
  fillFunction="lossFill" />
</mx:series>
</mx:ColumnChart>

<mx:HBox paddingBottom="2" paddingTop="2" paddingLeft="5"
  paddingRight="5" backgroundColor="#62ABCD"
  backgroundAlpha="0.6" borderColor="#62ABCD" borderStyle="solid"
  borderThickness="2" top="40" left="5">
<mx:Label text="{data.yearid}" fontWeight="bold" fontSize="14" />
</mx:HBox>

</mx:Canvas>
```

PieRenderer1 is an MXML component that derives from a Canvas. Within that, there is a Degrafa surface to render the background as a blue rounded rectangle. Then there are absolutely positioned PieChart3D and ColumnChart controls. The PieChart3D control shows the relative contributions of doubles, triples, and home runs. The ColumnChart (provided by the Flex framework) displays this year in the context of all of the years, where all of the years except for the current year are shown in 20% alpha to deemphasize them.

The resulting application, when run from Flex Builder 3, is shown in Figure 9-5.

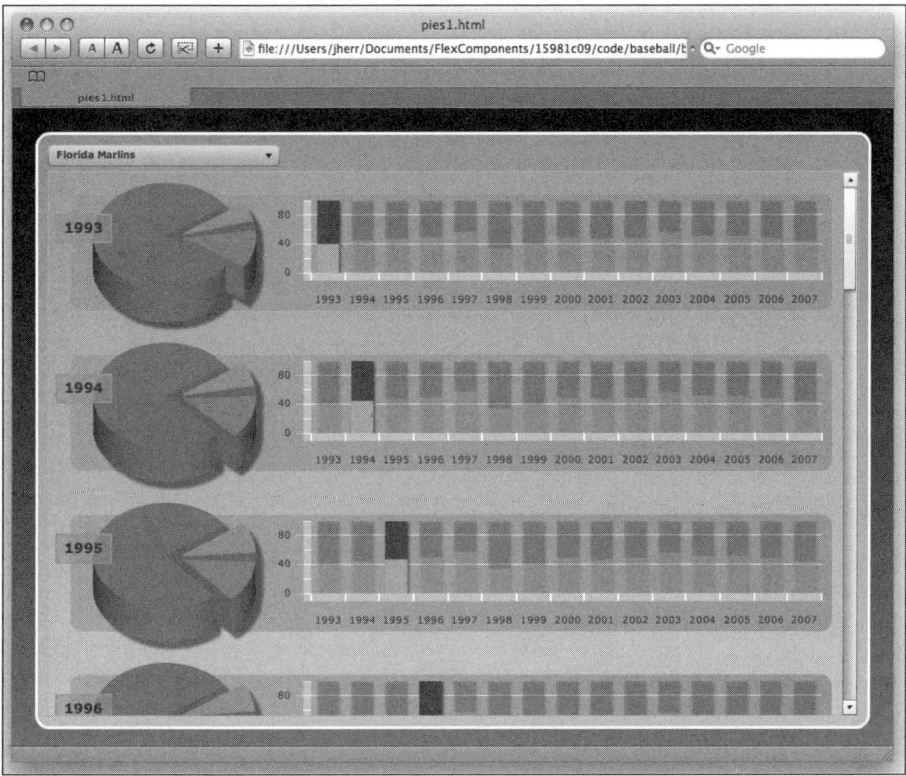

**Figure 9-5.** The List control, which uses 3D pie charts and column charts

This application shows the power of using renderers within the standard data display controls like the List control. List elements don't have to have text—they can have any type of control, regardless of complexity, as you can see here.

# Scientific charts in 3D

While some people were mesmerized by the computational power of Mathematica, I was blown away by the graphics. Math can produce some striking graphics, particularly in three dimensions. Flash doesn't have 3D drawing built in, but its 2D drawing API is strong enough to make quick work of rendering 3D graphics.

I found a scientific charting package online that was architected as components and had example source code. The following application uses the 3D plotting component to render a user-entered equation in 3D space:

```
<?xml version="1.0" encoding="utf-8"?>
<mx:Application xmlns:mx="http://www.adobe.com/2006/mxml"
  layout="vertical" creationComplete="onStartup()">
<mx:Script>
<![CDATA[
import bkde.as3.boards.GraphingBoard3D;
import bkde.as3.parsers.MathParser;
import bkde.as3.parsers.CompiledObject;
import bkde.as3.utilities.MatrixUtils;
import bkde.as3.utilities.StringUtils;
import bkde.as3.parsers.RangeObject;
import bkde.as3.parsers.RangeParser;

private var board:GraphingBoard3D;

private function onStartup() : void {
  board = new GraphingBoard3D(
    Math.min( plotHost.width, plotHost.height ) );
  plotHost.addChild( board );
  runPlot();
}

private function isLegal(a:*):Boolean {
  return ((typeof a)!="number" || isNaN(a) || !isFinite(a)) == false;
}

private function prepGraph() : Boolean {
  board.resetBoard();

  if( funcText.text.length == 0 )
    return false;

  var procFun:MathParser = new MathParser(["x","y"]);
  var compObj:CompiledObject = procFun.doCompile(funcText.text);
  if ( compObj.errorStatus == 1 ) {
    board.showError(compObj.errorMes);
    return false;
  }

  var xmin:Number = -1;
  var xmax:Number = 1;
  var zmin:Number = -1;
  var zmax:Number = 1;
  var fArray:Array = [];
  var yArray:Array = [];

  for( var j:int = 0; j<=board.nMesh;j++ ) {
    fArray[j] = [];
    var curz:Number = zmin+j*(zmax-zmin)/board.nMesh;
```

```
      for( var i:int = 0; i<=board.nMesh; i++){
      var curx:Number = xmin+i*(xmax-xmin)/board.nMesh;
      var cury:Number = procFun.doEval(
        compObj.PolishArray,[curz,curx]);
      fArray[j][i] = [curx,cury,curz];
      if(isLegal(cury)) yArray.push(cury);
    }
  }

  var ymin:Number = -1;
  var ymax:Number = 1;
  if ( yArray.length != 0 ) {
     yArray.sort(Array.NUMERIC);
     ymin = yArray[0];
     ymax = yArray[yArray.length-1];
  }
  if ( ymax == ymin ) { ymax+=0.5; ymin+=-0.5; }

  var size:Number = board.getCubeSize();
  var pArray:Array=[];

  for(j=0; j<=board.nMesh;j++) {
    pArray[j]=[];
    for(i=0; i<=board.nMesh;i++) {
      pArray[j][i]=[
        toPixel(xmin,xmax,size,fArray[j][i][0]),
        toPixel(ymin,ymax,size,fArray[j][i][1]),
        toPixel(zmin,zmax,size,fArray[j][i][2])
      ];
      if(isLegal( fArray[j][i][1]) && fArray[j][i][1]<=ymax &&
        fArray[j][i][1]>=ymin){
          pArray[j][i][3]=0;
      } else
        pArray[j][i][3]=1;
    }
  }

  board.nOpacity = opacitySlider.value;
  board.setPixArray(pArray);
  return true;
}

private function toPixel(min:Number,max:Number,
  size:Number,fun:Number):Number {
  return size-(max-fun)*(2*size/(max-min));
}

private function runPlot() : void
{
```

9

```
    board.width = Math.min( plotHost.width, plotHost.height );
    board.height = Math.min( plotHost.width, plotHost.height );
    board.setColorType("function");
    board.enableAxesLabels();

    var Ver:Array = MatrixUtils.MatrixByVector(
    MatrixUtils.rotMatrix(1,0,0,-15.2*Math.sqrt(2)),[0,1,0]);
    var iniMatrix:Array = MatrixUtils.MatrixByMatrix(
      MatrixUtils.rotMatrix(Ver[0],Ver[1],Ver[2],15*Math.PI/2),
       MatrixUtils.rotMatrix(1,0,0,-15.2*Math.sqrt(2)));

    if( !prepGraph() ) return;
    board.drawSurface(iniMatrix);
    board.drawAxes(iniMatrix);
  }

  private function onResize() : void {
    if ( initialized == false ) return;
    runPlot();
  }
]]>
</mx:Script>
<mx:Panel width="100%" height="100%" title="Math Plotter"
  paddingBottom="5" paddingLeft="5" paddingRight="5" paddingTop="5">
<mx:HBox>
  <mx:TextInput id="funcText" text="x^2+sin(y*5)" />
  <mx:Button label="Plot" click="runPlot()" />
  <mx:HSlider id="opacitySlider" minimum="0" maximum="1" value="0.7"
  change="runPlot()" />
</mx:HBox>
  <mx:UIComponent id="plotHost" width="100%" height="100%"
  resize="onResize()" />
</mx:Panel>
</mx:Application>
```

I won't pretend to understand all of the math here. Suffice it to say that the runPlot and prepGraph functions are the two primary methods involved in drawing the graph. These functions use the GraphingBoard3D control that comes with the library to draw an equation, which is interpreted by the MathParser object (also part of the library).

The opacity slider adjusts the opacity setting in the graph and replots to allow the user to create see-through graphs like the one shown in Figure 9-6.

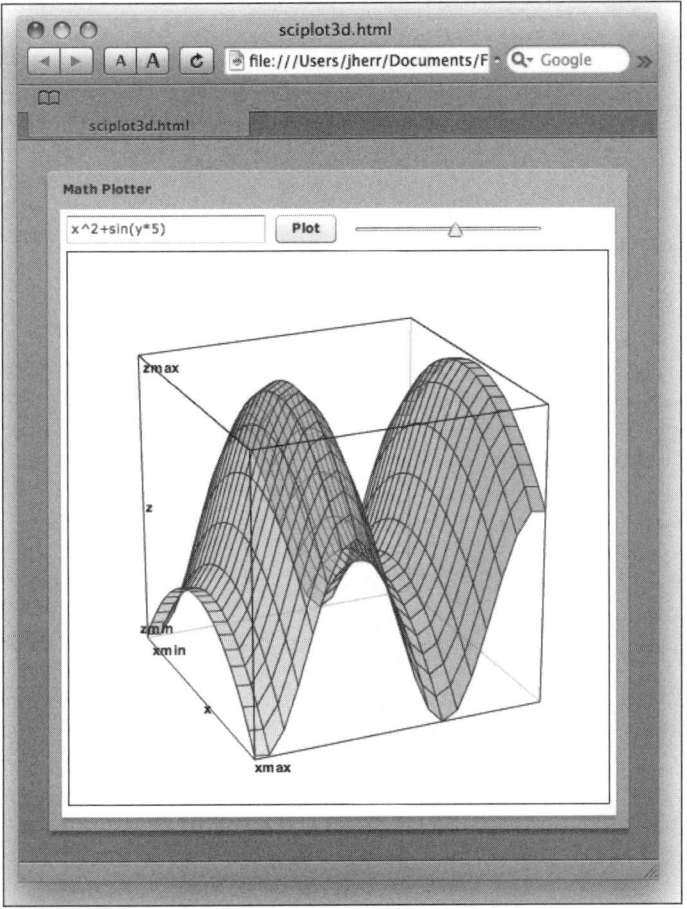

**Figure 9-6.** The 3D graph, which is only semi-opaque

If I up the opacity and type in another equation, I can get a more solid-looking graph that has a few more bumps in it—like the one shown in Figure 9-7.

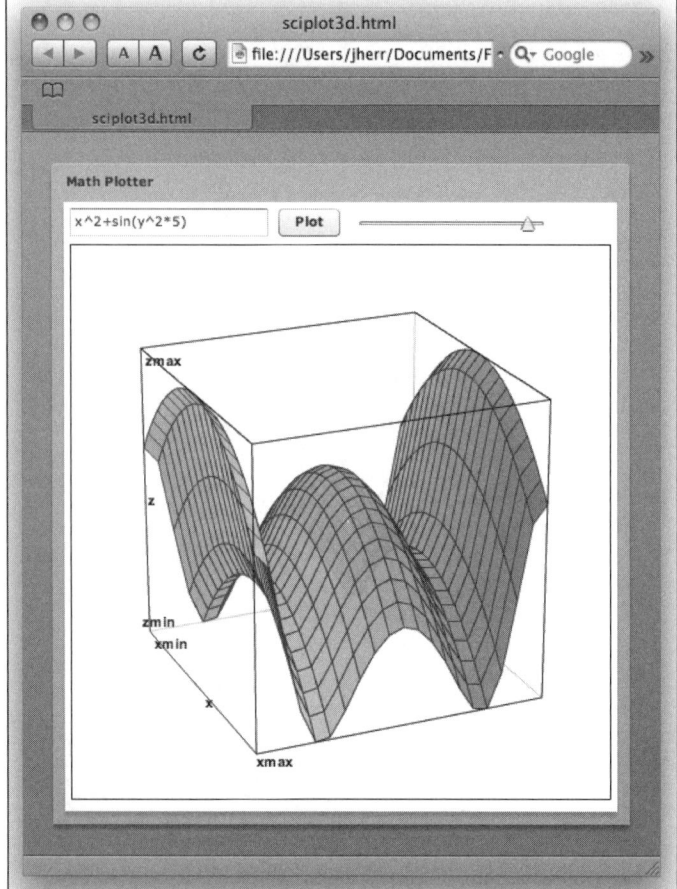

**Figure 9-7.** A lumpy opaque graph

With a little mouse handling code, you could have the graph spinning around on mouse control.

The nice thing about this particular library is that it comes as source code, so if you don't like the implementation, you can tweak it and send it back to the original authors.

# Faking 3D with Google SketchUp

I'd like to extend the view of components for at least this one example to include any set of tools that makes your life easier as an application developer. In this case, the tool I will include is Google's free SketchUp (http://sketchup.google.com) 3D modeling software. The problem I will solve in this example is the high CPU cost of 3D rendering.

Papervision3D is an excellent open source 3D rendering engine for Flex and Flash, no doubt. But it can be slow to render very elaborate models with lots of polygons and textures no matter how fast the machine.

Take as an example the Colonial Viper model, shown in Figure 9-8, that I downloaded from Google's 3D Warehouse (http://sketchup.google.com/3dwarehouse/).

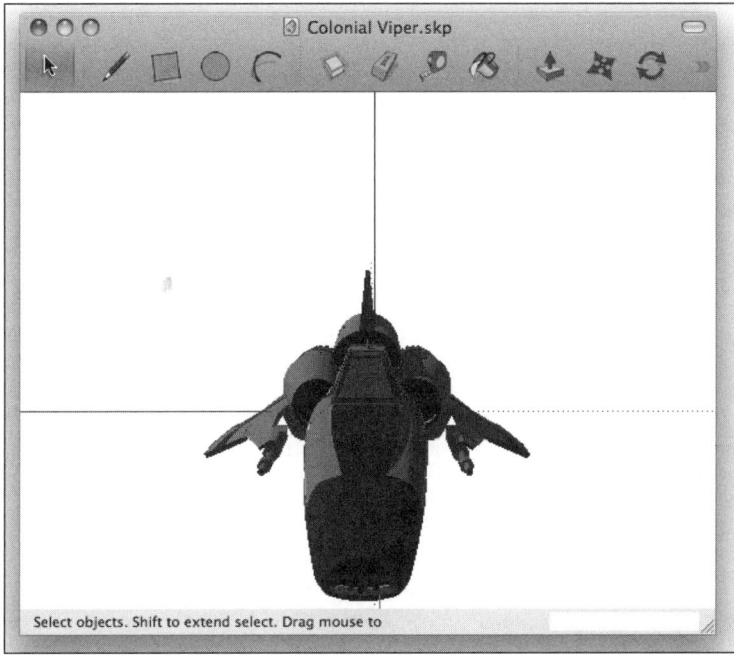

**Figure 9-8.** The Colonial Viper model

This is a nontrivial model with a lot of polygons. The XML file to describe the model is big. And it takes a lot of time in Papervision3D to render the model with the nice shading you see here.

Now let's say that I want to allow the user to spin this model around as if she were in a car showroom and watching a car spin around on a plate on the floor. How can I do that with this complex of a model? Can I cheat? Well, yes I can.

I can script SketchUp to take a snapshot of the model at every 5 degrees for 360 degrees. Then I can flip those images like a deck of cards in response to someone dragging the mouse. The model will spin as quickly as it takes to flip an image, which is really quick. That means no matter how complex the model, it will always spin at the same rate in my application because all I'm doing is flipping pre-rendered frames (like in a movie).

SketchUp has a Ruby interpreter built in. This Ruby interpreter can be used to do all kinds of things: add components to the model, rotate the model, change the camera angle, save snapshots of the model to an image file, and so on. The following Ruby code will spin the selected model around 360 degrees by units of 5 degrees and take a snapshot after each spin:

```
# Install with:
# require_all( File.join( File.expand_path( "~" ), "Sketchup" ) )

require 'sketchup.rb'

class PanoBuilder3

def initialize
  @distance = nil
  @frame = 0
  @angle = 0
end

def nextFrame(view)
  v = Geom::Vector3d.new(0,0,1)
  ss= Sketchup.active_model.selection
  ss.each do |e|
    pt = e.bounds.center
    tr = Geom::Transformation.rotation(pt,v,5 * 0.0174532925)
    Sketchup.active_model.active_entities.transform_entities(tr,e)
  end

  view.show_frame

  fpath = File.join( File.expand_path( "~" ),
   "Sketchup/images/#{@frame}.png" )
  view.write_image( fpath, 300, 250, true )

  @angle = @angle + 5
  @frame = @frame + 1
  @angle < 360
end

end

def buildpano3
    Sketchup.active_model.active_view.animation = PanoBuilder3.new
end

if( not file_loaded?("panobuilder3.rb") )
    UI.menu("Camera").add_item("Build Panorama 3") {buildpano3}
end

file_loaded("panobuilder3.rb")
```

I install this panobuilder3.rb file in my home directory within a folder called Sketchup. I then bring up the Ruby console in SketchUp and run the install line that is in the comment at the top of the script. The result is shown in Figure 9-9.

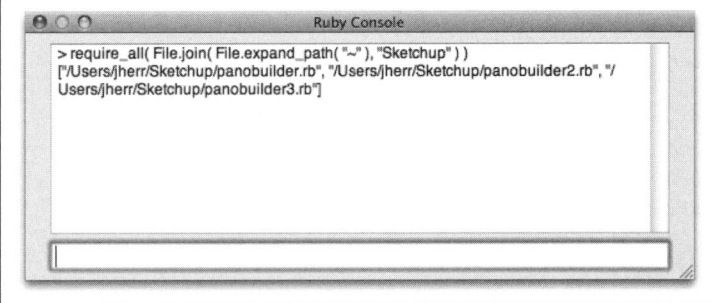

**Figure 9-9.** The Ruby console

From there, I just select the model I want to spin and then select Build Panorama 3 from the Camera menu as you can see in Figure 9-10.

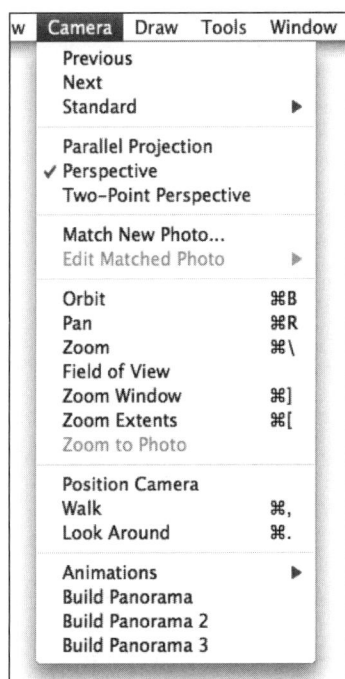

**Figure 9-10.** The Camera menu

That will build a series of images in the Sketchup/images directory. From there, I copy the images directory into my Flex project and use the following application code to display the model and allow the user to rotate it using the mouse:

```
<?xml version="1.0" encoding="utf-8"?>
<mx:Application xmlns:mx="http://www.adobe.com/2006/mxml"
  layout="vertical" creationComplete="onStartup()">
<mx:Script>
<![CDATA[
  import mx.controls.Image;
[Embed(source="images/0.png")] private var img0:Class;
[Embed(source="images/1.png")] private var img1:Class;
...
[Embed(source="images/70.png")] private var img70:Class;
[Embed(source="images/71.png")] private var img71:Class;
public var frames:Array = [
new img0(),
new img1(),
new img2(),
...
new img69(),
new img70(),
new img71()];

private var frame:int = 0;
private var lastX:int = 0;
private var tracking:Boolean = false;
private var lastImage:Image = null;
private var images:Array = [];

private function onStartup() : void {
  for each ( var bm:Bitmap in frames ) {
    var img:Image = new Image();
    img.source = bm;
    img.visible = false;
    images.push( img );
    pnl.addChild( img );
  }
  onDegreeChange();
}
private function onMouseDown(event:MouseEvent ) : void {
  lastX = event.localX;
  tracking = true;
}
private function onMouseMove(event:MouseEvent) : void {
  if ( tracking ) {
    if ( event.localX < lastX ) frame--;
    else frame++;
    if ( frame >= frames.length ) frame = 0;
    if ( frame < 0 ) frame = frames.length - 1;

    lastX = event.localX;
```

```
      onDegreeChange();
    }
}
private function onMouseUp(event:MouseEvent) : void {
  tracking = false;
}
private function onDegreeChange() : void {
  if ( lastImage != null ) lastImage.visible = false;
  images[ frame ].visible = true;
  lastImage = images[ frame ];
}
]]>
</mx:Script>
  <mx:Panel title="Colonial Viper" paddingBottom="0" paddingLeft="0"
    paddingRight="0" paddingTop="0"
    mouseDown="onMouseDown(event)" mouseUp="onMouseUp(event)"
    mouseMove="onMouseMove(event)" backgroundColor="black">
    <mx:Canvas id="pnl" width="300" height="250" />
  </mx:Panel>
</mx:Application>
```

There isn't much to this code. The onStartup method adds the individual images to the canvas and then sets visible on only one of them to true. The onMouseUp, onMouseDown, and onMouseMove messages respond to the mouse click and use the onDegreeChange method to change the active image to a different degree.

The finished application is shown in Figure 9-11.

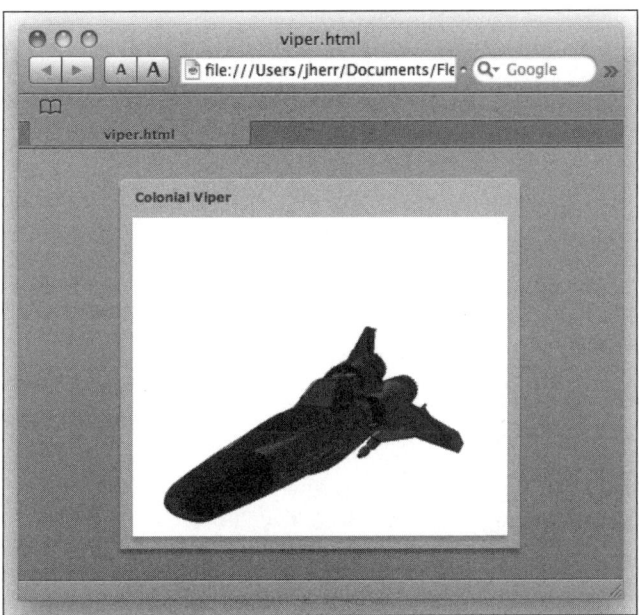

**Figure 9-11.** The model spinner

The effect is actually quite striking. There is no way to tell that there is no genuine 3D rendering going on.

I tried various effects when building the Ruby code for this application. The first was to rotate the camera around the model. What I found was that you would see a "light side" and a "dark side" to the model because of the single light source in SketchUp. It felt as if I were walking around a car in a showroom.

In the end, I found that rotating the model itself and maintaining the position of the camera, as I do in this example, provides the best result. It's as if the model were on a plate and you were standing still and watching it rotate in front of you. Thus, the model is always well lit.

# Where we will go from here

3D is great, but it can be overused. Some of the example graphs in this chapter work just as well in 2D as they do in 3D. If anything, the added dimension acts to distract from the data being presented. At the end of the day, I always recommend using the right visualization that imparts the information in the most comprehensible way possible.

That being said, I think we have all been in the situation when 2D just isn't sexy enough to get people's attention. When that's the case, it's nice to have a set of tools like the ones presented in this chapter that make 3D easy.

# 10 **VISUALIZING TIME AND SPACE**

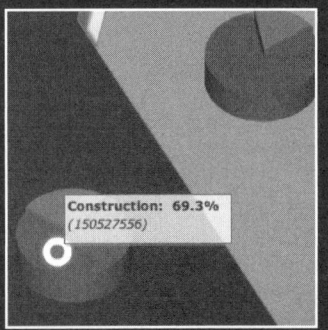

Updated 6/22/08

There is more to visualizations than just charts and graphs. There are all kinds of ways to visualize data. Component vendors, like ILOG, with their Elixir package, provide a bunch of Flex controls that present data effectively but don't look like what people expect to see in graphs. In this chapter, I'll show several examples of using these custom controls to present data in interesting combinations. We start off using gauges to present data in a visceral way, move on to some mapping demonstrations that show how to use maps to break up data geographically, then get into visualizing time, and wrap it up with a video display with overlaid gauges.

## Analog gauges

One of the most popular data display types is the gauge, like the kind you might find in a car to tell you that you are running on empty. Gauges have an almost visceral quality and provide a good at-a-glance snapshot for people. For these reasons, they have become a very popular feature of the executive dashboard.

In this example application, we use the gauge in a more traditional sense, as the kind of display you might see in a car. The code for the application is shown here:

```
<?xml version="1.0" encoding="utf-8"?>
<mx:Application xmlns:mx="http://www.adobe.com/2006/mxml"
  layout="absolute"
  xmlns:ilog="http://www.ilog.com/2007/ilog/flex" xmlns:local="*"
  creationComplete="onStartup()"
  width="748" height="416">
<mx:Script>
<![CDATA[
private function onStartup() : void {
  var t:Timer = new Timer( 1000, 0 );
  t.addEventListener(TimerEvent.TIMER,onTimer);
  t.start();
}
private function onTimer( event:Event ) : void {
  mph.value += ( Math.random() * 3 ) - 1;
  rpm.value += ( Math.random() * 50 ) - 25;
  fuel.value += ( Math.random() ) - 0.5;
  battery.value += ( Math.random() * 3 ) - 0.5;

  mph.value = Math.floor( Math.round( mph.value * 100 ) / 100.0 );
  rpm.value = Math.floor( Math.round( rpm.value * 100 ) / 100.0 );
  fuel.value = Math.floor( Math.round( fuel.value * 100 ) / 100.0 );
  battery.value = Math.floor( Math.round( battery.value * 100 )/100.0);
}
]]>
</mx:Script>
<mx:Image source="@Embed('back.png')" />
<ilog:SimpleCircularGauge id="mph" x="46" y="42" width="265"
  height="265" value="55" minimum="0" maximum="200"
```

```
      minorTickInterval="10" majorTickInterval="20"
      animationDuration="200"/>
   <ilog:SimpleCircularGauge id="rpm" x="421" y="42" width="265"
      height="265" minimum="0" maximum="10000"
      majorTickInterval="1000" minorTickInterval="500" value="1000"
      animationDuration="200"/>
   <ilog:SimpleVerticalGauge id="fuel" x="334" y="31" width="63.75"
      height="265" fontSize="10" majorTickInterval="25"
      minorTickInterval="5" showLabels="false" value="80"
      showTrack="true" showMinorTicks="false" showMajorTicks="false"/>
   <mx:Label x="151" y="246" text="MPH" color="#FFFFFF"
      fontWeight="bold" fontSize="20"/>
   <mx:Label x="112" y="327" text="Battery" color="#FFFFFF"
      fontWeight="bold" fontSize="20"/>
   <mx:Label x="526" y="246" text="RPM" color="#FFFFFF"
      fontWeight="bold" fontSize="20"/>
   <mx:Label x="341" y="291" text="Fuel" color="#FFFFFF"
      fontWeight="bold" fontSize="20"/>
   <local:LightRampRectangularGauge id="battery" width="400"
      height="36" animationDuration="250" x="204" y="326"
      minimum="0" maximum="100" value="50"  color="#FFFFFF"/>
   </mx:Application>
```

We use two of ILOG's SimpleCircularGauge controls to present the RPM and MPH. We also use a VerticalGauge to present the remaining fuel, and our own custom control, called the LightRampRectangularGauge, to present the battery charge in the car (I guess this is a hybrid car).

The ActionScript code, located at the top of the file, uses a timer to move the gauges around every second to give the whole display the sense that it's really hooked up to something.

To make the display a little more effective, I used Adobe's Fireworks application to build a custom image to sit in the background. To build the graphic, I first took a screenshot of the controls without a background. I then use that as the background of the graphic that I built and set my new graphic to an alpha of 50% so that I could see the original controls and where they fit. When I was finished designing the graphic, I set the alpha to 100% and saved the file into the project directory as a PNG.

Here is the custom gauge that we use to show the battery life:

```
   <?xml version="1.0" encoding="utf-8"?>
   <ilog:NumericRectangularGauge xmlns:mx="http://www.adobe.com/2006/mxml"
      xmlns:ilog="http://www.ilog.com/2007/ilog/flex"
      xmlns:local="*" showTrack="false"
      showMinorTicks="false" showLabels="false">
   <ilog:scaleRenderer>
     <ilog:RectangularScaleRenderer majorTickWidth="20">
       <ilog:majorTickRenderer>
         <mx:Component>
```

10

```
            <local:LightRectangularTickRenderer/>
          </mx:Component>
        </ilog:majorTickRenderer>
      </ilog:RectangularScaleRenderer>
    </ilog:scaleRenderer>
    <ilog:valueRenderer>
      <local:LightRectangularValueRenderer/>
    </ilog:valueRenderer>
</ilog:NumericRectangularGauge>
```

This is an MXML component just like you would use anywhere else, with the exception that in this case we are deriving the control from a NumericRectangularGauge and defining it from there. The rest of the classes that this control uses are provided with the download code associated with this book.

As with the core of the Flex framework, the ILOG controls use **renderers** to build the graphics for the components. You can override these renderers with your own custom code to change how the controls look and feel.

When I bring this application up in Flex Builder 3, I see something like Figure 10-1.

**Figure 10-1.** The hybrid car dashboard using Elixir gauges

There are a couple of things to take away from this example. The first is that you can use other Adobe tools, like Fireworks or Photoshop, in combination with Flex to create some very cool interfaces. The second is that you can, and probably should, use Elixir as a framework for building custom controls, like the battery life counter.

# Graphing on maps

Maps provide a remarkably compelling visual tool, and Elixir's support for mapping is very complete. Not only are there several common built-in map classes, but you can also import your own map data into Elixir's custom map creation tool. You can then use the Map classes to show the map and bind graphing data to it.

In the example applications that follow, I will use the map not only to graph data using colors on each of the states of the map (the data applies to the United States), but also to overlay controls onto each state to demonstrate how that is done.

The following application uses the US data source that we installed in Chapter 3. It then assigns each state a color based on the amount of money generated by the information technology (IT) sector in that state. It also overlays a pie chart that shows the percentages of IT, real estate, and construction sales in the state.

The code for this application is shown here:

```
<?xml version="1.0" encoding="utf-8"?>
<mx:Application xmlns:mx="http://www.adobe.com/2006/mxml"
  layout="vertical"
  xmlns:ilog="http://www.ilog.com/2007/ilog/flex"
  creationComplete="onStartup()"
  backgroundGradientColors="[#ffffff,#bbbbff]">
<mx:Script>
<![CDATA[
import ilog.charts3d.series.PieSeries3D;
import ilog.charts3d.PieChart3D;
import mx.effects.Zoom;
import mx.effects.Effect;
import ilog.maps.MapEvent;
import ilog.maps.MapSymbol;
import mx.controls.Label;
import mx.graphics.SolidColor;

import ilog.utils.ColorUtil;
import ilog.maps.MapFeature;
import mx.rpc.events.ResultEvent;

private function onStartup() : void {
  _reqTable = 'it';
  usdataRO.getAll.send( _reqTable );
}

private function scaleColor( minColor:Object, maxColor:Object,
  percent:Number ) : uint {
  var color:Object = {
    r: maxColor.r - ( ( 1.0 - percent ) * ( maxColor.r - minColor.r )),
    g: maxColor.g - ( ( 1.0 - percent ) * ( maxColor.g - minColor.g )),
```

10

```
          b: maxColor.b - ( ( 1.0 - percent ) * ( maxColor.b - minColor.b ))
      }
    return ColorUtil.RGBToUint( color );
  }

  private var _usObject:Object = null;

  private function getValue( stateData:Object ) : Number {
    return parseFloat( stateData.sales ) / parseFloat( _usObject.sales );
  }

  private var _reqTable:String = '';
  private var _usData:Object = {};

  private function onGetAllResult() : void {
    _usData[ _reqTable ] = usdataRO.getAll.lastResult;
    _reqTable = null;
    if ( _usData[ 'it' ] == null ) _reqTable = 'it';
    if ( _usData[ 'realestate' ] == null ) _reqTable = 'realestate';
    if ( _usData[ 'construction' ] == null ) _reqTable = 'construction';
    if ( _reqTable != null ) usdataRO.getAll.send( _reqTable );
    else updateMap();
  }

  private function getState( table:String, state:String ) : Object {
    for each( var sO:Object in _usData[table] ) {
      if ( sO.state == state )
        return sO;
    }
    return null;
  }

  private function updateMap() : void {
    var minColor:Object = { r: 0, g: 255, b: 0 };
    var maxColor:Object = { r: 255, g: 0, b: 0 };

    for each ( var sO:Object in _usData['it'] ) {
      if ( sO.state == 'United States' ) {
        _usObject = sO;
      }
    }

    var minVal:Number = Number.MAX_VALUE;
    var maxVal:Number = Number.MIN_VALUE;
    for each ( var s1:Object in _usData['it'] ) {
      if ( s1.state == 'United States' ) continue;
      var emp1:Number = getValue( s1 );
      minVal = Math.min( minVal, emp1 );
      maxVal = Math.max( maxVal, emp1 );
```

```
    }

    for each ( var featName:String in mymap.featureNames ) {
      var feat1:MapFeature = mymap.getFeature( featName );
      if ( feat1 )
        feat1.setStyle('fill',new SolidColor( scaleColor( minColor,
        maxColor, 0 ), 1 ) );
    }

  var symbols:Array = [];
  for each ( var s2:Object in _usData['it'] ) {
    var emp2:Number = getValue( s2 );
    var feat2:MapFeature = mymap.getFeatureFromLocaleName( s2.state );
    if ( feat2 )
    {
      var per:Number = ( emp2 - minVal ) / ( maxVal - minVal );
      feat2.setStyle('fill',new SolidColor( scaleColor( minColor,
      maxColor, per ), 1 ) );

      var pc:PieChart3D = new PieChart3D();
          pc.flatnessFactor = 1.5;
          pc.showDataTips = true;
          pc.width = 50;
          pc.height = 50;

          var data:Array = [];
          if ( getState('it',s2.state) != null ) data.push(
              { field: 'IT', value: getState('it',s2.state).sales } );
          if ( getState('realestate',s2.state) != null ) data.push(
              { field: 'Real Estate', value: getState('realestate', ➥
s2.state).sales } );
          if ( getState('construction',s2.state) != null ) data.push(
              { field: 'Construction', value: getState('construction', ➥
s2.state).sales } );

          var series:PieSeries3D = new PieSeries3D();
          series.field = "value";
          series.nameField = "field";
          series.explodeRadius = 0.03;
          pc.series = [ series ];
          pc.dataProvider = data;

      var ms:MapSymbol = new MapSymbol();
      ms.key = feat2.key;
      ms.component = pc;

      symbols.push( ms );
    }
  }
```

10

```
      mymap.symbols = symbols;
    }

    private var _effects:Array = new Array();

    private function createEffect(f:MapFeature):Effect {
      var z:Zoom = new Zoom();
      z.zoomWidthFrom = 1;
      z.zoomWidthTo = 1.5;
      z.zoomHeightFrom = 1;
      z.zoomHeightTo = 1.5;
      z.duration = 300;
      return z;
    }

    private function play(s:MapFeature, io:Boolean):void {
      var z:Effect = _effects[s];
      if(z == null) {
        z = createEffect(s);
        _effects[s] = z;
      }
      if(z.isPlaying) {
        z.reverse();
      } else {
        z.play([s], io);
      }
    }

    public function rollOver(event:MapEvent):void {
      var m:MapFeature = event.mapFeature;
      m.parent.setChildIndex(m, m.parent.numChildren - 1);
      play(m, false);
    }

    private function rollOut(e:MapEvent):void {
      var m:MapFeature = e.mapFeature;
      play(m, true);
    }
    ]]>
  </mx:Script>

  <mx:RemoteObject id="usdataRO"
    endpoint="http://localhost/amfphp/gateway.php"
    source="usdata.USDataService" destination="usdata.USDataService"
    showBusyCursor="true">
```

```
<mx:method name="getAll" result="onGetAllResult()">
<mx:arguments>
  <mx:Table />
</mx:arguments>
</mx:method>
</mx:RemoteObject>

<ilog:USStatesMap width="100%" height="100%" id="mymap"
  mapItemRollOver="rollOver(event)"
  mapItemRollOut="rollOut(event)" allowNavigation="true"
  animationDuration="300" zoomableSymbols="true"
  clipContent="false">
<ilog:filters>
  <mx:DropShadowFilter distance="10" alpha="0.5" />
</ilog:filters>
<ilog:backgroundFill>
  <mx:SolidColor alpha="0" />
</ilog:backgroundFill>
</ilog:USStatesMap>

</mx:Application>
```

The code for this application is broken into three parts. The ActionScript at the top of the file references the RemoteObject tags in the middle section of the file to get the data from the server. The user interface, defined by the US map, is at the bottom of the file.

The ActionScript code at the top of the file does the majority of the work. The onStartup method starts requesting one of the three data sources. All three data tables are requested from the server for this application. The onGetAllResult takes the returned data and stores it. The updateMap method is what's called when all of the data is finally loaded. It does all of the work of updating the map colors and adding the pie charts to the graph.

The scaleColor method is a generic method that takes two color values and a percentage and returns a color that is somewhere between the two colors based on the percentage. This is a handy little function that you can reuse wherever you like.

At the bottom of the ActionScript block are four methods, rollOver, rollOut, play, and createEffect, which are all involved in zooming the states as you move over them. If you don't like that effect, you can simply remove the code and its connections to the mymap object.

When I first bring this up from Flex Builder 3, I see something like Figure 10-2.

**10**

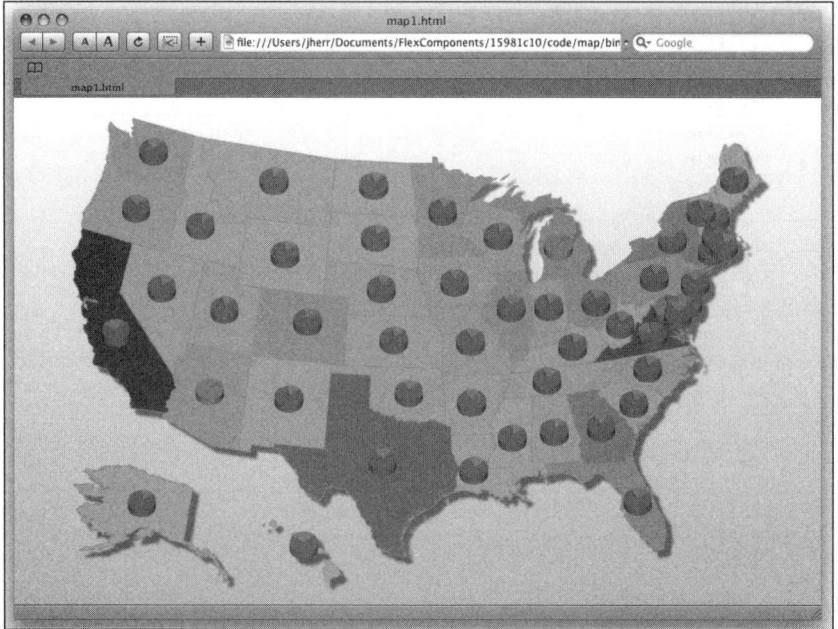

**Figure 10-2.** The initial state of the map showing percentages in pie charts of IT, real estate, and construction sales by state

When I use + to zoom in on the map, I see something like Figure 10-3.

**Figure 10-3.** The map zoomed in on the western US

The map control handles scrolling around the map with the cursor as well as the mouse wheel. When I mouse over a state, like California, the state pops out as shown in Figure 10-4.

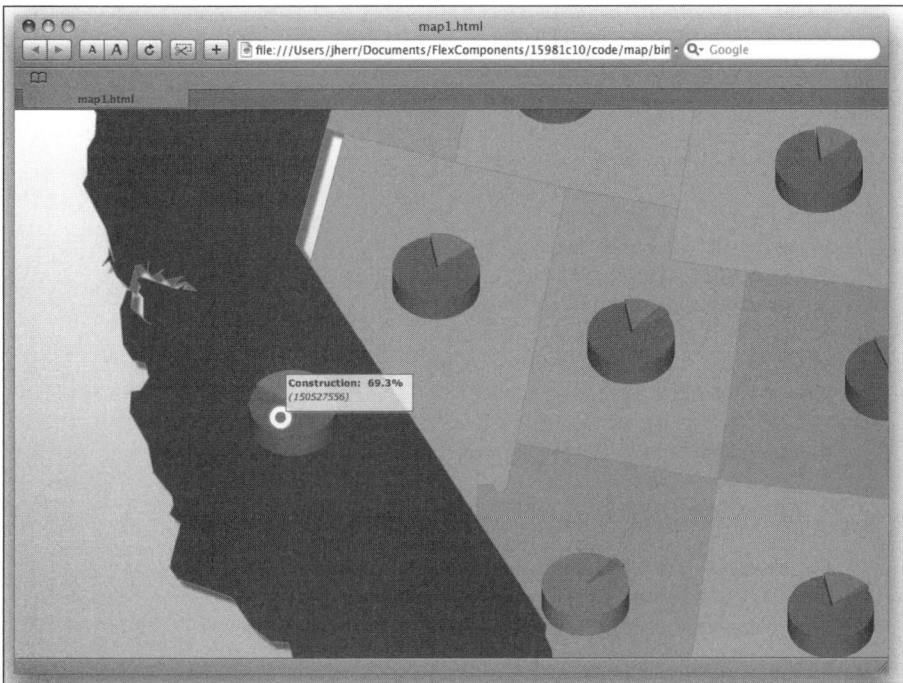

**Figure 10-4.** States pop out from the map when you roll over them.

Using the map as a data visualization tool and host for other controls is one option. Another is to use the map itself as a data selector and then provide additional information about the selected region in adjoining controls.

## Adding knobs and dials

In this next example, I'll allow the user to select how the map is shaded using an Elixir knob control, and then show the sales revenue values for IT, real estate, and construction in related semicircular gauges.

```
<?xml version="1.0" encoding="utf-8"?>
<mx:Application xmlns:mx="http://www.adobe.com/2006/mxml"
  layout="absolute"
  xmlns:ilog="http://www.ilog.com/2007/ilog/flex"
  creationComplete="onStartup()" width="1000" height="800"
  horizontalScrollPolicy="off"
  verticalScrollPolicy="off"
  backgroundGradientColors="[#ddddff,#3333ff]">
<mx:Script>
```

**261**

```
<![CDATA[
import ilog.maps.MapEvent;
import ilog.gauges.circular.renderers.*;
import mx.effects.Zoom;
import mx.effects.Effect;
import mx.controls.Label;
import mx.graphics.SolidColor;

import ilog.utils.ColorUtil;
import ilog.maps.MapFeature;
import mx.rpc.events.ResultEvent;

private var salesMin:Number;
private var salesMax:Number;
private var populationMin:Number;
private var populationMax:Number;
private var companiesMin:Number;
private var companiesMax:Number;

private function onStartup() : void {
  _reqTable = 'it';
  usdataRO.getAll.send( _reqTable );

  for each( var elem:Object in selData.elements ) {
    if ( ( elem as CircularScaleRenderer ) != null ) {
      var circLabel:CircularScaleRenderer = elem as ➥
CircularScaleRenderer;
        circLabel.percentLabelFontSize = 35;
        circLabel.setStyle('fontWeight','bold');
        circLabel.setStyle('color',0xffffff);
    }
  }
}

private function scaleColor( minColor:Object, maxColor:Object,
  percent:Number ) : uint {
  var color:Object = {
    r: maxColor.r - ( ( 1.0 - percent ) * ( maxColor.r - minColor.r)),
    g: maxColor.g - ( ( 1.0 - percent ) * ( maxColor.g - minColor.g)),
    b: maxColor.b - ( ( 1.0 - percent ) * ( maxColor.b - minColor.b))
  }
  return ColorUtil.RGBToUint( color );
}

private function getValue( stateData:Object ) : Number {
  return parseFloat( stateData.sales );
}
```

```
private var _reqTable:String = '';
private var _usData:Object = {};

private function onGetAllResult() : void {
  _usData[ _reqTable ] = usdataRO.getAll.lastResult;
  _reqTable = null;
  if ( _usData[ 'it' ] == null ) _reqTable = 'it';
  if ( _usData[ 'realestate' ] == null ) _reqTable = 'realestate';
  if ( _usData[ 'construction' ] == null ) _reqTable = 'construction';
  if ( _reqTable != null ) usdataRO.getAll.send( _reqTable );
  else updateMap();
}

private function getState( table:String, state:String ) : Object {
  for each( var s0:Object in _usData[table] ) {
    if ( s0.state == state )
      return s0;
  }
  return null;
}

private function updateMap() : void {
  var minColor:Object = { r: 0, g: 255, b: 0 };
  var maxColor:Object = { r: 255, g: 0, b: 0 };

  salesMin = Number.MAX_VALUE;
  salesMax = Number.MIN_VALUE;
  populationMin = Number.MAX_VALUE;
  populationMax = Number.MIN_VALUE;
  companiesMin = Number.MAX_VALUE;
  companiesMax = Number.MIN_VALUE;

  var minVal:Number = Number.MAX_VALUE;
  var maxVal:Number = Number.MIN_VALUE;
  for each ( var s1:Object in _usData[selData.value] ) {
    if ( s1.state == 'United States' ) continue;
    var emp1:Number = getValue( s1 );
    minVal = Math.min( minVal, emp1 );
    maxVal = Math.max( maxVal, emp1 );

    var sales:Number = parseFloat( s1.sales );
    salesMin = Math.min( salesMin, sales );
    salesMax = Math.max( salesMax, sales );
    var companies:Number = parseFloat( s1.companies );
    companiesMin = Math.min( companiesMin, companies );
    companiesMax = Math.max( companiesMax, companies );
    var population:Number = parseFloat( s1.payroll );
```

**10**

```
          populationMin = Math.min( populationMin, population );
          populationMax = Math.max( populationMax, population );
        }

      for each ( var featName:String in mymap.featureNames ) {
        var feat1:MapFeature = mymap.getFeature( featName );
        if ( feat1 )
          feat1.setStyle('fill',new SolidColor( scaleColor( minColor,
          maxColor, 0 ), 1 ) );
      }

      for each ( var s2:Object in _usData[selData.value] ) {
        var emp2:Number = getValue( s2 );
        var feat2:MapFeature = mymap.getFeatureFromLocaleName( s2.state );
        if ( feat2 )
        {
          var per:Number = ( emp2 - minVal ) / ( maxVal - minVal );
          feat2.label = s2.state;
          feat2.setStyle('fill',new SolidColor( scaleColor( minColor,
          maxColor, per ), 1 ) );
        }
      }
    }

    private function onValueChange() : void {
      updateMap();
    }

    private function onMouseOver( event:MapEvent ) : void {
      var stateData:Object = getState( selData.value,
       event.mapFeature.label );
      if ( stateData )
      {
        gSales.value = Math.floor( ( ( parseFloat( stateData.sales ) -
        salesMin ) / ( salesMax - salesMin ) ) * 100.0 );
        gCompanies.value = Math.floor( ( (
        parseFloat( stateData.companies ) - companiesMin ) /
        ( companiesMax - companiesMin ) ) * 100.0 );
        gPopulation.value = Math.floor(
        ( ( parseFloat( stateData.payroll ) - populationMin ) /
        ( populationMax - populationMin ) ) * 100.0 );
      }
    }
  }
  ]]>
</mx:Script>

<mx:RemoteObject id="usdataRO"
  endpoint="http://localhost/amfphp/gateway.php"
  source="usdata.USDataService" destination="usdata.USDataService"
```

```
    showBusyCursor="true">
<mx:method name="getAll" result="onGetAllResult()">
<mx:arguments>
   <mx:Table />
</mx:arguments>
</mx:method>
</mx:RemoteObject>

<ilog:USStatesMap left="20" top="20" width="95%" height="95%"
   id="mymap" allowNavigation="true"
   animationDuration="300" mapItemRollOver="onMouseOver(event)">
<ilog:backgroundFill>
   <mx:SolidColor alpha="0" />
</ilog:backgroundFill>
<ilog:filters>
   <mx:DropShadowFilter distance="10" alpha="0.5" />
</ilog:filters>
</ilog:USStatesMap>

<ilog:BlackKnob top="610" left="580" height="120" width="200"
   categories="{['it','construction','realestate']}"
   value="it" valueCommit="onValueChange();" id="selData"
   titleStyleName="myTtleStyle">
</ilog:BlackKnob>

<mx:HBox paddingBottom="10" paddingLeft="10" paddingRight="10"
   paddingTop="10"
   backgroundColor="#bbbbff" backgroundAlpha="0.8" cornerRadius="15"
   borderStyle="solid"
   borderColor="#9999ff" borderThickness="2" x="289" y="10">
<ilog:BlackSemiCircularGauge width="180" height="120" title="Sales"
   id="gSales" />
<ilog:BlackSemiCircularGauge width="180" height="120"
   title="Companies" id="gCompanies" />
<ilog:BlackSemiCircularGauge width="180" height="120"
   title="Population" id="gPopulation" />
</mx:HBox>

</mx:Application>
```

The ActionScript code in this example shares some of its code with the previous example. As before, it downloads all three data sets before starting the visualization. The updateMap method in this new version uses the selected data set from the selData control, which is the BlackKnob located near the bottom of the file. It updates the map colors. The gauge controls are set by the onMouseOver method located at the bottom of the ActionScript code.

The user interface definition, located at the bottom of the application, has a Panel object to provide a wrapper for the entire interface. Then there is a VBox container to provide two horizontal rows. The first row is populated with an HBox that contains a knob to select the data and the three semicircular gauges to display the currently moused-over data. Below this is the map, which takes up the rest of the available space.

When we bring this up in Flex Builder 3, we see something like Figure 10-5.

**Figure 10-5.** The US map with the data selector knob and gauges

This example shows a few things that you should be able to reuse in your application. First is the KnobControl, which I think is very novel. Elixir has a few knob styles built in, but you are free to create your own styles if you want. The reflected glass look of the knob is very appealing.

The second is the dynamic nature of the mouseover connection between the map and the gauges. It creates a fun interaction experience for users that encourages them to play with the visualization more and find out more about the data.

# Timelines: The fourth dimension for data

Time can present some interesting problems for visualizations. On the one hand, you might want to see a wide swath of time to get an idea how various events interrelate in the large. Or, on the other hand, you might be looking at your schedule and want accuracy down to just a few minutes, or you will miss that appointment with the doctor and get charged a fine.

In this section, I'll show two example controls, one that is free and one that is a commercial product. The first is the ScheduleViewer from the FlexLib (http://flexlib.googlecode.com/). The application that shows the schedule viewer, with some randomly generated events, is shown here:

```
<?xml version="1.0" encoding="utf-8"?>
<mx:Application
    xmlns:mx="http://www.adobe.com/2006/mxml"
    xmlns:flexlib="http://code.google.com/p/flexlib/"
    creationComplete="onStartup();">

<mx:Script>
<![CDATA[
import flexlib.scheduling.samples.ScheduleData;
import flexlib.scheduling.util.DateUtil;
import mx.collections.ArrayCollection;
import mx.events.ScrollEvent;
import mx.events.ScrollEventDirection;

[Bindable]
private var startDate : Date;
[Bindable]
private var endDate : Date;
[Bindable]
private var zoom : Number;

private function onStartup() : void
{
    startDate=DateUtil.clearTime( new Date() );
    endDate=new Date(startDate.getTime()+DateUtil.DAY_IN_MILLISECONDS);
    scheduleViewer.dataProvider = new ScheduleData().➥
createRandomColoredScheduleEntries( 20 );
}

private function onScrollTimeline( position : Number ) : void
{
    scheduleViewer.xPosition = position;
}
```

**10**

```
    private function onScrollScheduleViewer( event : ScrollEvent ) : void
    {
        if( event.direction == ScrollEventDirection.HORIZONTAL )
            timeline.xPosition = event.position;
    }
]]>
</mx:Script>

<mx:Panel title="Timeline" width="100%" height="100%"
    paddingBottom="5" paddingLeft="5" paddingRight="5" paddingTop="5">
<mx:HBox paddingBottom="10">
<mx:Label text="Zoom:"/>
<mx:HSlider id="zoomSlider" minimum="0" maximum="1000" value="100"
    liveDragging="true" change="zoom=zoomSlider.value;" />
</mx:HBox>

<flexlib:Timeline width="100%" startDate="{startDate}"
    endDate="{endDate}" id="timeline"
    zoom="{zoom}" scroll="onScrollTimeline( event.position );" />

<flexlib:ScheduleViewer id="scheduleViewer" width="100%" height="100%"
    startDate="{startDate}" endDate="{endDate}" zoom="{zoom}"
    entryRenderer="flexlib.scheduling.scheduleClasses.renderers.➥
ColoredGradientScheduleEntryRenderer"
    horizontalScrollPolicy="off"
    pixelScroll="onScrollScheduleViewer( event );" />

</mx:Panel>

</mx:Application>
```

There are two primary controls: the Timeline, which provides an x-axis header, and the ScheduleViewer, which displays a set of ScheduleItem objects. Both of these controls take a start date, an end date, and a zoom factor. Much of the ActionScript code is dedicated to keeping these two controls in sync. For example, the onScrollScheduleViewer and onScrollTimeline both respond to scroll events and force a scroll in the other control.

The zoom control, which is located in the HBox at the top of the user interface, sets the zoom value, which is data bound to both the timeline and the schedule viewer.

When we launch this from Flex Builder 3, we see something like Figure 10-6.

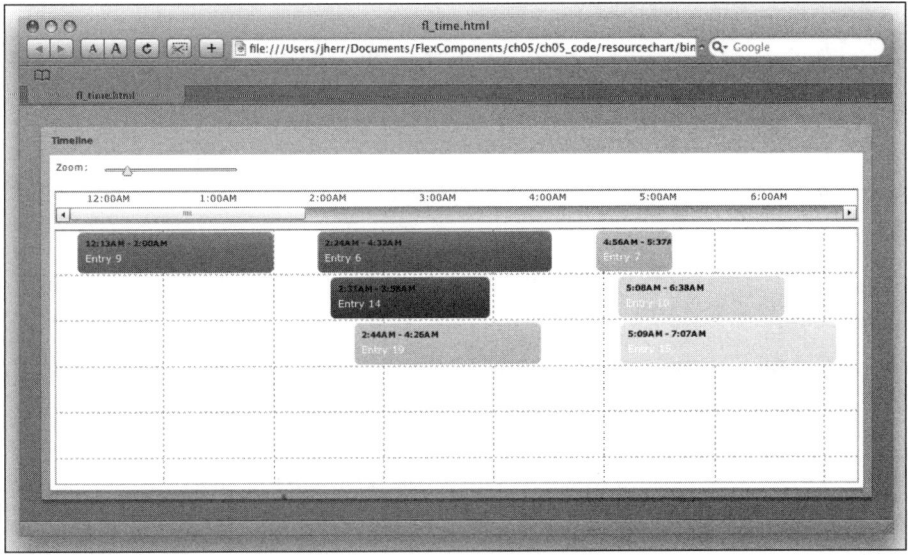

**Figure 10-6.** The FlexLib timeline viewer

As the events are randomly generated, you will get different events than what I've pictured here. But your results should be roughly similar.

As with the base Flex controls, this schedule viewer is very flexible in how you can render each of the schedule items. That means that you can draw images into the items, present graphs within them, change the display styling, and so on.

## The ILOG Resource Chart

Another timeline viewer comes from the Elixir toolkit with their Resource Chart. It's a little easier to get data into, and there is only one control, so you don't have to do any synchronization. Following is the code for the demonstration application:

```xml
<?xml version="1.0"?>
<mx:Application xmlns:mx="http://www.adobe.com/2006/mxml"
    xmlns:ilog="http://www.ilog.com/2007/ilog/flex">

<mx:Style>
.myTaskItemStyle {
  textStyleName : "myTextStyle";
  textRollOverColor : white;
  textSelectedColor : green;
  textSelectedRollOverColor : blue;
  background-color: #ee99ee;
}
.myTextStyle {
  color: #333333;
```

```
        fontWeight : "bold";
    }
    </mx:Style>

    <mx:Script>
    <![CDATA[
    import mx.collections.ArrayCollection;

    [Bindable]
    public var resources:ArrayCollection = new ArrayCollection([
        { id: "lori", name: "Lori" },
        { id: "jack", name: "Jack" },
        { id: "megan", name: "Megan" }
    ] );

    [Bindable]
    public var tasks:ArrayCollection = new ArrayCollection([
        { resourceId: "lori", name: "Investigate new offices",
          startTime: "1/14/2008 8:0:0", endTime: "1/17/2008 17:0:0" },
        { resourceId: "jack", name: "Clean current office",
          startTime: "1/16/2008 2:0:0", endTime: "1/16/2008 20:0:0" },
        { resourceId: "jack", name: "Move office",
          startTime: "1/18/2008 2:0:0", endTime: "1/18/2008 20:0:0" },
        { resourceId: "megan", name: "Help move office",
          startTime: "1/18/2008 2:0:0", endTime: "1/18/2008 20:0:0" }
    ]);
    ]]>
    </mx:Script>

    <ilog:ResourceChart id="resourceChart" width="100%" height="100%"
       resourceDataProvider="{resources}" taskDataProvider="{tasks}"
       taskItemStyleName="myTaskItemStyle">
    <ilog:timeScale>
       <ilog:TimeScale backgroundColors="{['white', '#999999']}"
       rollOverAlpha="0.5" rollOverColor="green" />
    </ilog:timeScale>
    </ilog:ResourceChart>
    </mx:Application>
```

The ResourceChart takes two data sources: the resources and the tasks. The "resources" can be people, things (e.g., trucks, trains, computers, etc.), or really anything you want. The tasks are what the "resources" are meant to accomplish and when. In this case, all the ActionScript code does is create two arrays, resources and tasks, which are defined as Bindable. These are then bound to the ResourceChart using the Flex data binding syntax. The rest of the tags are just to refine the styles a little bit to make it all look a little cleaner.

When we bring this up in Flex Builder 3, we see something like Figure 10-7.

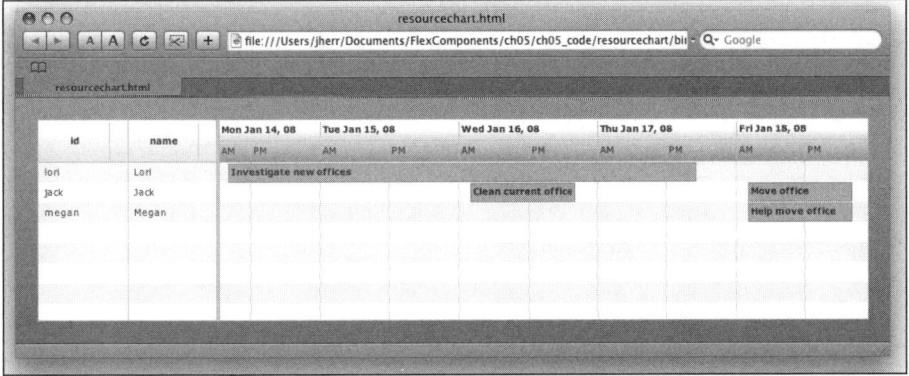

**Figure 10-7.** The Elixir Resource Chart

This resource chart is a more vertically purposed timeline than the one presented in the FlexLib. Resource charts do have a specific business purpose, and this control was clearly designed to make it easy to accomplish it. But as with all of these controls, you can view them as a framework that handles the interaction basics and allows you to override certain aspects of the interface to customize it to work in your application.

# Synchronizing media and controls

The final example in this chapter shows how to synchronize the display of data with the playback of video. In this case, I'll use a racing video that I found online and put it together with two gauge controls to create a nice little display that shows how fast a car is going at each step in the playback of the video.

The code for this application is shown here:

```
<?xml version="1.0" encoding="utf-8"?>
<mx:Application xmlns:mx="http://www.adobe.com/2006/mxml"
  layout="absolute" width="640" height="480"
  xmlns:ilog="http://www.ilog.com/2007/ilog/flex"
  horizontalScrollPolicy="off" verticalScrollPolicy="off">
<mx:Script>
<![CDATA[
import mx.events.VideoEvent;

private var telemetryData:Array = [
  { time: 0, rpm: 3000, mph: 0 },
  { time: 1000, rpm: 2500, mph: 0 },
  { time: 3000, rpm: 3000, mph: 0 },
  { time: 5000, rpm: 4000, mph: 0 },
  { time: 7000, rpm: 6000, mph: 70 },
  { time: 8000, rpm: 7000, mph: 90 },
```

```
          { time: 9000, rpm: 6000, mph: 110 }
      ];

      private function onPlayheadUpdate( event:VideoEvent ) : void {
        var curMPH:int = 0;
        var curRPM:int = 0;
        for each ( var telObj:Object in telemetryData ) {
          if ( telObj.time < ( event.playheadTime * 1000 )  ) {
            curMPH = telObj.mph;
            curRPM = telObj.rpm;
          }
        }
        mph.value = curMPH;
        rpm.value = curRPM;
      }
    ]]>
    </mx:Script>
    <mx:VideoDisplay width="640" height="480"
      source="http://localhost/flexcomp/racing/racing.f4v" autoPlay="true"
      playheadUpdate="onPlayheadUpdate( event )" />
      <ilog:SimpleCircularGauge id="rpm" x="467" y="311" minimum="2000"
       maximum="10000" startAngle="190" endAngle="70"
       majorTickInterval="2000" width="250" height="250"/>
      <ilog:SimpleCircularGauge id="mph" x="-109" y="290" width="300"
        height="300" startAngle="-10" endAngle="100"
        orientation="cclockwise" minimum="0" maximum="200"
        majorTickInterval="30"/>
      <mx:HBox x="0" y="0" width="650" height="70"
        backgroundColor="#B91C1C" backgroundAlpha="0.5" borderStyle="none">
        <mx:Text text="Pocono Speedway" fontSize="40" color="#C5C5C5"
        fontWeight="bold" textAlign="left"/>
      </mx:HBox>
    </mx:Application>
```

This code breaks out into two large sections. The ActionScript code at the top has a list of RPM and speed values associated with a time that is relative to the start of the movie. So, for example, the car was going at 110 MPH and revving at 6,000 RPM about nine seconds into the movie. The onPlayheadUpdate then uses this array to set the RPM and MPH gauge depending on where the movie is in its playback.

At the bottom of the file is the user interface definition. It's a layered interface with the video display sitting at the bottom of the stack. Then layered on top are two big circular gauges for the RPM and the MPH, as well as a semi-opaque title box that sits over the video.

The result is shown in action in Figure 10-8.

**Figure 10-8.** Data from the movie synched with and displayed in two gauges

I love how Flex and Elixir together make this display not only look good, but also easy to construct. Very little has been done with the ability to synchronize video display with controls. I think this represents a huge opportunity to extend the value of video applications that have already proven their popularity.

## Where we will go from here

This chapter provides a number of examples that you can use as starting points to add some unique data visualizations to your applications. Gauges and maps are great ways to convey information quickly. And they are the kind of thing that used to take weeks to develop. Now it's as fast as pointing the control's dataProvider at your data. The timeline controls make it easy to display data on a timeline. And the gauge and knob controls will satisfy the executives and their eternal cravings for a "real-time business dashboard."

# 11 INTERACTIVE MAPPING CONTROLS

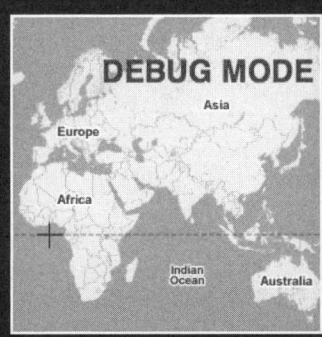 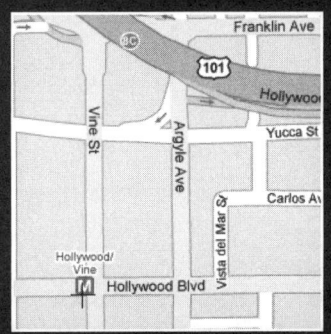 

Updated 7/3/08

# Three cool mapping controls

Mapping has been commoditized. It's gone from something that only big companies could afford to do, with the hardware requirements and the maps licensing, to something that can be done by anyone on any budget. Why? Because of Google Maps.

Google Maps revolutionized mapping with both its easy user interface and its wonderful API that allowed maps to be placed on any web page. Success breeds competition, of course, and now there are several similar mapping services from companies including Yahoo! and Microsoft.

In this chapter, I'll demonstrate how to use the Flex version of the APIs provided from Google and from Yahoo!, as well as how to use an independently produced control, the UMap from Advanced Flash Components (http://afcomponents.com).

We will start with Google Maps, and that means going to the Google Maps home page for Flash (http://code.google.com/apis/maps/documentation/flash), which is shown in Figure 11-1, and getting yourself a Google Maps API key.

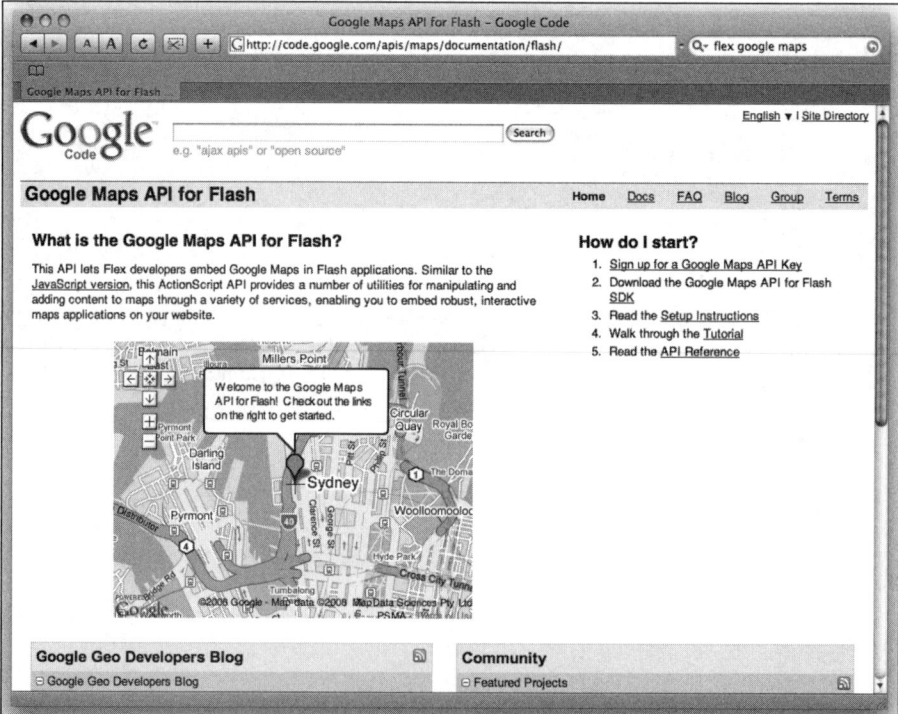

**Figure 11-1.** The Google Maps home page for Flash

From there, you click the Sign up for a Google Maps API key link on the left-hand side of the page, and that will take you to the signup page shown in Figure 11-2.

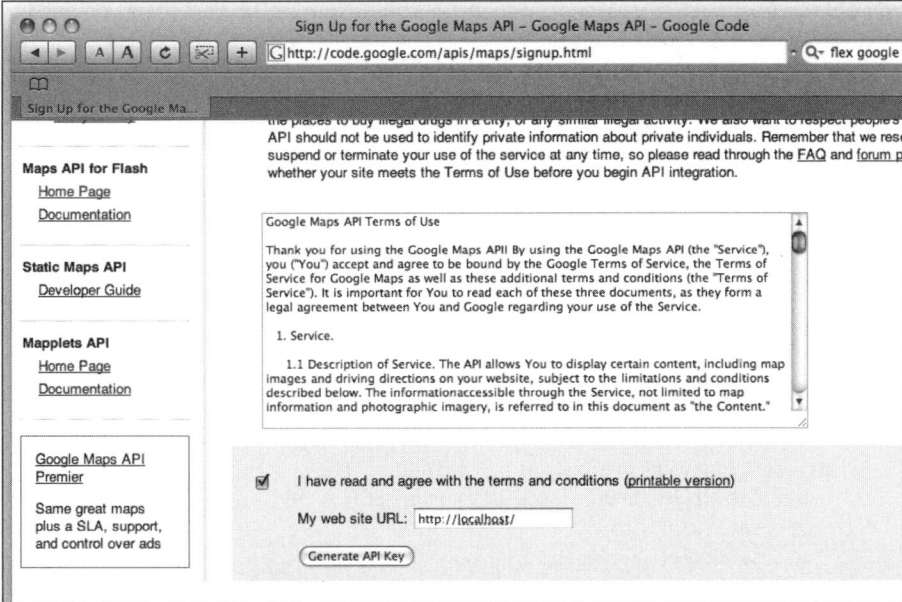

**Figure 11-2.** The API key signup page

You will want to get at least two keys, the first for your testing machine, which I presume is http://localhost, and the other for your production site. If you don't have a production site at the moment, you can just forgo that.

After you input the URL in the My web site URL field, you click the Generate API Key button, and that will bring up a third page that gives you your API key and some sample JavaScript code. An example is shown in Figure 11-3.

**Figure 11-3.** Your new Google API key

You can forget about the JavaScript code; it's worthless to you. The next thing you need to do is download the Google Flash API for Maps and install it in your Flex project.

From there, you should be able to write some code like the application shown here:

```
<?xml version="1.0" encoding="utf-8"?>
<mx:Application xmlns:mx="http://www.adobe.com/2006/mxml"
  layout="absolute"
  creationComplete="onStartup()">
<mx:Script>
<![CDATA[
import com.google.maps.Map;
import mx.core.UIComponent;

private var map:Map = new Map();

private function onStartup() : void {
  var uic:UIComponent = new UIComponent();
  uic.setStyle( 'top', 0 );
  uic.setStyle( 'left', 0 );
  uic.width = width;
  uic.height = height;
  addChild( uic );

  map.key = 'Maps Key';
  map.width = width;
  map.height = height;
  uic.addChild( map );
}
]]>
</mx:Script>
</mx:Application>
```

This is the simplest possible Google Maps implementation for Flex. The code first creates a UIComponent and adds it to the application frame. That UIComponent is required to host Flash Sprite objects. Then it sets the map key, resizes the Sprite, and adds it to the UIComponent.

When we bring this up from Flex, it appears as shown in Figure 11-4.

Oops, this isn't so good. So what's wrong? The secret is in the URL of the page. Instead of being http://localhost/... the page is file:///..., and the Google Maps component is expecting localhost with the key we gave it.

That means we need to run the page out of localhost. So we need to go to the Source Path tab on the Flex Build Path panel in the Project Properties dialog. From there, we need to input the directory within the localhost web server's document directory where the Flex Builder IDE should write the output files.

On my Macintosh, this looks like Figure 11-5.

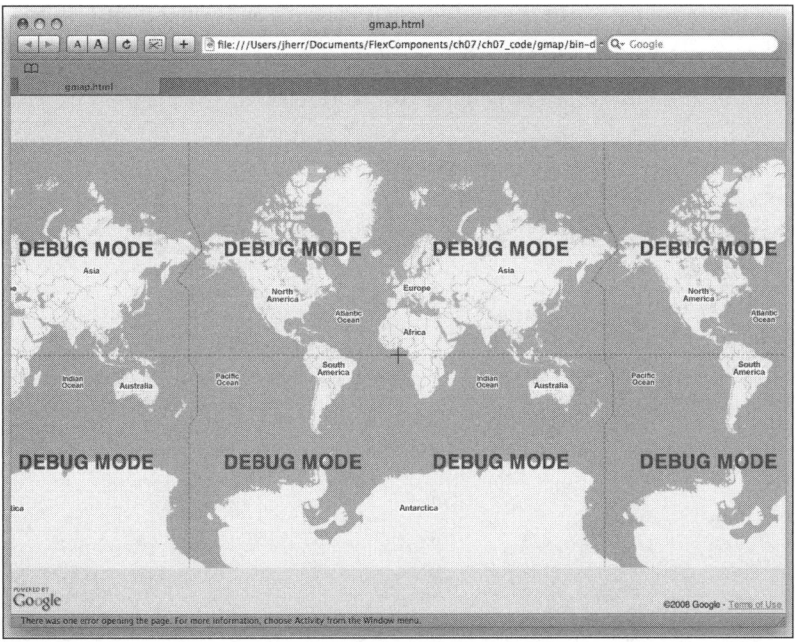

**Figure 11-4.** The Google Maps control in debug mode

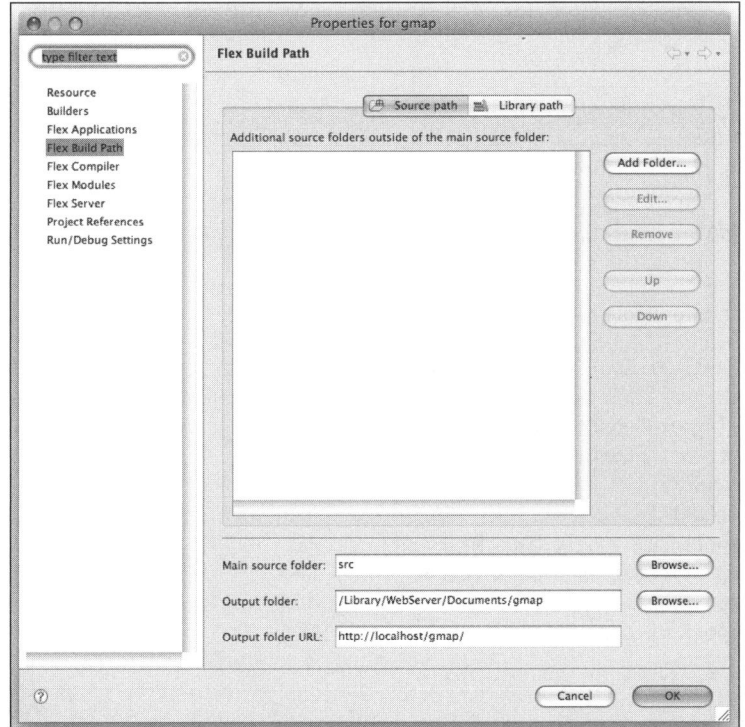

**Figure 11-5.** The Flex Build Path panel

The web server root is /Library/WebServer/Documents and within that I have a folder called gmap where I want the output files to be placed.

Now when we run this, we see something like Figure 11-6.

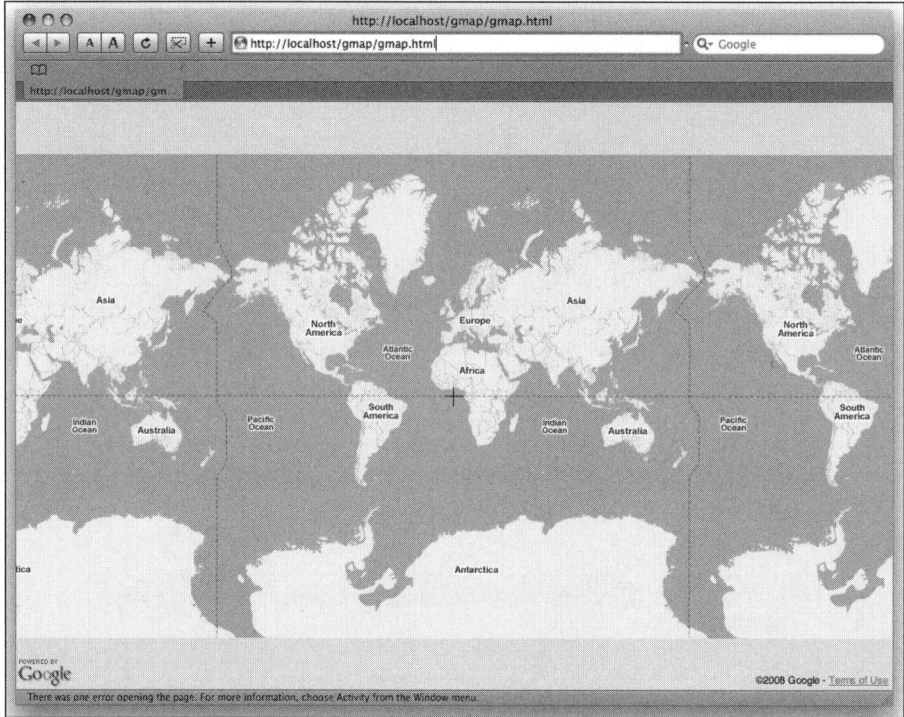

**Figure 11-6.** The map in nondebug mode

Ah, now we are cooking with gas. No more of that crazy "debug mode" stuff.

I don't think it's very interesting to look at one big map of the world. So let's zoom in on someplace interesting. Here's the code to do just that:

```
<?xml version="1.0" encoding="utf-8"?>
<mx:Application xmlns:mx="http://www.adobe.com/2006/mxml"
  layout="absolute"
  creationComplete="onStartup()">
<mx:Script>
<![CDATA[
import com.google.maps.MapEvent;
import com.google.maps.LatLng;
import com.google.maps.Map;
import mx.core.UIComponent;
```

```
    private var map:Map = new Map();

    private function onStartup() : void {
      var uic:UIComponent = new UIComponent();
      uic.setStyle( 'top', 0 );
      uic.setStyle( 'left', 0 );
      uic.width = width;
      uic.height = height;
      addChild( uic );

      map.key = 'Google Maps Key';
      map.width = width;
      map.height = height;
      map.addEventListener( MapEvent.MAP_READY, onMapReady );
      uic.addChild( map );
    }
    private function onMapReady( event:MapEvent ) : void {
      map.setCenter( new LatLng( 34.101509, -118.32691 ) );
      map.setZoom( 16 );
    }
    ]]>
    </mx:Script>
    </mx:Application>
```

This is similar to the original code, but in this case we have some extra code that watches for the MapEvent.READY message from the map control. When that happens, we set the middle of the map to the latitude and longitude somewhere in the US. Then we set the zoom factor to something fairly close. In Google Maps parlance, a zoom of 1 is the whole world, while a zoom of 18 is what you would use to place the sprinklers in your backyard.

The result of this is shown in Figure 11-7.

11

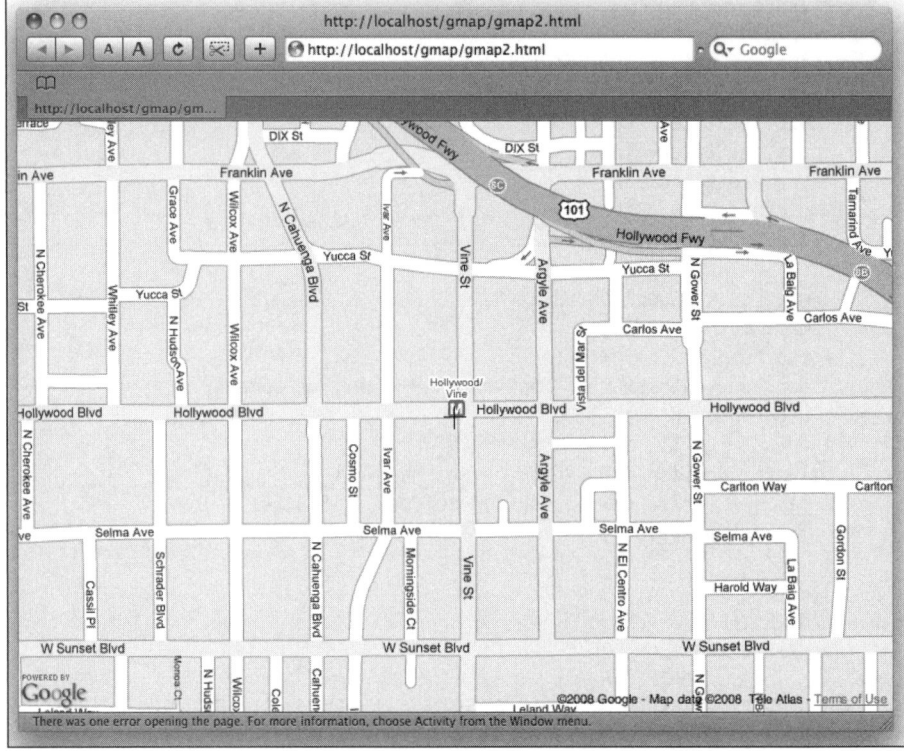

**Figure 11-7.** The corner of Hollywood and Vine in Los Angeles

Oh, look, we are at Hollywood and Vine. Get out the star maps!

Next, let's add a few controls to the map, as shown in the following application code:

```
<?xml version="1.0" encoding="utf-8"?>
<mx:Application xmlns:mx="http://www.adobe.com/2006/mxml"
  layout="absolute"
  creationComplete="onStartup()">
<mx:Script>
<![CDATA[
import com.google.maps.controls.ZoomControl;
import com.google.maps.controls.MapTypeControl;
import com.google.maps.MapEvent;
import com.google.maps.LatLng;
import com.google.maps.Map;
import mx.core.UIComponent;

private var map:Map = new Map();

private function onStartup() : void {
...
```

```
}
private function onMapReady( event:MapEvent ) : void {
  map.setCenter( new LatLng( 34.101509, -118.32691 ) );
  map.setZoom( 16 );

  map.addControl( new MapTypeControl() );
  map.addControl( new ZoomControl() );
}
]]>
</mx:Script>
</mx:Application>
```

This code adds two controls to the map: a type control where you can select from Map, Satellite, Hybrid, or Terrain mode, and a zoom control that allows the user to adjust the zoom factor of the map.

Figure 11-8 shows the application after it launches; I have zoomed out a little and changed to Terrain mode.

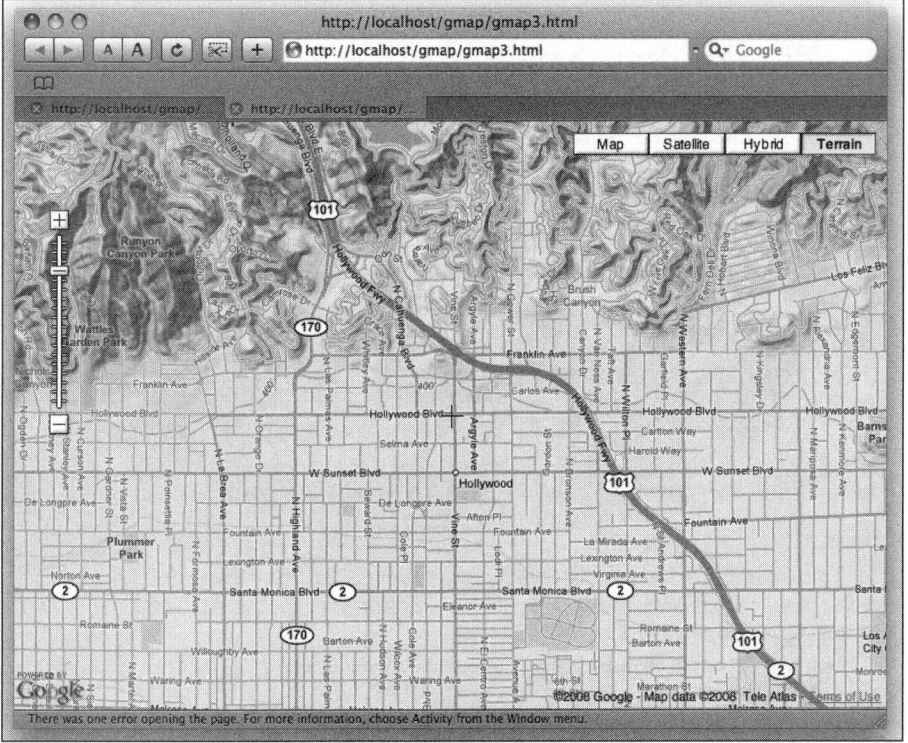

**Figure 11-8.** Terrain mode in the Google Maps control

I love Terrain mode. It's really pretty and not usually the type of thing you see on every other mapping page.

Now at this, point we have a genuinely usable map. It starts in Hollywood, but then you can zoom in and out and use the mouse to move around, as well as change the type of map so that you can see different types of detail.

To finish off the Google Maps example, I'll show how to add geocoding that will allow the user to type in an address, press Return, and have the map zoom to that location. **Geocoding** is the process of turning an address into a set of latitude and longitude coordinates. Thankfully, the Google Maps servers handle all of the gritty details for us, and we can concentrate on putting a nice interface on it.

The application code that handles geocoding is shown here:

```
<?xml version="1.0" encoding="utf-8"?>
<mx:Application xmlns:mx="http://www.adobe.com/2006/mxml"
  layout="absolute"
  creationComplete="onStartup()">
<mx:Script>
<![CDATA[
import com.google.maps.services.GeocodingEvent;
import com.google.maps.services.ClientGeocoder;
import com.google.maps.controls.ZoomControl;
import com.google.maps.controls.MapTypeControl;
import com.google.maps.MapEvent;
import com.google.maps.LatLng;
import com.google.maps.Map;
import mx.core.UIComponent;

private var map:Map = new Map();

private function onStartup() : void {
...
  locPanel.setStyle( 'top', height - locPanel.height - 20 );
}
private function onMapReady( event:MapEvent ) : void {
...
}
private function onGeocodeSuccess( event:GeocodingEvent ) : void {
  map.setCenter( event.response.placemarks[0].point );
}
private function onKeyDown( event:KeyboardEvent ) : void {
  if ( event.keyCode == Keyboard.ENTER ) {
    var cg:ClientGeocoder = new ClientGeocoder( "USA" );
    cg.addEventListener( GeocodingEvent.GEOCODING_SUCCESS,
    onGeocodeSuccess );
    cg.geocode( loc.text );
  }
}
```

```
     ]]>
   </mx:Script>
   <mx:Panel id="locPanel" title="Location" top="500" left="20"
     borderAlpha="0.95">
     <mx:TextInput id="loc" keyDown="onKeyDown( event )" width="300" />
   </mx:Panel>
</mx:Application>
```

The application now includes an additional Panel that has a TextInput for holding the address. This TextInput watches for a return in the onKeyDown method. Once it gets a return, it starts up a ClientGeocoder object and gives it the address specified by the user. When the geocoder returns with the data, it calls the onGeocodeSuccess method, which moves the map to the location that was returned by the server.

When I first launch the application, it looks like Figure 11-9.

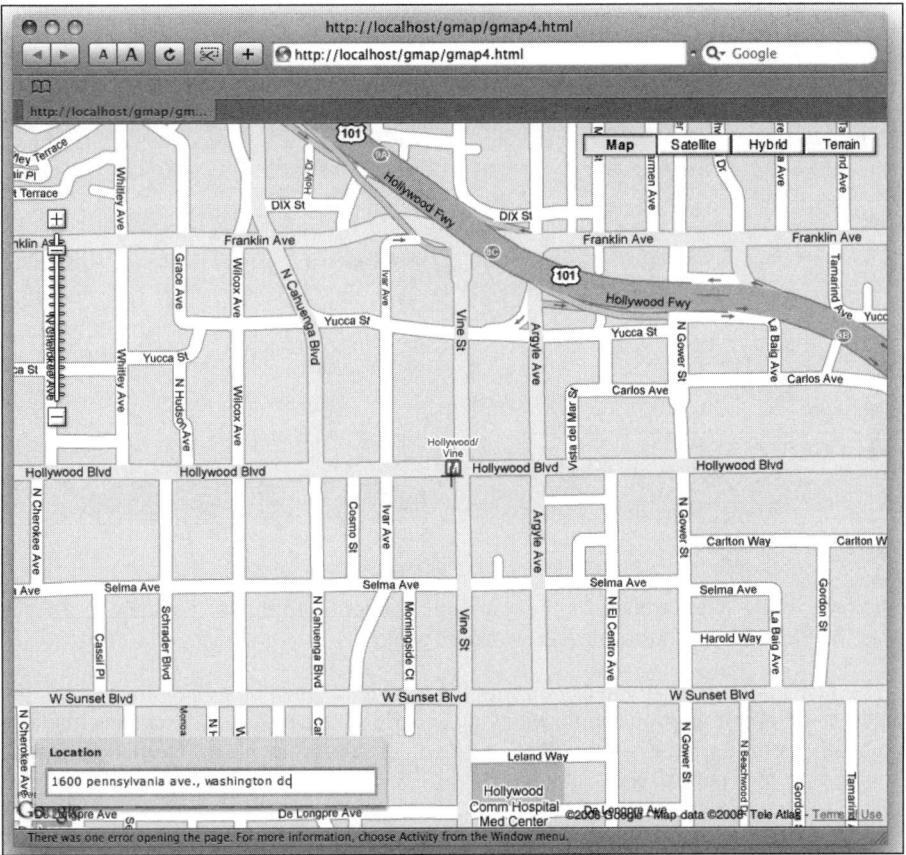

**Figure 11-9.** The application with the Address panel

You can see the location input in the lower-right corner of the display. We can now type in a familiar address, say 1600 Pennsylvania Ave., Washington DC, press Return, and be transported right to it as shown in Figure 11-10.

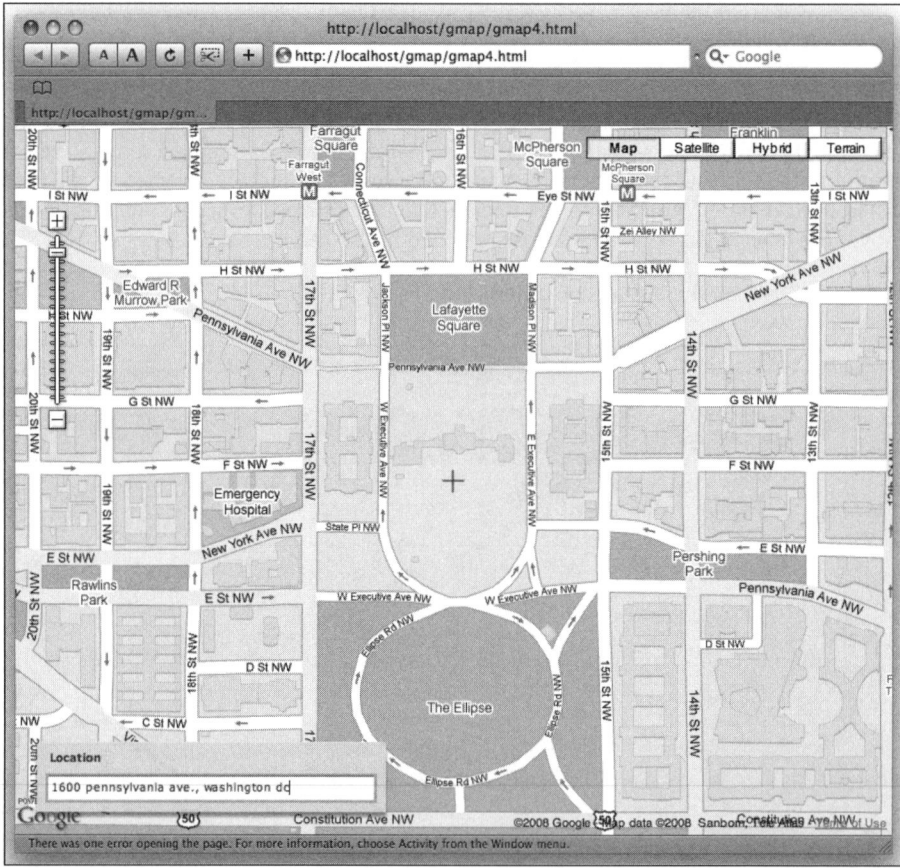

**Figure 11-10.** The White House

Welcome to the White House. All the way from Hollywood to the White House in a single press of a key! Even Schwarzenegger would be envious!

This is just a taste of what you can do with the Google Maps API for Flash. It gives you the ability to do everything you can do with the JavaScript API, which includes adding markers, embedding small windows with HTML marked up data, responding to marker events, adding your own control types, and so on.

## Yahoo! Maps

The Yahoo! Maps API is similar to the Google Maps API, though it's a little easier to use in some cases and includes an integrated search feature that maps the Yahoo! search results.

As with the Google Maps API, we start by downloading the Flash component and getting the Yahoo! application ID. So we first navigate to `http://developer.yahoo.com/maps/flash/flexGettingStarted.html`. This page is shown in Figure 11-11.

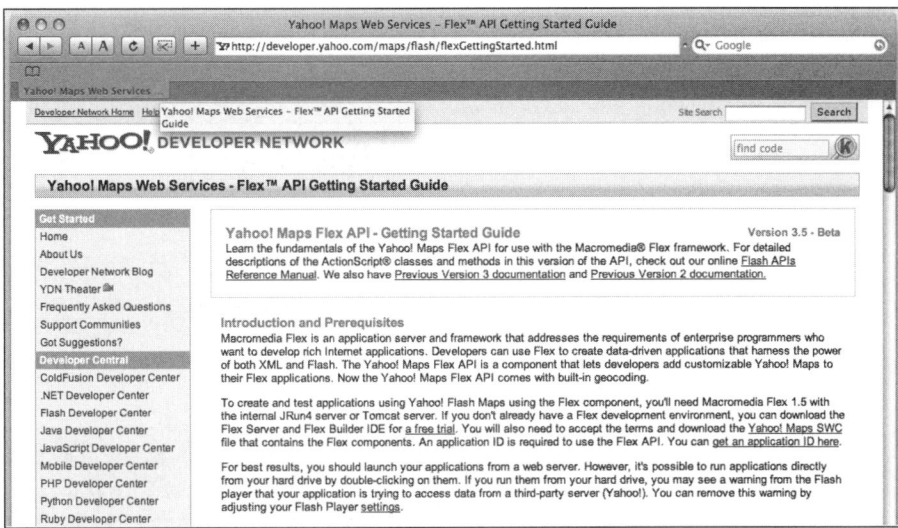

**Figure 11-11.** The Yahoo! Flash Maps landing page

From here, we need to register with the Yahoo! web services by following the link on the page. You will need a Yahoo ID to even start the process. So get one of those if you don't have one. When you do, the developer registration page looks like Figure 11-12.

**Figure 11-12.** The developer registration page

Fill in all the required fields in that form and submit it, and that will take you to another page that shows the application ID. As with the Google Maps key, this is relative to a URL. So you will likely want two application IDs: one for testing on localhost and the other for your production web site.

The application ID page is shown in Figure 11-13.

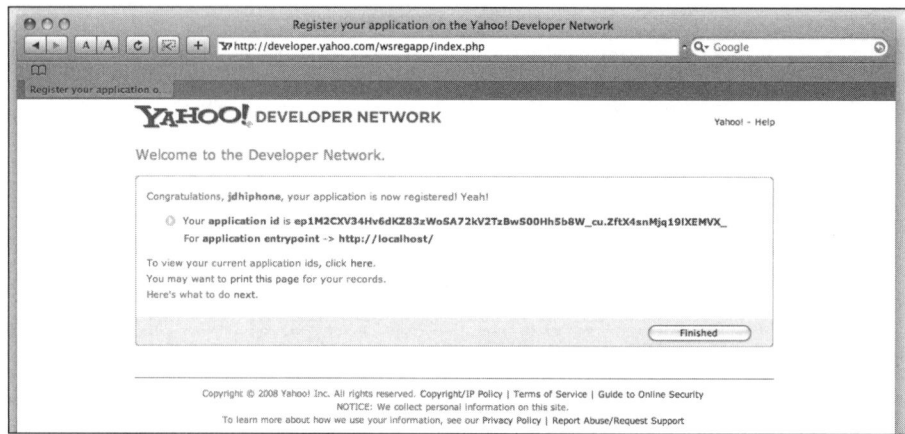

**Figure 11-13.** The application ID page

The next step is to create the simplest possible Yahoo! Maps Flex application. The code for that is shown here:

```
<?xml version="1.0" encoding="utf-8"?>
<mx:Application xmlns:mx="http://www.adobe.com/2006/mxml"
  creationComplete="onStartup();"
  layout="absolute">
<mx:Script>
<![CDATA[
import com.yahoo.maps.api.core.location.LatLon;
import mx.core.UIComponent;
import com.yahoo.maps.api.*;

private var map:YahooMap = new YahooMap();

private function onStartup() : void {
  var uic:UIComponent = new UIComponent();
  uic.width = width;
  uic.height = height;
  uic.setStyle('top',0);
  uic.setStyle('left',0);
  addChild( uic );
```

```
      map.init('Yahoo App ID',width,height);
      map.addEventListener( YahooMapEvent.MAP_INITIALIZE, onMapInit );
      map.addPanControl();
      map.addTypeWidget();
      uic.addChild( map );
    }
    private function onMapInit( event:YahooMapEvent ) : void {
      map.centerLatLon = new LatLon(41,-105);
    }
    ]]>
    </mx:Script>
    </mx:Application>
```

Because the Yahoo! Maps API is a Flash API, the control is based on Sprite. That means you need to wrap it in a UIComponent to embed it in a Flex application. This is done in the onStartup method.

The code also listens for the YahooMapEvent.MAP_INITIALIZE event with the onMapInit method. When that method is called, it sets the center of the map to somewhere around the middle of the United States.

As with the Google Maps API, we have to set the Source Build Path to the local web server before the map will show any data for the given application ID.

The result is shown in Figure 11-14.

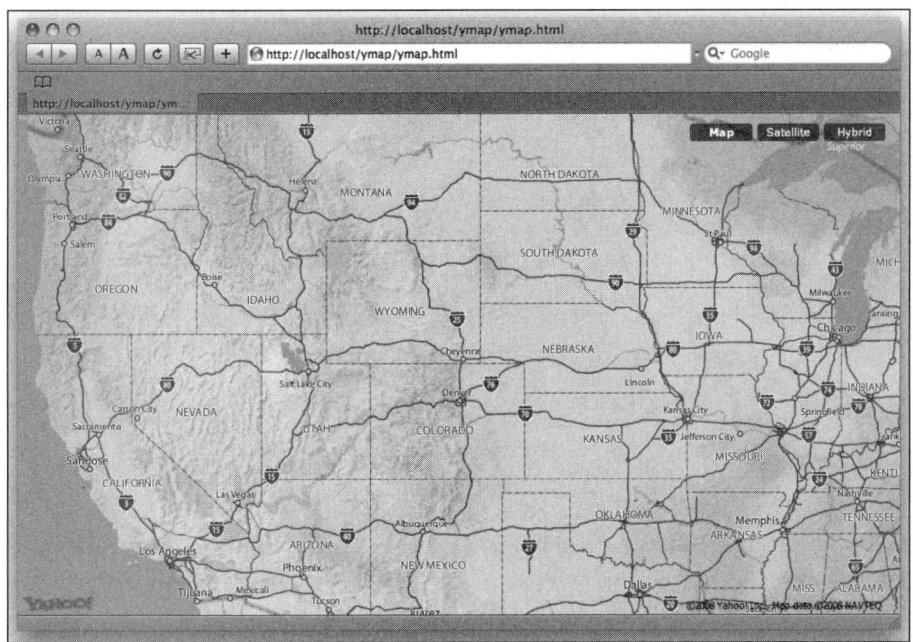

**Figure 11-14.** The initial version of the application

That's not a bad place to start. It's certainly a very pretty map right from the get-go.

The next step is to look at the geocoding capabilities of the Yahoo! Maps API. The following application code finds the White House and zooms in on it:

```
<?xml version="1.0" encoding="utf-8"?>
<mx:Application xmlns:mx="http://www.adobe.com/2006/mxml"
  creationComplete="onStartup();"
  layout="absolute">
<mx:Script>
<![CDATA[
import com.yahoo.maps.api.core.location.Address;
import com.yahoo.maps.webservices.geocoder.events.GeocoderEvent;
import com.yahoo.maps.webservices.geocoder.Geocoder;
import com.yahoo.maps.api.core.location.LatLon;
import mx.core.UIComponent;
import com.yahoo.maps.api.*;

private var map:YahooMap = new YahooMap();

private function onStartup() : void {
...
  map.init('Yahoo App ID',width,height);
  map.addEventListener( YahooMapEvent.MAP_INITIALIZE, onMapInit );
  map.addPanControl();
  map.addTypeWidget();
  uic.addChild( map );
}
private function onMapInit( event:YahooMapEvent ) : void {
  map.centerLatLon = new LatLon(41,-105);
  map.zoomLevel = 3;

  var gc:Geocoder = new Geocoder();
  gc.addEventListener(GeocoderEvent.GEOCODER_SUCCESS,onGeocodeSuccess);
  gc.geocode( new Address( "1600 pennsylvania ave., washington dc" ) );
}
private function onGeocodeSuccess( event:GeocoderEvent ) : void {
  map.centerLatLon = event.data.firstResult.latlon;
}
]]>
</mx:Script>
</mx:Application>
```

After the map signals that it's ready with the MAP_INITIALIZE event, the onMapInit method then creates a Geocoder object and searches for the address of the White House. The onGeocodeSuccess method is called when addresses are resolved to latitude and longitude pairs successfully. It then centers the map on that location.

The result of this example code is shown in Figure 11-15.

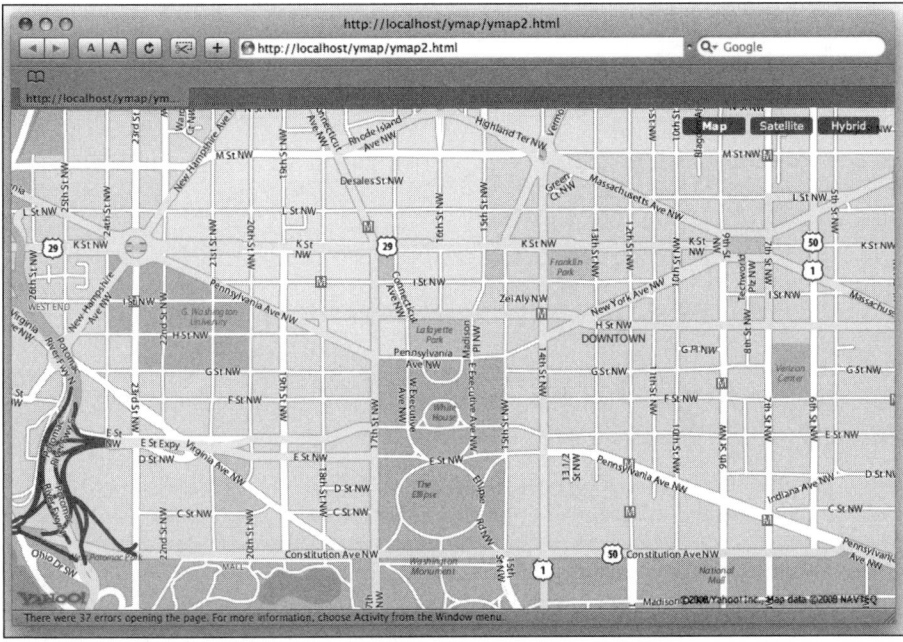

**Figure 11-15.** The final version of the application

That works very nicely.

An interesting aspect of this mapping API is its integration with the Yahoo! search results. The application in the following code uses this searching API to place markers for various search results on the map:

```xml
<?xml version="1.0" encoding="utf-8"?>
<mx:Application xmlns:mx="http://www.adobe.com/2006/mxml"
  creationComplete="onStartup();"
  layout="absolute">
<mx:Script>
<![CDATA[
import com.yahoo.maps.webservices.local.LocalSearchResults;
import com.yahoo.maps.api.markers.SearchMarker;
import com.yahoo.maps.webservices.local.LocalSearchItem;
import com.yahoo.maps.webservices.local.events.LocalSearchEvent;
import com.yahoo.maps.webservices.local.LocalSearch;
import com.yahoo.maps.api.core.location.Address;
import com.yahoo.maps.webservices.geocoder.events.GeocoderEvent;
import com.yahoo.maps.webservices.geocoder.Geocoder;
import com.yahoo.maps.api.core.location.LatLon;
import mx.core.UIComponent;
import com.yahoo.maps.api.*;

private var map:YahooMap = new YahooMap();
```

11

```
      private function onStartup() : void {
      ...
        map.init('Yahoo App ID',width,height);
        map.addEventListener( YahooMapEvent.MAP_INITIALIZE, onMapInit );
        map.addPanControl();
        map.addTypeWidget();
        uic.addChild( map );

        searchPanel.setStyle( 'top', height - searchPanel.height - 20 );
      }
      private function onMapInit( event:YahooMapEvent ) : void {
      ...
      }
      private function onGeocodeSuccess( event:GeocoderEvent ) : void {
      ...
      }
      private function onKeyDown( event:KeyboardEvent ) : void {
        if ( event.keyCode == Keyboard.ENTER ) runSearch();
      }
      private function runSearch( ) : void {
        var ls:LocalSearch = new LocalSearch();
        ls.addEventListener(LocalSearchEvent.SEARCH_SUCCESS,
        onSearchSuccess );
        ls.searchLocal( search.text, 3, map.centerLatLon );
      }
      private function onSearchSuccess( event:LocalSearchEvent ) : void {
        map.markerManager.removeAllMarkers();
        var lsr:LocalSearchResults = event.data as LocalSearchResults;
        for each( var lsi:LocalSearchItem in lsr.results )
          map.markerManager.addMarker( new SearchMarker( lsi ) );
      }
    ]]>
    </mx:Script>
    <mx:Panel id="searchPanel" title="Location" top="500" left="20"
      borderAlpha="0.95">
      <mx:TextInput id="search" text="starbucks"
        keyDown="onKeyDown( event )" width="300" />
    </mx:Panel>
    </mx:Application>
```

Much of the code remains the same, but now we have a search panel located at the bottom of the application frame. Within the panel is a TextInput where the user can type in a search term. The onKeyDown method listens for a return and calls the runSearch method when it finds one. The runSearch method uses the LocalSearch class to perform a search geographically centered around the current map location. The onSearchSuccess method is called when search results are found. That method creates markers for each of the search results returned by the Yahoo! servers.

When we run this application from Flex Builder, we see something like Figure 11-16.

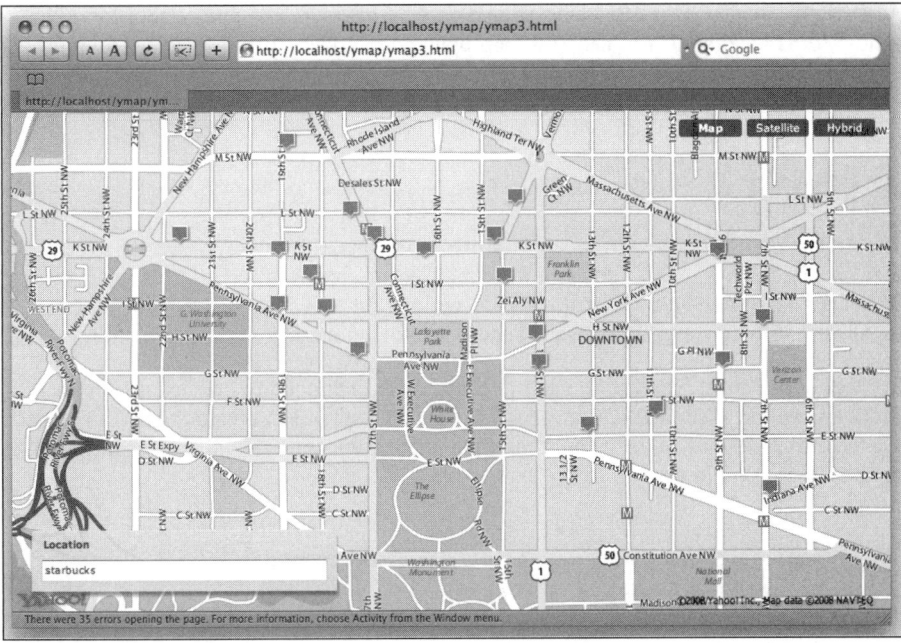

**Figure 11-16.** The map showing search results for Starbucks

This shows all of the Starbucks locations around the White House. If we want to do some reading, we might want to look for any Borders locations. The hits for that are shown in Figure 11-17.

**Figure 11-17.** The Borders stores around the White House

**293**

As with the Google Maps API, I have shown only a fraction of the potential of the API presented to us by Yahoo!. You can add map polygon overlays, custom overlays, support for GeoRSS, and much more.

# The UMap

The UMap control from Advanced Flash Components (http://afcomponents.com) will feel familiar initially, but is fundamentally a different approach to Flash mapping. Instead of being a Flash API from the map service vendors, the Advanced Flash team started with its API and layered it on top of any mapping service, geocoding service, or map source.

But let's start with the basics. To use the control, you will need to convert it from its MXP form. Follow the MXP to SWC conversion recipe in Chapter 3 to create the SWC. Then add the SWC to your libs folder. From there, the application code shown here uses the UMap control in the simplest way it can:

```
<?xml version="1.0" encoding="utf-8"?>
<mx:Application xmlns:mx="http://www.adobe.com/2006/mxml"
    layout="absolute"
    creationComplete="onStartup()">
<mx:Script>
<![CDATA[
import com.afcomponents.umap.core.UMap;
import mx.core.UIComponent;

private var map:UMap = new UMap();

private function onStartup() : void {
  var uic:UIComponent = new UIComponent();
  uic.setStyle( 'top', 0 );
  uic.setStyle( 'left', 0 );
  uic.width = width;
  uic.height = height;
  addChildAt( uic, 0 );

  map.setSize( width, height );
  uic.addChild( map );
}
]]>
</mx:Script>
</mx:Application>
```

Because the UMap control is based on Sprite, we need to create a UIComponent to host the control, and then add the new UMap Sprite to that control. The result of this application is shown in Figure 11-18.

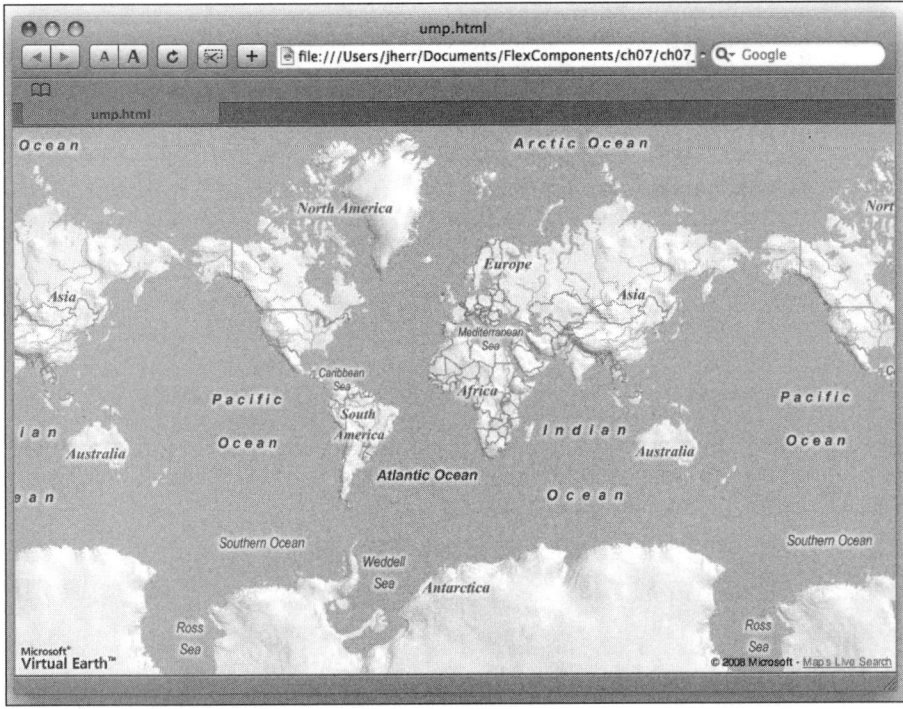

**Figure 11-18.** The initial state of the map

One important point to note is that we didn't have to request any API keys to get this to work. Nor did we have to host it on localhost. This component just works right out of the bag.

The next step is to add some mapping controls and zoom in on the United States. The application code for this is shown here:

```
<?xml version="1.0" encoding="utf-8"?>
<mx:Application xmlns:mx="http://www.adobe.com/2006/mxml"
    layout="absolute"
    creationComplete="onStartup()">
<mx:Script>
<![CDATA[
import com.afcomponents.umap.types.LatLng;
import com.afcomponents.umap.gui.*;
import com.afcomponents.umap.events.MapEvent;
import com.afcomponents.umap.core.UMap;
import mx.core.UIComponent;

private var map:UMap = new UMap();

private function onStartup() : void {
  ...
```

```
        map.setSize( width, height );
        map.addEventListener(MapEvent.READY, onMapReady);
        uic.addChild( map );
    }
    private function onMapReady( event:MapEvent ) : void {
      map.addControl( new ZoomControl() );
      map.addControl( new MapTypeControl() );
      map.addControl( new PositionControl() );
      map.setCenter( new LatLng( 41, -105 ) );
      map.setZoom( 4 );
    }
    ]]>
    </mx:Script>
    </mx:Application>
```

This code adds a zoom control, a map type control where you can choose between road, aerial, or hybrid map types, and a position control to the map. Now when we bring up the Flex application, it looks like Figure 11-19.

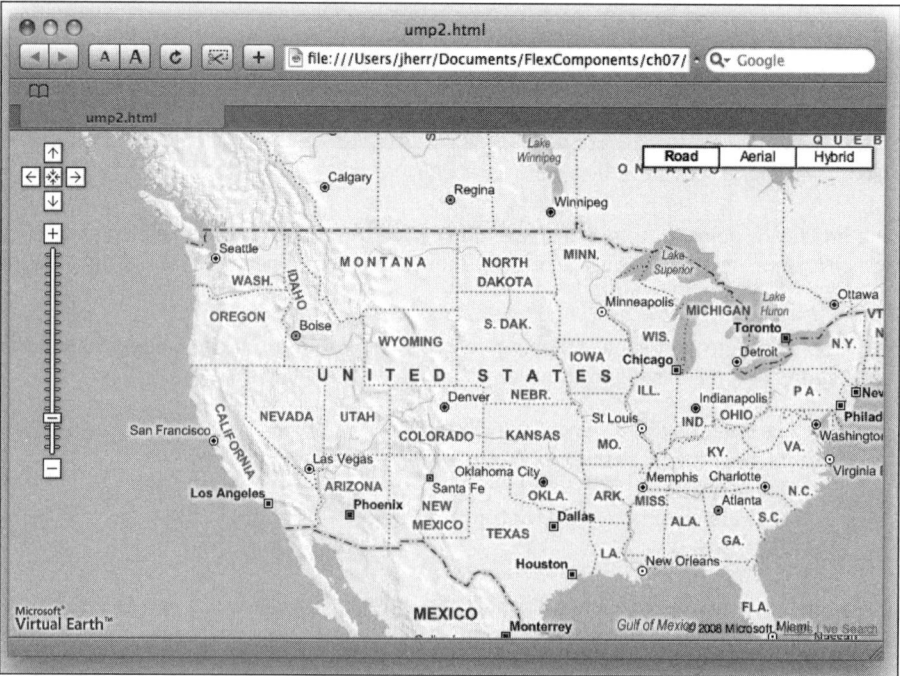

**Figure 11-19.** The UMap component displaying the map of the United States

OK, now we have a fully functional map with a full set of controls. The next step is to check out the UMap's geocoding functionality. UMap can support several different geocoding sources. The following application uses the default geocoding source:

```
<?xml version="1.0" encoding="utf-8"?>
<mx:Application xmlns:mx="http://www.adobe.com/2006/mxml"
    layout="absolute"
    creationComplete="onStartup()">
<mx:Script>
<![CDATA[
import com.afcomponents.umap.overlays.Layer;
import com.afcomponents.umap.display.geocodermanager.GeoNamesService;
import com.afcomponents.umap.events.GeocoderEvent;
import com.afcomponents.umap.display.geocodermanager.GeocoderManager;
import com.afcomponents.umap.types.LatLng;
import com.afcomponents.umap.gui.*;
import com.afcomponents.umap.events.MapEvent;
import com.afcomponents.umap.core.UMap;
import mx.core.UIComponent;

private var map:UMap = new UMap();

private function onStartup() : void {
...
}
private function onMapReady( event:MapEvent ) : void {
    ...
    var dgs:GeocoderManager = new GeocoderManager();
    dgs.addEventListener( GeocoderEvent.SUCCESS, onGeocodeSuccess );
    dgs.service.geocodeAddress( 'washington dc', 20,
      {verbosity:GeoNamesService.FULL} );
}
private function onGeocodeSuccess( event:GeocoderEvent ) : void {
    map.setCenter( new LatLng( event.results[0].position.lat,
      event.results[0].position.lng ) );
    map.setZoom( 15 );
}
]]>
</mx:Script>
</mx:Application>
```

11

In the UMap model, you can get several results back for a single query to the GeocoderManager. The geocodeAdress method takes three values: the address, the maximum number of results to return, and any options for the query. This version of the application will set the position of the map to the first result. You can see the result for the "Washington, DC" query shown in Figure 11-20.

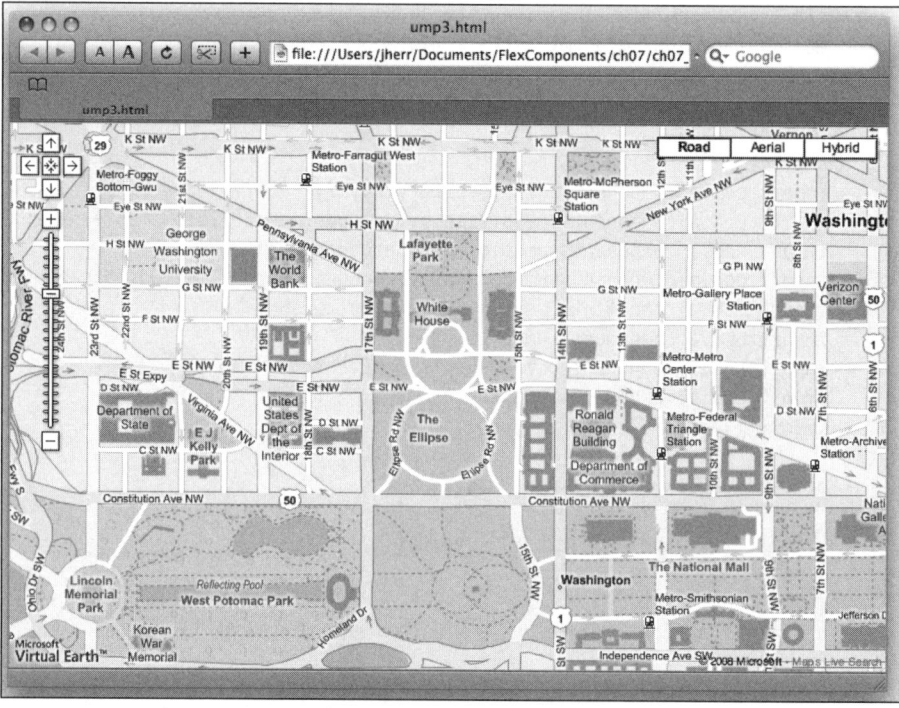

**Figure 11-20.** The UMap component displaying the first result from the "Washington, DC" query

To view all of the results from the query, we can create a new overlay layer on the UMap. The application code shown here demonstrates how this is done:

```
<?xml version="1.0" encoding="utf-8"?>
<mx:Application xmlns:mx="http://www.adobe.com/2006/mxml"
  layout="absolute"
   creationComplete="onStartup()">
<mx:Script>
<![CDATA[
import com.afcomponents.umap.overlays.Layer;
import com.afcomponents.umap.display.geocodermanager.GeoNamesService;
import com.afcomponents.umap.events.GeocoderEvent;
import com.afcomponents.umap.display.geocodermanager.GeocoderManager;
import com.afcomponents.umap.types.LatLng;
import com.afcomponents.umap.gui.*;
import com.afcomponents.umap.events.MapEvent;
import com.afcomponents.umap.core.UMap;
import mx.core.UIComponent;

private var map:UMap = new UMap();
private var dgs:GeocoderManager = new GeocoderManager();
```

```
    private function onStartup() : void {
    ...
    }
    private function onMapReady( event:MapEvent ) : void {
    ...
    }
    private function onGeocodeSuccess( event:GeocoderEvent ) : void {
      var layer:Layer = dgs.getLayer(event.results);
      map.addOverlay(layer);
      map.setBounds(layer.getBoundsLatLng());
    }
    ]]>
    </mx:Script>
    </mx:Application>
```

The GeocoderManager can turn the search results into a layer for us. That's done with the getLayer method. We then add that overlay to the map with the addOverlay method and use the setBounds method to size the map appropriately for the results.

The results of applying this new application code to the "Washington, DC" query are shown in Figure 11-21.

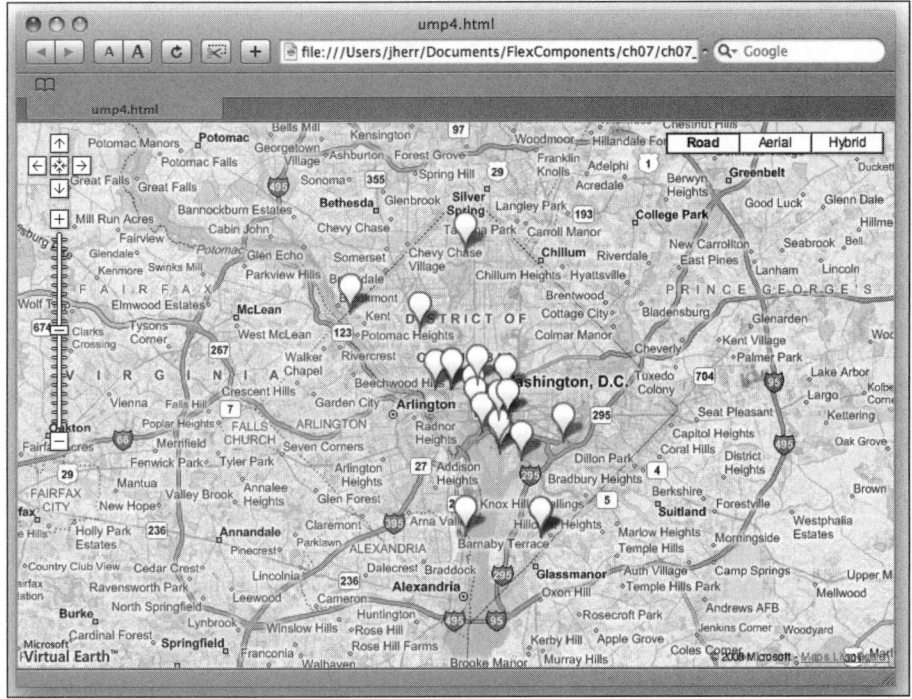

**Figure 11-21.** The map overlay with the search results

This shows markers for the first 20 search results on the "Washington, DC" query. If we zoom in on one of them and click it, we get a pop-up that looks like Figure 11-22.

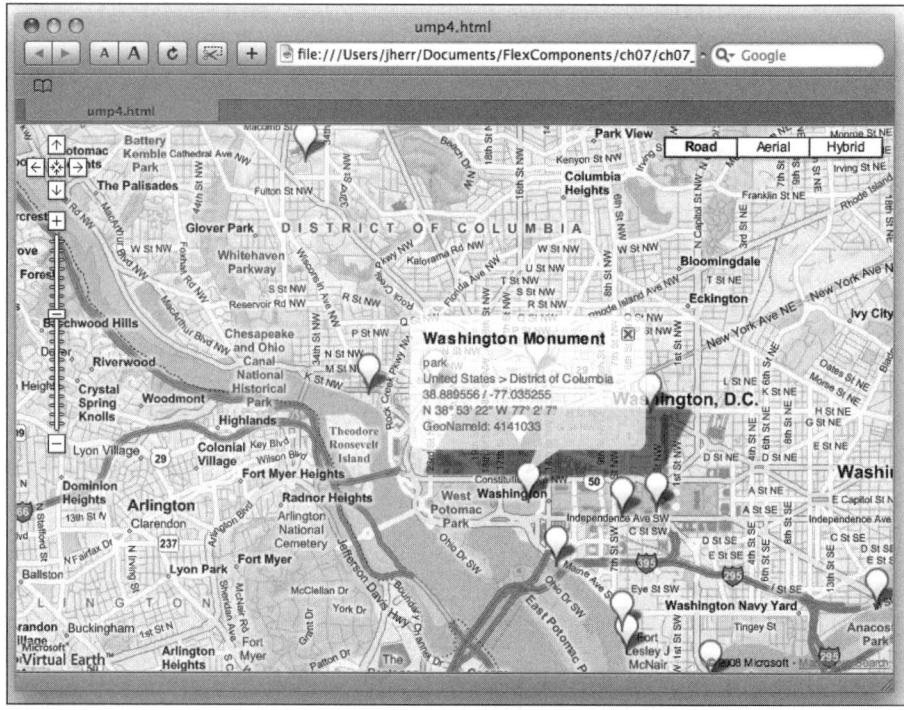

**Figure 11-22.** More information about the Washington Monument

To demonstrate how you can use multiple maps in conjunction with each other, the next example shows two maps. The first is the original map from the previous UMap examples, the second is a zoomed-in satellite map that is synced to the mouse location on the big map.

Here's the code for this application:

```
<?xml version="1.0" encoding="utf-8"?>
<mx:Application xmlns:mx="http://www.adobe.com/2006/mxml"
    layout="absolute"
    creationComplete="onStartup()">
<mx:Script>
<![CDATA[
import com.afcomponents.umap.overlays.Layer;
import com.afcomponents.umap.display.geocodermanager.GeoNamesService;
import com.afcomponents.umap.events.GeocoderEvent;
import com.afcomponents.umap.display.geocodermanager.GeocoderManager;
import com.afcomponents.umap.types.LatLng;
import com.afcomponents.umap.gui.*;
import com.afcomponents.umap.events.MapEvent;
```

```actionscript
import com.afcomponents.umap.core.UMap;
import mx.core.UIComponent;

private var map:UMap = new UMap();
private var zoomMap:UMap = new UMap();
private var dgs:GeocoderManager = new GeocoderManager();

private function onStartup() : void {
  var uic:UIComponent = new UIComponent();
  uic.setStyle( 'top', 0 );
  uic.setStyle( 'left', 0 );
  uic.width = width;
  uic.height = height;
  addChildAt( uic, 0 );

  map.setSize( width, height );
  map.addEventListener(MapEvent.READY, onMapReady);
  map.addEventListener(MouseEvent.MOUSE_MOVE,onMapMouseMove);
  uic.addChild( map );

  var uic2:UIComponent = new UIComponent();
  uic2.width = 250;
  uic2.height = 300;
  zoomPnl.addChild( uic2 );

  zoomMap.setSize( uic2.width, uic2.height );
  zoomMap.addEventListener(MapEvent.READY, onZoomMapReady);
  uic2.addChild( zoomMap );
}
private function onZoomMapReady( event:MapEvent ) : void {
  zoomMap.setCenter( new LatLng( 41, -105 ) );
  zoomMap.setMapType( "aerial" );
  zoomMap.setZoom( 18 );
}
private function onMapMouseMove( event:MouseEvent ) : void {
  zoomMap.setCenter( map.getMouseLatLng( 18 ) );
}
private function onMapReady( event:MapEvent ) : void {
  map.addControl( new ZoomControl() );
  map.addControl( new MapTypeControl() );
  map.addControl( new PositionControl() );
  map.setCenter( new LatLng( 41, -105 ) );
  map.setZoom( 4 );

  dgs.addEventListener( GeocoderEvent.SUCCESS, onGeocodeSuccess );
  dgs.service.geocodeAddress( 'washington dc', 20,
    {verbosity:GeoNamesService.FULL} );
}
private function onGeocodeSuccess( event:GeocoderEvent ) : void {
```

**11**

```
    var layer:Layer = dgs.getLayer(event.results);
    map.addOverlay(layer);
    map.setBounds(layer.getBoundsLatLng());
    zoomMap.setCenter( map.getCenter() );
}
]]>
</mx:Script>
<mx:Panel id="zoomPnl" title="Zoom In" top="30" left="80"
    borderAlpha="0.9">
</mx:Panel>
</mx:Application>
```

This application is an extension to the other UMap examples. In this case, a Panel is added to the display, which will host a second UIComponent, which will in turn host the zoomMap Sprite. That zoomMap object is initialized to a fixed zoom-in the onZoomMapReady method. From there, the zoomMap is synced to the mouse position on the original map object by the onMapMouseMove method. That method uses the getMouseLatLng helper method that returns a LatLng object for the current mouse coordinates.

You can see the results in Figure 11-23.

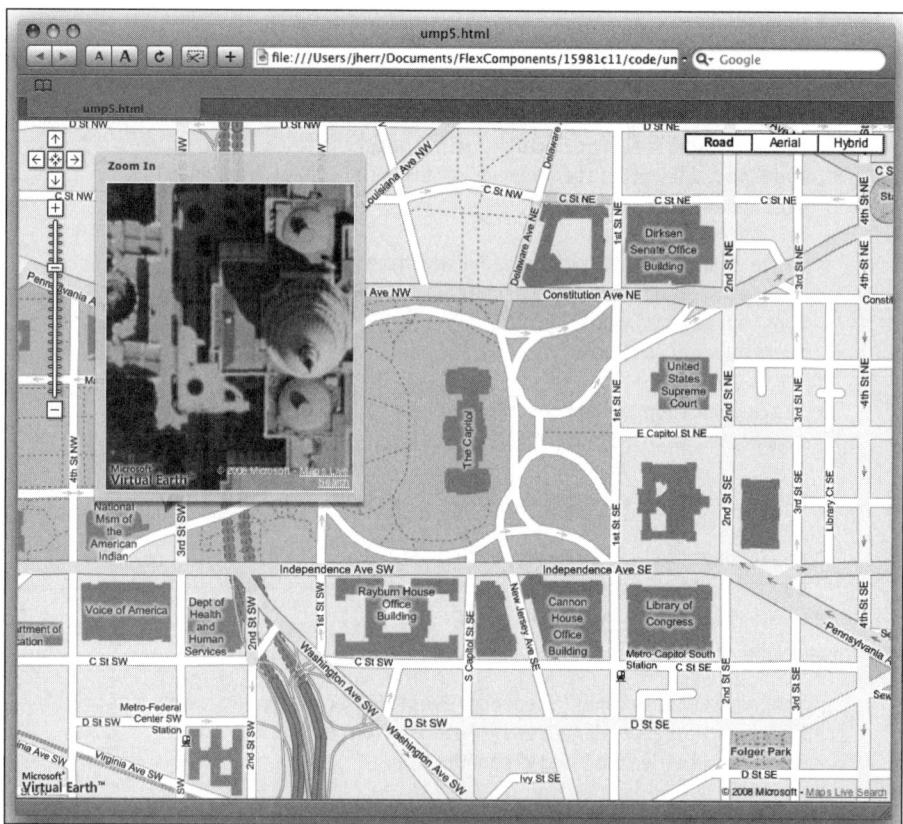

**Figure 11-23.** The two maps with the zoom-in centered on the US Capitol building

The UMap component is very powerful—certainly more powerful than the introductory demonstration I've shown here. It's particularly useful when your customer wants to display custom maps. You can grab map tiles from any source and use a custom map converter that comes with the UMap component to build a custom map for just your area of interest. Because the UMap still knows the geographical boundaries of the map, you can continue to use the latitude- and longitude-based services, like geocoding, when viewing the custom maps.

# Where we will go from here

Just a couple of years ago, online mapping was at odds with Flash and Flex. Now we have several components that integrate so seamlessly you would think that maps are integrated into the Flex core (and maybe they will be). Taking advantage of mapping, particularly with components like UMap, is very easy. Use the code in this chapter as a starting point with your applications, and you will have dynamic interactive mapping in no time flat.

11

# 12 INTRODUCING HIERARCHAL DATA AND COMPONENTS

Data is often structured into hierarchies. You have one or more root nodes, with each node having subnodes, and nodes of subnodes, and so on. The directory structure on your hard drive is organized this way. Most categorization systems are organized this way. Even your organizational tree at work is likely structured this way.

The Flex 3 framework already has support for hierarchal data display, with the Tree control. This chapter contains a few more controls to make the best use of your hierarchal data.

# Tree Maps

Tree Maps are a popular way of visualizing data that's structured into hierarchal trees. A Tree Map shows a set of nested rectangles. The nesting corresponds to the nodes of the tree. It's as if you took the tree, looked at it from the top, and flattened it. The size of the boxes depends on the weight of each node. So you have to not only have the tree, but also have a weight associated with each of the nodes in the tree. Of course, that weight metric is completely up to you.

The application code shown here uses the RaVis library from the BirdEye project (http://birdeye.googlecode.com/) to visualize the Tree Map:

```
<?xml version="1.0" encoding="utf-8"?>
<mx:Application xmlns:mx="http://www.adobe.com/2006/mxml"
  xmlns:qavis="org.un.cava.birdeye.qavis.treemap.controls.*"
  width="100%" height="100%" initialize="onStartup();">

<qavis:TreeMap id="treeMap" width="100%" height="100%" showRoot="false"
  dataProvider="{testData}" labelField="@name" weightField="@x"
  colorFunction="{itemToColor}" />

<mx:RemoteObject id="usdataRO"
  endpoint="http://localhost/amfphp/gateway.php"
  source="usdata.USDataService" destination="usdata.USDataService"
  showBusyCursor="true">
<mx:method name="getAll" result="onGetAllResult()">
<mx:arguments>
  <mx:Table />
</mx:arguments>
</mx:method>
</mx:RemoteObject>

<mx:Script>
<![CDATA[
import mx.collections.ArrayCollection;

import org.un.cava.birdeye.qavis.treemap.controls.treeMapClasses.*;

[Bindable]
private var testData:XML;
```

```
private const MIN_COLOR:uint = 0x4f94cd;
private const ZERO_COLOR:uint = 0;
private const MAX_COLOR:uint = 0x00008b;

private var _maxAbsoluteChange:Number;

private var _reqTable:String = '';
private var _usData:Object = {};

private function onGetAllResult() : void {
  _usData[ _reqTable ] = usdataRO.getAll.lastResult;
  _reqTable = null;
  if ( _usData[ 'it' ] == null ) _reqTable = 'it';
  if ( _usData[ 'realestate' ] == null ) _reqTable = 'realestate';
  if ( _usData[ 'construction' ] == null ) _reqTable = 'construction';
  if ( _reqTable != null ) usdataRO.getAll.send( _reqTable );
  else updateMap();
}

private function onStartup() : void {
  _reqTable = 'it';
  usdataRO.getAll.send( _reqTable );
}

private function updateMap() : void {
  testData = <data />;

  var par_it:XML = <parent name="Information Technology" />;
  testData.appendChild( par_it );
  for each( var obj1:Object in _usData['it'] ) {
    if ( obj1.state == 'United States' ) continue;
    par_it.appendChild( <child name={obj1.state}
    x={obj1.companies} /> );
  }
  var par_construction:XML = <parent name="Construction" />;
  testData.appendChild( par_construction );
  for each( var obj2:Object in _usData['construction'] ) {
    if ( obj2.state == 'United States' ) continue;
    par_construction.appendChild( <child name={obj2.state}
      x={obj2.companies} /> );
  }
  var par_real:XML = <parent name="Real Estate" />;
  testData.appendChild( par_real );
  for each( var obj3:Object in _usData['realestate'] ) {
    if ( obj3.state == 'United States' ) continue;
    par_real.appendChild( <child name={obj3.state}
      x={obj3.companies} /> );
  }
```

12

```
        var children:XMLList = testData..child;
        this._maxAbsoluteChange = 0;
        for each(var child:XML in children)
        {
                var change:Number = Number(child.@x);
                this._maxAbsoluteChange = Math.max(this._maxAbsoluteChange,
                  Math.abs(change));
        }
}

private function itemToColor(item:Object):uint {
  var change:Number = Number(item.@x);
  if(change < 0) {
    return this.blendColors(MIN_COLOR, ZERO_COLOR,
      Math.abs(change) / this._maxAbsoluteChange);
  }
  else if(change > 0) {
    return this.blendColors(ZERO_COLOR, MAX_COLOR,
      1 - (Math.abs(change) / this._maxAbsoluteChange));
  }
  return ZERO_COLOR;
}

private function blendColors(color1:uint, color2:uint,
    percent:Number = 0.5) : uint {
  var remaining:Number = 1 - percent;

  var red1:uint = (color1 >> 16) & 0xff;
  var green1:uint = (color1 >> 8) & 0xff;
  var blue1:uint = color1 & 0xff;

  var red2:uint = (color2 >> 16) & 0xff;
  var green2:uint = (color2 >> 8) & 0xff;
  var blue2:uint = color2 & 0xff;

  color1 = ((red1 * percent) << 16) + ((green1 * percent) << 8) ➥
+ blue1 * percent;
  color2 = ((red2 * remaining) << 16) + ((green2 * remaining) << 8) ➥
+ blue2 * remaining;

  return color1 + color2;
}
]]>
</mx:Script>
</mx:Application>
```

The application first requests the three tables from the usdata service: the it (information technology) table, the realestate table, and the construction table. It then creates the XML hierarchy in the testData object. The graph responds to the change in the data by updating the graph.

The application displaying the data in the tables is shown in Figure 12-1.

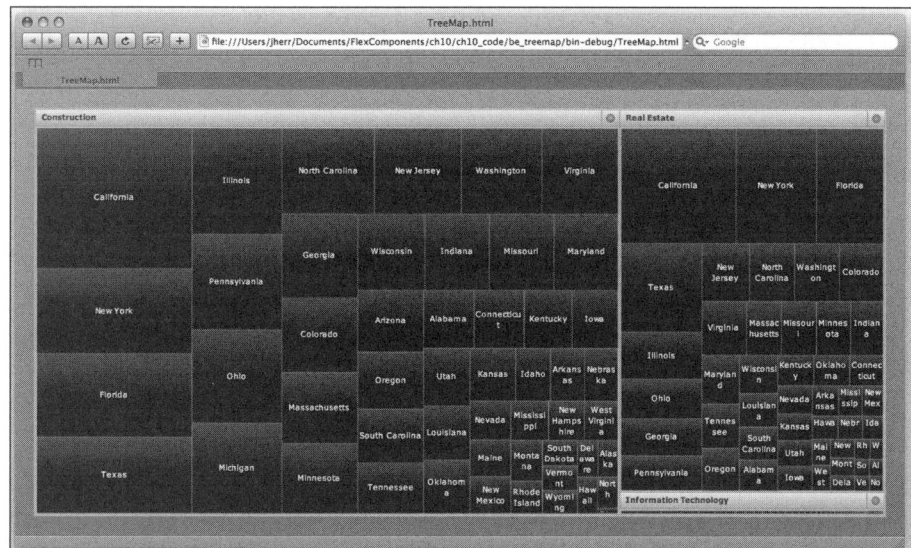

**Figure 12-1.** The usdata data displayed in a Tree Map

You can double-click one of the titles and zoom in on a particular sector, as shown in Figure 12-2.

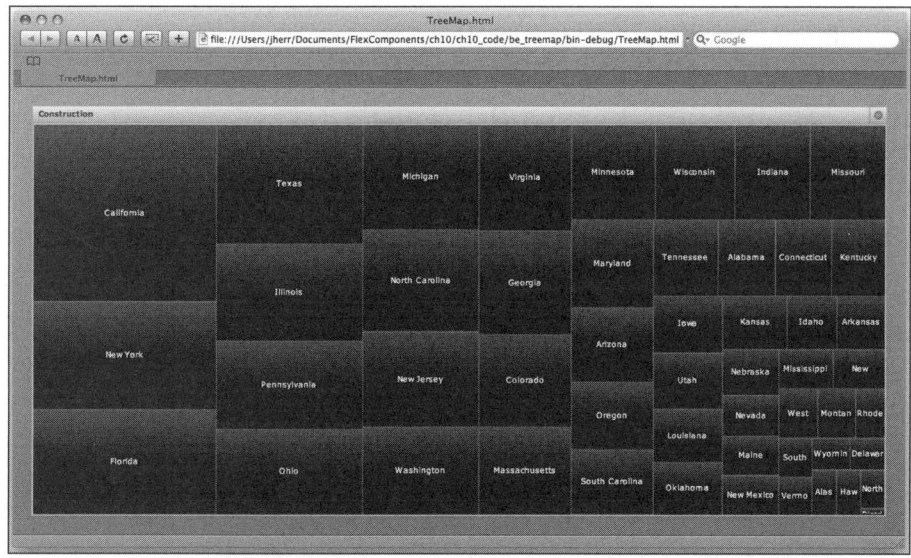

**Figure 12-2.** The zoomed-in graph

You can then zoom back by clicking the Close button associated with a particular industry vector.

## The ILOG Elixir TreeMap control

The ILOG Elixir component framework also has a TreeMap control. Following is the same application as before, but this time using Elixir's TreeMap control:

```
<?xml version="1.0" encoding="utf-8"?>
<mx:Application xmlns:mx="http://www.adobe.com/2006/mxml"
  layout="absolute"
  creationComplete="onStartup()"
  xmlns:ilog="http://www.ilog.com/2007/ilog/flex">

<mx:RemoteObject id="usdataRO"
  endpoint="http://localhost/amfphp/gateway.php"
  source="usdata.USDataService" destination="usdata.USDataService"
  showBusyCursor="true">
<mx:method name="getAll" result="onGetAllResult()">
<mx:arguments>
  <mx:Table />
</mx:arguments>
</mx:method>
</mx:RemoteObject>

<mx:Script>
<![CDATA[
private var _reqTable:String = '';
private var _usData:Object = {};

private function onGetAllResult() : void {
  _usData[ _reqTable ] = usdataRO.getAll.lastResult;
  _reqTable = null;
  if ( _usData[ 'it' ] == null ) _reqTable = 'it';
  if ( _usData[ 'realestate' ] == null ) _reqTable = 'realestate';
  if ( _usData[ 'construction' ] == null ) _reqTable = 'construction';
  if ( _reqTable != null ) usdataRO.getAll.send( _reqTable );
  else updateMap();
}

private function onStartup() : void {
  _reqTable = 'it';
  usdataRO.getAll.send( _reqTable );
}
private function buildChildren( table:String ) : Array {
  var elems:Array = [];
  for each( var obj:Object in _usData[table] ) {
    if ( obj.state == 'United States' ) continue;
    elems.push( { name: obj.state, size: obj.companies } );
  }
  return elems;
}
```

```
private function updateMap() : void {
  var items:Array = [];
  items.push( { name: "Information Technology",
  children: buildChildren('it') } );
  items.push( { name: "Construction",
   children: buildChildren('construction') } );
  items.push( { name: "Real Estate",
  children: buildChildren('realestate') } );
  tm.dataProvider = items;
}
]]>
</mx:Script>
<ilog:TreeMap id="tm" width="100%" height="100%" colorField="size"
  labelField="name" labelThreshold="1" areaField="size"
  colorScheme="div-red-green" backgroundColor="0xFFFFFF"
  textBackgroundColor="0xFFFFFF" borderThreshold="1"
  borderThickness="1" maxTopMargin="20" neutral="0"
  animationDuration="500">
</ilog:TreeMap>
</mx:Application>
```

The Elixir TreeMap object works on a hierarchal ActionScript data structure. This is built by the updateMap method. The updateMap method is called when all of the data has been returned for the three usdata tables.

The application using the ILOG control is shown in Figure 12-3.

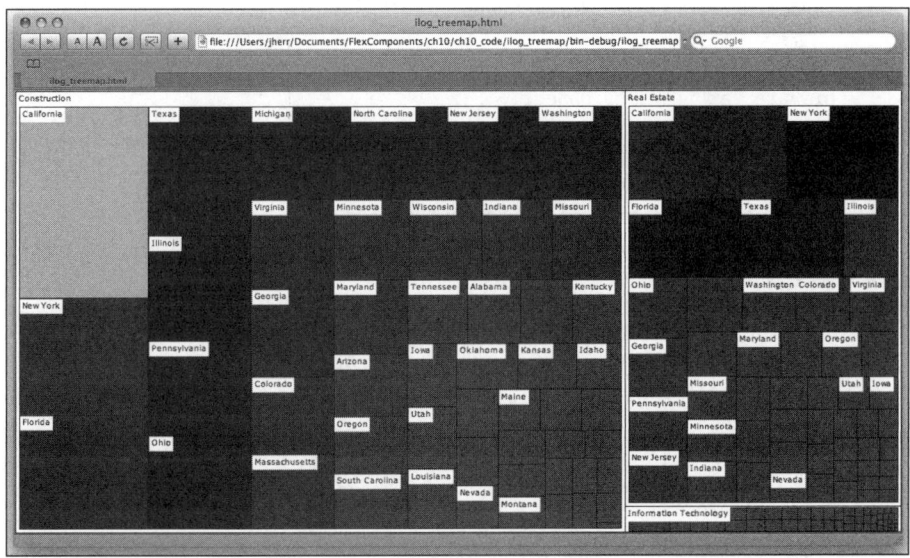

**Figure 12-3.** The ILOG Elixir TreeMap control showing the usdata tables

The nice thing about the ILOG TreeMap control is that it automatically handles coloring the data for you. It's also a little easier to get data into the control because the TreeMap takes a simple ActionScript 3 data structure instead of XML.

## Cascading lists

Another way to view a hierarchy is using a set of lists. The user is presented with the first list, which contains the root node. She can select a node, and a new list is presented right next to it with the contents of the subnodes of the selected root node. The process continues with more lists as the user goes deeper into the tree.

There is a CascadeList component on blog.widgets-lab.com (http://blog.widget-labs. com/2007/03/05/cascade-list-component/) that does just this. The application that uses this cascading list component on the album data (installed in Chapter 3) is shown here:

```
<?xml version="1.0" encoding="utf-8"?>
<mx:Application xmlns:mx="http://www.adobe.com/2006/mxml"
  layout="vertical"
  xmlns:cl="com.rd.widget.cascadelist.*"
  creationComplete="bands.send()">

<mx:HTTPService id="bands" url="http://localhost/music/music.xml"
  resultFormat="e4x" result="onBands(event);" />
<mx:Script>
<![CDATA[
import mx.rpc.events.ResultEvent;

[Bindable]
private var treeData:Object = [];

private function getMembers( band:XML ) : Array {
  var members:Array = [];
  for each ( var member:XML in band.member ) {
    members.push( { label: member.toString() } );
  }
  return members;
}
private function getBands( genre:XML ) : Array {
  var bands:Array = [];
  for each ( var band:XML in genre.band ) {
    bands.push( { label: band.@name, children: getMembers( band ) } );
  }
  return bands;
}
private function onBands( event:ResultEvent ) : void {
  var genres:Array = [];
```

```
    for each ( var genre:XML in event.result..genre ) {
    genres.push( { label: genre.@name, children: getBands( genre ) } );
    }
    treeData = {label:"root", root:true, children: genres };
}
]]>
</mx:Script>
<mx:Panel title="Cascade List">
    <cl:CascadeList dataProvider="{treeData}" initialNumberOfLevels="2"
    width="500" height="300" />
</mx:Panel>
</mx:Application>
```

This application requests the album XML data from the server. Once the data is down-loaded, the application uses the E4X syntax to build an ActionScript 3 object containing the hierarchal data.

When this application starts up and loads the XML, you see the interface shown in Figure 12-4.

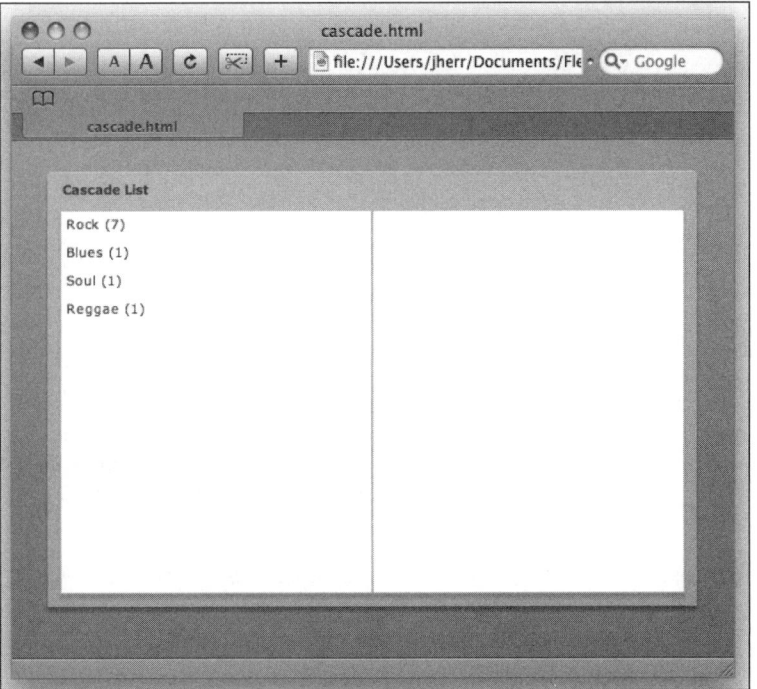

**Figure 12-4.** The cascading list showing the list of genres

By clicking around a little bit, you can dive deeper into the list as shown in Figure 12-5.

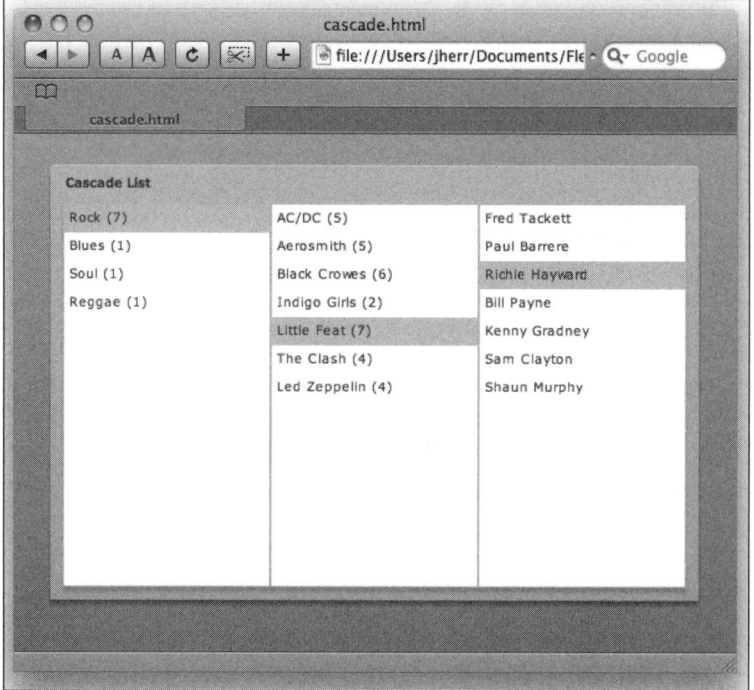

**Figure 12-5.** The cascade list showing the band members of Little Feat

As you can see, this is a nice way of allowing the user to easily traverse the structure of a hierarchal data set.

## Checkbox trees

Another way to navigate around in a hierarchy is by using the Tree control. As with other Flex controls, it supports using an itemRenderer to display the data. On Adobe Exchange is an itemRenderer component (http://www.adobe.com/cfusion/exchange/index.cfm?event=extensionDetail&extid=1047969) that allows us to add a check box to every node in the tree.

A checkbox tree can come in really handy for allowing the user to specify which parts of the tree should be included in some action. For example, the tree could show all of the folders on a user's hard drive and allow him to select which folders be backed up.

The application code shown here uses this checkbox itemRenderer component to display check boxes next to a simple hierarchal tree:

```
<?xml version="1.0" encoding="iso-8859-1"?>
<mx:Application xmlns:mx="http://www.adobe.com/2006/mxml">
<mx:XMLListCollection id="folderCollection">
<mx:XMLList xmlns="">
<folder state="unchecked" label="Images" isBranch="true" >
  <folder state="unchecked" isBranch="true" label="Home" >
      <folder state="unchecked" isBranch="false" label="Megan" />
      <folder state="unchecked" isBranch="false" label="Lori" />
      <folder state="unchecked" isBranch="false" label="Oso" />
  </folder>
  <folder state="unchecked" isBranch="true" label="Work" />
</folder>
<folder state="unchecked" label="Video" isBranch="true" >
  <folder state="unchecked" isBranch="false" label="Home" />
  <folder state="unchecked" isBranch="false" label="Work" />
</folder>
</mx:XMLList>
</mx:XMLListCollection>
<mx:Panel width="100%" height="100%" title="Checkbox Tree">
  <mx:Tree itemRenderer="CheckTreeRenderer" labelField="@label"
    dataProvider="{folderCollection}" width="100%" height="100%" />
</mx:Panel>
</mx:Application>
```

When the application first launches, you see the display shown in Figure 12-6.

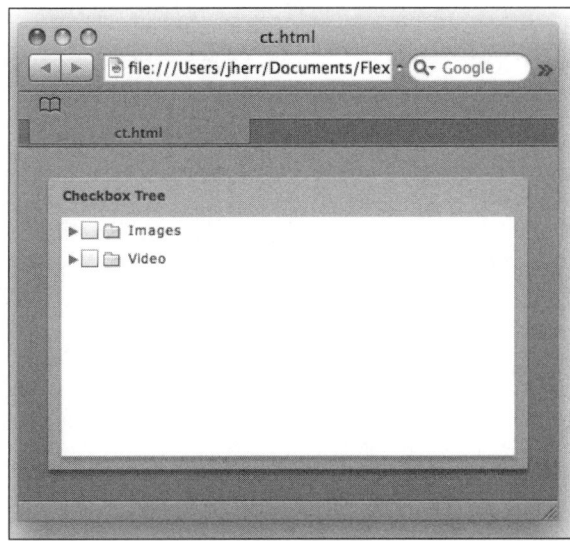

**Figure 12-6.** The hierarchal folder list with the check boxes

12

As with all tree controls, you can click to open up the various sublevels as shown in Figure 12-7.

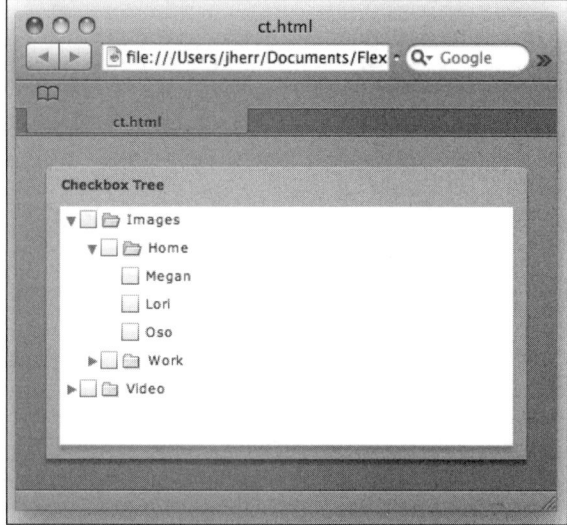

**Figure 12-7.** The hierarchal list expanded

If you check items in the leaf nodes, the parent items are displayed with a small black block indicating that there are selected items below. If you click parent items, all of the subitems are selected. You can see this effect in Figure 12-8.

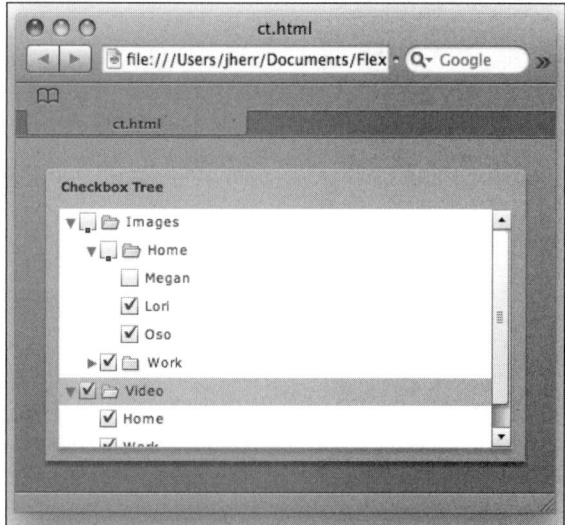

**Figure 12-8.** Selected elements of the tree

If a hierarchal tree is too big to fit in the user interface, you can use a drop-down box to show the hierarchy. Steve House has a component that does just that posted on his Random Ramblings of a Cyber-Soul blog (http://cyberdust.wordpress.com/2007/02/23/introducing-selecttree-the-drop-down-tree-control/).

The application shown here displays a Tree control in the drop-down using Steve's SelectTree component:

```
<?xml version="1.0" encoding="utf-8"?>
<mx:Application xmlns:mx="http://www.adobe.com/2006/mxml"
  xmlns:view="view.*" layout="vertical">

<mx:Script>
<![CDATA[
public function getSelectTreeItemText(o:Object):String {
  return o.@label;
}
public function treeChange(e:Event):void {
  if(selectTree.selectedItem != null)
    subjectMirror.text = selectTree.selectedItem.@label;
  else
    subjectMirror.text = "";
}
]]>
</mx:Script>

<mx:Style source="main.css" />

<mx:XMLListCollection id="folderCollection">
<mx:XMLList xmlns="">
<folder state="unchecked" label="Images" isBranch="true" >
  <folder state="unchecked" isBranch="true" label="Home" >
      <folder state="unchecked" isBranch="false" label="Megan" />
      <folder state="unchecked" isBranch="false" label="Lori" />
      <folder state="unchecked" isBranch="false" label="Oso" />
  </folder>
  <folder state="unchecked" isBranch="true" label="Work" />
</folder>
<folder state="unchecked" label="Video" isBranch="true" >
  <folder state="unchecked" isBranch="false" label="Home" />
  <folder state="unchecked" isBranch="false" label="Work" />
</folder>
</mx:XMLList>
</mx:XMLListCollection>

<mx:Panel width="100%" height="100%" title="Checkbox dropdown"
  paddingBottom="5" paddingLeft="5" paddingRight="5" paddingTop="5">

<mx:TextInput id="subjectMirror" text="" />
```

12

```
<view:SelectTree id="selectTree" dataProvider="{folderCollection}"
  change="treeChange(event)" labelField="@label" tabEnabled="true"
  textFunction="getSelectTreeItemText" />

</mx:Panel>
</mx:Application>
```

This application uses the same XML data source as in the check box example as the hierarchal data source for the drop-down. When the application first comes up, it shows the combo and a text item that will be set to the value of the control selected from the tree. You can see the drop-down in Figure 12-9.

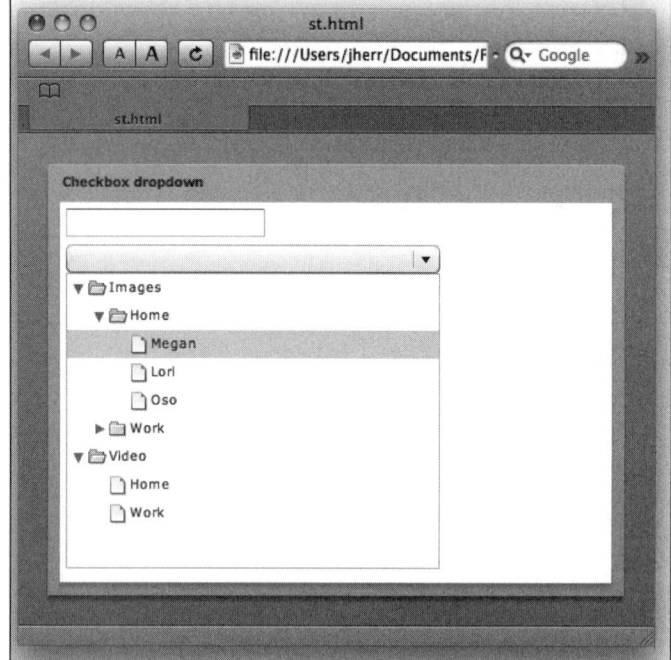

**Figure 12-9.** The drop-down Tree control

When you select something from the tree in the drop-down, the combo is set to the value of the node, and the text box is updated with the new value as well. This is shown in Figure 12-10.

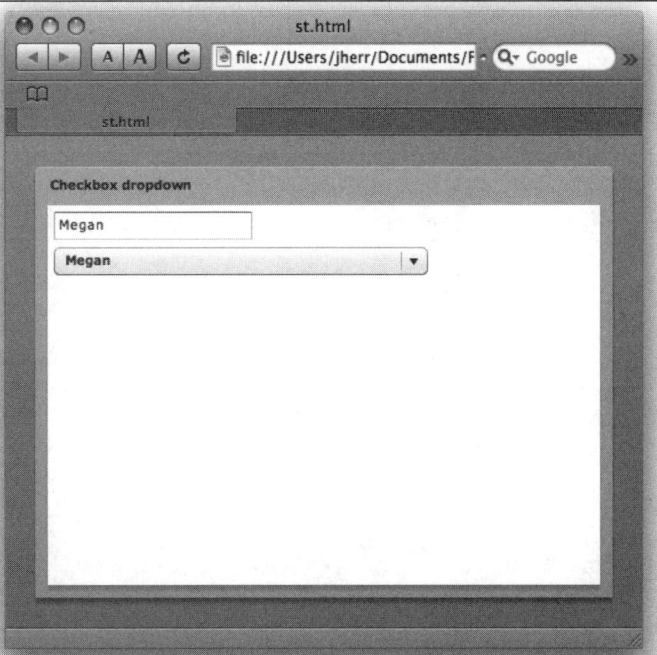

**Figure 12-10.** The combo and text box after selecting Megan from the tree

This control makes it a lot easier to fit big hierarchal trees into small form factors in your user interface.

# Where we will go from here

Hierarchies are just one way to organize a list of nodes. Another way to structure data is as a set of connections between nodes. This is called a network map or node graph. It's the kind of structure that appears in the Friends network on Facebook (http://facebook.com), for example. In the next chapter, I show some cool controls that visualize these types of data structures.

**12**

# 13 **NETWORK GRAPH COMPONENTS**

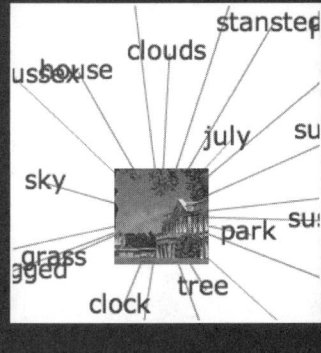 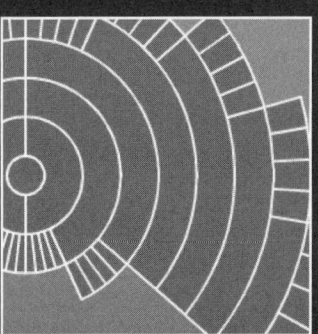 

Don't let the title of this chapter keep you from digging in; "network" doesn't always mean a computer network. In fact, a network graph is any set of interconnected nodes. For example, Facebook (http://facebook.com) is one big network graph. If I know you, and you know me, and we know another person, then our graph can be represented as three nodes with six connections (or edges) between the three nodes.

In this chapter, I present several controls that not only visualize network graphs, but also allow you to interact with the graphs in a dynamic way.

# Graphing Flickr with SpringGraph

The SpringGraph component (http://mark-shepherd.com/blog/springgraph-flex-component/) makes it easy to build a set of nodes, create links between those nodes, and display them in a dynamic network graph. You can customize the display of the nodes using an itemRenderer.

Flickr makes for an interesting data source for node graphs because you have images connected to tags, which in turn connect to other tags with more images. For example, the tag "dog" might lead to images of someone walking their dog in a park, which is also tagged with "park" and has its own set of pictures.

A spring graph, like the one in this application, allows you to associate text nodes with image nodes and move them around interactively. You can then double-click the node to dig down even further.

In the following application code, we use the SpringGraph component to visualize all of the results from Flickr (http://flickr.com) to a particular query:

```
<?xml version="1.0" encoding="utf-8"?>
<mx:Application xmlns:mx="http://www.adobe.com/2006/mxml"
  xmlns:fc="http://www.adobe.com/2006/fc"
  layout="absolute" creationComplete="onStartup()">
<mx:Script>
<![CDATA[
import com.adobe.flex.extras.controls.springgraph.Graph;
import com.adobe.webapis.flickr.methodgroups.Photos;
import com.adobe.webapis.flickr.events.FlickrResultEvent;
import com.adobe.webapis.flickr.*;

private var flickrSvc:FlickrService = new FlickrService(
  "Your Flickr Key" );

private var items:Graph = new Graph();
private var rootItem:FlickrItemData;
private var searchText:String = 'dog';

public static var instance:flickrspring = null;
```

```
public function openNode( item:FlickrItemData ) : void {
  if ( item.photo != null ) {
    flickrSvc.photos.getInfo( item.photo.id );
  }
  if ( item.text != null ) {
    searchText = item.text;
    onSearch();
  }
}

private function onStartup() : void {
  instance = this;

  flickrSvc.permission = AuthPerm.NONE;
  flickrSvc.addEventListener( FlickrResultEvent.PHOTOS_SEARCH,
  onPhotoSearchResult );
  flickrSvc.addEventListener( FlickrResultEvent.PHOTOS_GET_INFO,
  onPhotoInfoResult );

  rootItem = new FlickrItemData( searchText );
  rootItem.text = searchText;
  items.add( rootItem );
  s.dataProvider = items;

  onSearch();
}
private function onSearch() : void {
  flickrSvc.photos.search( "", searchText, "", "", null, null, null,
  null, License.ATTRIBUTION, "tags", 10 );
}
private function onPhotoInfoResult( event:FlickrResultEvent ) : void {
  for each( var t:PhotoTag in event.data.photo.tags ) {
    if ( items.find( t.tag ) == null ) {
    var item:FlickrItemData = new FlickrItemData( t.tag );
    item.text = t.tag;
    items.add( item );
    items.link( items.find( event.data.photo.id ), item );
    }
  }
}
private function onPhotoSearchResult( event:FlickrResultEvent ) : void{
  for each( var p:Photo in event.data.photos.photos ) {
    var item:FlickrItemData = new FlickrItemData( p.id );
    item.photo = p;
    items.add( item );
    items.link( items.find( searchText ), item );
  }
}
]]>
```

13

```
      </mx:Script>
      <fc:SpringGraph id="s" backgroundColor="#ffffff"
        lineColor="#333388CC" left="0" right="0" top="0" bottom="0"
        itemRenderer="FlickrItem" repulsionFactor="0.4" width="100%"
          height="100%">
      </fc:SpringGraph>
    </mx:Application>
```

The application uses the AS3 Flickr Library (http://as3flickrlib.googlecode.com) to run initial requests. The application also fields requests to open subnodes and make subqueries. In both cases, it creates new FlickrItemData nodes, which are defined by the AS3 class shown here:

```
    package
    {
      import com.adobe.flex.extras.controls.springgraph.Item;
      import com.adobe.webapis.flickr.*;

      public class FlickrItemData extends Item
      {
        public var photo:Photo = null;

        public var text:String = null;

        public function FlickrItemData(id:String=null)
        {
          super(id);
        }

      }
    }
```

Associated with each of the nodes is a Flickr Photo object that comes from the AS3 Flickr Library. If there is no photo associated with the node, the text field must be nonnull.

The itemRenderer that displays these nodes is shown in the following code:

```
    <?xml version="1.0" encoding="utf-8"?>
    <mx:Canvas xmlns:mx="http://www.adobe.com/2006/mxml" width="75"
      height="75" dataChange="onDataChange()"
      creationComplete="onDataChange()" horizontalScrollPolicy="off"
      verticalScrollPolicy="off"
      doubleClickEnabled="true" doubleClick="onDblClick()">
    <mx:Script>
    <![CDATA[
    import com.adobe.webapis.flickr.Photo;
```

```
      private function onDblClick() : void {
        flickrspring.instance.openNode( data as FlickrItemData );
      }
      private function onDataChange() : void {
        if ( data == null || !initialized ) return;
        if ( data.photo != null ) {
          var p:Photo = data.photo as Photo;
          img.source = "http://static.flickr.com/"+p.server+"/"+p.id+"_"+➡
p.secret+"_s.jpg";
          textItem.visible = false;
        }
        if ( data.text != null ) {
          img.visible = false;
          var tl:TextLineMetrics = textItem.measureText( data.text );
          textItem.text = data.text;
          textItem.width = tl.width + 10;
          textItem.height = tl.height + 10;
          width = tl.width + 10;
          height = tl.height + 10;
        }
      }
    ]]>
    </mx:Script>
    <mx:Image id="img" width="75" height="75" />
    <mx:Label id="textItem" fontSize="20" />
  </mx:Canvas>
```

This MXML component takes a FlickrItemData object as data. If the photo field of the object is defined, it uses the image tag to display the photo. If the text is set, the textItem label is set and the box is resized to show the whole text.

## Getting set up with Flickr

To get this application to work, you need a Flickr API key (which is free). Once you have it, you can run the application, and you should see something like Figure 13-1.

13

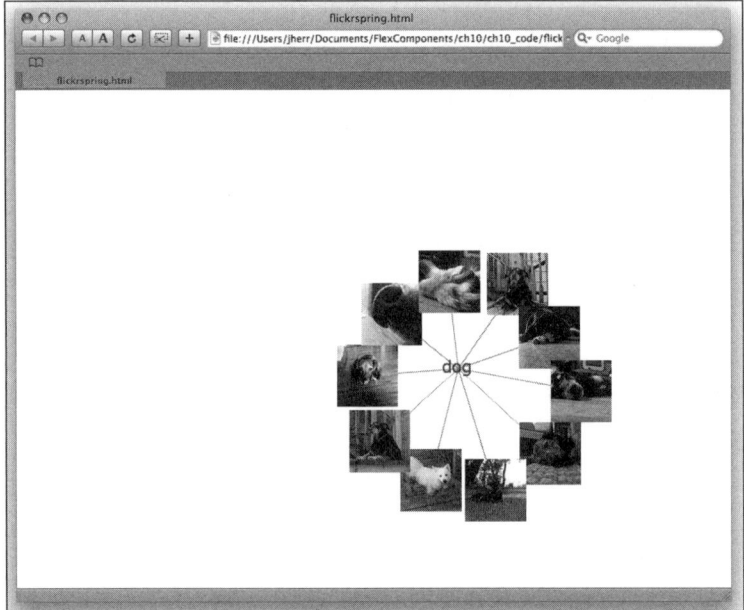

**Figure 13-1.** The result of the "dog" query

From here you can double-click one of the dog images to bring up the tags associated with that image. This is shown in Figure 13-2.

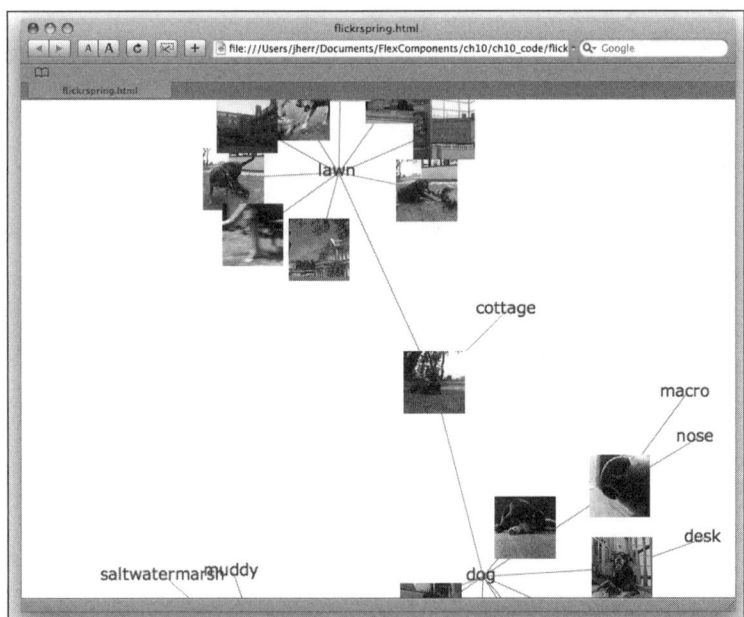

**Figure 13-2.** More text and image nodes in the SpringGraph

As you can see from Figure 13-3, the number of nodes with text and graphics can get fairly large.

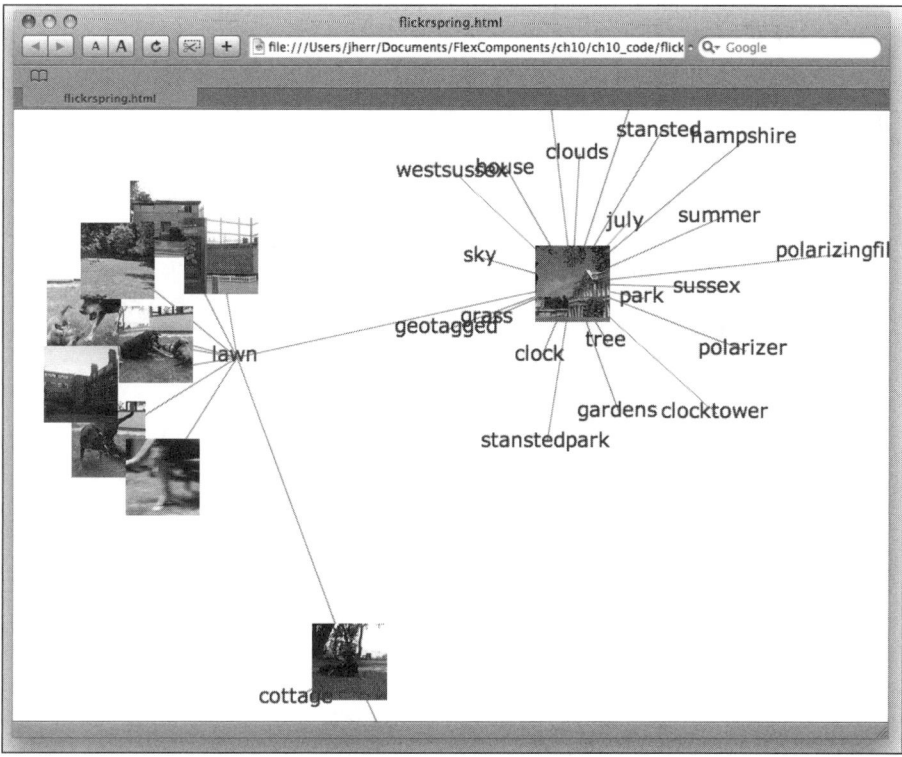

**Figure 13-3.** A SpringGraph with a bunch of open nodes

As the node tree grows, the SpringGraph automatically adjusts to show the new data. If you don't like where it's going, you can just grab a node and move it around for yourself.

As you can see for yourself, the SpringGraph is a robust and easy-to-use node graph viewer.

# Flare for displaying tree structures

The Flare library (http://flare.prefuse.org/) is the Flash version of the Prefuse library (http://prefuse.org/) that's used to display data structures like node graphs. Actually, it can do a whole bunch of things, of which displaying tree structures is just a part.

The Flare project is more about computer science than it is about front-end user-facing features. Where the SpringGraph project is about showing things like pictures or people as nodes, the Flare project is more about showing tree graphs in a more mathematical context.

13

The Flex application code that hosts the Flare graph is shown here:

```
<?xml version="1.0" encoding="utf-8"?>
<mx:Application xmlns:mx="http://www.adobe.com/2006/mxml"
  layout="absolute"
  creationComplete="onStartup()">
<mx:Script>
<![CDATA[
import flex.FlexGraph;
import mx.core.UIComponent;
import flare.demos.*;

private var graph:FlexGraph = new FlexGraph();

private function onStartup() : void {
  var uic:UIComponent = new UIComponent();
  addChild( uic );
  uic.addChild( graph );
}
]]>
</mx:Script>
<mx:ApplicationControlBar dock="true">
  <mx:Button label="Starburst" click="graph.starbust();" />
  <mx:ButtonBar id="treeType"
    itemClick="graph.changeLayout(treeType.selectedIndex)"
    dataProvider="{['Force Directed','Node Link Tree',
     'Indented Tree','Radial Tree','Circle']}"
    selectedIndex="0" />
</mx:ApplicationControlBar>
</mx:Application>
```

The FlexGraph component is a wrapper for the Flare library's Visualization Flash object. Following is the code for this class:

```
package flex
{
  import flare.animate.Sequence;
  import flare.animate.Transition;
  import flare.animate.Transitioner;
  import flare.util.Button;
  import flare.util.GraphUtil;
  import flare.vis.Visualization;
  import flare.vis.controls.DragControl;
  import flare.vis.data.Data;
  import flare.vis.data.NodeSprite;
  import flare.vis.operator.OperatorSwitch;
  import flare.vis.operator.layout.CircleLayout;
  import flare.vis.operator.layout.ForceDirectedLayout;
  import flare.vis.operator.layout.IndentedTreeLayout;
  import flare.vis.operator.layout.NodeLinkTreeLayout;
```

```
import flare.vis.operator.layout.Orientation;
import flare.vis.operator.layout.RadialTreeLayout;
import flare.vis.util.graphics.Shapes;

import flash.display.Sprite;
import flash.events.MouseEvent;
import flash.geom.Point;
import flash.geom.Rectangle;

public class FlexGraph extends Sprite
{
  private var vis:Visualization;
  private var os:OperatorSwitch;
  private var anchors:Array;
  private var shape:int = 0;

  public var WIDTH:Number = 800;
  public var HEIGHT:Number = 550;

  public function FlexGraph() {
    name = "FlexGraph";
    var w:Number = WIDTH;
    var h:Number = HEIGHT;

    var data:Data = GraphUtil.diamondTree(5,3,5);
    vis = new Visualization(data);
    vis.bounds = new Rectangle(0,0,w,h);

    os = new OperatorSwitch(
      new ForceDirectedLayout(),
      new NodeLinkTreeLayout(Orientation.LEFT_TO_RIGHT, 20, 5, 10),
      new IndentedTreeLayout(20),
      new RadialTreeLayout(50, false),
      new CircleLayout()
    );
    anchors = [
      null,
      new Point(40, h/2),
      new Point(40, 40),
      new Point(w/2, h/2),
      new Point(0, 0)
    ];
    os.index = 1;
    vis.marks.x = anchors[1].x;
    vis.marks.y = anchors[1].y;

    vis.operators.add(os);
    vis.tree.nodes.visit(function(n:NodeSprite):void {
      n.size = 1.5;
```

13

```actionscript
        n.fillColor = 0x666666; n.fillAlpha = 0.8;
        n.lineColor = 0x999999; n.lineAlpha = 0.9;
        n.lineWidth = 2;
        n.buttonMode = true;
    });
    vis.update();
    addChild(vis);

    vis.controls.add(new DragControl());
}

public function changeLayout( index:int ) : void {
    switchLayout( index ).play();
}

public function starbust() : void {
    toStarburst().play();
}

private function switchLayout(idx:int):Transition
{
    vis.operators.clear();
    vis.operators.add(os);
    vis.continuousUpdates = false;
    vis.operators[0].index = idx;

    var seq:Sequence;
    if (shape != 0) {
        seq = new Sequence(
            vis.data.nodes.setProperties({scaleX:0, scaleY:0}, 0.5),
            vis.data.nodes.setProperties({shape:0,
                lineColor:0xffdddddd}, 0.5),
            vis.data.nodes.setProperties({scaleX:1, scaleY:1}, 0),
            vis.data.edges.setProperties({lineColor:0xffcccccc}, 0.5)
        );
    } else {
        seq = new Sequence();
    }

    shape = 0;
    if (idx > 0) {
        seq.onEnd = function():void {
            var t:Transitioner = new Transitioner(2);
            t.$(vis.marks).x = anchors[idx].x;
            t.$(vis.marks).y = anchors[idx].y;
            vis.update(t).play();
        };
    } else {
        seq.onEnd = function():void { vis.continuousUpdates = true; };
```

```
    }
    return seq;
  }

  private function toStarburst():Transition
  {
    vis.operators.clear();
    vis.operators.add(new RadialTreeLayout(50,false));
    var t0:Transitioner = new Transitioner(2);

    t0.$(vis.marks).x = WIDTH/2;
    t0.$(vis.marks).y = HEIGHT/2;
    if (shape == Shapes.WEDGE) {
      return vis.update(t0);
    } else {
      shape = Shapes.WEDGE;
      return new Sequence(
        vis.update(t0),
        vis.data.edges.setProperties({lineColor:0}, 0.5),
        vis.data.nodes.setProperties({scaleX:0, scaleY:0}, 0.5),
        vis.data.nodes.setProperties({shape:Shapes.WEDGE,
          lineColor:0xffffffff}, 0),
        vis.data.nodes.setProperties({scaleX:1, scaleY:1}, 0.5)
      );
    }
  }

  public function play():void
  {
    var os:OperatorSwitch = vis.operators.getOperatorAt(0) as➡
OperatorSwitch;
    if (os.index == 0)
      vis.continuousUpdates = true;
  }

  public function stop():void
  {
    vis.continuousUpdates = false;
  }
  }
}
```

It looks like there is a lot to it, but it's actually fairly straightforward code. Most of the work is done in the constructor, where the data for the graph is set up along with additional controls. The switchLayout method changes the display mode of the graph and animates that transition to create some very cool effects. The toStarburst method changes from a traditional node display to a "starburst" display, which is shown a little later in Figure 13-6.

When the application first starts up, it looks like Figure 13-4.

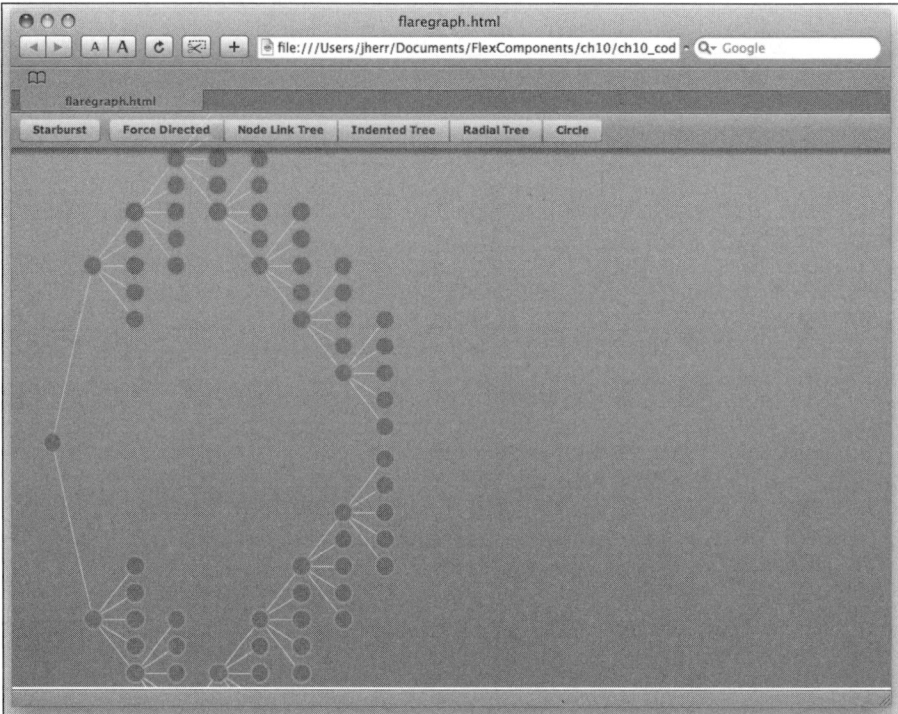

**Figure 13-4.** The initial startup state of the application

You can click the buttons in the application control bar at the top of the window to change how the nodes are displayed. Figure 13-5 shows the result of clicking the Radial Tree button.

Clicking the Starburst button results in a very cool transition from whatever the current state of the graph is to the Radial Tree design first, and then on to the slicing design shown in Figure 13-6.

The Flare library is an amazingly cool library filled with unique visualizations, effects, and more. It's definitely worth your time to look into.

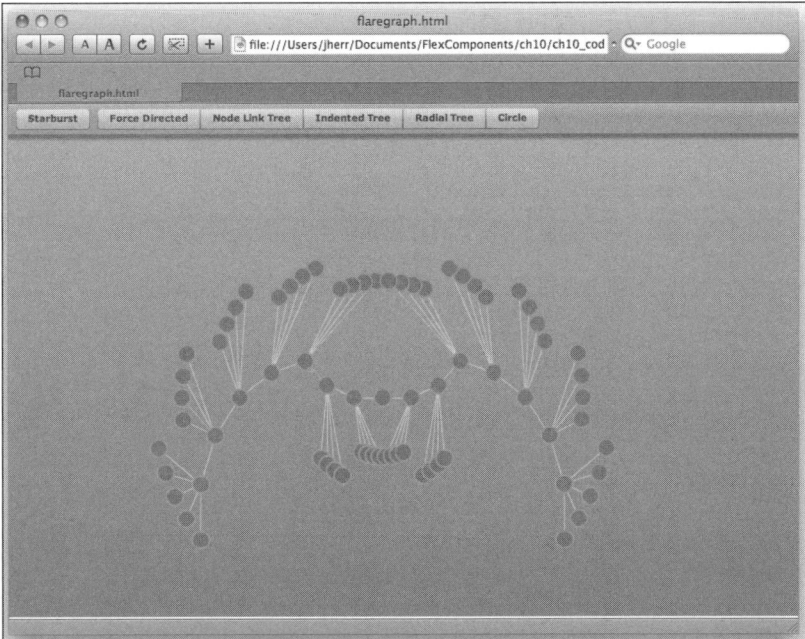

**Figure 13-5.** The Radial Tree design

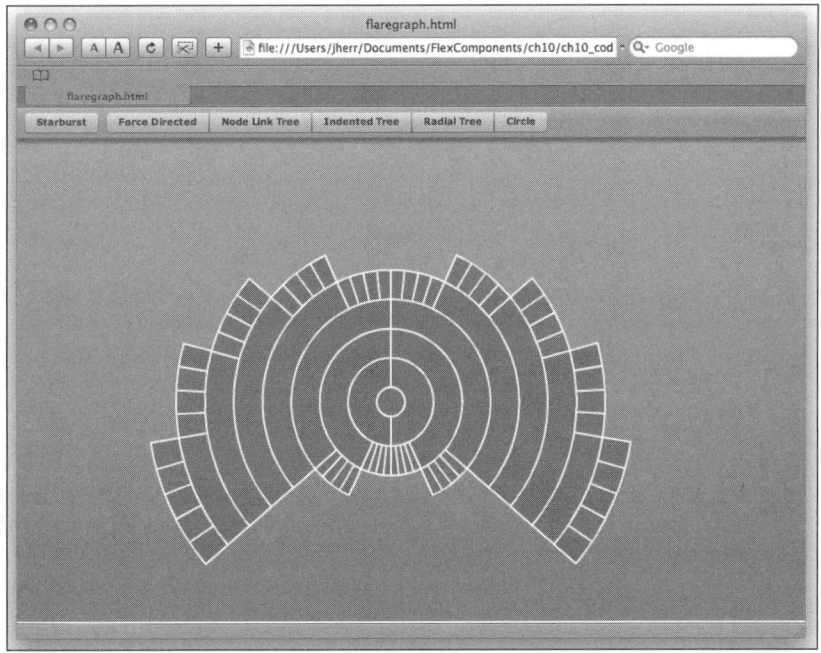

**Figure 13-6.** The Starburst pattern

# The RaVis node graph

The BirdEye library (http://birdeye.googlecode.com/) contains a growing set of visualizations, including a node graph. The following application code visualizes the band data from the music database as a set of nodes in a node graph:

```
<?xml version="1.0" encoding="utf-8"?>
<mx:Application xmlns:mx="http://www.adobe.com/2006/mxml"
  layout="vertical"
  xmlns:vg="org.un.cava.birdeye.ravis.graphLayout.visual.*"
  creationComplete="bands.send()">
<mx:HTTPService id="bands" url="http://localhost/music/music.xml"
  resultFormat="e4x" result="onBands(event);" />
<mx:Script>
<![CDATA[
import org.un.cava.birdeye.ravis.graphLayout.visual.edgeRenderers.➡
BaseEdgeRenderer;
import org.un.cava.birdeye.ravis.graphLayout.layout.➡
ConcentricRadialLayouter;
import org.un.cava.birdeye.ravis.graphLayout.data.Graph;
import org.un.cava.birdeye.ravis.graphLayout.visual.IVisualNode;
import mx.rpc.events.ResultEvent;

private function addMembers( parent:IVisualNode, band:XML ) : void {
  for each( var member:XML in band.member ) {
    var memberNode:IVisualNode = vgraph.createNode(member.toString());
    memberNode.data = { name: member.toString(), color: 0x0000FF,
      image:null };
    vgraph.linkNodes( parent, memberNode );
  }
}
private function addBands( parent:IVisualNode, genre:XML ) : void {
  for each( var band:XML in genre.band ) {
    var bandNode:IVisualNode = vgraph.createNode(➡
band.@name.toString());
    bandNode.data = { name: band.@name.toString(), color: 0x00FF00,
      image: 'http://localhost/music/'+band.@image.toString() };
    vgraph.linkNodes( parent, bandNode );
    addMembers( bandNode, band );
  }
}
private function onBands( event:ResultEvent ) : void {
  vgraph.graph = new org.un.cava.birdeye.ravis.graphLayout.data.Graph(
    "genres");

  var rootNode:IVisualNode = vgraph.createNode("root");
  rootNode.data = { name: 'Genres', color: 0x333333, image:null };
  for each ( var genre:XML in event.result..genre ) {
    var genreNode:IVisualNode = vgraph.createNode(
```

```
                genre.@name.toString());
            genreNode.data = { name: genre.@name.toString(), color: 0xFF0000 };
            vgraph.linkNodes( rootNode, genreNode );
            addBands( genreNode, genre );
        }

        vgraph.layouter = new ConcentricRadialLayouter(vgraph);
        vgraph.layouter.autoFitEnabled = true;
        vgraph.edgeRenderer = new BaseEdgeRenderer(vgraph.edgeDrawGraphics);
        vgraph.maxVisibleDistance = 2;
        vgraph.displayEdgeLabels = false;
        vgraph.currentRootVNode = rootNode;
        vgraph.draw();
    }
]]>
</mx:Script>
<mx:Panel width="100%" height="100%" title="Bands">
<vg:VisualGraph id="vgraph" width="100%" height="100%"
    itemRenderer="MyNodeRenderer" />
</mx:Panel>
</mx:Application>
```

The application first starts up by requesting the XML for the music library. The onBands method creates a graph, and then creates the root node for the data. From there, it iterates over each genre, creating a node for it, and then calling the addBands method to add the bands to the node. The addBands method adds a node for each band to the graph and calls the addMembers method to add nodes for all of the members.

## Rendering the nodes

After creating the graph, the onBands method sets up the rest of the vgraph member variables and calls the draw method to render the graph. If you don't like how the graph is laid out, you can change the object that is set in the layouter member variable to a different layouter type.

The itemRenderer that renders each node is shown in the following code:

```
<?xml version="1.0" encoding="utf-8"?>
<mx:VBox xmlns:mx="http://www.adobe.com/2006/mxml" width="100"
    height="20" horizontalScrollPolicy="off"
    verticalScrollPolicy="off" creationComplete="onData()"
    dataChange="onData()" paddingBottom="3"
    paddingLeft="3" paddingRight="3" paddingTop="3" cornerRadius="5"
    borderColor="#999999" borderStyle="solid"
    backgroundColor="#cccccc" backgroundAlpha="0.7" borderThickness="1"
    horizontalAlign="center">
<mx:Script>
<![CDATA[
private function onData() : void {
```

**13**

```
          if ( !initialized || !data ) return;
          var met:TextLineMetrics = txt.measureText( data.data.name );
          width = met.width + 15;
          height = met.height + 8;

          setStyle( 'backgroundColor', data.data.color );
          setStyle( 'borderColor', data.data.color );

          if ( data.data.image != null ) {
            img.source = data.data.image;
            img.width = 50;
            img.height = 50;
            img.visible = true;
            img.includeInLayout = true;
            height += 60;
          }
        }
      }
    ]]>
    </mx:Script>
    <mx:Image id="img" visible="false" height="0" width="0"
      includeInLayout="false" />
    <mx:Label id="txt" text="{data.data.name}" fontSize="14"
      fontWeight="bold" color="white" />
    </mx:VBox>
```

This is a pretty simple component. It just takes the name of the node and puts it into the label. It then uses the measureText method to figure out just how big the name is and adjusts the size of the container accordingly. If there is an image associated with the node, it sets the local image object and resizes the node to match.

It also sets the colors so that genres are in red, bands are in green, and band members are in blue.

When the application first starts up, it looks like Figure 13-7.

From here, you can double-click any of the nodes to navigate along the tree. In this case, I double-clicked The Clash, and you can see the result in Figure 13-8.

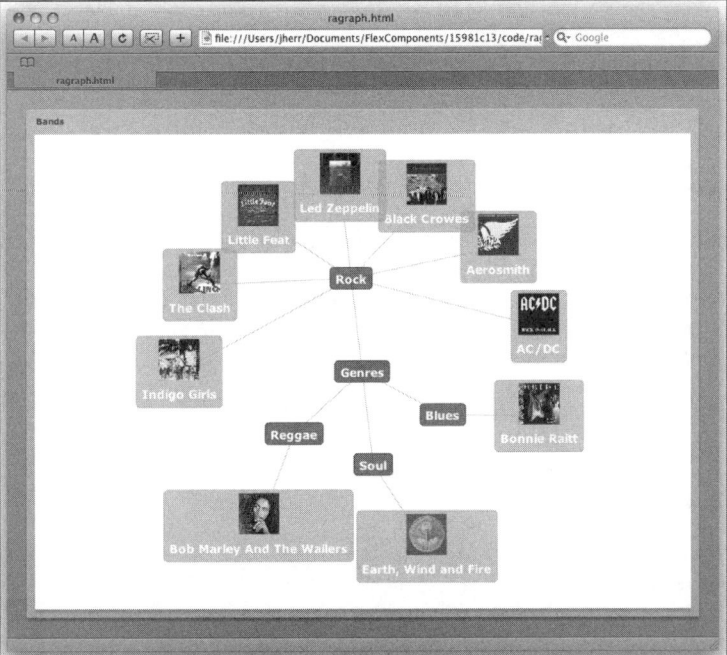

**Figure 13-7.** The startup state of the application after the music database has been downloaded

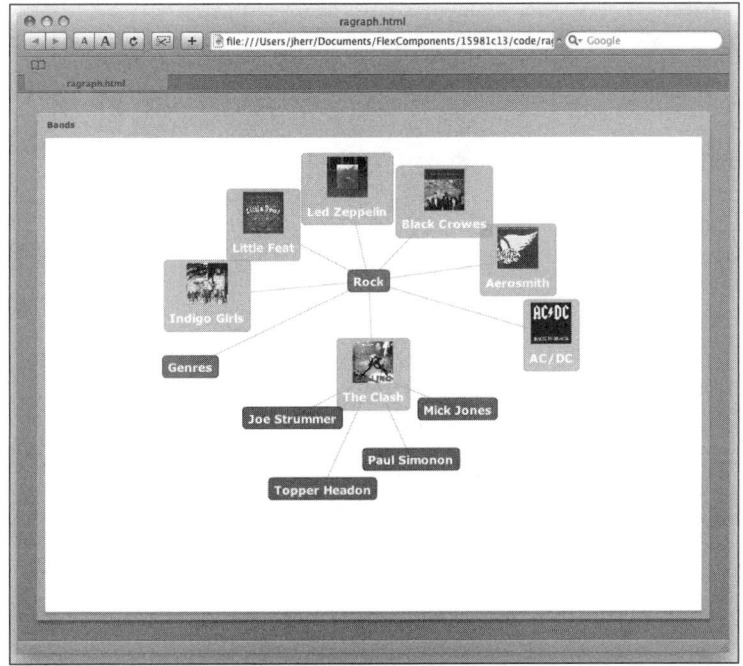

**Figure 13-8.** The members of The Clash

One very nice thing about the RaVis network graph component is that it automatically hides nodes that aren't in the area you are currently navigating. That way it kind of cleans up after you as you navigate around big node graphs.

## yFiles FLEX

The yFiles FLEX framework (http://www.yworks.com/en/products_yfilesflex_about. html) is the pinnacle of node graph systems. It's an OEM product that has both a client and a server component to it. The client does the basic rendering of the graph and the editing. The server does the graph layout and maintains the persistent state of the network so that multiple users can edit a central graph simultaneously.

You can see the yFiles node graph in action in Figure 13-9.

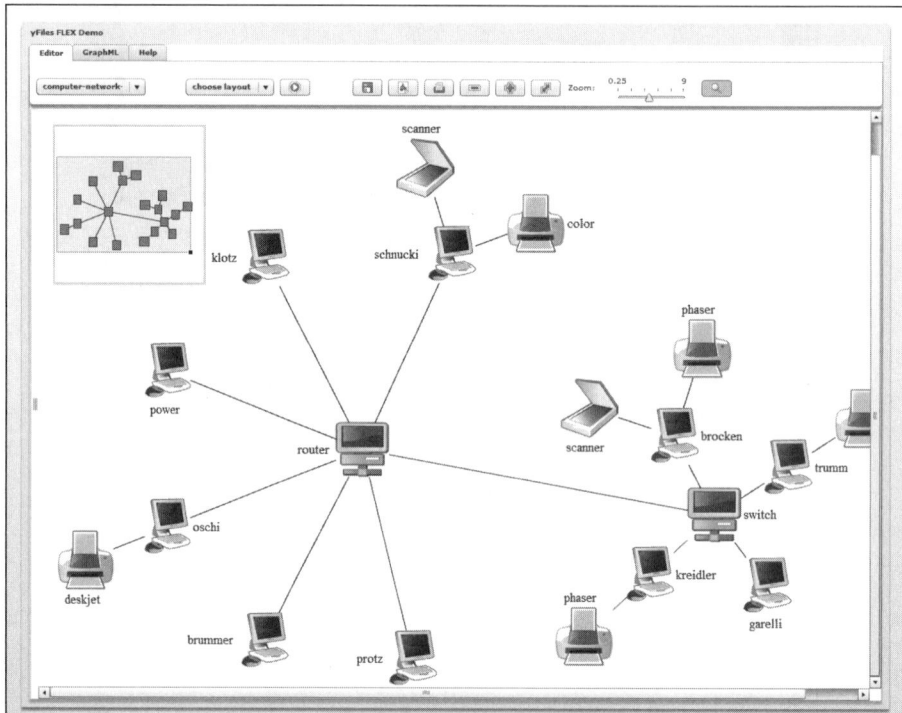

**Figure 13-9.** A network map shown in the yFiles node graph

The yFiles FLEX framework is a serious piece of work. It's well worth considering if you are looking to build an industrial-strength application that has serious multiuser diagramming requirements.

# Where we will go from here

The few examples in this chapter barely scratch the surface of what you can do with some creativity and these components. Even if this type of dynamic graphing isn't your thing, you should try some of these examples out anyway as they demonstrate what can be done in terms of interactivity with Flex and Flash applications. This kind of thing would be insanely difficult to do with DHTML and Ajax.

In the next chapter, I'll show how to reskin your application to give the whole thing a completely different look and feel with very little effort.

13

# 14  COOL PREMADE SKINS

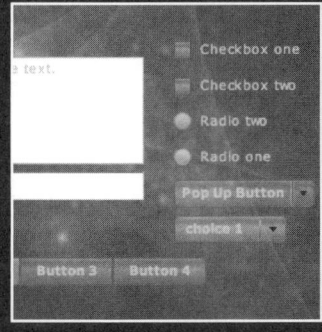 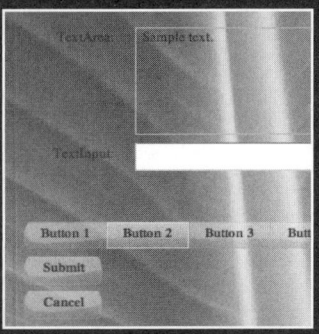 

Updated 7/2/08

The Halo skin, which is the default look and feel of Flex, is very professional, but it may not be right for your application. Changing the look and feel of the controls, the containers, the layout, the fonts, and colors en masse is called **reskinning**. The idea is that you implement the functionality of your application in ActionScript and MXML, and then define the text, colors, images, and so on using Flex CSS.

In this chapter, I use skins downloaded primarily from the ScaleNine Flex skin archive (http://scalenine.com) to change the look and feel of all of the Flex controls.

## Skinning basics

Skins usually come packaged in a .zip or .tar.gz file. So the first step is to extract all of the files from these archives. From there you need to add any CSS, PNG, AS, TTF, or SWC files to your Flex application. The following list explains these types of files and their relationship to the skinning of your application:

- **CSS**: The CSS tells the Flex framework what fonts, style settings, images, and programmatic skins to apply to which controls.
- **PNG, JPG**: These are the image files that the CSS skins apply to the controls.
- **AS, SWC**: These files contain the ActionScript classes that define the programmatic skins applied to the controls.
- **SWF**: SWF files contain extra classes or Flash assets that the skin will be using to modify the display of the Flex controls.
- **TTF**: These are the font files used by the skin.

To make sure everything compiles properly, you need to ensure the file hierarchy is maintained between the compressed file that you downloaded and where the files sit in your Flex project.

## A simple form to play with skins

To try out these different skins, I'll use the same form (or pretty close to the same form) with all of the different skins.

This simple example form, which contains a window panel and several example controls, is shown here:

```
<?xml version="1.0" encoding="utf-8"?>
<mx:Application xmlns:mx="http://www.adobe.com/2006/mxml"
  layout="absolute" width="800" height="600">

<mx:MenuBar x="10" y="20" width="339">
<mx:dataProvider>
  <mx:String>File</mx:String>
  <mx:String>Edit</mx:String>
```

```
        <mx:String>View</mx:String>
        <mx:String>Modify</mx:String>
        <mx:String>Text</mx:String>
        <mx:String>Window</mx:String>
    </mx:dataProvider>
</mx:MenuBar>

<mx:Panel id="panel1" x="80" y="120" width="510" height="330"
    layout="vertical" title="Panel" paddingTop="30" paddingLeft="10">
<mx:HBox paddingBottom="5" paddingLeft="5" paddingRight="5"
    paddingTop="5">
<mx:Form>
<mx:FormItem label="TextArea:">
    <mx:TextArea height="84" width="150">
    <mx:text><![CDATA[ Sample text. ]]></mx:text>
    </mx:TextArea>
</mx:FormItem>
<mx:FormItem label="TextInput:">
    <mx:TextInput width="150"/>
</mx:FormItem>
</mx:Form>
<mx:VBox>
<mx:CheckBox label="Checkbox one" />
<mx:CheckBox label="Checkbox two" />
<mx:RadioButton label="Radio two" groupName="radiogroup1" />
<mx:RadioButton label="Radio one" groupName="radiogroup1" />
<mx:PopUpButton label="Pop Up Button"/>
<mx:ComboBox>
    <mx:dataProvider>
        <mx:String>choice 1</mx:String>
        <mx:String>choice 2</mx:String>
        <mx:String>choice 3</mx:String>
        <mx:String>choice 4</mx:String>
    </mx:dataProvider>
</mx:ComboBox>
</mx:VBox>
    </mx:HBox>
<mx:ToggleButtonBar selectedIndex="1">
    <mx:dataProvider>
        <mx:String>Button 1</mx:String>
        <mx:String>Button 2</mx:String>
        <mx:String>Button 3</mx:String>
        <mx:String>Button 4</mx:String>
    </mx:dataProvider>
</mx:ToggleButtonBar>
<mx:Button label="Submit" />
<mx:Button label="Cancel"/>
</mx:Panel>

</mx:Application>
```

14

When you bring this up from Flex Builder 3, you see something like Figure 14-1.

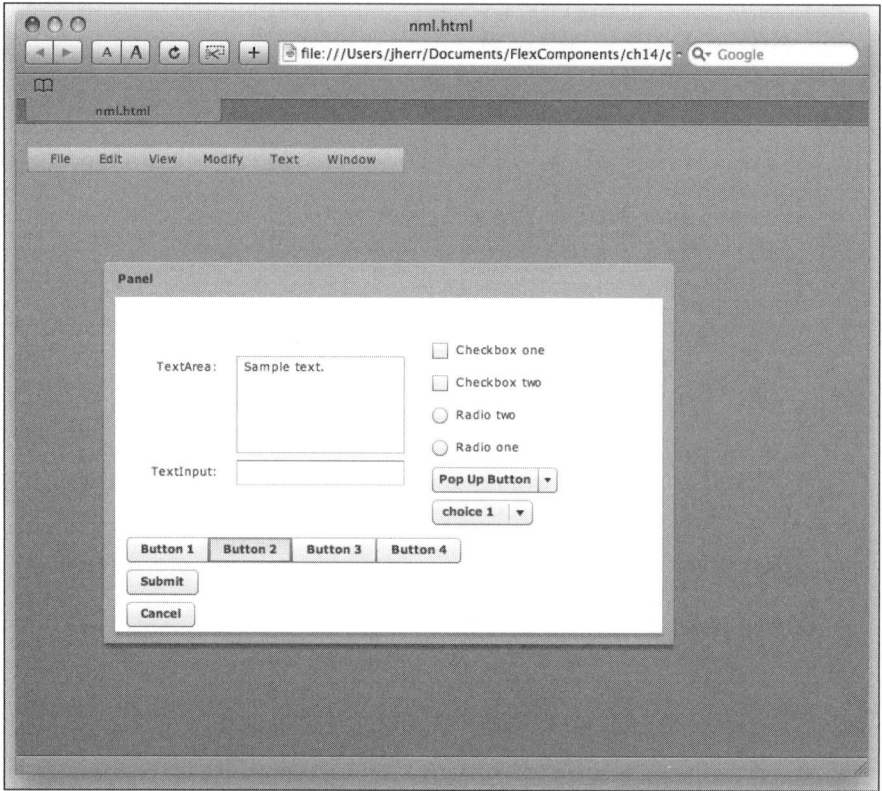

**Figure 14-1.** The application with no skin

From here, we are going to apply the newly downloaded skin to the application to see just how it looks.

## Blue Plastic

The first skin we are going to look at is the Blue Plastic Flex skin (http://fleksray.org/ Flex_skin.html#Blue%20Plastic). As with all of the skins, we need to make some minor modifications to the application code to make the best use of the skin. This can be seen in the following application code:

```
<?xml version="1.0" encoding="utf-8"?>
<mx:Application xmlns:mx="http://www.adobe.com/2006/mxml"
  xmlns:ext="nl.wv.extenders.panel.*" horizontalScrollPolicy="off"
 verticalScrollPolicy="off"
  layout="absolute" width="864" height="554"
  backgroundImage="blueglass.jpg">
```

```
<mx:Style source="blue_plastic.css"/>

<ext:ReflectionManager id="reflection"  target="{panel1}"
  width="{this.panel1.width}"
  height="{(this.panel1.height / 100) * 50}" fadeFrom="0.35"
  fadeTo="0" blur="0.3"/>
...

<ext:SuperPanel id="panel1"
  x="80" y="120" width="510" height="330"
  showControls="true" enableResize="true"
  layout="vertical" title="Panel" paddingTop="30" paddingLeft="10">
...
</ext:SuperPanel>

</mx:Application>
```

The application tag now includes the blueglass.jpg background image. We have also included the blue_plastic.css file, which defines this skin. To wrap the whole thing, we've added a ReflectionManager tag that gives the whole application a reflection.

You can check out the result in Figure 14-2.

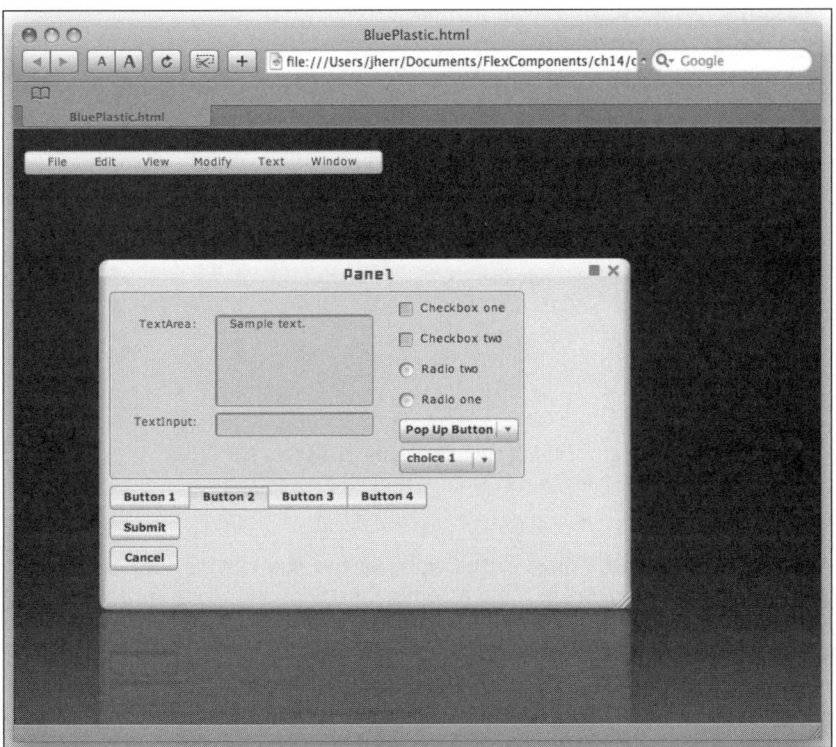

**Figure 14-2.** The Blue Plastic skin applied to the application

Personally I'm not all that happy with the soft look of the panel. But I really like the reflected image. The `ReflectionManager` that comes packaged with this skin could come in very handy.

To give a feel for what the CSS for a skin looks like, I've included some of the CSS code here:

```
TextArea {
  focusSkin: Embed(source="blue_plastic.swf", symbol="focus");
  borderSkin: Embed(source="blue_plastic.swf", symbol="layout one");
  paddingLeft: 8;
  paddingRight: 4;
}
AccordionHeader
{
  disabledSkin: Embed(source="blue_plastic.swf",
    symbol="Button_disabledSkin");
  downSkin: Embed(source="blue_plastic.swf", symbol="Button_downSkin");
  overSkin: Embed(source="blue_plastic.swf", symbol="Button_overSkin");
  selectedDisabledSkin: Embed(source="blue_plastic.swf",
  symbol="Button_disabledSkin");
  selectedDownSkin: Embed(source="blue_plastic.swf",
  symbol="Button_downSkin");
  selectedOverSkin: Embed(source="blue_plastic.swf",
  symbol="Button_overSkin");
  selectedUpSkin: Embed(source="blue_plastic.swf",
  symbol="Button_upSkin");
  upSkin: Embed(source="blue_plastic.swf", symbol="Button_upSkin");
  focusSkin: Embed(source="blue_plastic.swf", symbol="focus");
  fontFamily: franci;
  fontWeight: normal;
  fontSize: 12;
  fontAntiAliasType: advanced;
  fontSharpness: -100;
  fontgridFitType: subpixel;
}
Application
{
  backgroundImage: Embed(source="blue_plastic.swf",
  symbol="BackgroundImage");
}
```

As you can see, in this case most of the work for the skin is done with assets from the included `blue_plastic.swf` file, though some alterations are made with just some CSS basics, like the change of the font family, weight, size, and so on of the AccordionHeader control (as well as many others).

# Darke Nite

The Darke Nite skin (http://fleksray.org/Flex_skin.html#Darke%20Nite) has a kind of wondrous night feel to it. It's very easy to use, as you can see in the following application code:

```
<?xml version="1.0" encoding="utf-8"?>
<mx:Application xmlns:mx="http://www.adobe.com/2006/mxml"
    layout="absolute" width="1024" height="680"
    backgroundImage="dark_nite.jpg">

<mx:Style source="flex_skins.css"/>

...

</mx:Application>
```

All we need to do is set the background image and include the flex_skins.css file. You can see the result in Figure 14-3.

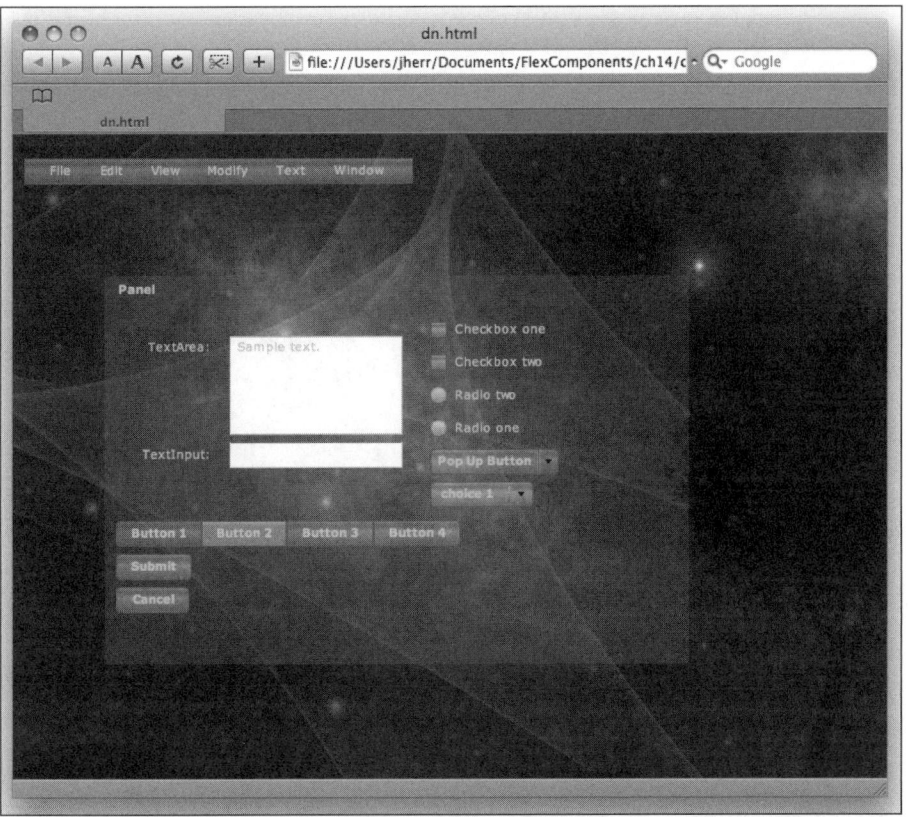

**Figure 14-3.** The Darke Nite skin applied to the application

**347**

I really like this skin. It's easy to use, has a nice, consistent look, and doesn't change the control scheme too much. You could argue that it's too dark, but everything has its time and place.

## Darkroom

In fact, you could go even a little darker with the Darkroom skin (http://www.scalenine.com/themes/darkroom/darkroom.html), which was inspired by Adobe's Darkroom imaging product. As with the Darke Nite skin, using the Dark Room skin is very easy, as shown in the following updated application code:

```
<?xml version="1.0" encoding="utf-8"?>
<mx:Application xmlns:mx="http://www.adobe.com/2006/mxml"
  layout="absolute" backgroundGradientColors="[#222222, #222222]">

<mx:Style source="style/darkroom.css"/>

...

</mx:Application>
```

The only modifications to the application were the change to the background gradient colors and the addition of the CSS source. The result can be seen in Figure 14-4.

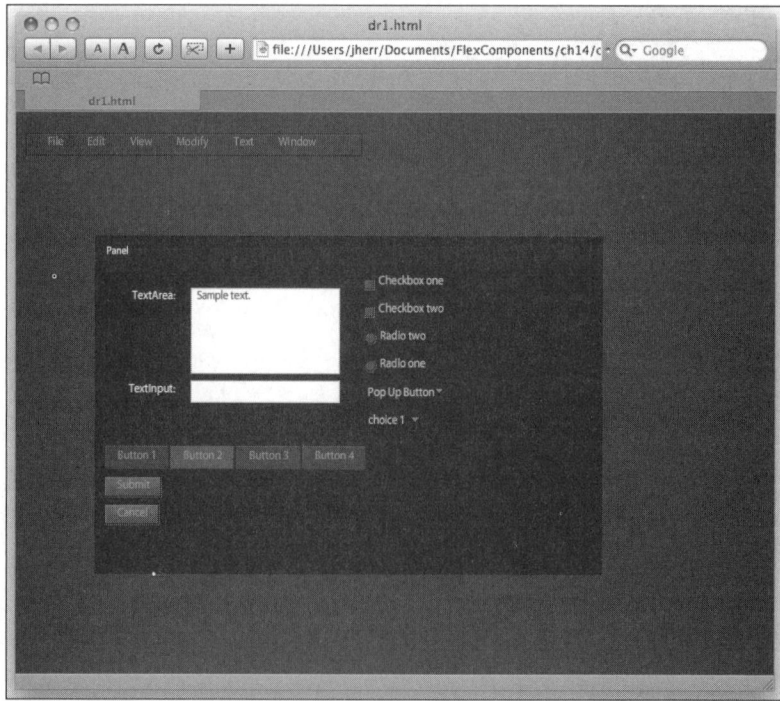

**Figure 14-4.** The Darkroom skin applied to the application

Dark, stark, and very sleek. This is the kind of skin that you can use if you are looking for something avant-garde.

# Flekistral

The Flekistral skin (http://fleksray.org/Flex_skin.html#Flekristal) has a decidedly more upbeat feel. The updated application to use this skin is shown here:

```
<?xml version="1.0" encoding="utf-8"?>
<mx:Application xmlns:mx="http://www.adobe.com/2006/mxml"
  layout="absolute" width="800" height="600"
  backgroundImage="backgrounds/palmleaf.jpg">

<mx:Style source="flekristal.css"/>

...

</mx:Application>
```

There are quite a few backgrounds packaged with this skin download. To start out, I picked the palmleaf.jpg background. The result is shown in Figure 14-5.

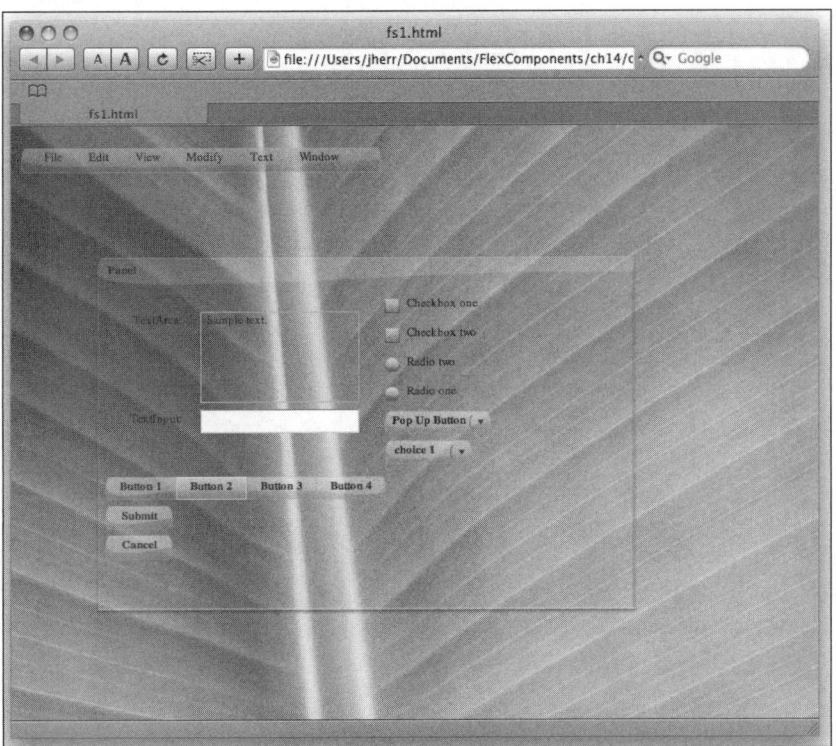

**Figure 14-5.** The palm leaf background

I certainly like the bevels on the buttons. That's very nice. Plus the use of a serif font for the text is a nice change from the ordinary.

The application shown next is another background for the Flekistral skin:

```
<?xml version="1.0" encoding="utf-8"?>
<mx:Application xmlns:mx="http://www.adobe.com/2006/mxml"
  layout="absolute" width="800" height="600"
  backgroundImage="backgrounds/space2.jpg">

<mx:Style source="flekristal.css"/>

...

</mx:Application>
```

This one is kind of spacey. It's shown in Figure 14-6.

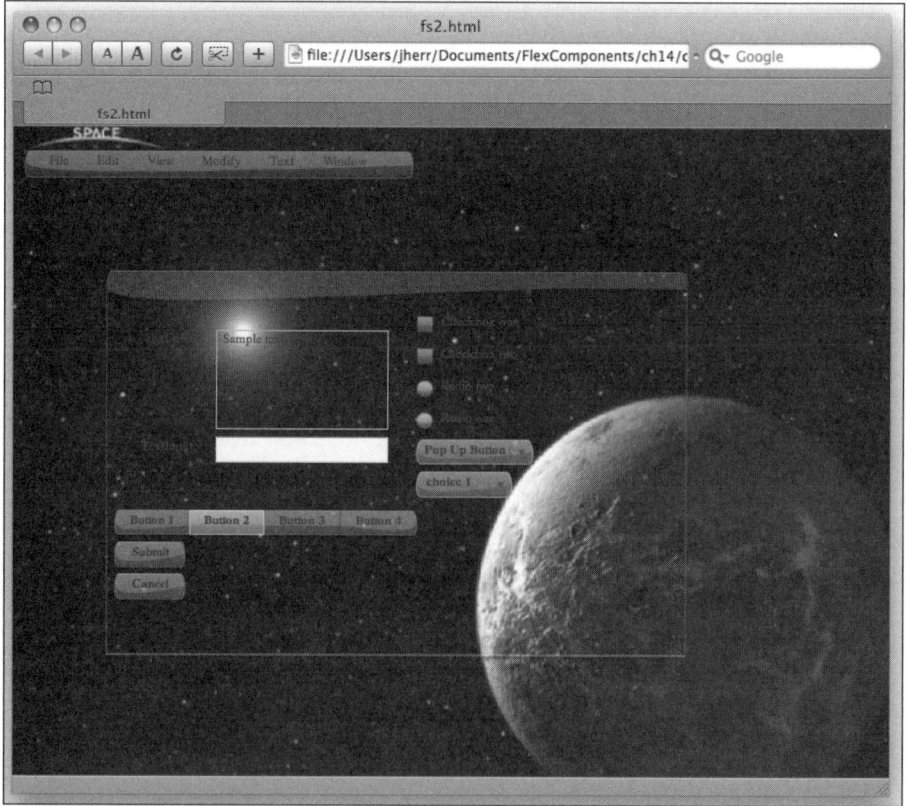

**Figure 14-6.** The space background

This might be a little too much, but it would probably be good for a kiosk of a space and science museum.

# Obsidian

The Obsidian skin (http://www.scalenine.com/themes/obsidian/obsidian.html) is a very nice dark-themed design with some glossy button effects. Following is the application code to use this skin:

```
<?xml version="1.0" encoding="utf-8"?>
<mx:Application xmlns:mx="http://www.adobe.com/2006/mxml"
  layout="absolute" width="800" height="600">

<mx:Style source="obsidian.css"/>

...

</mx:Application>
```

All that we needed to do for this skin was to add the CSS file included with the download. The results can be seen in Figure 14-7.

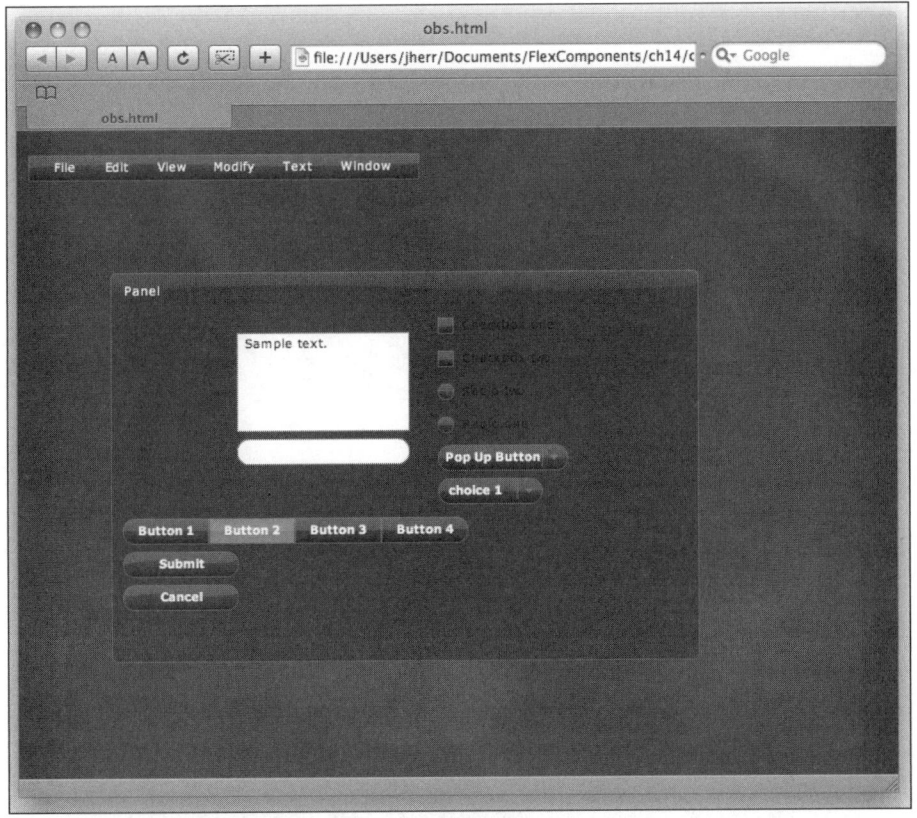

**Figure 14-7.** The Obsidian skin applied to the application

14

I really like the look of this skin. It's very clean. It's a little too dark in this example, but that could easily be cleaned up with a few well-placed applications of some white or light gray background.

# OS X

The OS X skin (http://weblogs.macromedia.com/mc/archives/2006/05/mac_os_x-lookin. html) attempts to put a Mac OS X look and feel onto Flex applications. The updated application code to use this skin is shown here:

```
<?xml version="1.0" encoding="utf-8"?>
<mx:Application xmlns:mx=http://www.adobe.com/2006/mxml
  layout="absolute" width="800" height="600">

<mx:Style source="OSX.css"/>

...

</mx:Application>
```

As with some of the other skins, this one is very easy to use. You only need to add a reference to the CSS file. The result is shown in Figure 14-8.

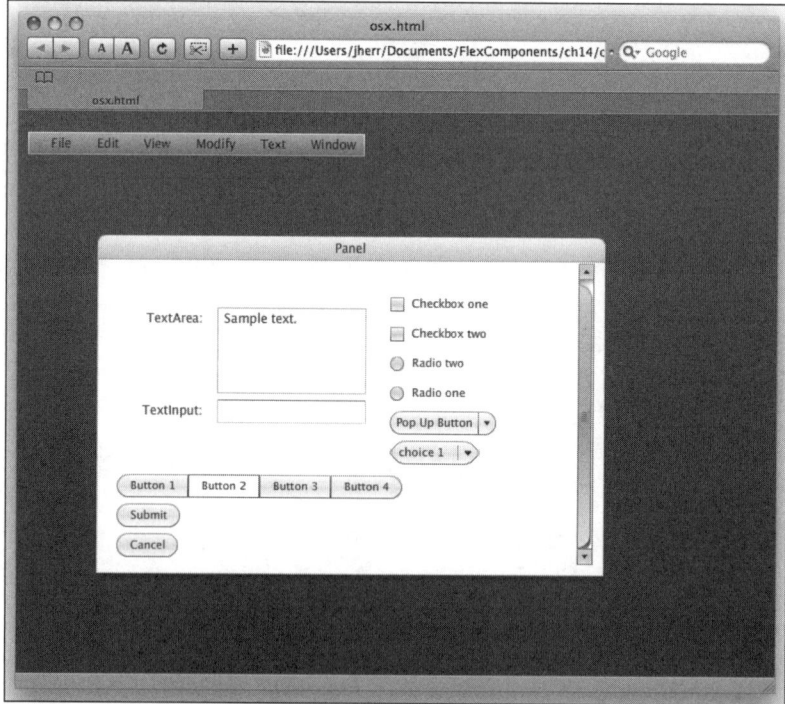

**Figure 14-8.** The OS X skin applied to the application

A few things need some cleanup, like the skin on the ComboBox that clips where the top of the button meets the bottom of the button.

# Treasure Map

The final skin I will show off is the Treasure Map skin (http://www.adobe.com/cfusion/exchange/index.cfm?event=extensionDetail&loc=en_us&extid=1268018) from the Flex Exchange graphics section. This one is a fancy skin that overhauls a lot of the interface with big fonts and updated panels. Following is the complete application code that demonstrates the Treasure Map skin:

```
<?xml version="1.0" encoding="utf-8"?>
<mx:Application xmlns:mx="http://www.adobe.com/2006/mxml"
  xmlns:ext="nl.wv.extenders.panel.*"
  layout="absolute" width="800" height="600">

<mx:Style source="treasuremap.css"/>

<ext:SuperPanel x="30" y="50" width="343" height="298"
  title="Controls" layout="absolute">
<mx:TextInput width="150" top="60" left="30" />
<mx:CheckBox label="Checkbox one" top="90" left="30" />
<mx:RadioButton label="Radio two" groupName="radiogroup1"
  top="150" left="30" />
<mx:Button label="Submit" top="210" left="30" />
</ext:SuperPanel>

</mx:Application>
```

In this case, the fonts and controls were just too big to show them all.

When we launch this application from Flex Builder 3, we see something like Figure 14-9.

14

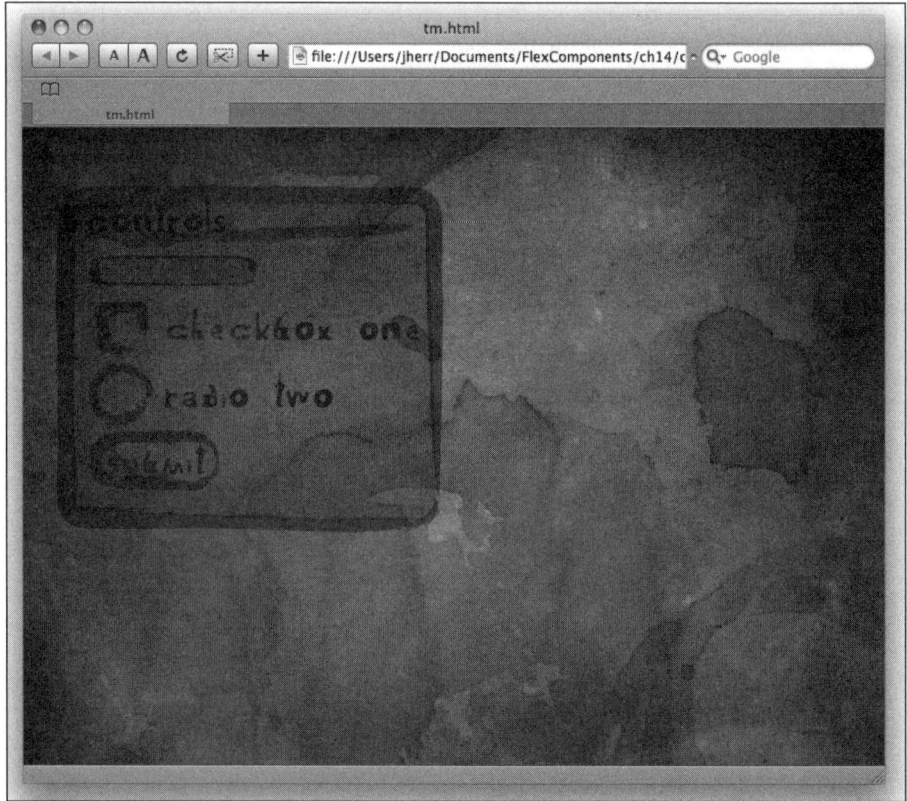

**Figure 14-9.** The Treasure Map skin

It may not be for every application, but it does show you just how far you can take the reskinning of the Flex controls.

## Where we will go from here

There are lots of things you can do with Flex skinning. The Flex Builder 3 IDE makes it fairly easy to develop skins. And you can use these skins as starting points for developing new skins of your own. If you do develop a new skin and want to publicize it, I recommend using the ScaleNine site (http://scalenine.com). That site is the Flex developer's best resource for finding new skins to use.

In the next chapter, I discuss how to create your own Flex components.

# 15  BUILDING YOUR OWN COMPONENTS

Updated 7/6/08

After reading about all these cool Flex components (and hopefully using a few), I would be surprised if you weren't inspired to build a few components of your own. In this chapter, I'll walk you through the process of using Flex Builder 3 to build your own components.

Before we begin, I should note that building components in Flex is a topic that could take up volumes. What I'll do in this chapter is take you through the process of building your own audio player component, and you can take it from there.

# Building one component requires two projects

When you build a component, you will have two projects. The first is the MXML application that you will use to test the component. In this case, we will name that project "audiotest." The second project is the component itself. That project will be a Flex Library called "miniaudio."

The first step is to create the test project. Create a Flex project just as you normally would, as shown in Figure 15-1.

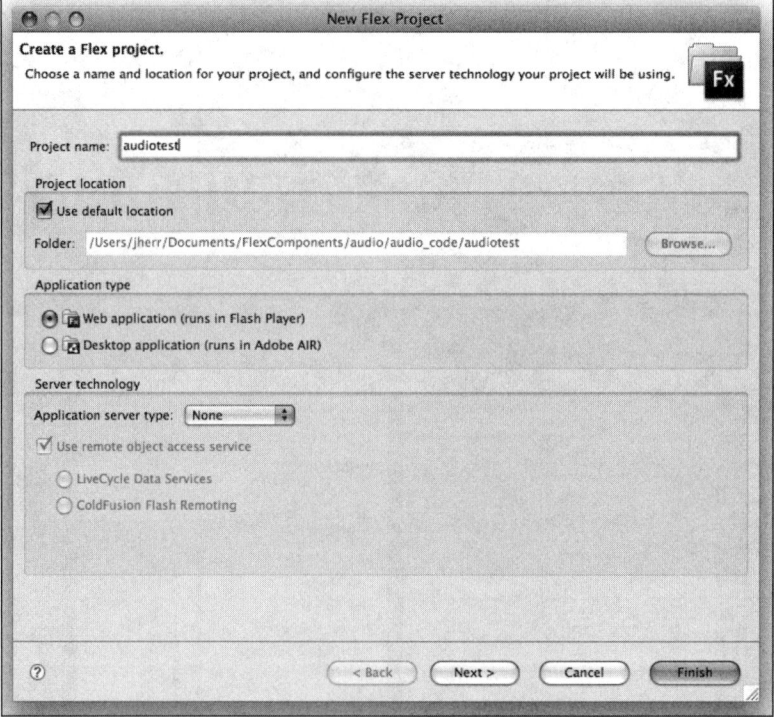

**Figure 15-1.** Creating the test project

The second step is to create the Flex Library project to host the component code. This is shown in Figure 15-2.

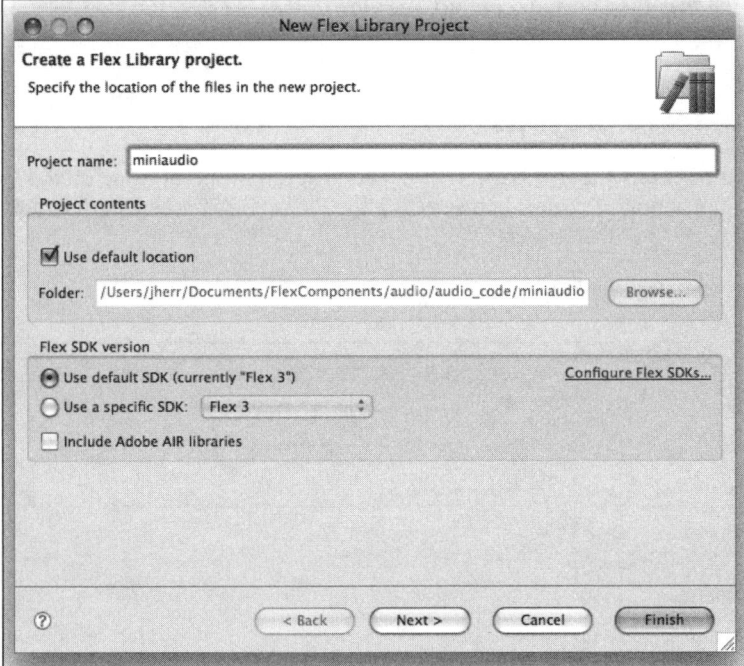

**Figure 15-2.** Creating the Flex Library project for the component

At this point, your Flex Builder environment should look like Figure 15-3.

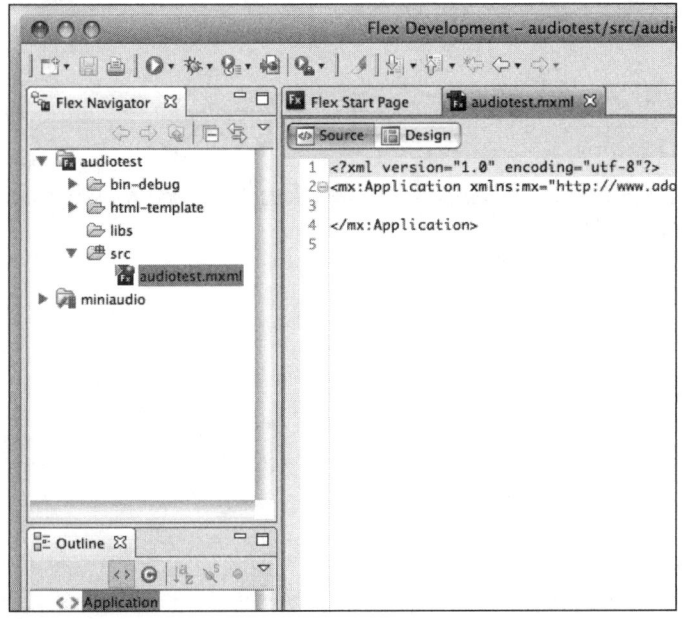

**Figure 15-3.** The Flex Builder environment after the two projects have been created

You can tell that the miniaudio project is a Flex Library because the icon for the project has the little books superimposed on it.

## Linking the two projects

Now we need to link the two projects together. That starts with bringing up the Properties dialog on the audiotest project and selecting the Project References tab. Here you will see the list of all of the other projects.

This is shown in Figure 15-4.

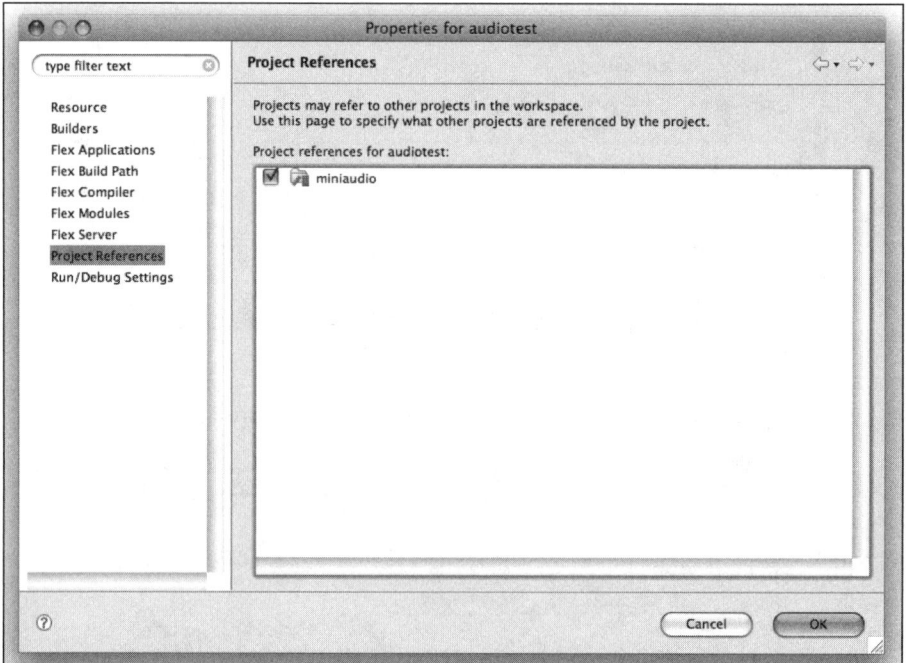

**Figure 15-4.** The Project References panel

Make sure that the miniaudio project is checked. Then head over to the Flex Build Path tab and select the Library Path tab in that panel. This is shown in Figure 15-5.

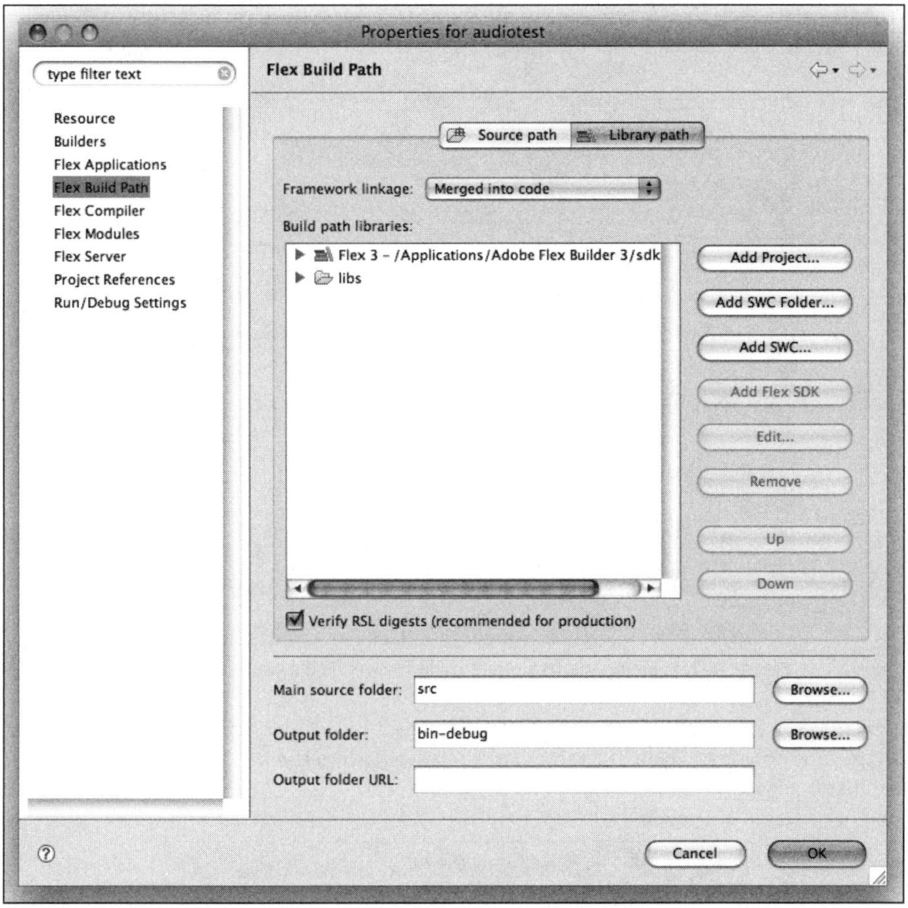

**Figure 15-5.** The Library Path tab for the audiotest project

The next step is to click the Add SWC button, which will bring up the Add Folder dialog shown in Figure 15-6.

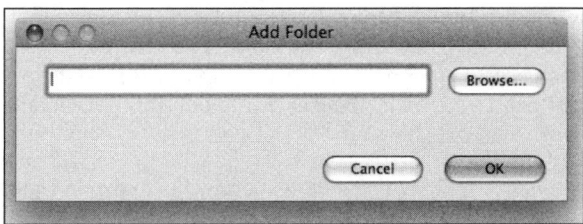

**Figure 15-6.** The Add Folder dialog launched from the Add SWC button

From here we click the Browse button and navigate over to the bin directory in the mini-audio project. You can see that in Figure 15-7.

**Figure 15-7.** Locating the bin directory in the miniaudio project

With that set you click the Choose button. This will return you to the Add Folder dialog where you should see the bin directory in a relative path to the miniaudio project. You can see that in Figure 15-8.

**Figure 15-8.** The updated Add Project dialog

Click the OK button, and you should see the miniaudio/bin directory has now been added to the list of paths where Flex Builder 3 will look for SWC libraries to add to this project.

The updated Library Path panel for the audiotest project is shown in Figure 15-9.

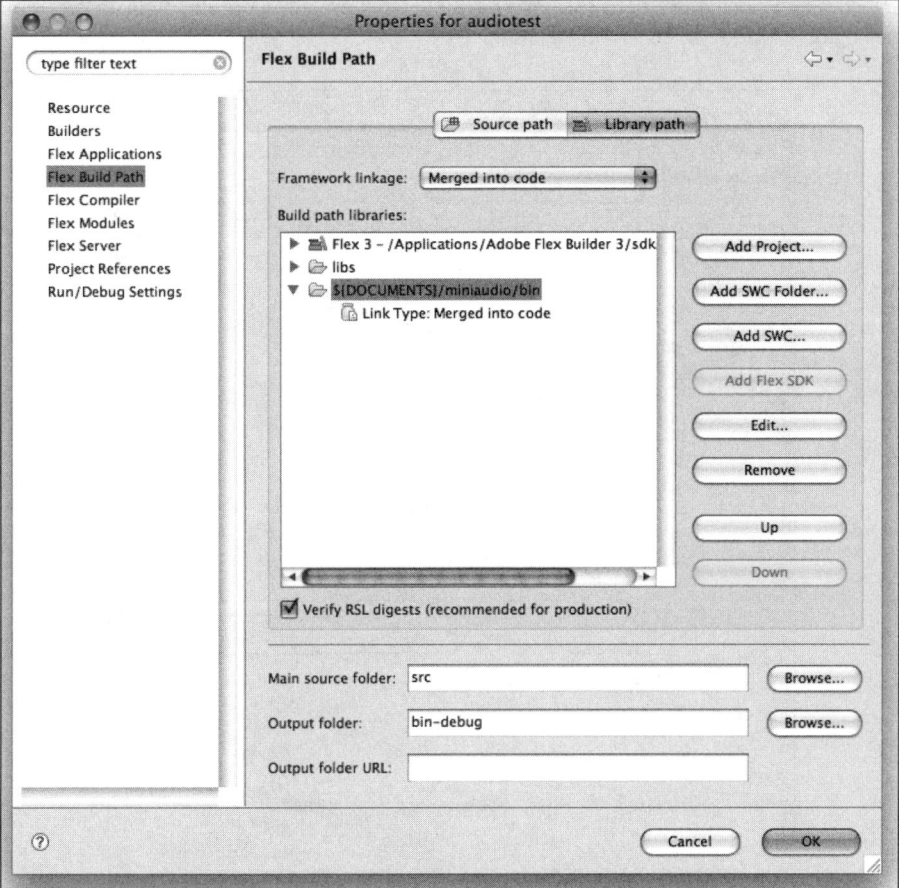

**Figure 15-9.** The updated Library Path panel

# Setting up the component

To start writing the code for the component, we need to create a directory where the source code will go. For this project, I'm going to use src/com/jherrington/miniaudio. This maps to the com.jherrington.miniaudio namespace for the project.

15

Select New Folder after right-clicking the miniaudio project icon and type in src/com/jherrington/miniaudio as shown in Figure 15-10.

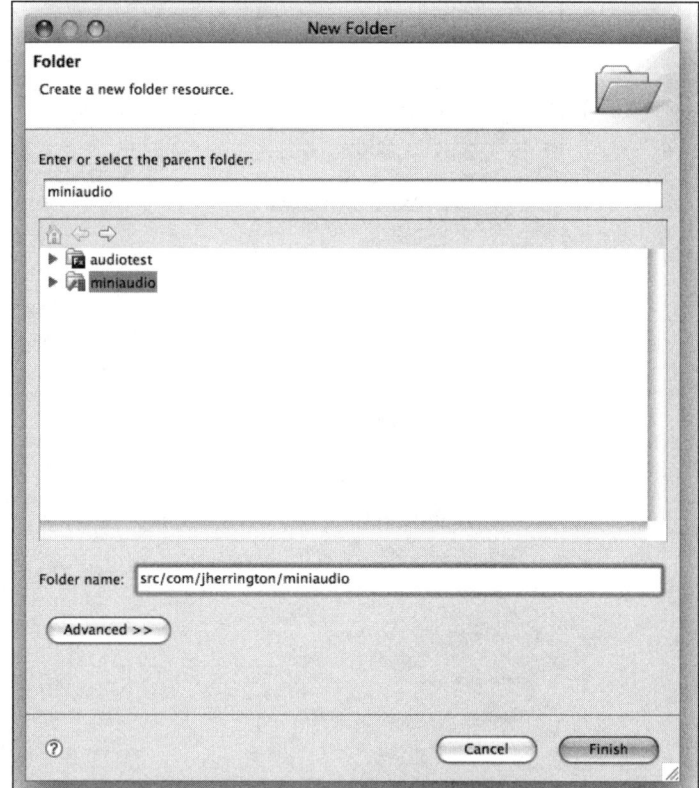

**Figure 15-10.** Creating the directory for the miniaudio source

Once the src directory has been created, we need to select the Flex Library Build Path tab from the Properties dialog. Then select the src item and click OK.

You can see the result in Figure 15-11.

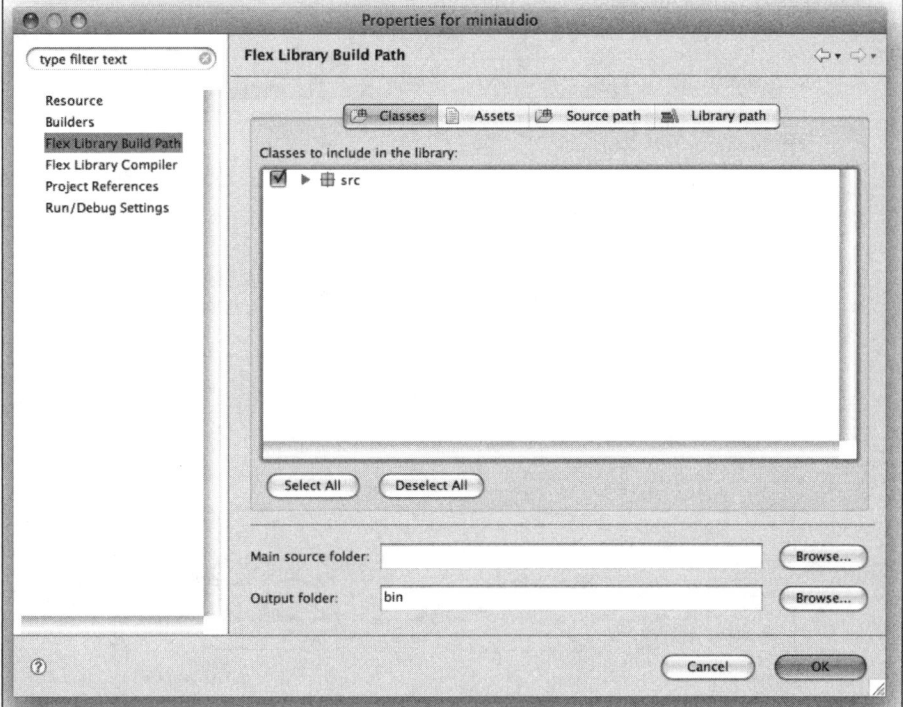

**Figure 15-11.** The Flex Library Build Path panel

## Using MXML to assemble the user interface

We are going to use MXML to put together the user interface for the miniaudio player. So the next step is to create the Player.mxml file in the miniaudio project. This should be located in the com/jherrington/miniaudio folder.

You can see the MXML wizard in Figure 15-12.

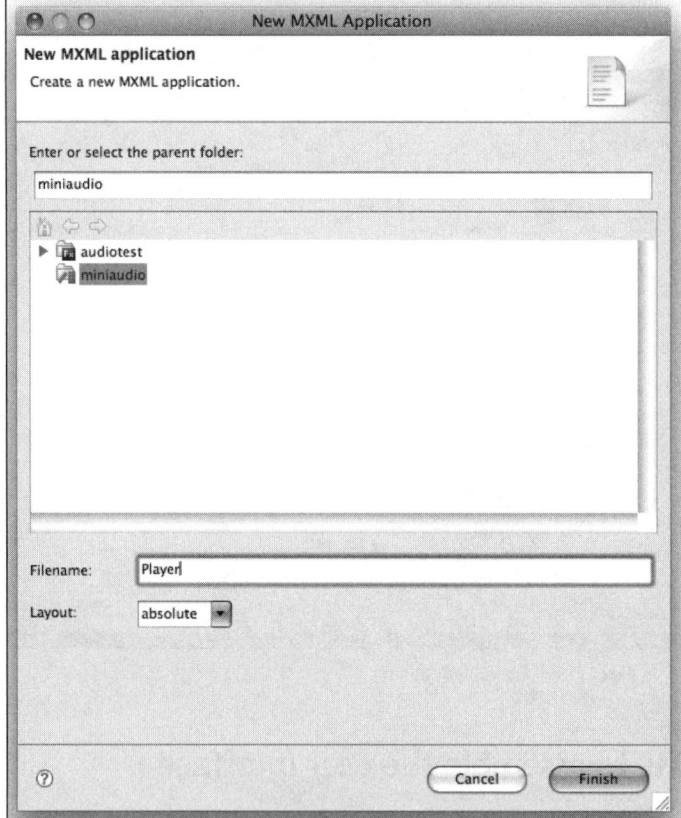

**Figure 15-12.** Creating the Player application

One more thing to set up before we can get into coding this project is the source path in the miniaudio project. This needs to be set so that the project doesn't think that the namespace is src.com.jherrington.miniaudio. You just need to set the Main source folder setting to src in the Source path panel. You can see that in Figure 15-13.

Just to make sure that everything is set up properly, have a look at Figure 15-14 and make sure the Flex Navigator panel it shows looks the same as what you have in your Flex Builder application.

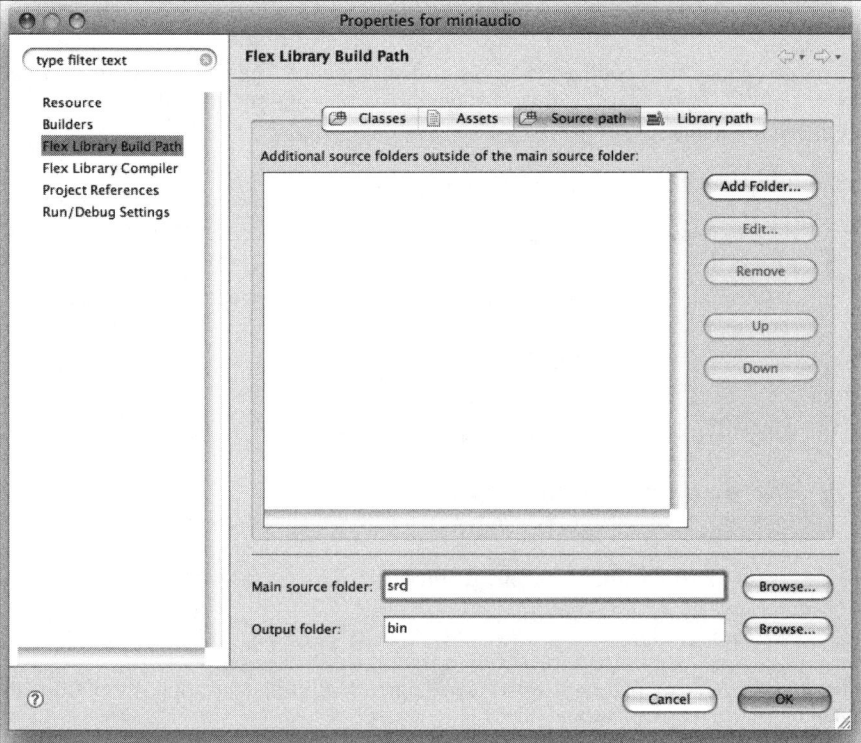

**Figure 15-13.** The Source path panel

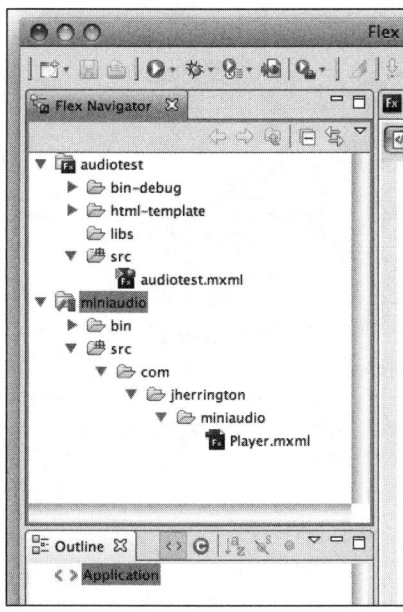

**Figure 15-14.** The fully set up environment with both of the projects ready to go

## Writing the component code

Now we can finally start coding the miniaudio component. The first version of this component is just going to be a "hello world" type thing to make sure that the audiotest project can see the miniaudio project.

The initial code for the Player.mxml file is shown here:

```
<?xml version="1.0" encoding="utf-8"?>
<mx:Panel mlns:mx="http://www.adobe.com/2006/mxml" layout="vertical"
  width="200" height="50" borderColor="black" borderStyle="solid"
  borderThickness="1">
<mx:Label text="MP3 Player" />
</mx:Panel>
```

And the initial version of the audiotest.mxml file is here:

```
<?xml version="1.0" encoding="utf-8"?>
<mx:Application xmlns:mx="http://www.adobe.com/2006/mxml"
  layout="vertical"
  xmlns:ma="com.jherrington.miniaudio.*">
<ma:Player />
</mx:Application>
```

If everything works as planned, when you launch the audiotest application from Flex Builder, you should see something like Figure 15-15.

**Figure 15-15.** The "hello world" for the MP3 component

The next version of the miniaudio code will actually do the work of loading in an MP3 sound and controlling the playback with some Flex controls.

Here is the updated code for Player.mxml:

```
<?xml version="1.0" encoding="utf-8"?>
<mx:Module xmlns:mx="http://www.adobe.com/2006/mxml" layout="vertical"
  horizontalScrollPolicy="off"
  verticalScrollPolicy="off" creationComplete="onStartup()">
<mx:Script>
<![CDATA[
private var _playing:Boolean = false;
private var _autoPlay:Boolean = false;
private var _sound:Sound = null;
private var _soundChan:SoundChannel = null;
private var _source:Object = null;
private var _resumePoint:Number = 0;

public function get playing( ) : Boolean {
  return _playing;
}

public function get autoPlay( ) : Boolean {
  return _autoPlay;
}

public function set autoPlay( play:Boolean ) : void {
  _autoPlay = play;
}

public function get sound( ) : Sound {
  return _sound;
}

public function get source( ) : Object {
  return _source;
}

public function set source( src:Object ) : void {
  _source = src;
  if ( _source as Sound != null )
    _sound = _source as Sound;
  else
    _sound = new Sound( new URLRequest( _source as String ) );
  _sound.addEventListener(Event.ID3, onTags);
  _sound.addEventListener(Event.OPEN, onLoad);
}

private function onLoad( event:Event ) : void {
  if ( autoPlay && playing == false )
    onPlay();
}
```

15

```
private function onStartup() : void {
}

private function onTags( event:Event ) : void {
  mp3Name.text = _sound.id3.songName;
}

private function onPlayComplete( event:Event ) : void {
  _soundChan = null;
  _playing = false;
  updateUI();
}

private function onPlay() : void {
  if ( _playing ) {
    _resumePoint = _soundChan.position;
    _soundChan.stop();
    _soundChan = null;
    _playing = false;
  } else {
    _soundChan = _sound.play( _resumePoint );
    var transform:SoundTransform = _soundChan.soundTransform;
    transform.volume = vol.value;
    _soundChan.soundTransform = transform;
    _soundChan.addEventListener(Event.SOUND_COMPLETE,onPlayComplete);
    _playing = true;
  }
  updateUI();
}
private function onVolumeChange( ) : void {
  if ( playing ) {
    var transform:SoundTransform = _soundChan.soundTransform;
    transform.volume = vol.value;
    _soundChan.soundTransform = transform;
  }
}
private function updateUI( ) : void {
  playBtn.label = _playing ? 'Pause' : 'Play';
}
]]>
</mx:Script>
<mx:Label id="mp3Name" text="" width="100%" truncateToFit="true" />
<mx:HBox>
<mx:Button id="playBtn" label="Play" click="onPlay();" />
<mx:HSlider id="vol" width="50" minimum="0" maximum="1" value="1"
  change="onVolumeChange()"
  showDataTip="false" />
</mx:HBox>
</mx:Module>
```

The code for this component is split into two segments. At the top is the ActionScript portion, and the user interface is located in the MXML tags at the bottom of the file. The ActionScript code is mainly getters and setters for the various properties of the component. The most important property is source. It defines the location of the MP3 file to play. The autoPlay property sets whether the sound should start playing as soon as it's loaded. And the sound property is a read-only accessor for the sound object.

There are no public methods. The only methods are event handlers for the sound object and for the user interface controls.

Once we have updated the Player.mxml file, we add a source value to the audiotest.mxml file that points to an MP3 file.

```
<?xml version="1.0" encoding="utf-8"?>
<mx:Application xmlns:mx="http://www.adobe.com/2006/mxml"
  layout="vertical"
  xmlns:ma="com.jherrington.miniaudio.*">
<ma:Player source="http://localhost/music/02 Shirley Bassey - ➥
Where Do I Begin (Away Team Mix).mp3"
  autoPlay="true" width="200" />
</mx:Application>
```

In my case, it's a track from the *Hotel Costes, Etage 3* album by Stephane Pompougnac.

With that done, we can once again launch the audiotest project, and you should see something like Figure 15-16.

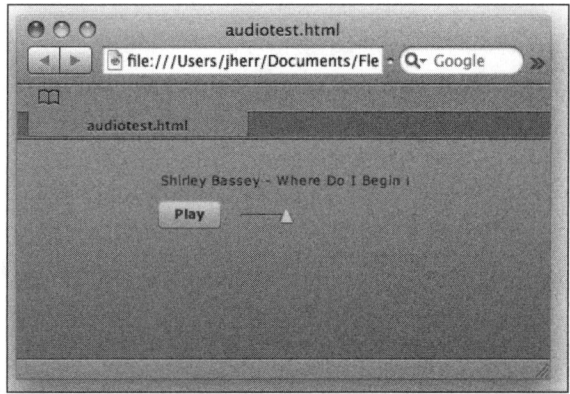

**Figure 15-16.** The basic audio player

# Perfecting the well-designed component

A well-designed component dispatches messages whenever its state changes. So the first thing we need to do is define a new Event type and add some custom message values.

15

The code for the new AudioPlayerEvent class is shown here:

```
package com.jherrington.miniaudio
{
  import flash.events.Event;
  import flash.media.SoundChannel;

  public class AudioPlayerEvent extends Event
  {
    public static const PLAY:String = "PLAY";

    public static const PAUSE:String = "PAUSE";

    public static const FINISHED:String = "FINISHED";

    public static const LOADED:String = "LOADED";

    public var channel:SoundChannel = null;

    public function AudioPlayerEvent(type:String,
    chan:SoundChannel = null, bubbles:Boolean=false,
    cancelable:Boolean=false)
    {
      super(type, bubbles, cancelable);
      channel = chan;
    }
  }
}
```

We've defined four new event names: play, pause, finished, and loaded. These are fired when the component starts playing, pauses playback, finishes playback, and finishes loading the sound.

We've also added a new member variable that will hold the sound channel that will be set when the audio player starts playing and a sound channel is created.

The updated Player.mxml file that uses the new AudioPlayerEvent class is shown in the following code:

```
<?xml version="1.0" encoding="utf-8"?>
<mx:Module xmlns:mx="http://www.adobe.com/2006/mxml" layout="vertical"
  horizontalScrollPolicy="off"
  verticalScrollPolicy="off" creationComplete="onStartup()">
<mx:Script>
<![CDATA[
private var _playing:Boolean = false;
private var _autoPlay:Boolean = false;
private var _sound:Sound = null;
private var _soundChan:SoundChannel = null;
private var _source:Object = null;
private var _resumePoint:Number = 0;
```

```
[Event("AudioPlayerEvent.LOADED")]
[Event("AudioPlayerEvent.FINISHED")]
[Event("AudioPlayerEvent.PLAY")]
[Event("AudioPlayerEvent.PAUSE")]

public function get playing( ) : Boolean {
  return _playing;
}

public function get autoPlay( ) : Boolean {
  return _autoPlay;
}

public function set autoPlay( play:Boolean ) : void {
  _autoPlay = play;
}

public function get sound( ) : Sound {
  return _sound;
}

public function get source( ) : Object {
  return _source;
}

public function set source( src:Object ) : void {
  _source = src;
  if ( _source as Sound != null )
    _sound = _source as Sound;
  else
    _sound = new Sound( new URLRequest( _source as String ) );
  _sound.addEventListener(Event.ID3, onTags);
  _sound.addEventListener(Event.OPEN, onLoad);
}

private function onLoad( event:Event ) : void {
  if ( autoPlay && playing == false )
    onPlay();
}

private function onStartup() : void {
  dispatchEvent( new AudioPlayerEvent( AudioPlayerEvent.LOADED ) );
}

private function onTags( event:Event ) : void {
  mp3Name.text = _sound.id3.songName;
}
```

15

```
    private function onPlayComplete( event:Event ) : void {
      _soundChan = null;
      _playing = false;
      updateUI();

      dispatchEvent( new AudioPlayerEvent( AudioPlayerEvent.FINISHED ) );
    }

    private function onPlay() : void {
      if ( _playing ) {
        _resumePoint = _soundChan.position;
        _soundChan.stop();
        _soundChan = null;
        _playing = false;

        dispatchEvent( new AudioPlayerEvent( AudioPlayerEvent.PAUSE ) );
      } else {
        _soundChan = _sound.play( _resumePoint );
        var transform:SoundTransform = _soundChan.soundTransform;
        transform.volume = vol.value;
        _soundChan.soundTransform = transform;
        _soundChan.addEventListener(Event.SOUND_COMPLETE,onPlayComplete);
        _playing = true;

        dispatchEvent( new AudioPlayerEvent( AudioPlayerEvent.PLAY,
        _soundChan ) );
      }
      updateUI();
    }
    private function onVolumeChange( ) : void {
      if ( playing ) {
        var transform:SoundTransform = _soundChan.soundTransform;
        transform.volume = vol.value;
        _soundChan.soundTransform = transform;
      }
    }
    private function updateUI( ) : void {
      playBtn.label = _playing ? 'Pause' : 'Play';
    }
  ]]>
</mx:Script>
<mx:Label id="mp3Name" text="" width="100%" truncateToFit="true" />
<mx:HBox>
<mx:Button id="playBtn" label="Play" click="onPlay();" />
<mx:HSlider id="vol" width="50" minimum="0" maximum="1" value="1"
    change="onVolumeChange()"
    showDataTip="false" />
</mx:HBox>
</mx:Module>
```

# Spiffing up the look with CSS

The final thing to do is add some CSS to the audio player to spiff up the interface a little bit.

The updated code that has classes for the player and the label for the name of the song is shown in the code that follows:

```
<?xml version="1.0" encoding="utf-8"?>
<mx:Module xmlns:mx="http://www.adobe.com/2006/mxml" layout="vertical"
  horizontalScrollPolicy="off"
  verticalScrollPolicy="off" creationComplete="onStartup()"
  styleName="player">
<mx:Style>
.player {
  paddingTop: 5;
  paddingBottom: 5;
  paddingLeft: 5;
  paddingRight: 5;
  borderColor: #cccccc;
  borderStyle: solid;
  borderThickness: 1;
  backgroundColor: white;
}
.songName {
  fontSize: 14;
  fontWeight: bold;
}
</mx:Style>
<mx:Script>
<![CDATA[
...
]]>
</mx:Script>
<mx:Label id="mp3Name" text="" width="100%" truncateToFit="true"
  styleName="songName" />
<mx:HBox>
<mx:Button id="playBtn" label="Play" click="onPlay();"
  styleName="playButton" />
<mx:HSlider id="vol" width="50" minimum="0" maximum="1"
  value="1" change="onVolumeChange()"
  showDataTip="false" styleName="volumeSlider" />
</mx:HBox>
</mx:Module>
```

When we bring this final version up in the browser from Flex Builder 3, we see something like Figure 15-17.

**15**

**Figure 15-17.** The finished player component

Of course, the name of the song will be dependent on where you point the audiotest.mxml application.

## Completing the visualization

To make this whole component even cooler, we are going to finish it off by adding Ben Stucki's visualization component (http://www.adobe.com/cfusion/exchange/index.cfm?event=extensionDetail&loc=en_us&extid=1034708) that is available on Adobe's Flex Exchange.

To use the visualization component, we add the source to the audiotest project and then add it to the interface in a box below the player component.

```
<?xml version="1.0" encoding="utf-8"?>
<mx:Application xmlns:mx="http://www.adobe.com/2006/mxml"
  layout="vertical"
  xmlns:ma="com.jherrington.miniaudio.*" xmlns:vis="com.fusiox.ui.*"
  creationComplete="onStartup()">
<mx:Script>
<![CDATA[
private function onStartup() : void {
  vis.start();
}
]]>
</mx:Script>
<ma:Player source="http://localhost/music/02 Shirley Bassey - ➥
Where Do I Begin (Away Team Mix).mp3"
  autoPlay="true" width="200" />
<mx:HBox backgroundColor="white" borderColor="#cccccc"
  borderStyle="solid" borderThickness="1">
<vis:Visualization id="vis" width="200" height="50" type="bars" />
</mx:HBox>
</mx:Application>
```

In an interesting twist, these two components don't need to know about each other because the visualizer simply shows whatever is coming out of the speaker.

When we run this from Flex Builder, we should see something like Figure 15-18.

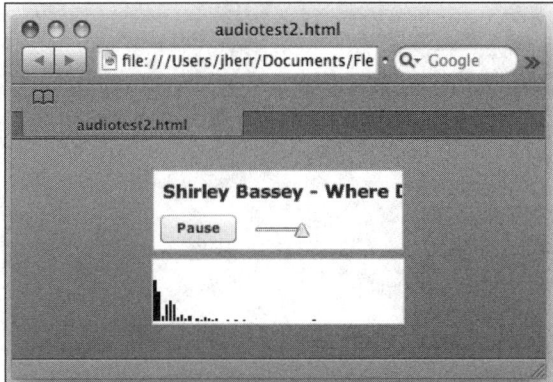

**Figure 15-18.** The completed player component

Of course, if you use a Metallica song, the spectrum will look radically different. But then, hey, that's the point.

# Where we will go from here

Building components with Flex is actually a lot of fun. Not only is it easy to build something cool, but it's also fun to get a component out on the Internet somewhere and to get some feedback from folks who use it. I suggest getting your component up on the Adobe Exchange as soon as you have something that's reasonably solid and getting some feedback on it. Be sure to blog about it as well and let an Adobe Flex evangelist know about what you are doing. That's a great way to get the word out.

15

Some data about states and what not

| State | Companies E | |
|---|---|---|
| United States | 18589 | 5 |
| Alabama | 162 | 4 |
| Alaska | 39 | 3 |
| Arizona | 353 | 1 |
| Arkansas | 124 | 5 |
| California | 2808 | 7 |
| Colorado | 470 | 1 |
| Connecticut | 243 | 5 |
| Delaware | 59 | 2 |

State data

| companies | employees | payr |
|---|---|---|
| 18589 | 514046 | 2571 |
| 162 | 4875 | 2193 |
| 39 | 392 | 1523 |
| 353 | 11389 | 4355 |
| 124 | 5976 | 2948 |
| 2808 | 76323 | 4319 |
| 470 | 12681 | 6446 |
| 243 | 5512 | 2232 |
| 99 | 2297 | 1239 |

| sales | state | statepopulat |
|---|---|---|
| 74507785 | United States | 288368698 |
| 562931 | Alabama | 4486508 |
| 48620 | Alaska | 643786 |
| 1483611 | Arizona | 5456453 |
| 567506 | Arkansas | 2710079 |
| 12415051 | California | 35116033 |
| 1898223 | Colorado | 4506542 |
| 454126 | Connecticut | 3460503 |
| 366915 | Delaware | 807385 |

Updated 7/2/08

I've been on enough projects to know that if you attempt to bring Flex into a project by first going to the suits and saying "Hey, I want to use Flex," you will run into a roadblock. The best way to bring Flex in is to do a skunkworks-style Flex project, and then show it to the suits and say, "Look at this kick-butt thing—let's use Flex." Concepts are easy to ignore, while working prototypes that rock are much more effective.

Using Flex the skunkworks way is easy; the Flex SDK is free, Flex Builder 3 is free for a trial period, even most of the components in this book are free to preview. The problem comes in connecting your Flex application to your web application. Not every web application has XML-based web services. And if you ask someone in the server group to create the services, well, you'll probably be waiting a while.

The trick is to hack into the data, to use the web interfaces that are available and scrape the data off them for display. This chapter will show you how to scrape the data off both an HTML web page and a JSON-based web service, the two most common Web 2.0 data sources.

## Hacking HTML data

Demonstrating how to get access to data that's hidden within HTML pages starts with building a simple HTML page that we can parse in Flex. The following PHP script takes the information technology data from the usdata data set and exports it as HTML:

```
<html><head><title>State Data</title></head>
<body>
<p>Some data about states and what not
<table>
<tr>
<th>State</th>
<th>Companies</th>
<th>Employees</th>
<th>Payroll</th>
<th>Sales</th>
<th>State Population</th>
</tr>
<?php
require_once("MDB2.php");
$dsn = 'mysql://root@localhost/usdata';
$mdb2 =& MDB2::factory($dsn);
$sth =& $mdb2->prepare( "SELECT * FROM it" );
$res = $sth->execute();
$rows = array();
while ($row = $res->fetchRow(MDB2_FETCHMODE_ASSOC)) {
?>
<tr>
<td><?php echo( $row['state'] ) ?></td>
<td><?php echo( $row['companies'] ) ?></td>
<td><?php echo( $row['employees'] ) ?></td>
```

```
<td><?php echo( $row['payroll'] ) ?></td>
<td><?php echo( $row['sales'] ) ?></td>
<td><?php echo( $row['statepopulation'] ) ?></td>
</tr>
<?php } ?>
</table></body>
```

You may have to change the login credentials for the database access in this code from `root` and `password` to whatever your MySQl credentials are.

You can see the HTML this page generates in a browser in Figure 16-1.

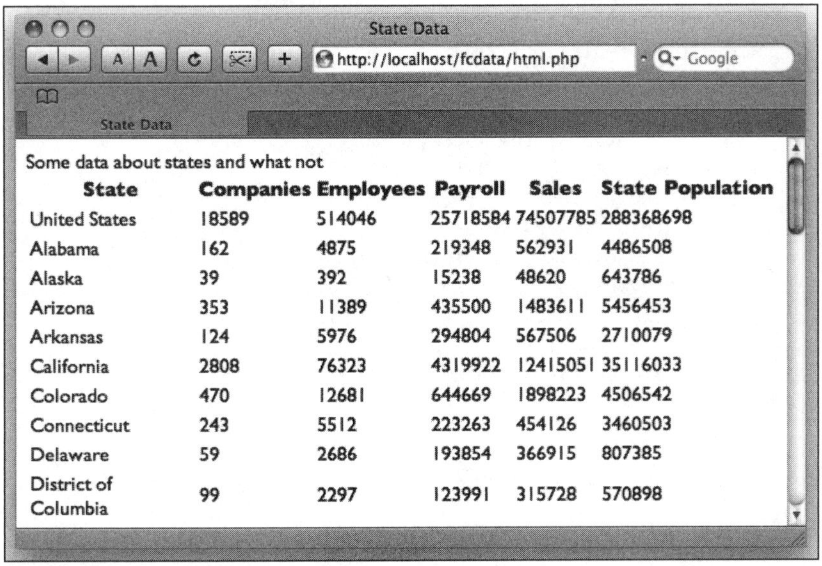


| State | Companies | Employees | Payroll | Sales | State Population |
|---|---|---|---|---|---|
| United States | 18589 | 514046 | 25718584 | 74507785 | 288368698 |
| Alabama | 162 | 4875 | 219348 | 562931 | 4486508 |
| Alaska | 39 | 392 | 15238 | 48620 | 643786 |
| Arizona | 353 | 11389 | 435500 | 1483611 | 5456453 |
| Arkansas | 124 | 5976 | 294804 | 567506 | 2710079 |
| California | 2808 | 76323 | 4319922 | 12415051 | 35116033 |
| Colorado | 470 | 12681 | 644669 | 1898223 | 4506542 |
| Connecticut | 243 | 5512 | 223263 | 454126 | 3460503 |
| Delaware | 59 | 2686 | 193854 | 366915 | 807385 |
| District of Columbia | 99 | 2297 | 123991 | 315728 | 570898 |

**Figure 16-1.** The HTML page in the browser

If your web application exports XHTML, you can use XML instead of text and parse it with the E4X syntax extension built into ActionScript. But most web applications don't export XHTML. The PHP script isn't exporting XHTML because of the unbalanced `<p>` tag at the top of the page. So we have to bring the page in as text and then use regular expressions to parse the data out of the page.

## Parsing the HTML

The code for the Flex application that reads the HTML page and then displays the resulting data is shown here:

```
<?xml version="1.0" encoding="utf-8"?>
<mx:Application xmlns:mx="http://www.adobe.com/2006/mxml"
  layout="vertical"
  creationComplete="htmlData.send()">
```

```
<mx:Script>
<![CDATA[
import mx.collections.ArrayCollection;
import mx.rpc.events.ResultEvent;

[Bindable]
private var stateData:ArrayCollection = new ArrayCollection();

private function stripTags( htmlString:String ) : String {
  return htmlString.replace( /<.*?>/g, '' );
}
private function onHTMLResult( event:ResultEvent ) : void {
  var html:String = event.result.toString();
  html = html.replace( /\r/g, '' );
  html = html.replace( /\n/g, '' );
  for each ( var row:String in html.match( /<tr>(.*?)<\/tr>/g ) ) {
    var cells:Array = row.match( /<td>(.*?)<\/td>/g );
    if ( cells.length > 0 ) {
        stateData.addItem( {
        state:stripTags(cells[0]),
        companies:Number(stripTags(cells[1])),
        employees:Number(stripTags(cells[2])),
         payroll:Number(stripTags(cells[3])),
         sales:Number(stripTags(cells[4])),
         statepopulation:Number(stripTags(cells[5]))
        } );
    }
  }
}
]]>
</mx:Script>
<mx:HTTPService id="htmlData" resultFormat="text"
  url="http://localhost/fcdata/html.php"
  result="onHTMLResult(event);" />
<mx:Panel title="State data" width="100%" height="100%">
  <mx:DataGrid dataProvider="{stateData}" width="100%" height="100%" />
</mx:Panel>
</mx:Application>
```

There are four important elements to this code. The first is that the resultFormat of the HTTPService is set to text so that the entire page is returned as one big string. The second element is the first set of regular expressions in onHTMLResult:

```
html = html.replace( /\r/g, '' );
html = html.replace( /\n/g, '' );
```

These expressions remove the line breaks and turn the page into one big string that is easier to parse.

These two regular expressions find every row in the document, and then break each row into their individual cells:

```
for each ( var row:String in html.match( /<tr>(.*?)<\/tr>/g ) ) {
  var cells:Array = row.match( /<td>(.*?)<\/td>/g );
```

From here we extract the data one cell at a time with the stripTags function, which removes any remaining tags from the content of each cell.

At the end of onHTMLResult we have an array that we can pass to the DataGrid that will display the data.

The result of this Flex application is shown in Figure 16-2.

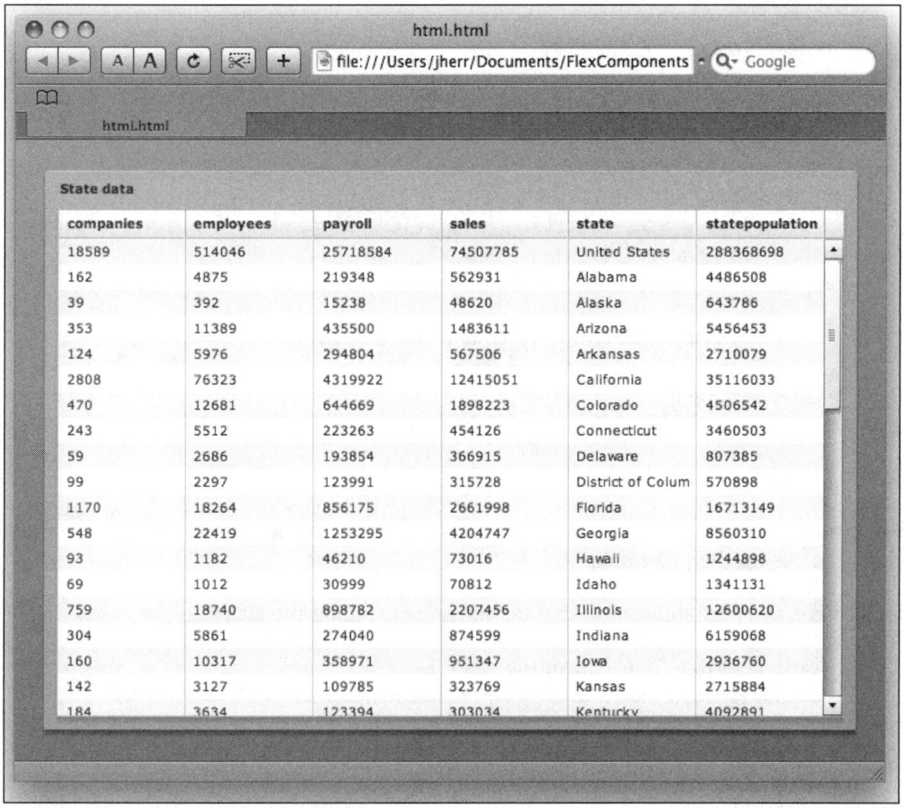


| companies | employees | payroll | sales | state | statepopulation |
|---|---|---|---|---|---|
| 18589 | 514046 | 25718584 | 74507785 | United States | 288368698 |
| 162 | 4875 | 219348 | 562931 | Alabama | 4486508 |
| 39 | 392 | 15238 | 48620 | Alaska | 643786 |
| 353 | 11389 | 435500 | 1483611 | Arizona | 5456453 |
| 124 | 5976 | 294804 | 567506 | Arkansas | 2710079 |
| 2808 | 76323 | 4319922 | 12415051 | California | 35116033 |
| 470 | 12681 | 644669 | 1898223 | Colorado | 4506542 |
| 243 | 5512 | 223263 | 454126 | Connecticut | 3460503 |
| 59 | 2686 | 193854 | 366915 | Delaware | 807385 |
| 99 | 2297 | 123991 | 315728 | District of Colum | 570898 |
| 1170 | 18264 | 856175 | 2661998 | Florida | 16713149 |
| 548 | 22419 | 1253295 | 4204747 | Georgia | 8560310 |
| 93 | 1182 | 46210 | 73016 | Hawaii | 1244898 |
| 69 | 1012 | 30999 | 70812 | Idaho | 1341131 |
| 759 | 18740 | 898782 | 2207456 | Illinois | 12600620 |
| 304 | 5861 | 274040 | 874599 | Indiana | 6159068 |
| 160 | 10317 | 358971 | 951347 | Iowa | 2936760 |
| 142 | 3127 | 109785 | 323769 | Kansas | 2715884 |
| 184 | 3634 | 123394 | 303034 | Kentucky | 4092891 |

**Figure 16-2.** The data extracted from the HTML page

This is a fairly simple example of parsing data from an HTML page. If your web application works in a similar way, you might be able to make slight modifications to the regular expressions in this application and get it to work.

Things can get more complicated if the data table is paginated and split across several pages. If that's the case, you will need to make several requests to get all of the data.

If your web application requires a login, you are going to need to manage the cookie return from the server and apply it to subsequent HTTPService requests.

# Accessing JSON services

Web services that use the JavaScript Object Notation (JSON) standard (e.g., Flickr) are much easier to access. All you need to do is use the JSONDecoder class included with the AS3 Core Lib (http://as3corelib.googlecode.com) library.

To demonstrate this, we need a PHP page that exports JSON for the contents of the it table in the usdata data set. This PHP code is shown here:

```php
<?php
require_once("MDB2.php");
$dsn = 'mysql://root@localhost/usdata';
$mdb2 =& MDB2::factory($dsn);
$sth =& $mdb2->prepare( "SELECT * FROM it" );
$res = $sth->execute();
$rows = array();
while ($row = $res->fetchRow(MDB2_FETCHMODE_ASSOC)) { $rows []= $row; }
echo( json_encode( $rows ) );
?>
```

When we run this PHP script on the command line, it looks like this:

```
% php json.php
[{"state":"United States","companies":"18589","employees":"514046",
  "payroll":"25718584","sales":"74507785",
  "statepopulation":"288368698"}...]
```

To read the JSON web service, we use the resultFormat set as text and the JSONDecoder class to parse up the JSON data.

Following is the Flex application that demonstrates reading the JSON service:

```xml
<?xml version="1.0" encoding="utf-8"?>
<mx:Application xmlns:mx="http://www.adobe.com/2006/mxml"
  layout="vertical"
  creationComplete="htmlData.send()">
<mx:Script>
<![CDATA[
import mx.rpc.events.ResultEvent;
import com.adobe.serialization.json.JSONDecoder;

private function onHTMLResult( event:ResultEvent ) : void {
  var js:String = event.result.toString();
  var jsd:JSONDecoder = new JSONDecoder( js );
  stateGrid.dataProvider = jsd.getValue();
```

```
      }
    ]]>
  </mx:Script>
  <mx:HTTPService id="htmlData" resultFormat="text"
    url="http://localhost/fcdata/json.php"
    result="onHTMLResult(event);" />
  <mx:Panel title="State data" width="100%" height="100%">
    <mx:DataGrid id="stateGrid" width="100%" height="100%" />
  </mx:Panel>
</mx:Application>
```

As you can see, it's pretty simple to get access to the data. You need to create a JSONDecoder object and pass it the JSON data as a string. We then call the getValue method on the JSONDecoder to get access to the data.

The resulting Flex application is shown in Figure 16-3.

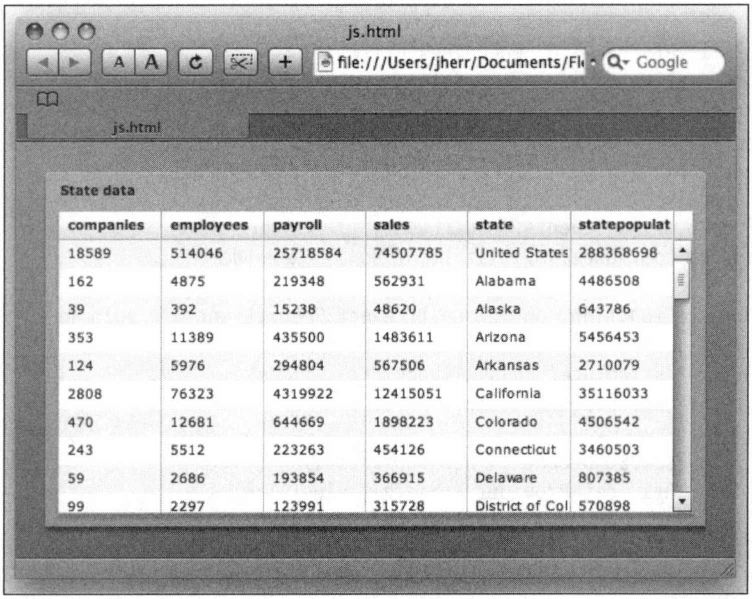

**Figure 16-3.** The JSON reader Flex application in action

This is just one way that JSON can be returned from the server. Another common way that JSON is returned is as a JavaScript function call. The PHP script to emulate that type of service is shown here:

```
<?php
require_once("MDB2.php");
$dsn = 'mysql://root@localhost/usdata';
$mdb2 =& MDB2::factory($dsn);
$sth =& $mdb2->prepare( "SELECT * FROM it" );
$res = $sth->execute();
```

```php
$rows = array();
while ($row = $res->fetchRow(MDB2_FETCHMODE_ASSOC)) { $rows []= $row; }
echo( "jsCallback( ".json_encode( $rows )." );" );
?>
```

When we run this script on the command line, you can see the following results:

```
% php json_func.php
jsCallback( [{"state":"United States","companies":"18589",
"employees":"514046","payroll":"25718584",
 "sales":"74507785","statepopulation":"288368698"}, ... ] );
```

As you can see, the jsCallback function is invoked by this JSON script. If we were a JavaScript application on a web page, this might mean something to us. Unfortunately, our application isn't JavaScript, so we need to strip that jsCallback stuff off before running the JSONDecoder.

The Flex application that consumes this second type of JSON data is shown here:

```xml
<?xml version="1.0" encoding="utf-8"?>
<mx:Application xmlns:mx="http://www.adobe.com/2006/mxml"
  layout="vertical"
  creationComplete="htmlData.send()">
<mx:Script>
<![CDATA[
import mx.rpc.events.ResultEvent;
import com.adobe.serialization.json.JSONDecoder;

private function onHTMLResult( event:ResultEvent ) : void {
  var js:String = event.result.toString();
  js = js.replace( /^jsCallback\( /, '' );
  js = js.replace( /\);$/, '' );

  var jsd:JSONDecoder = new JSONDecoder( js );
  stateGrid.dataProvider = jsd.getValue();
}
]]>
</mx:Script>
<mx:HTTPService id="htmlData" resultFormat="text"
  url="http://localhost/fcdata/json_func.php"
  result="onHTMLResult(event);" />
<mx:Panel title="State data" width="100%" height="100%">
  <mx:DataGrid id="stateGrid" width="100%" height="100%" />
</mx:Panel>
</mx:Application>
```

The only additions here are the two regular expressions that trim the callback function invocation off the JSON text before passing it to the decoder. When we run this application code, the result is exactly the same as with the previous example.

## Security issues

If you have security issues with calling the web server, there are two solutions. The ideal solution is to have the web application administrator add a crossdomain.xml file to the root of the web application. This will mean that any Flex or Flash application can access the site. The crossdomain.xml file is defined in more detail at http://crossdomainxml.org.

If adding anything to the web application is a no-no (which is probably the case), you will want to call the Security.allowDomain function when the application starts up with the name of the domain you are trying to access.

## Where we will go from here

With the combination of the data access recipes in this chapter and the cool components shown throughout the book, you have the tools to build some amazing Flex applications very quickly. I can't wait to see what you come up with.

# INDEX

Foundation
**XML for Flash**
Sas Jacobs

1-59059-543-2     $39.99 [US]

Foundation
**Actionscript Animation**
Making Things Move!
Keith Peters

1-59059-518-1     $39.99 [US]

Foundation
**Flash 8**
Sham Bhangal
and Kristian Besley

1-59059-542-4     $36.99 [US]

Foundation
**ASP.NET 2.0 for Flash**
Ryan Moore

1-59059-517-3     $39.99 [US]

Foundation
**Flash 8 Video**
Tom Green
Jordan Chilcott

1-59059-651-X     $44.99

EXPERIENCE THE
DESIGNER TO DESIGNER™
DIFFERENCE

Foundation
**Flash Applications for Mobile Devices**
Richard Leggett
Weyert du Boer
Scott Janousek

1-59059-558-0     $49.99 [US]

**New Masters of Flash**
Volume 3

1-59059-314-6     $59.99 [US]

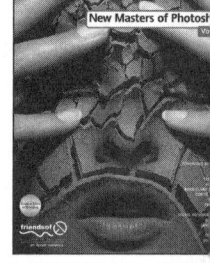

**New Masters of Photoshop**
Vol

1-59059-315-4     $59.99

**Object-Oriented ActionScript for Flash 8**
PETER ELST and TODD YARD

1-59059-619-6     $44.99 [US]

**Extending Flash MX 2004**
Complete Guide and Reference to JavaScript Flash
Keith Peters and Todd Yard

1-59059-304-9     $49.99 [US]

**Apache Essentials**
Install, Configure, Maintain

1-59059-355-3     $24.99 [US]

Macromedia
**Dreamweaver MX 2004 Design, Projects**
Rachel Andrew
Craig Grannell
Allan Kent
Christopher Schmitt

1-59059-409-6     $39.99 [US]

TOM GREEN & TIAG
From **After Effects to Flash**

1-59059-748-6     $49.99

ANTONIO DE DONATIS
AdvancED
**ActionScript Components**
Mastering the Flash Component Architecture

1-59059-593-9     $49.99 [US]

MICHAEL KEMPER
GUIDO ROSSI
BRIAN MONNONE
AdvancED
**Flash Interface Design**

1-59059-555-6     $44.99 [US]

**DOM Scripting**
Web Design with JavaScript and the Document Object Model
Jeremy Keith

1-59059-533-5     $34.99 [US]

FOREWORD BY MOLLY E. HOLZSCHLAG

**Web Accessibility**
Web Standards and Regulatory Compliance

1-59059-638-2     $49.99 [US]

**HTML Mastery**
Semantics, Standards, and Styling

Paul H

1-59059-765-6     $34.99

**Blog Design Solutions**

1-59059-581-5     $39.99 [US]

**CSS Mastery**
Advanced Web Standards Solutions
ANDY BUDD
with Cameron Moll & Simon Collison

1-59059-614-5     $34.99 [US]

**Flash Application Design Solutions**
The Flash Usability Handbook
KA WAI CHEUNG
CRAIG BRYANT

1-59059-594-7     $39.99 [US]

WEB STANDARDS SOLUTIONS
The Markup and Style Handbook

1-59059-381-2     $34.99 [US]

**PODCAST SOLUTIONS**
The Complete Guide to Podcasting
by MICHAEL W. GEOGHEGAN and DAN KLASS

1-59059-554-8     $24.9

# Selected screenshots

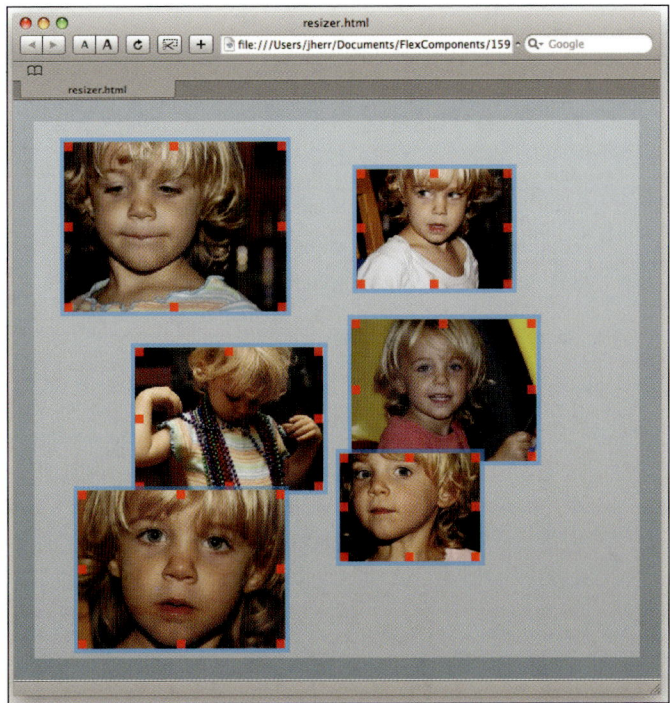

**Figure 4-6.** When the application first starts up

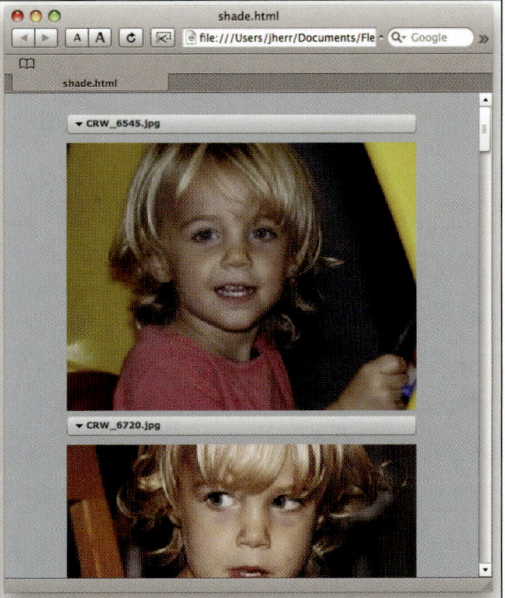

**Figure 4-9.** The application after startup with the images in WindowShade containers

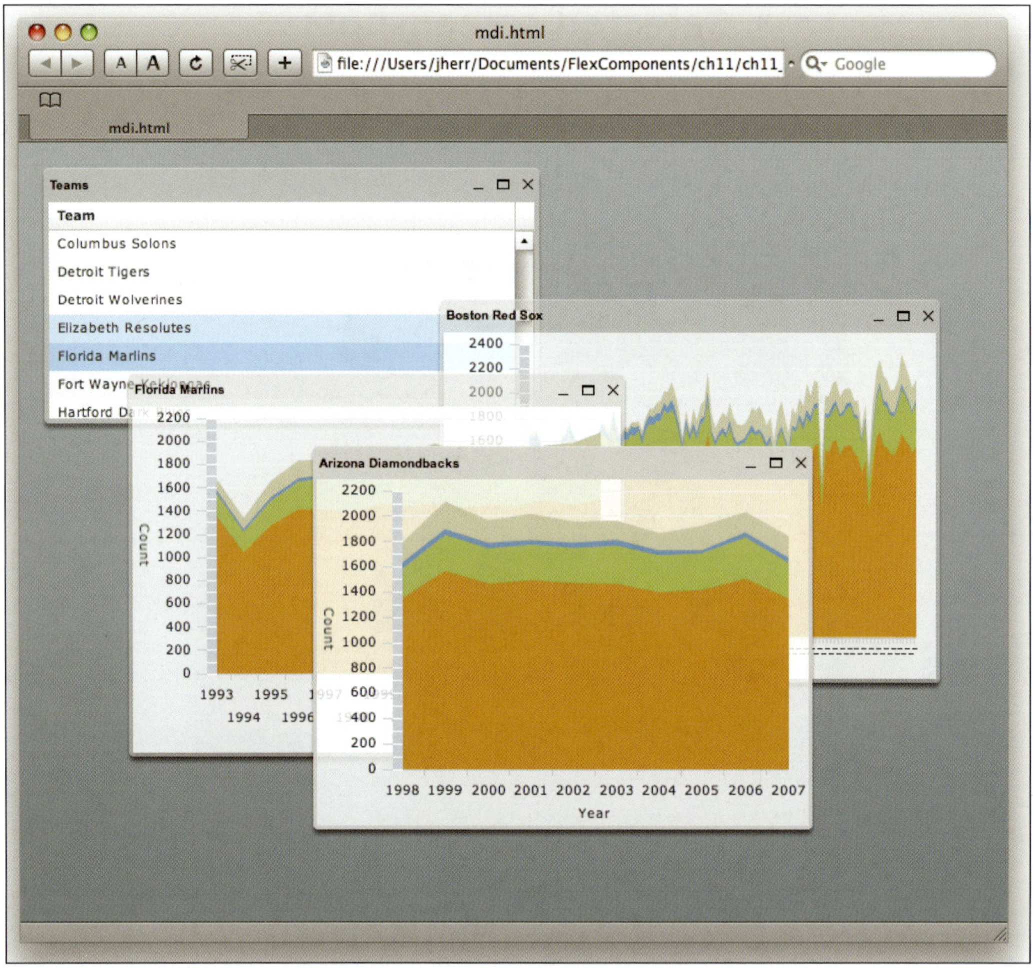

**Figure 4-23.** Four windows to show the list of teams and some team results

**Figure 5-4.** The EnhancedButtonSkin applied to a Button and a CanvasButton

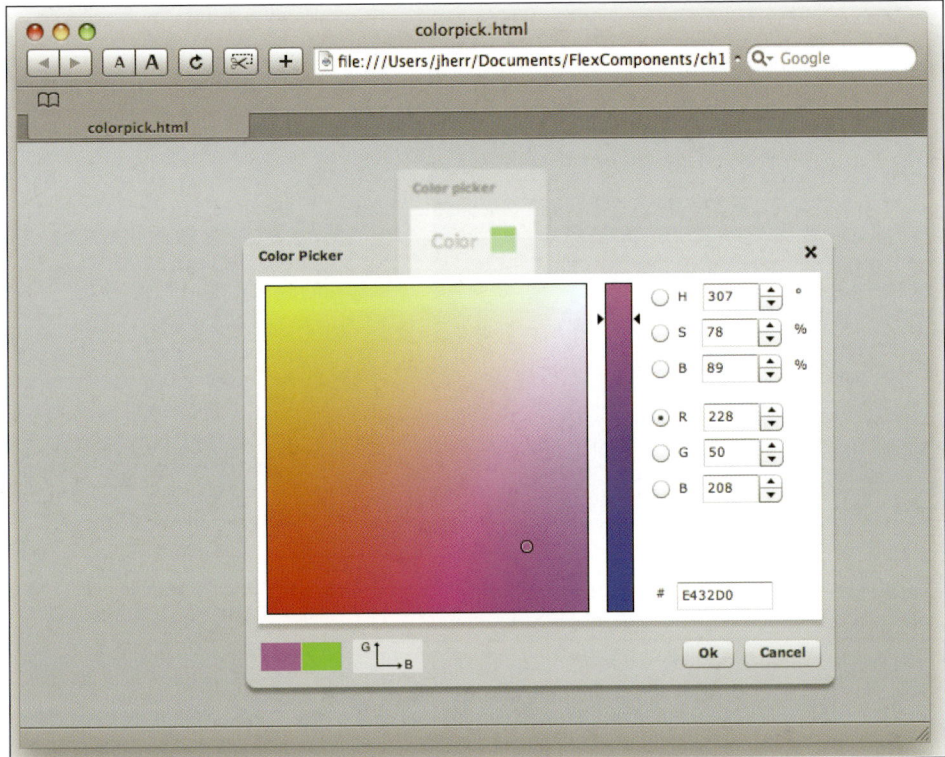

**Figure 5-6.** The Korax color selector window

**Figure 6-2.** Looking down into the carousel

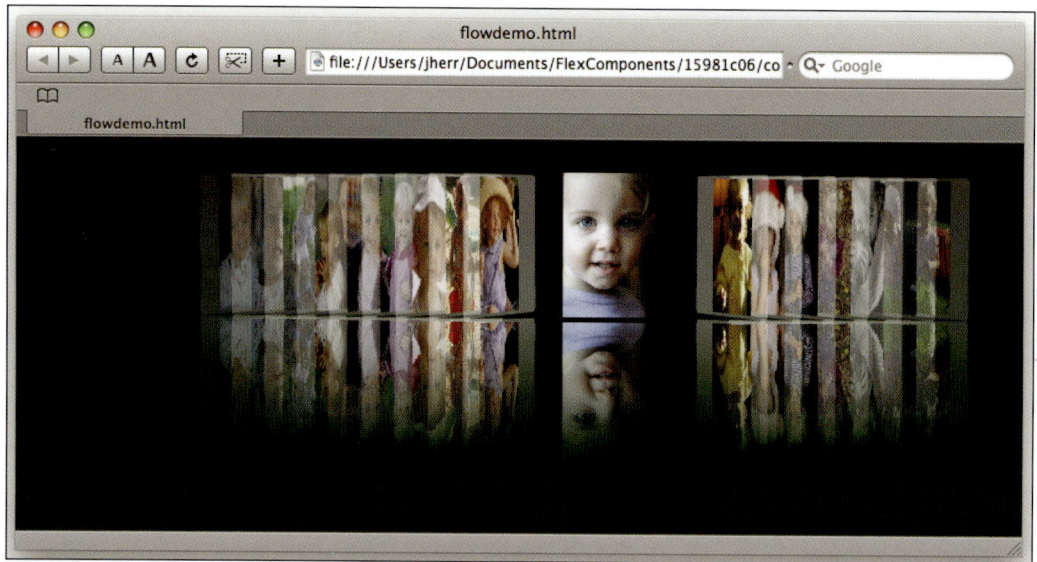

**Figure 6-3.** The 3D Flow List from Advanced Flash Components

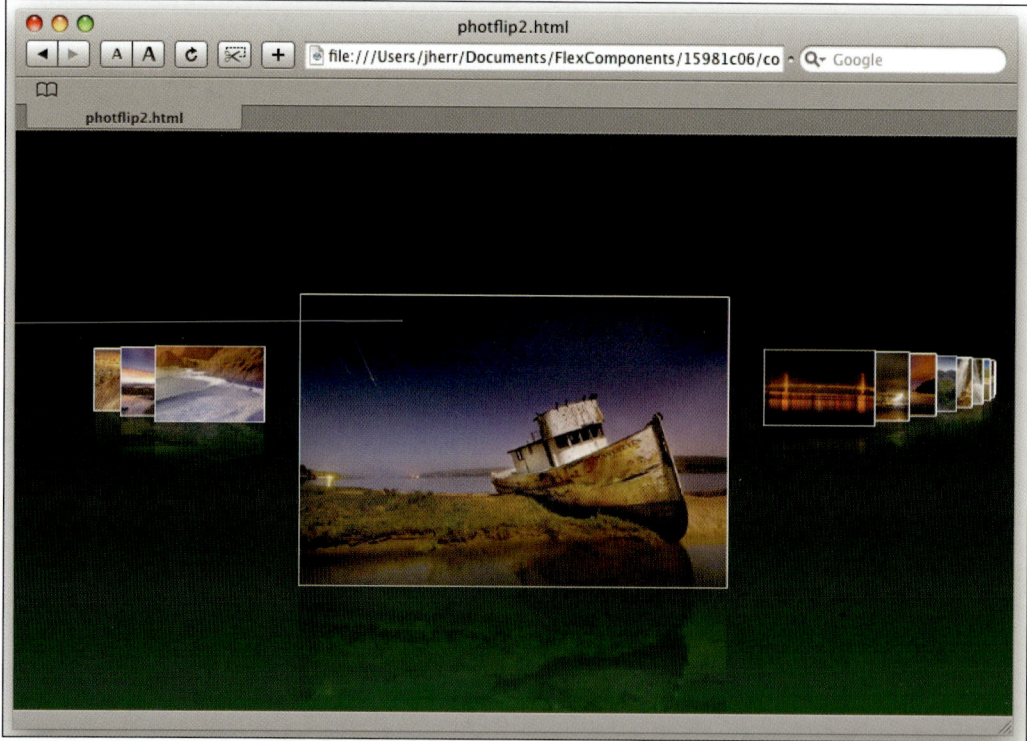

**Figure 6-6.** The selected image popped out

**Figure 6-9.** The vertical version of the RotationMenu

**Figure 6-10.** The startup state of the image grid

**Figure 6-12.** The startup state of the Flex SlideShow component

**Figure 6-14.** The Degrafa dynamic masking example

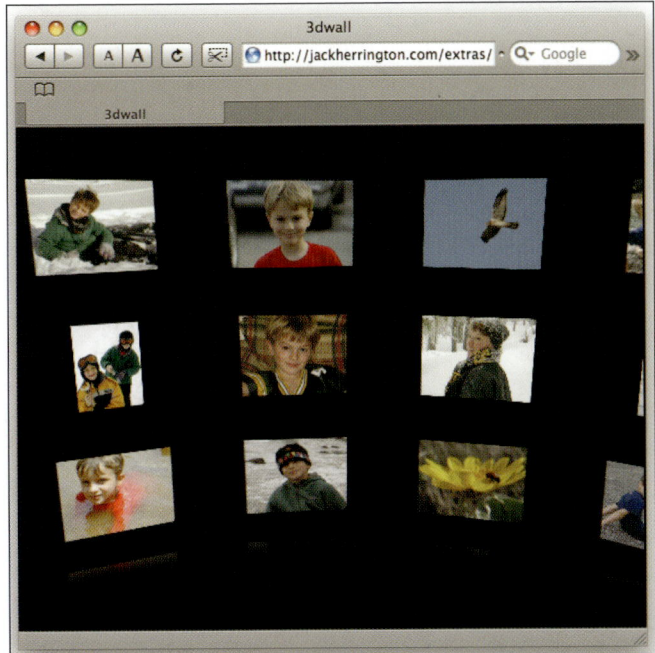

**Figure 6-15.** The 3D Wall from Flashloaded

**Figure 7-1.** The XML MP3 Player (photo courtesy
of Bo Boswell [http://blue-wire.com])

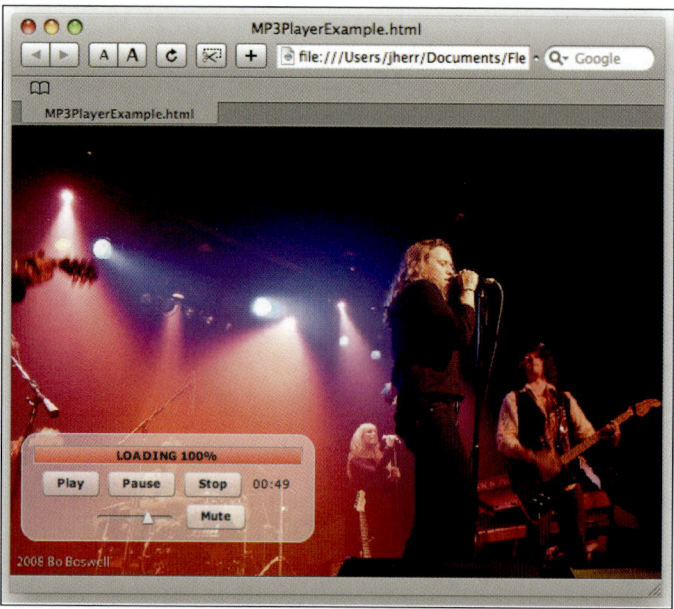

**Figure 7-2.** A simple MP3 player application that uses the MP3Player object

**Figure 7-4.** Going for a ride on the roller coaster player

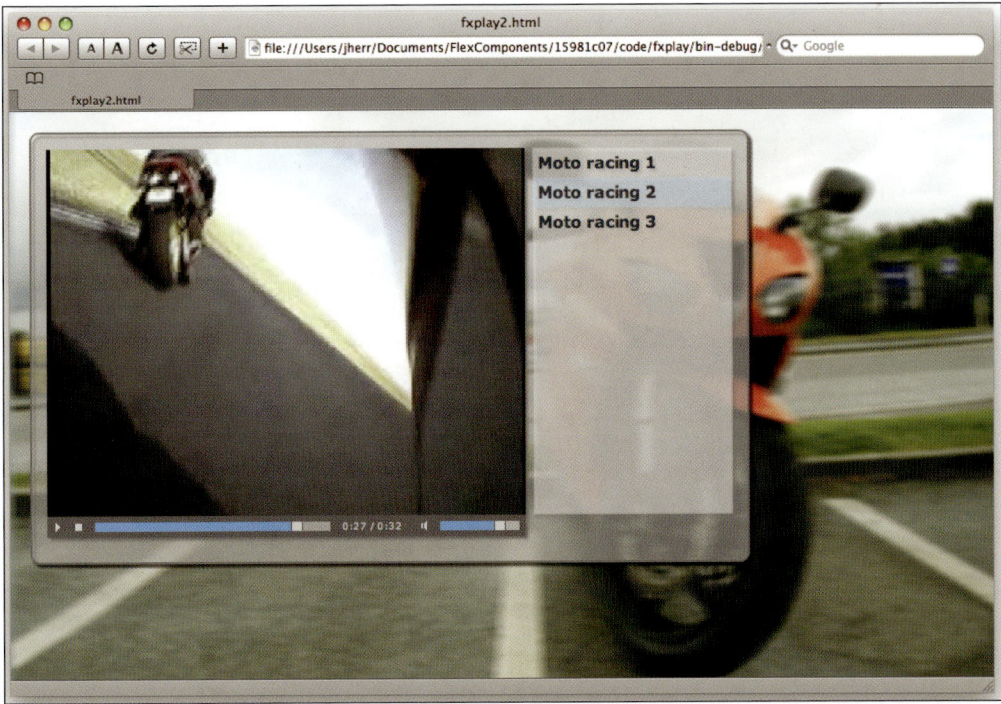

**Figure 7-5.** The motorcycle-themed video player with multiple movies

**Figure 7-6.** The first FLVPlayer example

**Figure 7-8.** The video player with both foreground and background graphics

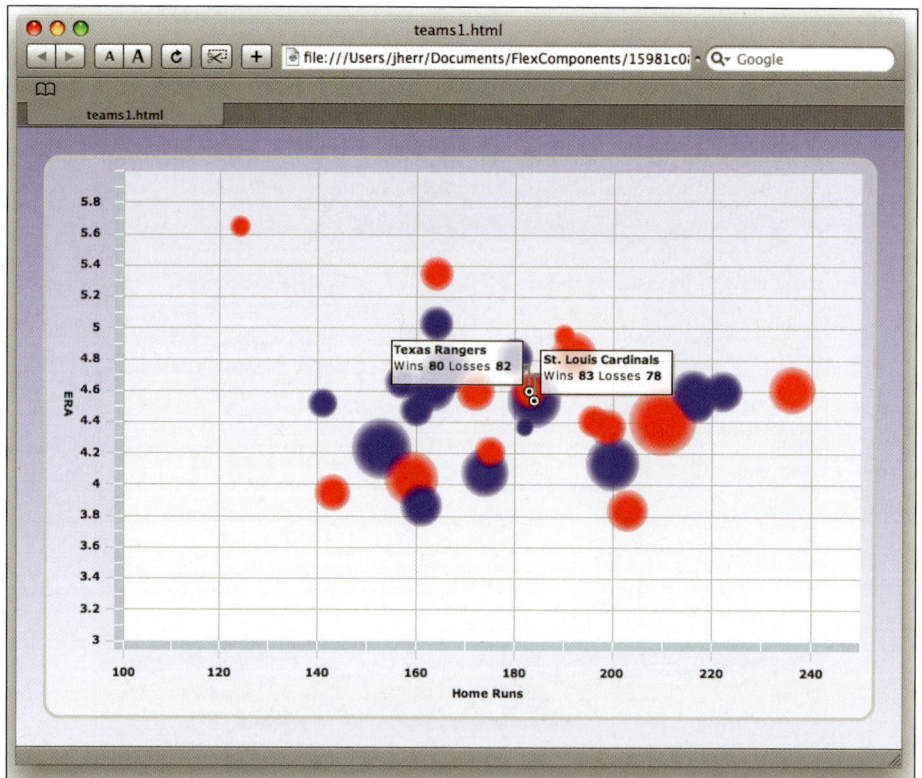

**Figure 8-2.** The bubble chart with the custom tooltips

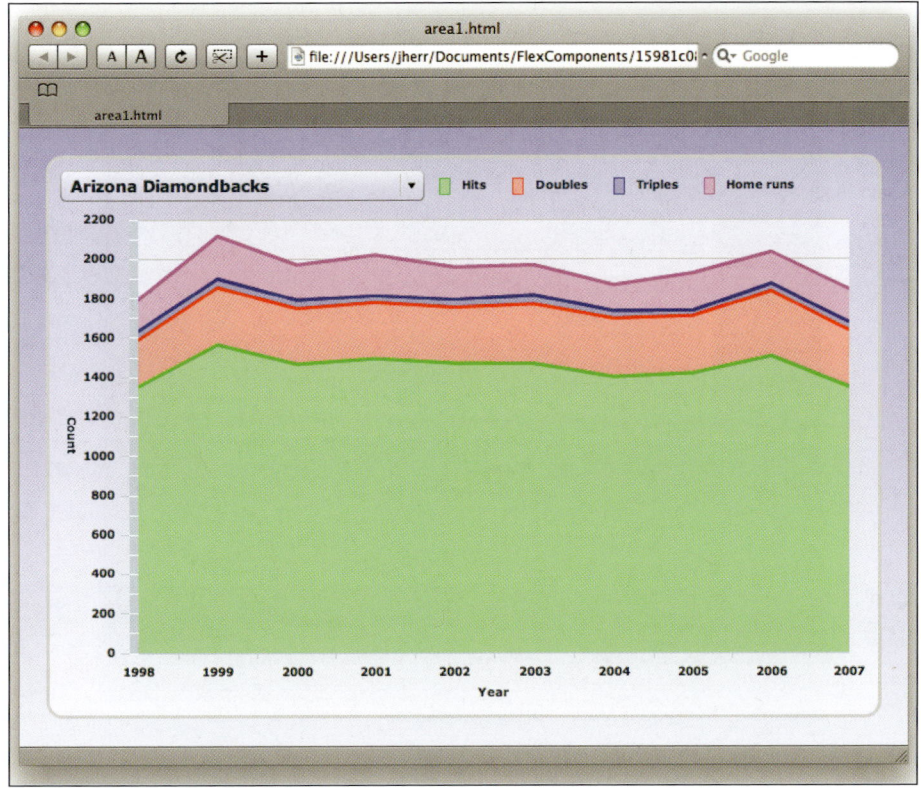

**Figure 8-4.** The batting counts for the Arizona Diamondbacks

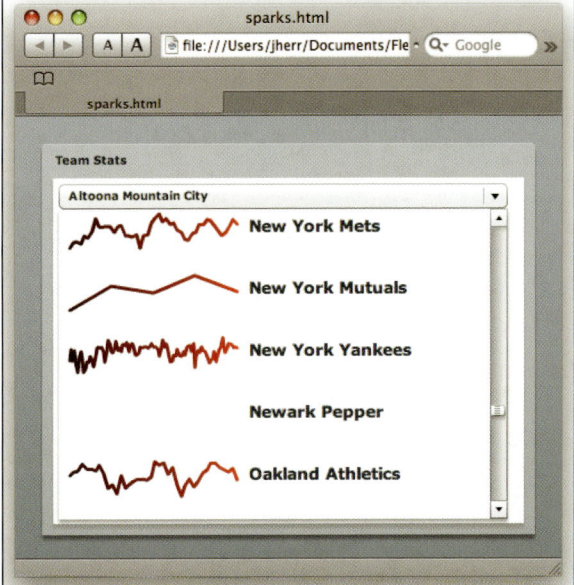

**Figure 8-10.** The sparkline combo box

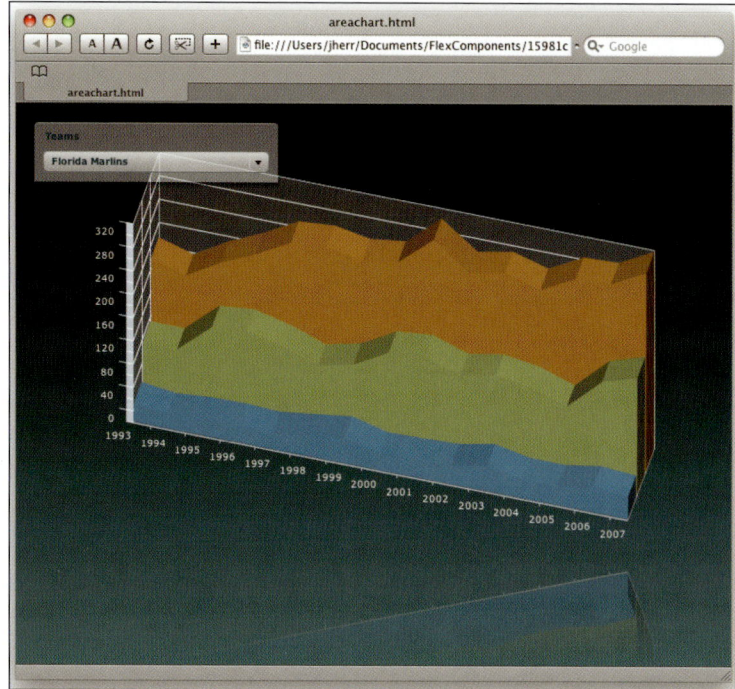

**Figure 9-1.** The Florida Marlins batting averages

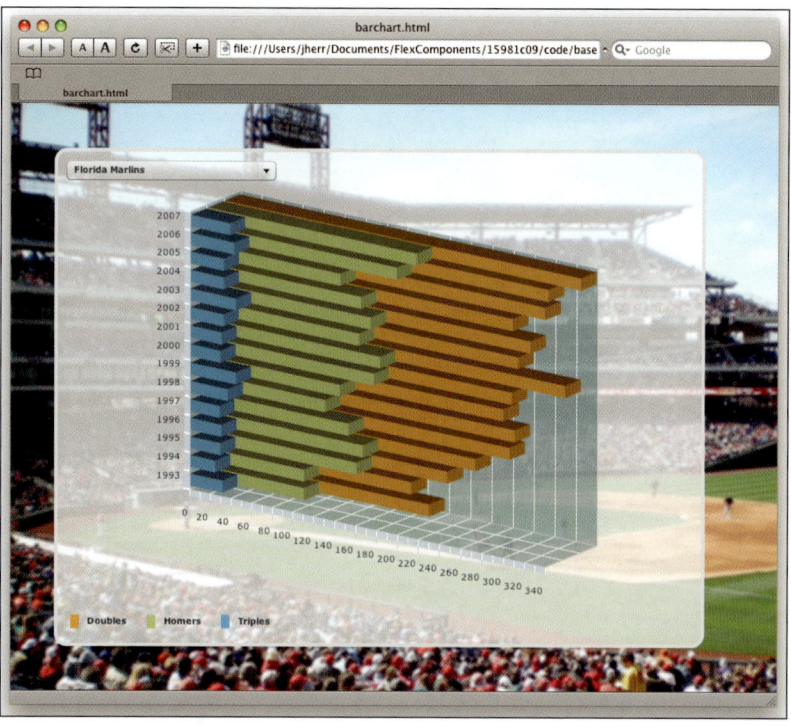

**Figure 9-4.** The bar chart example

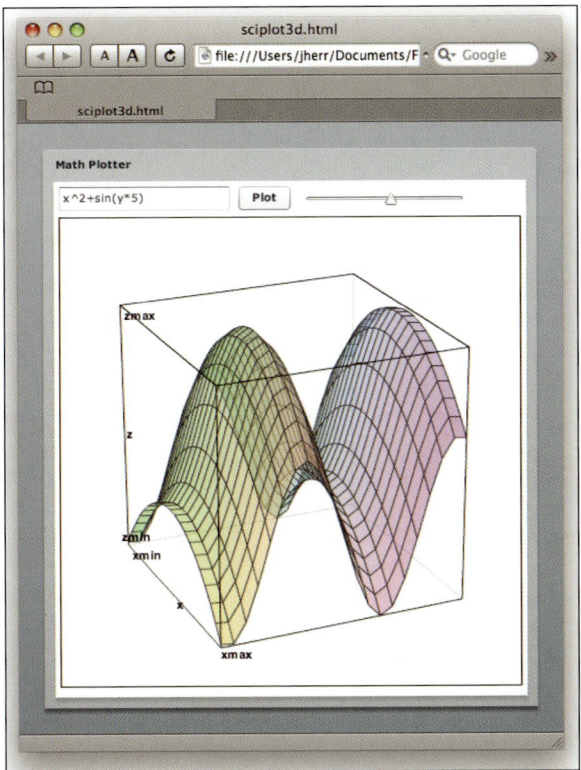

**Figure 9-6.** The 3D graph, which is only semi-opaque

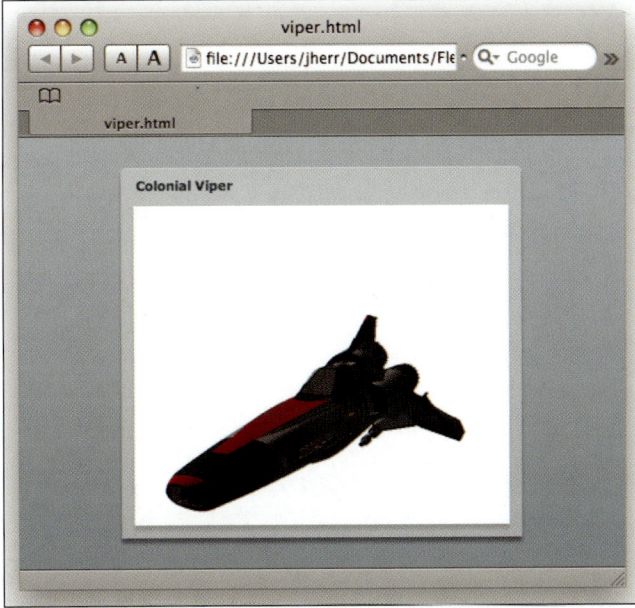

**Figure 9-11.** The model spinner

**Figure 10-1.** The hybrid car dashboard using Elixir gauges

**Figure 10-5.** The US map with the data selector knob and gauges

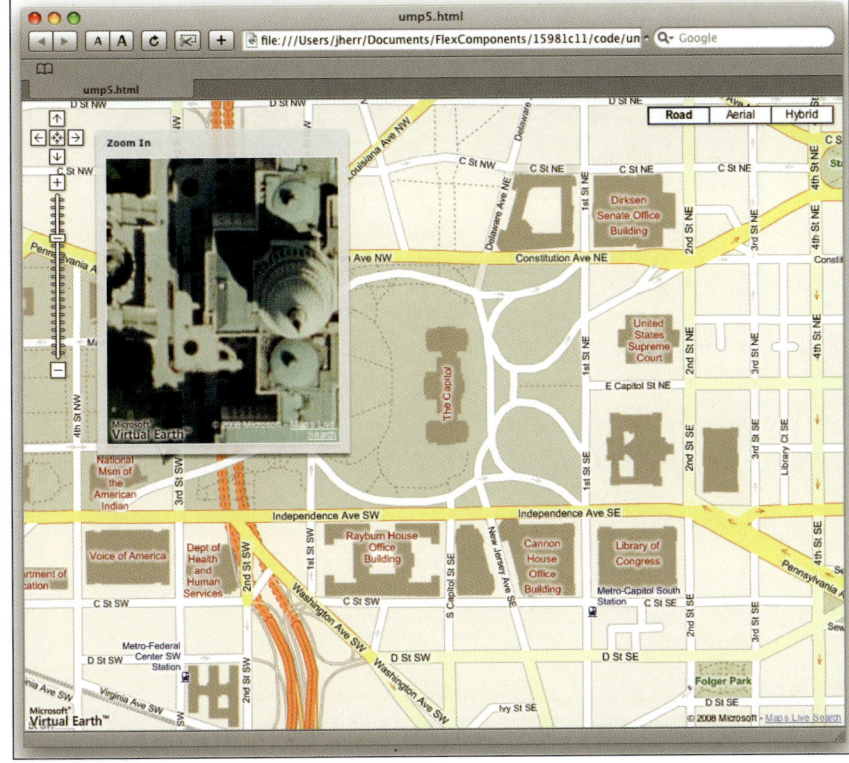

**Figure 11-23.** The two maps with the zoom-in centered on the US Capitol building

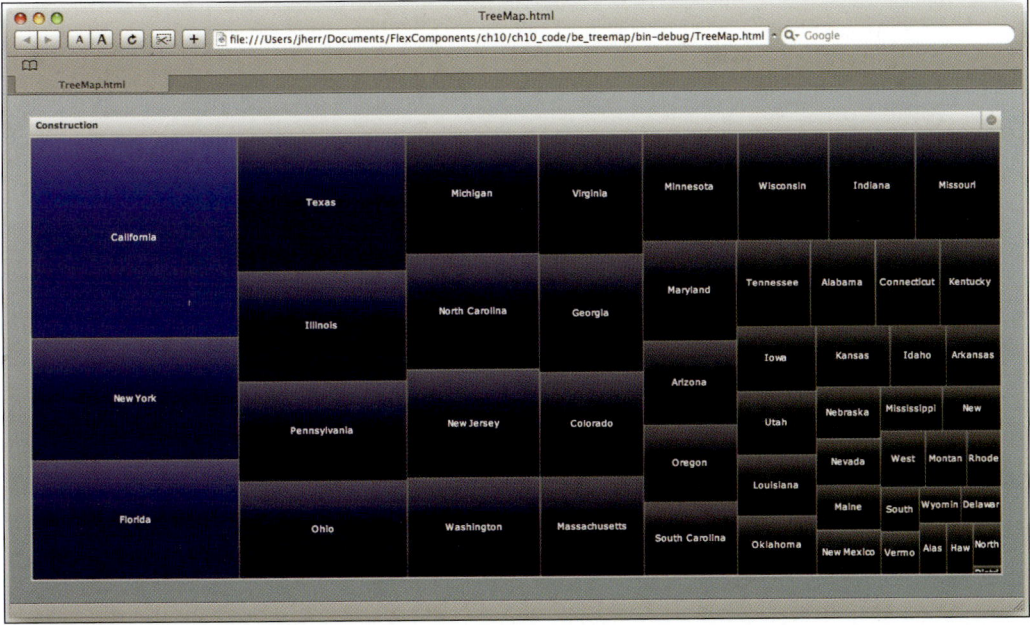

**Figure 12-2.** The zoomed-in graph

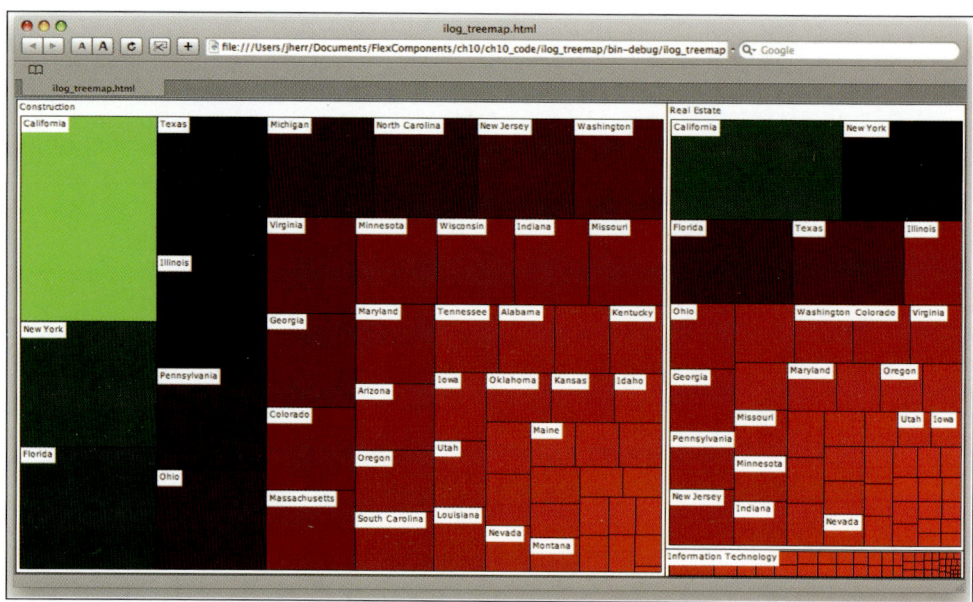

**Figure 12-3.** The ILOG Elixir TreeMap control showing the usdata tables

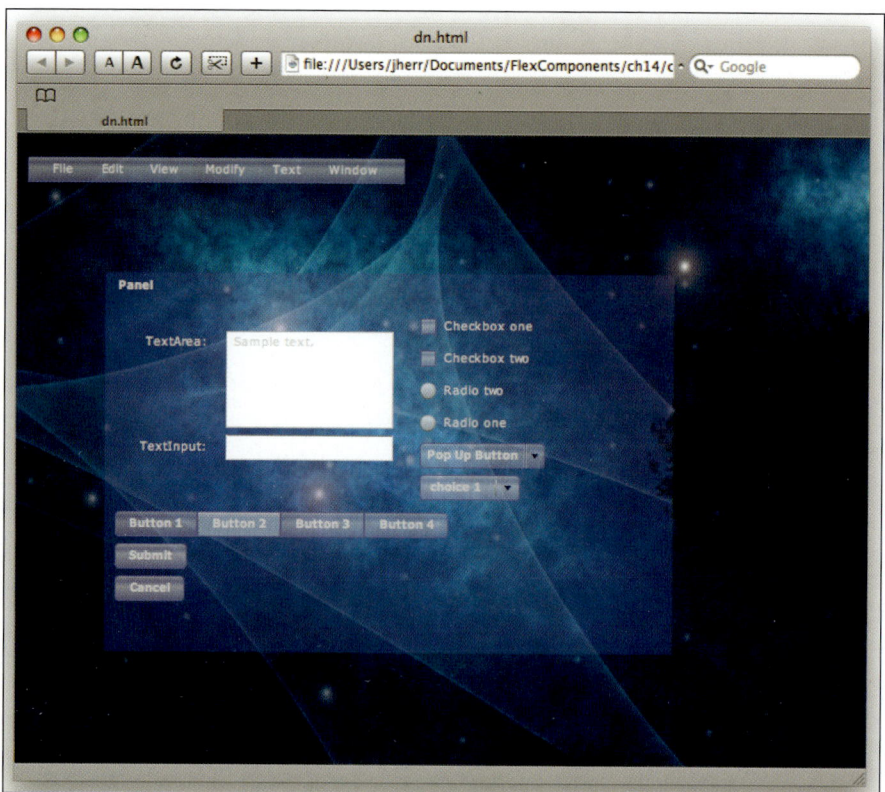

**Figure 14-3.** The Darke Nite skin applied to the application